Readings in Virtual Research Ethics: Issues and Controversies

Elizabeth A. Buchanan
University of Wisconsin-Milwaukee, USA

 Information Science Publishing

Hershey • London • Melbourne • Singapore

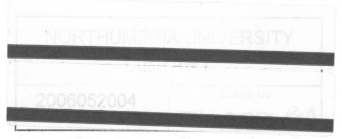

Readings in Virtual Research Ethics: Issues and Controversies

Table of Contents

Preface

INTRODUCTION
Virtual Research Ethics: Issues and Controversies

Researchers have for years looked to *The Belmont Report* for guiding principles of research ethics. This seminal report institutionalized three main areas of research ethics, namely, justice, beneficence and autonomy. Institutional review boards (IRBs) or ethics committees were established to oversee the conduct of research and to protect research subjects and, for the past 20 years, such mechanisms seemed adequate.

Enter the Internet, a hosting ground to virtual communities, locales and spaces and to populations of individuals who found new identities and new cultures, oftentimes, existing only in the virtual. Research fields that had no corresponding physicality became the objects of study. What were these new places and new communities? What did these populations have to say? And, how could researchers see, hear and document them through formal study? Moreover, how would traditional research ethics apply in these virtual realms? How would researchers and IRBs alike protect subjects in the virtual—and protect them from what? What dangers were posed in virtual fields? Was a new research ethic needed? What principles could be borrowed from the existing literature and guidelines? More questions than answers surfaced around virtual research ethics throughout the 1990s.

The 1990s gave way to various disciplines looking at these questions within their own parameters and from their own professional perspectives, and a body of albeit scattered literature began to emerge. A significant event occurred when The American Academy for the Advancement of Science in collaboration with the NIH Office for Protection from Research Risks convened a conference in 1999 around virtual research ethics, noting:

"The Office for Protection from Research Risks (OPPR) ... has received inquiries from researchers and Institutional Review Boards (IRBs) members seeking guidance regarding research in this area. Many IRBs recognize their unfamiliarity with the protocols. To both protect human subjects and promote innovative and scientifically sound research, it is important to consider the ethical, legal, and technical issues associated with this burgeoning area of research" (Frankel & Siang, 1999, p. 2).

What is this burgeoning area of research? What are the issues and controversies? Why is a collection of this type necessary and important? This volume brings together many faces of the ethical issues in virtual research from a multidisciplinary and multinational perspective. There are common and contradictory themes throughout the writings included herein, and these themes contribute to the complexity of virtual research ethics at this point in time, as seen through the lenses of discrete disciplines and countries. Such themes include informed consent; confidentiality and anonymity; privacy; public and private spaces; ownership, stewardship and the use of virtual data and virtual personae; participant recruitment; participant debriefing; virtual research with minors and the overarching theme of the changing roles of both researchers and researched in virtual environments. Contributors hail from Canada, Australia, Sweden, United Kingdom, Italy and the United States, and from such academic disciplines as English, women's studies, business, psychology, communications, interdisciplinary studies, education, sociology and others, representing the true diversity that is virtual research. Unique and diverse perspectives are gleaned by looking at virtual research ethics through multiple forms of media. Different types of Internet and Web platforms are explored as the conduits through which virtual communities and personae are studied and how these various channels—e-mail surveys and e-mail interviews, synchronous chat, newsgroups, MUDs, online support groups, Web pages—each engender specific ethical dilemmas.

The diverse contributions to this volume make it useful for many readers. Academics, who are new to this type of research but wish to pursue virtual research, will be introduced to its salient ethical issues, as well as to the conduct of virtual research through case studies. Researchers will encounter various methodological approaches, qualitative and quantitative, including such forms as ethnography, e-mail surveys, participatory action research and interviewing. Those sitting on IRBs or preparing to face their IRB will gain knowledge and practical guidance on this emerging research, and will be better poised to protect their virtual participants and subjects. Finally, readers of this volume will enter the growing discussion and debate surrounding virtual research ethics. Many further questions and areas for consideration are posed throughout these chapters—there is much fertile ground yet to be explored. There are many stones left unturned for future researchers in the virtual realm. It is my hope as editor of this collection that as more research is conducted, it will be done so with an awareness, attention and sensitivity to ethics as described by the contributions herein.

This book is organized accordingly: Section One, "Foundations of Virtual Research Ethics," begins with a contribution from Blaine Peden and Douglas Flashinski, who set the stage by providing the need for a volume such as this. While focusing on psychological experiments, the authors recognize a dramatic increase in the use of virtual experiments and surveys in the last few years. In this chapter, "Virtual Research Ethics: A Content Analysis of Surveys and Experiments Online," their main question— Are these sites compliant with ethical standards and guidelines?—is a significant one. Through a content analysis, Peden and Flashinski provide an insightful look at how psychological researchers, using virtual experiments and surveys, are—or are not— observing and conforming to the ethics of online research. Their ultimate predictions seem well grounded. They say that IRBs will continue to face more protocols employing online research and as such, IRBs must devote more time and attention to virtual research ethics and its specificity by acknowledging and learning about the issues raised through this volume. Further, the idea of an "online participants' bill of rights" holds great promise and potential in meeting many ethical concerns addressed throughout these chapters. What this bill of rights may ultimately look like is debatable—there is no one virtual research ethic, as we shall see. But, the idea is well taken.

Perhaps researchers will find the origins of an online participants' bill of rights in "Ethical Decision-Making and Internet Research: Recommendations from the AoIR Ethics Working Committee," presented by Charles Ess and Steve Jones. This statement represents the efforts of an international working group, which is indicative of the breadth and depth of the emerging study of virtual research ethics. In this excerpt from the full document, readers gain an overview of the pertinent issues online research entails as well as succinct guidelines for the conduct of virtual research. Guided by the philosophical perspective of ethical pluralism, this chapter is truly foundational: Many of the issues Ess and Jones confront will be explored, questioned, and tested in greater detail in subsequent chapters. In addition, a detailed resource list is included.

Following Ess and Jones, Malin Sveningsson offers an overview of online research ethics using the perspective of the Swedish Research Council's Ethics Committee for Research in the Humanities and Social Sciences. Although the specific methodology of ethnography grounds Sveningsson's discussion, her chapter, "Ethics in Internet Ethnography," is included in this Foundations section, as it provides a thorough consideration of pertinent ethical issues in the conduct of research online, regardless of methodological approach. Of import, this chapter highlights unique distinctions between online and offline research, calling the researcher's role into direct question. Ultimately, researchers are urged to follow Sveningsson's conclusion to be both reflexive and flexible in online research.

Finally, in this Foundations section, Maczewski, Storey and Hoskins delve into the virtual realm, which they suggest is constituted by three spheres: The online, onground and the technical. The interplay of these research spheres contributes to the specificity of virtual research ethics and should be considered carefully by researchers prior to the conduct of engagement in research. In this chapter, "Conducting Congruent, Ethical, Qualitative Research in Internet-Mediated Research Environments," the authors explore such issues as data collection, data use and ownership, trust, voice and confidentiality, and recommend that research practices undergo scrutiny and evaluation within the contexts of Internet-mediated spaces. This section of general insights and perspectives on virtual research ethics takes readers into the next where specific media are used as the backdrop for exploring virtual research ethics.

Section Two, "Media, Messages and Ethics," introduces readers to different approaches to virtual research. In Chapter 5, "Blurring the Boundaries: Ethical Considerations for Online Research Using Synchronous CMC Forums," Danielle Lawson, through a comprehensive review of the literature surrounding CMC, looks at synchronous CMC and the ethical challenges surrounding identity, privacy, informed consent and chat copyright in these realms. Lawson's contribution reveals that there is much debate in the literature around these issues. Moreover, she explores whether informed consent is indeed needed, and whether copyright provisions protect synchronous CMC. These are difficult questions to answer, as Lawson ascribes a new category to such synchronous CMC products—textural, a blurring of boundaries of speech and text online.

The next two chapters look at the use of e-mail as a method of data collection. In Chapter 6, "When the Ethic is Functional to the Method: The Case of E-Mail Qualitative Interviews," Nadia Olivero and Peter Lunt explore qualitative e-mail interviews, while in Chapter 7, "The Ethics of Conducting E-Mail Surveys," Sandeep Krishnamurthy investigates e-mail surveys.

Olivero and Lunt question the implications of establishing interview relationships based on written, asynchronous computer-mediated communication. In response to the unavoidable interviewer effect and to avoid an undesirable practice of strategic self-presentation by interviewees, the authors look to feminist ethics for guidance. In particular, they promote an interview model based on reciprocity and equal participation. The development of rapport based in a trusting relationship will promote more effective e-mail interviews.

In Krishnamurthy's contribution, the role of the subject as a consumer or participant in e-mail surveys is explored through the perspective of market research. How are academic e-mail surveys different from spam surveys? Is spam inherently unethical? How can respondent permission, which is explored throughout this chapter, lend to a more ethical form of e-mail survey research? The author proposes a permission-based program and advocates that academic researchers begin to think more thoroughly about permission before conducting such e-mail survey research.

The last chapter in Section Two, "Organizational Research Over the Internet: Ethical Challenges and Opportunities," presents readers with an in-depth look at the field of organizational research and its use of Internet-based research. W. Benjamin Porr and Robert Ployhart assert that while the use of virtual research in organizations is growing, an awareness of the concomitant ethical issues, such as privacy, informed consent, confidentiality and anonymity, and debriefing, needs attention. The authors conclude with a case study in the conduct of virtual organizational research, and with guidelines for those engaging in such forms of organizational research. Despite one's disciplinary perspective, Porr and Ployhart's discussion will particularly enlighten readers facing IRBs with virtual research protocols.

Porr and Ployhart's concluding case study leads readers directly into Section Three, "Researchers/Researched? Research Ethics in Practice," which consists of various disciplinary case studies of virtual research in action and the concurrent ethical issues each author encountered in his or her engagement in the virtual. Readers will see the process of virtual research and the ways in which ethical challenges and dilemmas arise through these chapters. The themes are oftentimes similar from one chapter to the next: informed consent, public and private, confidentiality, protection of subjects, and more. Yet, each chapter is unique and fruitful.

We first look at Lynne Roberts, Leigh Smith and Clare Pollock, who use grounded theory to study social interaction in MOOs. Their chapter, "Conducting Ethical Research Online: Respect for Individuals, Identities and the Ownership of Words," alerts readers to the ethical challenges faced throughout this study, including the distinction between public and private spaces, how the researchers identified themselves online, how informed consent and confidentiality were obtained and maintained and, finally, how the researchers dealt with distressing information conveyed through the MOO.

Mary Walstrom takes the issue of distressing information to the fore in her chapter on "Ethics and Engagement in Communication Scholarship: Analyzing Public Online Support Groups as Researcher/Participant-Experiencer." Walstrom provides an elaborate discussion of an engaged research approach and how, she suggests, it could lead to more ethically-based virtual research. She uses this engaged approach to study eating disorder support groups online, and concludes with a call to researchers of the virtual to consider this approach not only for their benefit, but for those we study. Underlying this chapter, Walstrom's researcher/participant-experiencer model shows the fluidity and subsequent complexity that arises when one is first a participant in the online arena which then becomes the object of study.

Next, Monica Whitty considers the ethical issues surrounding the study of Internet relationships and sexuality. She looks at the existent literature in this area to raise questions about the role of the researcher and the extent to which he or she assumes alternative identities in order to obtain data online. She too considers practical issues of informed consent, withdrawal of consent, confidentiality and distressing information in the context of studying Internet relationships and sexuality.

The next chapter, "Co-Construction and Field Creation: Website Development as both an Instrument and Relationship in Action Research," from Maximilian Forte, looks at virtual research ethics through an anthropological perspective using action research. Forte's work with the Santa Rosa Carib community in Trinidad and Tobago examines the process of co-construction through a website development project. The author looks critically at the intersection of online and offline research and the disparate research ethics each entails, while calling attention to the ethically questionable hierarchy typically seen in the researcher-researched relationship. Forte argues that online research places greater ethical demands on the researcher as well as the researched, and accordingly, both parties must recognize ethics as a negotiated process, as opposed to a rigid procedure that acknowledges only "scientific takers and native givers."

As Forte negotiated the online and offline realms in the process of data collection and research, David Clark too looks at this meeting of the virtual and the material in his ongoing study of a Linux community. In his chapter, "What If You Meet Face to Face? A Case Study in Virtual/Material Research Ethics," Clark struggles with such issues as informed consent, which of course is required for the material interviews throughout his study, but may not be necessary when he uses public listserv data. What happens when his participants "really" know each other and their virtual data becomes a source of embarrassment in their material meetings? Clark's focus on virtual/material ethics provides an interesting look at the ethical issues posed by such hybrid forms of research.

Finally, in Chapter 14 titled "Fact or Fiction: Notes of a Man Interviewing Women Online," Michael Ayers presents a case study of his e-mail interviews with participants from the National Organization of Women (NOW) Village site. This chapter may offend some, and indeed, as a woman and a feminist, I thought critically about the assertions made herein. Yet, it is significant as it presents intriguing ethical questions about rapport, trust, honesty, and researcher markers in virtual arenas. Ayers' relates his trials and tribulations of interviewing feminist activists through the NOW Village, which was a much different experience than he anticipated. He questions the complex issue of how rapport is created through e-mail interviews, asking how only two evident markers, masculinity and "researcher," impacted the responses he received to his interview questions. Ayers then asks a very fundamental question to virtual research: How do researchers know they are receiving "true" responses? Were the responses he ultimately received intended as shock value, a signal to him as a researcher to back off? Was it a gender issue in this case? In light of the uncertainties with which Ayers proceeded in his study, he proposes a reflexive cybersociology to acknowledge both the validity and potential falseness of virtual data.

Section Four, "Online Research with Minors—Special Considerations?" highlights two chapters of research with minors in the online arena. As we know, codified principles of research ethics dictate that minors receive special consideration, by virtue of their potential vulnerability and inability to comprehend research itself. Parental consent is one means by which we extend this special protection to children. With virtual research, researchers are presented with newfound difficulties in studying children. Susannah Stern and Magdalena Bober present their research and concomitant difficulties in this section.

Stern's chapter, "Studying Adolscents Online: A Consideration of Ethical Issues," describes her research on youth home pages, framed in a discussion of two traditional principles of research ethics, autonomy and beneficence. This chapter documents the challenges of obtaining parental consent, as well as calls into question the role of the researcher. Stern offers practical suggestions for those intending to use virtual research with minors; it is not as easy as one may have thought, as Stern details.

Then, in Chapter 16 titled "Virtual Youth Research: An Exploration of Methodologies and Ethical Dilemmas from a British Perspective," readers can observe cross-cultural differences in the study of minors, by contrasting Stern and Bober's chapters and their experiences as online researchers. Through a plethora of perspectives, Bober elucidates the ethics of youth research through such channels as interviews, website development, participant observation online and examination of Web-server logs. Both Stern and Bober's chapters provide important information for those considering virtual youth research, imparting useful guidelines to the conduct of such research, while raising awareness of the many questions and challenges that arise with this research.

In the concluding section, Section Five, "A Call to Researchers," two chapters of import reside. Both are a call to arms of sorts for researchers. Both recognize that researchers and researched share a new relationship within virtual spaces and these new relationships elicit new considerations while demanding new understandings. Acknowledging the cross-cultural and international characteristics of virtual research in Chapter 17, "International Digital Studies: A Research Approach for Examining International Online Interactions," Kirk St.Amant calls to question how communications take place in this international context and what ethical implications surface. This chapter's significance revolves around the role of researcher in the virtual environment—it is a call to researchers that a new model of study is indeed necessary, what St.Amant calls international digital studies. Will such a model help in the realm of virtual research ethics? Will researchers conduct more ethically-sound research following St.Amant's evaluative process of determining digital ethos conditions? Ultimately, St.Amant's model has the potential to assist researchers in understanding how cross-cultural factors influence online communications.

Then, Maria Bakardjieva, Andrew Feenberg and Janis Goldie resituate the subject and ask pointedly, "What do research subjects get out of it anyway?" In many ways, we have come full circle to Peden and Flashinski's call for an online participant's bill of rights. This chapter, "User-Centered Internet Research: The Ethical Challenge," forces us as virtual researchers to consider how to resituate our subjects in order to incorporate participant needs and benefits into research design. The authors call for the use of different research models—reflexive and collaborative approaches and participatory action research—to help balance the scales so that we can address with more ethical certainty exactly what the subject gets out of it. These approaches bring us closer to a user-centered model of virtual research, which ultimately heightens accountability, respect, sincerity, and honesty, and, thus, ethics.

The readings of this volume will take you, the reader, to many places. They encourage you to think about research and research ethics in a new context. Ultimately, this volume asks you to reflect on ethics and ask two significant questions: "Am I conducting ethical virtual research?" and "Do my participants believe I am conducting ethical research?" Readers will quickly see these are not easy questions to answer once we step foot in the virtual.

REFERENCE

Frankel, M. & Siang, S. (1999). *Ethical and legal aspects of human subjects research on the Internet.* A report presented at the American Association for the Advancement of Science, Washington, D.C. Retrieved from: http://www.aaas.org/spp/sfrl/projects/intres/report.pdf.

Acknowledgments

First and foremost, I would like to thank all of the contributors to this volume for their work and commitment. I have enjoyed working with each of you, and have enjoyed learning from the ideas and thoughts shared during the writing and review process. This has truly been a collaborative effort, and I thank all of you for the time and intellectual energies you have given to this volume.

I thank Idea Group Publishing for their support of this book, in particular, Michele Rossi, Jennifer Sundstrom and Amanda Appicello for their professionalism throughout this project.

I thank the School of Information Studies at the University of Wisconsin-Milwaukee for the resources used in the completion of this book and to my colleagues for their support and friendship.

As always, I dearly thank my parents, Gail and Jack Buchanan, for simply being who they are and for their never-ending support and love.

An extra special thanks goes to my husband, Bill Topritzhofer. His enduring support, assurances and old-fashioned love during the months of work made this volume possible. Thanks, Bill, for assuring me I was not crazy to propose a book while eight months pregnant, and for your belief that I could complete it even with an inquisitive baby around.

And, of course, to Zachary, my dear son, who somehow became a one year old during the process of this book. My love for you transcends all boundaries. May you grow and live in a peaceful and just world, real or virtual.

Elizabeth A. Buchanan, PhD
Milwaukee, WI
March 2003

Section I

Foundations of Virtual Research Ethics

Chapter I

Virtual Research Ethics: A Content Analysis of Surveys and Experiments Online

Blaine F. Peden
University of Wisconsin-Eau Claire, USA

Douglas P. Flashinski
University of Wisconsin-Eau Claire, USA

ABSTRACT

This chapter presents a content analysis of Internet surveys and experiments. Our study explores guidelines for the conduct of online research by describing the extent to which psychological studies comply with Reips' (2000) recommendations for Web researchers. Our study also explores ethical considerations and problems in the conduct of virtual research by describing the extent to which behavioral studies on the Internet comply with ethical standards for research (American Psychological Association, 2003). The chapter concludes with a discussion of aspects of virtual research ethics pertinent to future participants, Internet scientists and Institutional Review Boards.

"We need not invent new ethical rules for online research. We need only increase our awareness of and commitment to established ethical principles."

– Jim Thomas, 1999, p. 8

INTRODUCTION

This chapter reports on a content analysis of psychological research on the Internet. Our interest in studying how psychologists do surveys and experiments online derives from a professional involvement in both research and ethics. In the late 1990s, we became intrigued by other psychologists' use of the Internet as a tool for conducting research. At first we served as participants in some online surveys and experiments. Later we explored ways to implement our own research on the Web by talking to information technologists and by reading the scattered literature on Internet science.

Our experience as participants raised initial questions and concerns about virtual research ethics. For example, we participated in online studies that differed with respect to inducements for research participation. Although some researchers paid all their participants and others employed a lottery or random drawing for monetary prizes, many Internet scientists provided no inducements other than an opportunity for the participants to contribute to science. A discussion with Institutional Review Board (IRB) members initially revealed a genuine quandary about how participants, who should remain anonymous, could be paid. The IRB members also raised eyebrows when we asked about how students in the Psychology Department subject pool could receive credit for participating in online research.

Our experience with information technologists prompted further questions and concerns about virtual research ethics. The individuals who were helping us implement our own studies on the Internet did not understand our concerns about informed consent and debriefing. In fact, they often seemed to regard these pages as blemishes on the face of an otherwise attractive website.

While we were participating in online studies and exploring how to implement our own surveys and experiments, we began to search the literature. We quickly learned that relevant articles appeared in rather diverse and scattered sources. We also learned that many articles about psychological research on the Internet focused on methodological issues. Nonetheless, we detected an emerging awareness and interest in virtual research ethics, the topic of this volume.

Our contribution to this volume is empirical and analytical. First, we provide the rationale and method for our content analysis of Internet surveys and experiments conducted by psychologists in the early months of 2002. Our study explores guidelines for the conduct of online research, a goal of this volume, by describing the extent to which psychological studies comply with Reips' (2000) recommendations for Web researchers. Our study also explores ethical considerations and problems in the conduct of virtual research, another goal of this volume, by describing the extent to which behavioral studies on the Internet comply with ethical standards for research (American Psychological Association (APA), 2003). Second, we analyze and interpret specific findings in terms of recent comments and developments in the current literature on Internet science. Finally, we discuss the more general aspects of virtual research ethics pertinent to future participants, Internet scientists and IRBs.

BACKGROUND

What a difference a decade makes in terms of technology and behavior in cyberspace. In the early 1990s, the Internet was virtually unknown to the general public and the relatively exclusive province of academics and scientists (Musch & Reips, 2000). Within a few years the Internet evolved into the World Wide Web (Web) and began to attract more and more users. For example, one projection estimated 500 million "netizens" online in 2003. At present many people incorporate online activities into their daily routines and regard continuous, or 24/7, access to the Web as a necessity. The growing number of people and the incredible diversity of behavior in cyberspace also produced numerous opportunities for researchers in general and psychologists in particular. For example, researchers from different disciplines examined various aspects of online communities and other interactions in cyberspace (Jones, 1999). As early as 1995, clinical psychologists began to offer psychotherapy online and research psychologists began to conduct surveys and experiments online.

In the late 1990s, the authors became aware of the many ways psychologists used the Internet. As we examined the sites of online therapists and served as participants in Internet research, we soon realized that use of the Web by professionals for telehealth services and by social scientists for research raised a number of methodological and ethical questions. Quite predictably, the initial discussions regarding these methodological and ethical issues appeared in diverse and scattered sources. Below we review a portion of the literature that led to our content analysis of online surveys and experiments by psychologists.

An early article by Jones (1994) defined the domain of virtual research ethics. Jones expressed doubt that the guidelines for traditional face-to-face research could be applied directly to online research. He pointed out that traditional guidelines for obtaining informed consent via paper-and-pencil procedures did not translate unequivocally into the domain of cyberspace. For example, one the ethical standards of the APA (2003) indicates that consent procedures must use language comprehensible to the participants. Although a recent article by Paasche-Orlow, Taylor and Brancati (2003) demonstrates that accomplishing this goal is difficult in face-to-face medical research, the problem is greater in online research. The practical problem is that the pool of online participants is potentially demographically, geographically and linguistically quite diverse. As an aside, Jones (1994) also posed an interesting question: What kind of Internet research activities would constitute a clear violation of professional ethics?

Hewson, Laurent and Vogel (1996) discussed the Internet as a tool for research. These authors argued that the Web was a way to gain access to participants for surveys and experiments. To this end the authors translated the prevailing methodological guidelines for face-to-face research into the domain of online research. For example, they advocated an indirect method in which researchers solicit participants who, in turn, must contact the researcher to participate in the study. The indirect approach resembles conventional procedures for recruiting face-to-face participants. The indirect method also contrasts markedly with the now-dominant direct method in which researchers post their surveys and experiments on the Web. We note that these authors recommended the indirect approach on the basis of methodological, rather than ethical considerations. Indeed, Hewson et al. focused entirely on methodological issues and did not address ethical issues at all.

An article by Michalak and Szabo (1998) addressed both methodological and ethical issues in Internet research. These authors listed 30 guidelines for Internet researchers that were derived from an amalgamation of personal experience, general standards for research and the APA (1992) ethical standards regarding face-to-face research. For example, they advised Internet researchers to encourage participation by offering a promise to disseminate findings or papers. Apparently, the issue of payment to induce participation in Internet research is a controversial point. On one hand, the Department of Psychology at University of Calgary, for example, posted a policy statement regarding lotteries as participant remuneration ("Lotteries," 2000). This document notes that lotteries represent an alternative to paying all the participants; however, the practice should be used only after careful deliberation. An alternative perspective is that lotteries are a form of gambling and, therefore, are somewhat immoral and should be avoided— a sentiment expressed on the website for Jonathan Baron's questionnaires late in 2002. Interestingly, this statement had disappeared by February of 2003. Nonetheless, the issue of paying participants represented a genuine concern for Baron and Siepmann (2000), who devoted several pages to a discussion of this issue.

Eventually, new forums emerged for discussions about Internet research. Such forums included a new association and two new journals. For example, the Association of Internet Researchers formed in 1998, and *CyberPsychology and Behavior* and *The Journal of Online Behavior* published their first issues in 1999 and 2000, respectively.

One landmark event occurred in June 1999 when the American Association for the Advancement of Science (AAAS) convened a panel of social, behavioral and computer scientists, representatives from the legal and ethics communities and members of IRBs. The panel addressed ethical issues entailed in empirically assessing the Internet as an instrument and medium for research. Frankel and Siang's (1999) report of the panels' proceedings examined issues regarding benefits and risks, informed consent, privacy and confidentiality and justice. For example, the report indicated that the survey was the most common form of Internet research. The report also indicated that online surveys potentially entailed more risks with regard to privacy and confidentiality than more traditional survey methods. Furthermore, the report considered issues such as informed consent in online studies like those raised by Jones (1994). For example, the report raised the question whether a mouse click to "I agree" is a valid counterpart to a signature when the age, competency and comprehension of the online participant are unknown. The report concluded with a statement of goals. In particular, their agenda for action called for studies of Internet research practices, such as our content analysis.

The issues surrounding virtual research methods and ethics eventually were distilled and presented to the general audience of psychologists as emerging trends. For example, the *Monitor on Psychology* is a traditional forum exploring contemporary issues affecting the practice of psychologists that is read by many members of the APA. At first, reports in this publication focused on the novelty of research online (e.g., Bourke, 1998). Soon, however, a special issue focused on the various ways in which the Web was changing the complexion of contemporary psychology ("Psychology and the Internet," 2000). This special issue introduced readers to various aspects of online research in four articles. The first article ("A Web of Research," Azar, 2000a) reported methodological pros and cons of online surveys and experiments. The article ended with a list of tips for researchers who wanted to implement their own studies on the Internet. A second article ("A Web Experiment Sampler," Azar, 2000b) encouraged readers to examine and/or participate in online research by listing the Internet addresses for studies available as the special issue went to press. The third article ("Free of Charge, Open All Hours," Beans, 2002) described how an established online lab could be used for research by faculty and students in smaller psychology departments. The final article ("Online

Experiments: Ethically Fair or Foul," Azar, 2000c) specifically addressed issues of virtual research ethics. The latter article noted that informed consent and debriefing pose new challenges for the ethically responsible conduct of research in online studies. Furthermore, the article identified a new twist on the topic of virtual research ethics by delineating and discussing a potential risk to researchers. Quite simply, conducting a study online reveals a researcher's methods and procedures well in advance of publication and thereby provides an opportunity for intellectual piracy.

The domain of online behavioral research acquired a new status when psychologists started publishing books about online research. For example, Birnbaum (2000) published an edited volume about psychological experiments on the Internet and followed it the next year with a textbook (Birnbaum, 2001). Reips and Bosnjak (2001) contributed an international perspective regarding dimensions of Internet science. The content of all three volumes focused largely on methodological rather than ethical issues. For example, the term ethics does not appear in the index of the Reips and Bosnjak volume and the Birnbaum textbook devotes only two pages to a discussion of ethical review. On the other hand, the most recent volume about online research by Batinic, Reips and Bosnjak (2002) mentions ethical issues several times throughout the book.

However, several authors in the Birnbaum (2000) volume explicitly confronted ethical issues in their Internet research. Reips (2000) indicated that the public nature of Web experiments encourages compliance with ethical standards and further noted that the ethical regulations vary internationally. An example is that American and British institutions require a consent form for participants, whereas European institutions typically do not. Buchanan (2000) indicated that both practical and ethical considerations regarding test security and copyright issues influenced the choice of instruments in his online studies of personality. Mueller, Jacobsen and Schwarzer (2000) commented on some of the issues that arose when they tried to apply the paper-and-pencil informed consent procedures of face-to-face research to Internet studies. They recommended using brief consent forms and fostering a sense of anonymity by avoiding any requests for an e-mail address. The latter recommendation runs counter to the advice of Michalak and Szabo (1998). Moreover, Mueller et al. regarded clicking "I agree" as an acceptable analog to a signature and noted it was courteous to provide a debriefing statement after participants submit their responses to a survey. Finally, they opposed use of Reips' (2000) high entrance barrier technique, a procedure aiming to produce early dropouts and ensure the participants who remain actually complete the study. As an aside, Mueller (1997) posted one of the earliest statements about ethical issues entailed in human participant research on the Internet. While we were preparing this chapter, our Internet searches for policy statements by institutions revealed many more colleges and universities now have guidelines in place for Internet research (see, for example, "Guidelines," 2002).

Our reading of the then-current literature suggested two discernible trends. One trend was that behavioral researchers were soliciting participants for surveys, personality tests and experiments in ever-increasing numbers. For example, Birnbaum (2001) indicated that the number of psychological studies on the Internet doubled from 1998 to 1999, and Azar (2000b) stated that this number doubled again from 1999 to 2000. Further evidence of this trend comes from an examination of a prominent gateway or portal to psychological surveys and experiments: the Psychological Research on the Net page of the American Psychological Society (APS) hosted by John Krantz at Hanover College.

Early in 2002, the APS site listed 117 studies; however, one year later this number had grown by approximately 25 percent to 150 studies. The second trend was that the literature focused largely on how to do surveys and experiments on the Internet and whether the results obtained in laboratory studies compared favorably with those obtained in Internet studies (Birnbaum, 2001, 2002; Reips & Bosnjak, 2001).

Despite these clear trends, what seemed to be missing was an empirical assessment of what Internet researchers were actually doing, both with regard to methodological and ethical practices. One exception was a survey of the first generation of Web researchers by Musch and Reips (2000). These authors surveyed online researchers who had conducted an experiment as opposed to a survey online. Interestingly, Musch and Reips (2000) said "ethical problems were not considered a problem by most Web experimenters" (p. 71). Later in the chapter, they addressed the issue of inducement for participation in Internet research. Musch and Reips (2000) reported 13 of 34 experimenters said they offered a monetary reward to participants. The studies included 10 lotteries with prizes ranging from $11 to $1,224, and three studies that paid every participant a sum from $6 to $15 dollars. In light of Baron's comment and the University of Calgary guidelines mentioned previously, one must wonder what the criteria are for deciding whether the chance for $1,224 in a lottery represents an ethically excessive inducement.

A CONTENT ANALYSIS OF PSYCHOLOGICAL RESEARCH ON THE NET

In this section, we describe a content analysis of Internet surveys and experiments by psychologists. Specifically, we assessed how researchers conduct their studies online and also how well online researchers follow ethical guidelines. First, we used Reips (2000) list of recommendations for Web researchers to create a coding sheet that allows us to describe how psychologists conduct online surveys, personality tests and experiments. We used Reips' guidelines rather than those of Michalak and Szabo (1998) because the former guidelines were based on empirical analysis. It was also relatively easy to operationally define items that represented specific instances of the more general advice that Web researchers (a) create an attractive site, (b) emphasize the site's trustworthiness, (c) employ other features attractive to participants and (d) employ a high entrance barrier technique. Second, we used a draft of the pending version of what became the new APA (2003) ethics code to create a second coding sheet that allowed us to analyze and describe the extent to which these Internet researchers comply with fundamental ethical principles for research.

Sources

We identified 22 Internet labs or portals to surveys and experiments that were active in the early months of 2002. Table 1 lists the portals still active in February 2003 and the number of studies in our sample from each of these Internet labs. Originally, we located these sites by means of searching and linking. We entered various key words (e.g., online experiments, psychological research) into search engines, such as Alta Vista, Google and Yahoo, that led us to many portals. In turn, these portals often provided links to other Internet labs. As we were preparing this chapter, we discovered some new gateways to online surveys and experiments.

Table 1: Number of Studies in Sample from Online Portals Active in February 2003

10	Psychological Research on the Net http://psych.hanover.edu/research/exponnet.html
2	Yahoo Directory [for Tests and Experiments] http://dir.yahoo.com/Social_Science/Psychology/ Research/Tests_and_Experiments/
1	Psychological Science on the Net http://www.psychologicalscience.net/pages/Tests_-_ Research_Online/
2	Language Experiments: The Portal for Psychological ... http://surf.to/experiments
3	Web Experimental Psychology Lab http://www.psych.unizh.ch/genpsy/Ulf/Lab/WebExp PsyLab.html
2	Decision Research Center http://psych.fullerton.edu/mbirnbaum/dec.htm
1	Current Online Experiments U of Saarland, Germany http://www.uni-saarland.de/fak5/ronald/home.htm
4	SE Missouri State University http://www4.semo.edu/snell/survey.htm
1	Trier Experimental Server http://cogpsy.uni-trier.de:8000/TEServ-e.html
1	Interactive CyberLab for Web Experiments http://we-by-jiro.net/english/exp/exp_e.shtml
2	Online Surveys http://www.psych-central.com/online1.htm
1	UCI Cognitive Science Experiments http://psiexp.ss.uci.edu/
3	University of Nebraska-Lincoln http://psych.unl.edu/psychlaw/research.asp
1	Leaf Experiment: U of Liverpool in England http://wwwcgi.liv.ac.uk/~rlawson/leafH/leafHex.html
1	Theoretical Social Psychology Experiment http://www.iit.edu/~reevkev/hard/
1	Jonathon Baron's Questionnaire Studies http://www.psych.upenn.edu/~baron/qs.html
1	Laughlab: United Kingdom http://www.laughlab.co.uk/home.html
4	Social Psychology Network http://www.socialpsychology.org/expts.htm#studies
2	Social Psychology Research on the Internet at USC http://www.usc.edu/dept/LAS/psychology/socialpsycexpt/

Materials

We created two coding sheets. Table 2 presents data obtained from the first coding sheet. To accommodate the format of this volume, we rephrased some of the labels and statements and also omitted the demographic items for the rater, date of participation, portal, research topic, research method, investigator and country of origin. This coding sheet used simple "yes" or "no" questions to evaluate compliance with Reips' (2000) recommendations for Web researchers to (a) create an attractive site; (b) emphasize the site's trustworthiness; (c) employ other features attractive to participants and (d) employ a high entrance barrier technique.

We adapted Reips' (2000, pp. 110-111) guidelines by devising three to eight items for each of the four categories in Table 2. Our operational definitions for compliance assessed whether the website: (a) is generally attractive (e.g., No or Yes: website is free of advertising such as commercial banners); (b) emphasizes its trustworthiness (e.g., website emphasizes its scientific purpose); (c) employs features attractive to participants (e.g., No or Yes: website provides a chance of prize or payment such as a fee or lottery) and (d) uses high entrance barrier technique (e.g., No or Yes: Instructions say participation is serious and/or science needs good data).

Table 3 presents data obtained from the second coding sheet. Once again, we rephrased some of the labels and statements to accommodate the format of this volume. Table 3 omits the four items assessing ethical standard 8.07 regarding deception in research because no online study reported use of any deception. This coding sheet also used simple yes or no questions to evaluate compliance with the APA's (2003) ethical principles of psychologists and code of conduct. As above, we devised one to 12 items to assess compliance with each of the following 12 ethical standards that seemed applicable to online research:

Table 2: Ranked Percent Compliance with Reips' (2000) Recommendations

%	Website is generally attractive
2	Site offers alternative versions of a study in formats such as frames, no frames, or text
10	Site offers multilingual pages
33	There are signs that site could be interesting such as awards or comments
84	Site looks good: nice graphics, good functions, fast loads
96	Site is free of advertising such as commercial banners

%	Website emphasizes it trustworthiness
22	There is an active link to the institutional Web page
39	Site offers more than one study
39	Site allows asking for information before doing study
67	Site emphasizes its scientific purpose
78	Site ensures (and keeps) confidentiality
88	Site provides name of researcher's institution
90	Site provides contact information: e-mail or phone number
96	Study conducted by an academic or non-profit institution

Table 2: (continued) Ranked Percent Compliance with Reips' (2000) Recommendations

%	**Website employs other features to attract participants**
16	Site provides a chance of prize/payment: fee or lottery
	If YES, 2 of 8 (25%) guarantee certain payment or prize
	If YES, 7 of 8 (88%) say completion required for gratuity
36	Site tells participants "how near finish" they are [n = 42]
43	Site design results in shorter load times for ensuing pages [n = 23]

%	**Website employs high entrance barrier technique**
8	Instructions say participant can be traced by Internet Protocol (IP) address or cookie
35	Study employs an experimental manipulation
37	Says participation is serious and/or science needs good data
37	Instructions warn about sensitive aspects or risks [n = 30]
41	Instructions promote credibility of researcher: Who am I?
43	Instructions "personalize" by asking for e-mail or phone
74	Instructions state how long the study will take to complete
84	Instructions say compliance and/or completion is a requirement for gratuity [n = 8]
88	Instructions provide institutional affiliation

- 2.01 Boundaries of Competence: two items;
- 3.06 Conflict of Interest: one item;
- 3.10 Informed Consent: four items;
- 4.01 Maintaining Confidentiality: three items;
- 6.01 Documentation of ... Work, and Maintenance of Records: one item;
- 8.01 Institutional Approval: two items;
- 8.02 Informed Consent to Research: 12 items;
- 8.04 Client/Patient, Student and Subordinate Research Participants: one item;
- 8.05 Dispensing with Informed Consent for Research: one item;
- 8.06 Offering Inducements for Research Participation: one item;
- 8.07 Deception in Research: four items;
- 8.08 Debriefing: six items.

Procedure

Interrater Agreement. We evaluated our initial coding system and established interrater accuracy and reliability on several online studies. Initially, each of three raters independently evaluated the same studies for compliance with Reips' (2000) recommendations for Web researchers and for compliance with ethical standards for research (American Psychological Association, 2003). We discussed all disagreements and

Table 3: Ranked Percent Compliance with APA (2003) Ethical Standards

%	2.01 Boundaries of Competence
55	Site indicates the credentials (degree) of researcher/PI
57	Site provides a way to confirm these credentials easily

%	3.06 Conflict of Interest
2	Site declares any incentives or restrictions on publication

%	3.10 Informed Consent
22	Site permits asking a question at any point during study
45	Site states person must be 18 years old to participate
51	Site documents informed consent such as clicking: I Agree
63	Site permits asking questions before giving consent

%	4.01 Maintaining Confidentiality
19	Site says private and study data go in separate files [n = 21]
20	Study employs a secure site; a lock icon appears on site
45	Study asks for personal information: name, phone, e-mail

%	6.01 Documentation of Professional ... Records
39	Site describes data creation, maintenance, and disposal

%	8.01 Institutional Approval
27	Site provides way to confirm IRB approval by means of a case number or link to IRB contact person
31	Site states that the host institution approved the study

%	8.02 Informed Consent to Research
4	Site encourages participant to print or save consent form
16	Site offers financial or other inducements for participation
20	Site states foreseeable consequences of declining to participate or withdrawing anytime during the study
31	Site identifies IRB contact for any questions about rights
31	Site makes it easy to reach IRB contact by e-mail/phone
43	Sites states procedures for and limits of confidentiality
45	Site indicates potential benefits to participants or others
55	Site says one can decline to participate/withdraw anytime
71	Site states foreseeable factors affecting willingness to participate: potential risks, discomfort, or adverse effects
74	Site describes the expected duration of the research
76	Sites describes the procedures used in the research
84	Site states requirements to receive/qualify for incentive
86	Site describes the purpose of the research

Table 3: (continued) Ranked Percent Compliance with APA (2003) Ethical Standards

%	**8.04 Student and Subordinate Research Participants**
5	Site allows students to meet requirement or get extra credit [n = 42]

%	**8.05 Dispensing With Informed Consent for Research**
29	Sites dispenses with informed consent on grounds that study is truly anonymous

%	**8.06 Offering Inducements for Research Participation**
100	Site avoids excessive or inappropriate inducements

%	**8.08 Debriefing**
27	Site gives references or links for more information on topic
29	Site tries to minimize harm: says who can help [n = 17]
33	Study ends abruptly (dead end) with nowhere to navigate
40	Debriefing provides appropriate information about the study either at its conclusion or indicates a date when this information will be e-mailed or posted on the Internet
54	Study gives debriefing statement at end of data collection
85	Contact person answers e-mail inquiry promptly [n = 13]

revised our coding sheets. Subsequently repeating this entire process produced the final coding system depicted in Tables 2 and 3 and demonstrated that interrater agreement was high (i.e., > 90 percent for all three pairs of raters).

Content Analysis. The first author evaluated 19 sites, 12 of which were included in our sample, and the second author evaluated 26 sites, 18 of which were included in our sample. A third rater evaluated 14 sites, nine of which were included in our sample. Each rater surfed to a research portal, participated in one or more studies at each Internet lab or portal and then completed both coding sheets. In addition, each rater printed copies of all of the Web pages for archival purposes. Collectively, we evaluated 59 sites, 49 of which were unique and comprised our sample. Finally, our analysis of the 10 studies evaluated independently by two different raters revealed that we had maintained high levels of interrater accuracy and reliability during our content analysis of these online sites for surveys and experiments.

RESULTS AND DISCUSSION

Sample Demographics

We identified the demographic characteristics of the online studies in our sample such as the country of origin, investigator, method and topic area (after the categories on the APS Psychological Research on the Net website: http://psych.hanover.edu/ research/exponnet.html). We used N = 49 to calculate all of the percentages unless noted otherwise. The majority of the online studies originated in the USA (55 percent) followed by Germany (10 percent), United Kingdom (10 percent) and Canada (8 percent). The majority of investigators posting studies identified themselves as university faculty (35 percent), undergraduates (27 percent) or graduate students (14 percent); however, we were unable to identify the remaining 24 percent of the Internet researchers. Online surveys (65 percent) outnumbered online experiments (35 percent). Finally, the online studies represented 12 different content areas: biological psychology/neuropsychology, cognition, developmental psychology, emotions, forensic psychology, general issues, health psychology, industrial/organizational, personality, psychology and religion, sensation and perception, and social psychology.

Although previous studies have focused on the demographic characteristics of the participants, our study is the first to report the demographic characteristics of the Internet researchers. We found that the majority of the Internet researchers are from the USA and Canada. Our result superficially resembles those of Krantz and Dalal (2000) who indicated that 80 percent to 90 percent of the participants for online studies in English say they are North Americans. Our finding that surveys outnumber experiments is consistent with the claim of the AAAS report that the survey is the most common form of Internet research (Frankel & Siang, 1999). Finally, our sample included a few studies from the various content areas; however, our sampling was not proportional to the number of studies available in each category. For example, in February 2003 the APS portal listed over 40 social psychology studies and only five industrial/organizational studies.

Compliance with Reips' (2000) Recommendations for Web Researchers

We evaluated compliance with Reips' (2000) recommendations for Web researchers to (a) create an attractive site, (b) emphasize the site's trustworthiness, (c) employ other features attractive to participants and (d) employ a high entrance barrier technique. Setting the threshold for compliance at 50 percent, we found that Internet surveys and experiment sites did not achieve the threshold for compliance on 15 of the 25 (60 percent) recommendations. Table 2 describes "compliance" with Reips' suggestions within each of the four categories by ranking items from lowest to highest percent "Yes" scores. Overall, the studies complied most with the recommendation to emphasize trustworthiness and least with the recommendation to employ other features to attract participants.

Website is Generally Attractive. Three of the five recommendations about making the website attractive did not achieve the 50 percent threshold of compliance. The study sites produced low compliance with recommendations to provide alternative versions of a study (2 percent), offer multilingual pages (10 percent) and include awards and comments that signal the Web could be interesting (33 percent). These study sites achieved high compliance with recommendations to look nice in terms of graphics, functionality and loading quickly (84 percent), and avoiding commercial advertising (96 percent).

The dominance of North American researchers who themselves speak English and use current technology may explain why so few Internet research sites either offer multilingual pages or provide alternative versions of their study. Moreover, sites that did offer these amenities all originated in Europe. We seldom encountered commercial advertising. In one case, the website included a link (Amazon.com) to a book by the author, and in the other case the website included an advertisement for the foundation supporting the research.

Website Emphasizes its Trustworthiness. The online studies complied most with Reips' recommendations to emphasize the site's trustworthiness. Five of the eight recommendations in this category exceeded the 50 percent threshold of compliance. For example, the site indicated the study was a product of an academic or non-profit institution (96 percent), provided researcher contact information via e-mail or phone number (90 percent), named the researcher's institution (88 percent), ensured confidentiality (78 percent) and emphasized its scientific purpose (67 percent). On the other hand, the online studies produced low compliance with recommendations to ask for further information before doing the study (39 percent), offer more than one study (39 percent) and provide an active link to the institutional home page (22 percent).

Most of the higher scoring items reflect ethically appropriate activities; however, one exception pertains to allowing participants to ask questions before agreeing to do the study, an aspect of informed consent. Only a few sites offered a single study; however, a single study does not always indicate the site's trustworthiness. For example, Jonathan Baron offers a single study at a time; however, new studies appear at regular intervals. In addition, several online researchers, who previously listed a single study, have relocated their study to one of the larger portals such as the APS site or Reips' Web Experiment Psychology Lab.

Website Employs Other Features to Attract Participants. The online studies complied least with Reips' recommendations to employ other features to attract participants because all three items fell short of the 50 percent threshold for compliance. For example, the website provided a chance of prize or payment (16 percent), informed participants about how near they are to the finish (36 percent, where n = 42) and produced shorter loading times for successive pages (43 percent, where n = 23). Further examination of the eight studies offering any inducement revealed most employed a lottery (75 percent) and only 25 percent guaranteed a certain payment or prize for research participation. All but one of the eight studies (88 percent) clearly stated that participants had to complete the study to qualify for the gratuity.

Musch and Reips' (2000) survey revealed 13 of 34 (38 percent) of the experiments employed monetary incentives as opposed to 16 percent of our studies. Perhaps there is a systematic difference between experiments and surveys in this regard, and our lower percentage is influenced by the 2:1 ratio of surveys to experiments in our sample. Overwhelmingly, researchers preferred a lottery as a method for inducement for participation; however, two studies paid all the participants.

Website Employs High Entrance Barrier Technique. Six of the nine recommendations fell short of the 50 percent threshold for compliance. For example, the sampled studies indicated the participant could be traced by an Internet Protocol address or cookie (8 percent), employed an experimental manipulation (35 percent), stated participation is serious or science needs good data (37 percent), prepared the participant for any sensitive aspects of the study (37 percent where n = 30), promoted the credibility of the researcher (41 percent), and personalized the study by asking for an e-mail address or phone number (43 percent). On the other hand, the sampled sites performed above threshold by stating how long the study will take (74 percent), stating completion is required to qualify for a gratuity (84 percent where n = 8), and providing an institutional affiliation (88 percent).

The online studies in our sample did not appear to implement the high entrance barrier technique. This outcome is consistent with the sentiments of Mueller et al. (2000) and again may reflect the predominance of surveys that typically require shorter time commitments. The use of this technique may be much more appropriate for experiments that take some time to complete.

Compliance with APA (2003) Ethical Standards

We evaluated compliance with 12 ethical standards applicable to virtual research (APA, 2003). Again setting the threshold for compliance at 50 percent, we found that Internet surveys and experiment sites did not achieve the threshold for compliance on 22 of the 35 (63 percent) items. Table 3 describes "compliance" with 11 ethical standards by ranking items from lowest to highest percent "Yes" scores. Overall, the studies complied most with the items measuring avoidance of deception and excessive inducements and least with the items assessing informed consent and debriefing. Note that Table 3 omits the four items pertaining to Ethical Standard 8.08 (Deception in Research) because no online studies in our sample employed deception, and the other three questions about such things as allowing deceived participants to withdraw their data were inapplicable.

Boundaries of Competence (2.01). Both items exceeded the 50 percent threshold for compliance. For example, 55 percent of the studies indicated the credentials of the researcher or principal investigator and 57 percent of the studies provided a way to confirm these credentials easily.

Although the online studies in our sample scored above the 50 percent threshold for compliance, the scores could and should be higher. Quite simply, Internet studies that indicate the credentials of the researcher and make them easy to confirm comply with Reips' (2000) recommendation to promote trustworthiness. Also, these simple measures avoid any hint of deception that may arise from the perception that the researcher is cloaked in anonymity (Frankel & Siang, 1999). Furthermore, presenting appropriate credentials distinguishes the research from commercial endeavors and indicates the scientific legitimacy of the study that may promote the public perception of psychology.

Conflict of Interest (3.06). The one item about declaring any conflicts of interest, such as financial incentives for the research or restrictions on publication, did not achieve the threshold for compliance (2 percent). One reason for this low compliance score may be that social scientists receive relatively fewer corporate grants for research, especially in comparison to the biomedical disciplines. Hence, Internet researchers feel little need to make a formal statement about conflict of interest. Nonetheless, the issue is important as evidenced by the recent "Statement" (n.d.) of the American Association of University Professors that discusses prominent cases and reviews potential hazards.

Informed Consent (3.10). Two of the four items fell short of the 50 percent threshold for compliance. The lower scoring items pertained to allowing participants to ask questions anytime (22 percent) and to stating that you must be 18 years old to participate (45 percent). The above threshold items included appropriately documenting consent by clicking: "I Agree" (51 percent) and allowing participants to ask questions before consenting to participate (63 percent).

Although it is technically possible to allow participants to ask questions at any time by restricting the availability of the study to the time when the Internet researcher is online (e.g., in a chat room), this strategy would be difficult for studies that employ the direct method by posting their study on the Internet with an open invitation for anyone to participate (Hewson et al., 1996). A greater concern pertains to the age of participants. Nosek, Banaji and Greenwald (2002) discussed the issues of Internet research with children (under the age of 18 years old) and the more difficult issue of controlling participation in research not designed for children. To this end, they presented four strategies for minimizing the opportunity for children to participate in Internet studies. In addition, Nosek et al. advised Internet researchers to review the U.S. regulations regarding protection of the privacy of children under the age of 13.

We thought it noteworthy that only one-half of the studies in our sample formally documented consent (by clicking "I Agree"). In short, documentation of informed consent stands out as a focal issue especially when the age, competency and comprehension of the online participant is unknown (see Frankel & Siang, 1999). For example, the guidelines for conducting Web-based survey research from the University of New Hampshire ("Guidelines," 2002) specifically require Internet researchers to request the IRB waive the requirement for obtaining a signed consent from each participant (i.e., in order to use clicking on "I Agree").

Finally, many studies in our sample allowed participants to e-mail the researcher with questions before consenting to participate in the study. Unfortunately, we did not explore this option by systematically contacting researchers before participating in the study.

Maintaining Confidentiality (4.01). None of the three items achieved the 50 percent threshold for compliance. For example, personal information and responses will go into separate data files (19 percent, where n = 21); the study employs a secure site as indicated by a lock icon (20 percent) and the study asks for personal or private information such as name or phone number (45 percent).

Although psychologists are expected to protect confidential information, our results indicate considerable room for improvement. For example, Nosek et al. (2002) noted that one way to protect the privacy of online participants is to encrypt data; however, our results show use of a secure site to collect data is infrequent. These authors note that there are both more and less sophisticated and costly ways to effectively protect participant confidentiality. It is also discouraging to see that one-half of the studies that solicit personal information do not indicate that this information and the participant's responses will go into separate files. Nosek et al. also raised the important point that post-study interactions with participants pose problems with regard to confidentiality as well (see also Frankel & Siang, 1999).

Documentation of Professional and Scientific Work, and Maintenance of Records (6.01). The one item assessing whether the site states how the researcher will create, maintain and dispose of record and data fell short of the 50 percent threshold (39 percent). Nosek et al. (2002) noted that data stored on servers connected to the Internet pose more risks to the confidentiality of participants than data stored in locked file cabinets. Frankel and Siang (1999) noted that data disposal could be hazardous as well because erased material can often be recovered. The more general issue of safeguarding the privacy of participants by securing their data is an important one and one addressed at length in guidelines for Internet research (see, for example, "Guidelines," 2002). For example, this document specifically lists 10 questions that Internet researchers should ask their Web host. The list includes questions such as "What security measures are in place to protect data during transmission from the browser to the Web server?" and "What are the organization's data storage and back-up policies and processes?"

Institutional Approval (8.01). Neither of the two items achieved the 50 percent threshold. For example, only 27 percent provided a way to confirm IRB approval by providing a case number or link, and only 31 percent actually stated that the host institution had approved the study. It is noteworthy that only one-third of the studies indicated institutional approval of the online study, a statement that would emphasize the trustworthiness and scientific merit of the study (Reips, 2000). There may be several explanations for these low scores. First, some Internet researchers contend that Internet research is inherently innocuous and need not be reviewed (see ethical standard 8.05 below about dispensing with informed consent). Second, our sample included several European studies. As noted previously, ethical regulations vary internationally. For example, Elgesem (2002) noted that there is no ethical review of projects within the social sciences and the humanities in Norway. Finally, Internet researchers may have omitted this information inadvertently. On the other hand, we encountered one (medical) study during the development of our coding system that actually included a link to a readable copy of the IRB approval form. Furthermore, the majority of studies posted on the PSYCHEXPERIMENTS site (http://psychexps.olemiss.edu/) in February 2003 included a link to a copy of the IRB approval form.

Informed Consent to Research (8.02). Seven of the 13 items produced compliance scores below the 50 percent threshold. For example, only 4 percent of the online studies encouraged the participant to print or save the consent form, provided financial or other inducements to obtain participants, stated the foreseeable consequences of declining to participate or withdrawing anytime (20 percent), identified the IRB contact person for any questions (31 percent), made it easy to reach the IRB contact by providing an e-mail link or phone number (31 percent), stated the procedures for and limits of confidentiality (43 percent) and described potential benefits to participants or others (45 percent). Alternatively, the online studies exceeded the threshold for compliance by saying one can decline to participate or withdraw anytime (55 percent) and describing foreseeable factors affecting the willingness to participate (71 percent), the expected duration of the research (74 percent), the procedures to be used in the research (76 percent), requirements to receive or qualify for an incentive for participation (84 percent, where n = 8) and the purpose of the research (86 percent).

Appendix B in the guidelines for conducting Web-based survey research from the University of New Hampshire "Guidelines" (2002) provides a template for informed consent that incorporates all 12 of our items. To the extent that the New Hampshire guidelines represent the emerging trend, we would expect much higher compliance on all of these items by future Internet researchers.

The virtual research ethics literature revealed various concerns regarding the process of informed consent; however, one special concern is the extent to which virtual research participants fully comprehend the details of the research into which they are consenting to participate. The more general concern is heightened both in the case of medical research (Paasche-Orlow et al., 2003) and online (therapeutic) intervention research (Childress & Asamen, 1998). Recent articles have proposed some interesting solutions. For example, Nosek et al. (2002) indicated that consent forms could benefit from inclusion of FAQs (frequently asked questions) that anticipate potential questions and concerns. Stanton and Rogelberg (2001) suggested the use of streaming video in place of traditional text. The idea is that the video will engage the attention and interest of online participants and thereby better inform participants. Stanton and Rogelberg also suggested use of "quiz" items that participants must answer correctly (to indicate their comprehension) in order to gain access to the actual study materials. In fact, we encountered such quizzes in a couple of the studies in our sample.

Client/Patient, Student and Subordinate Research Participants (8.04). Only 5 percent of the studies (where n = 42) indicated that the site allowed students to meet a course requirement or get extra credit for participation. On one hand, the low scores on this item are surprising given that about one-half of the researchers were faculty or graduate students who previously might have recruited participants from institutional subject pools. On the other hand, the researchers may explicitly seek a more demographically diverse sample.

We wonder whether the rise of Internet studies will have some negative impact on institutional participant pools. We have encountered two solutions to the problem of protecting anonymity while giving students credit for participation in research. First, we recently learned about a study that allowed students to print a page documenting their participation in an online study as part of the debriefing procedure. Second, we also encountered a more secure solution (i.e., one not so amenable to counterfeit certificates of participation). One commercial site for Internet research advertises that it can handle "extra credit" for subject pools. Moreover, the Web master at personality/science.org (http://www.personalityscience.org/csh/PSO.nsf/about) collaborated with the IRB at the University of Minnesota in the development of this Internet site, and it certainly represents a model for others who aspire to comply ethically. Unfortunately, no studies were available at this site during our period of data collection.

Dispensing with Informed Consent for Research (8.05). About 29 percent of the sites included a statement that the study could dispense with informed consent because it entailed a truly anonymous survey. Further analysis revealed two things about the studies in our sample that dispensed with informed consent. First, 11 studies were surveys and three were experiments. Second, nine of the 14 studies in our sample involved investigators who were faculty or graduate students and only two involved undergraduates. The status of the remaining three investigators was unknown.

Offering Inducement for Research Participation (8.06). The one item determining whether the online studies avoided excessive or inappropriate inducements to obtain participants produced 100 percent compliance. In our sample, eight studies provided some form of financial incentive, and none seemed excessive. Participants received a certain payment in two studies ($3 in one study and $8 in the other) and entry into a random drawing for a larger sum ranging from $10 to $500 in six studies. One study actually paid all participants and awarded an additional $25 to a single participant. In some cases, the odds were clear: one participant of the 200 participants would receive $200. In other cases, both the odds and payment were uncertain. For example, a random process determines whether a payment of $500 goes to an individual or whether the same $500 goes in various sums to 19 different individuals (i.e., one at $100, three at $50, six at $25 and 10 at $10).

Our results resemble those of Musch and Reips (2000). They reported 13 of 34 studies entailed payments to participants: 10 studies with lotteries offering $11 to $1,224 and three studies that paid all participants a sum from $6 to $15. Clearly, the range of payments to all participants are comparable; however, the lottery for $1,224 is much larger than any one we encountered and again raises the question regarding the threshold for deciding whether the chance for $1,224 in a lottery represents an ethically excessive inducement. The random drawings in our sample generally conformed to the policy statement about use of lotteries for payment of participants mandated by the Department of Psychology at the University of Calgary ("Lotteries," 2000). They mandated that informed consent procedures must include:

- A clear statement of the amount of the reward(s) involved;
- A statement of the exact odds of a participant actually winning;
- A clear timetable of the draw(s);
- A clear description of the actual process of selection and
- An indication of exactly how and when payment will be made.

Debriefing (8.08). Four of the six items fell short of the 50 percent threshold for compliance. For example, the low scoring items included providing references or links for more information on the topic (27 percent), taking steps to minimize the harmful impact of procedures by saying who can help (29 percent, where n = 17), ending abruptly in a dead-end with nowhere to navigate (33 percent), debriefing that provides appropriate information about the study either at its conclusion or that indicates a date when this information will be e-mailed or posted on the Internet (40 percent). The above threshold items entailed providing a debriefing statement at the conclusion of the data collection (54 percent) and a contact person who responded to inquiries by e-mail in a timely manner (85 percent, where n = 13).

In many studies in our sample, the debriefing procedures were dismal. Quite simply, only about one-half of the studies even provided a debriefing statement, and one in every three studies ended abruptly and required closing and reopening the browser. Furthermore, most of the debriefing statements were cursory. We were not surprised by these results. First, our original interest in virtual research ethics was prompted, in part, by similar experiences during our informal period of participation in online research. Second, the early literature regarding Internet research ethics said little about debriefing. Third, Musch and Reips (2000) indicated that their online experimenters answered the question regarding feedback about the design of the experiment by saying: "About half of the experiments conveyed the experimental design to the participants, either immediately after participation (four) or with some temporal delay (12). Participants in 18 experiments were not informed about the design of the study in which they participated" (p. 81).

The current trend is toward much greater emphasis on more thorough debriefing procedures. This is markedly different from the view of Mueller et al. (2000) who said that it was a matter of simple courtesy to provide a debriefing statement after participants submit their responses to a survey. For example, the guidelines for conducting Web-based survey research from the University of New Hampshire's "Guidelines" (2002) mandated:

"Researchers should provide feedback (debriefing) to participants at the end of the survey. Effective feedback should: acknowledge participation, thank participants, sum up the purpose of the research, provide participants with instructions to request results (if applicable), relay any special instructions, provide hyperlinks to Web pages containing related information and provide an e-mail link to the researcher(s) in case of any questions. To ensure that after reading the debriefing information participants want to keep their submitted responses as part of the data file, researchers can present participants with options to either keep in, or remove from the data file their responses before exiting the site" (p. 2).

Recent articles (e.g., Nosek et al., 2002; Stanton & Rogelberg, 2001) specifically address additional concerns about Internet debriefings. For example, both articles note that participants can opt out of an online study without reading the debriefing. Furthermore, no experimenter is there to help in the case of either confusion or adverse reactions of the participants who complete the study. The latter concern is heightened in the case of online (therapeutic) intervention research (Childress & Asamen, 1998). Both articles listed several options for Internet researchers to enable debriefing even if participants withdraw early from the study. Suggestions included: (a) e-mailing debriefing statements, (b) use of a "leave the study" button on every Web page that directs participants to the debriefing materials and (c) programming that overrides closing the browser prematurely. Stanton and Rogelberg (2001) also proposed use of FAQs and multimedia, such as streaming video, to better engage participants in the debriefing process and even limiting the time that the research was available online to a time when the researcher could be available in a chat room to address concerns or answer questions.

Recent guidelines for Internet research (see, for example, "Guidelines," 2002) also forcefully address the issue of debriefing in online studies. For example, the "Ethics Handbook for Psychology Students" at http://www.psych.ucalgary.ca/Research/ethics/apply/handbook.doc emphasizes the importance of meaningful educational gains for participants, apparently in response to skepticism from the university community regarding the value of participation in research by students. Specifically, this document calls for face-to-face interaction with participants (a) outlining the aspects of your content area, (b) answering participant questions and (c) discussing the study and how it relates to the content. A similar emphasis is apparent in the guidelines for Internet research in the "Guidelines" from the University of New Hampshire (2002). Its Appendix C provides an example for a substantive Debriefing Sheet for Internet surveys. Furthermore, the debriefing sheet says: "Click here if you have read this information and want to keep your responses to the survey" as opposed to "Click here if you have read this information and want to remove your responses from the data file." No studies in our sample allowed participants to remove the data after the debriefing. In fact, submitting the data always preceded any debriefing.

One obvious question is why Internet researchers do a less-than-adequate job of debriefing their participants? First, we speculate that the researchers believe the details of their study are transparent and require little further explanation. That is, researchers are egocentric and fail to realize that their participants are not immersed in the culture of psychology. Second, Internet researchers do not think about the value-added aspects of participation in research that may encourage participants in their study to return in the future. Perhaps Internet researchers should regard participants as a renewable resource rather than as a limited commodity. In short, psychologists must realize that the prospects for future research may be limited if the growth in the number of individuals who will participate in research does not exceed the growth in the number of Internet researchers.

FUTURE TRENDS AND CONCLUSION

We have reported the methods and findings for our content analysis of Internet surveys and experiments by psychologists. In review, we have described the extent to which psychological studies comply with Reips' (2000) recommendations for Web researchers and the extent to which behavioral studies on the Internet comply with ethical standards for research (APA, 2003).

We are confident about our findings even though our sample of online psychology studies is not exhaustive. First, our method was sound because our coding system was simple, and we established high levels of interrater agreement prior to the study and maintained them during the study. Second, our sample represented a relatively generous proportion of the Internet studies available during our period of data collection, even though the absolute number of studies in our sample may appear small. Third, our results resemble those from prior studies whenever we have comparable data. On the other hand, we acknowledge some limitations with regard to our methods and conclusions. Our sample did not include studies that either target specific populations or employ psycho-therapeutic Internet interventions (see Childress & Asamen, 1998); however, these studies should comprise only a small portion of those online at any one time. In addition, our sample did not include any studies from PSYCHEXPERIMENTS (http://psychexps.olemiss.edu/), a site that listed nine studies in February 2003. Despite attempts to access these studies by different coders from different computers, we repeatedly encountered problems with incompatible software. Finally, we neglected to examine compliance with ethical guidelines regarding assessment issues such as the use of obsolete tests and test security.

In the previous section we presented and discussed our results in the narrower context of specific recommendations for Web researchers and also compliance with specific ethical standards. In the remainder of the chapter, we address emerging trends and larger issues pertinent to online participants, Internet scientists and IRBs.

Participants

In addition to other advantages of Web research (Reips, 2000), Internet researchers benefit from easy access to a large number of demographically diverse participants and online participants benefit from easy access to surveys and experiments. In some sense, the motivation for online researchers is much more apparent than the motivation for online participants. We forecast two trends with respect to participants in the next decade. One trend will entail much greater interest in the psychology of participation (Buchanan, 2000). The second trend will focus on the rights of online participants.

To date the literature on the psychology of participation in Internet research is sparse. For example, Buchanan (2000) reported the results from two experiments in which participants explain why they were subjects. Some 45 percent of the participants indicated that they were "curious or interested" or "enjoy tests or surveys" and only 9 percent indicated they were "helping research." Other evidence indicates that participants appear to be motivated by monetary compensation. For example, Musch and Reips (2000) indicated significantly more participants completed studies that offered an individual payment or lotteries as opposed to no monetary compensation. In addition, offering financial incentives tended to generate higher rates of participation than in ones with no monetary compensation.

A couple of studies in our sample included questions related to the psychology of participation. One study assessed participants' agreement with items such as:

* I am interested in the subject matter of this study.

* I am participating in this study for the chance to win money.

* It is important to help researchers conducting psychological experiments.

Another study asked participants:

* Did you enjoy filling out the questionnaire?

* In the future, would you like to participate in another study?

* To what degree do you think your answers are anonymous?

* How would you rate the seriousness of your submission (i.e., you gave honest answers)?

Future Internet researchers should consider including such items as well as items asking about participants' online research history.

The second trend concerns the rights of online participants. In our introduction we noted that Jones (1994) posed the rhetorical question: What kind of Internet research activities would constitute a clear violation of professional ethics? Although our study identified various shortcomings with respect to compliance with ethical standards in virtual research, we do not regard these as clear violations as much as they are a product of the newness of Internet research. On the other hand, an important question is whether these shortcomings affect participants adversely. We do know that despite good intentions and the researchers' best efforts, harm can be done to participants in Internet research (Bier, Sherblom, & Gallo, 1996). What we do not know is how online subjects balance a sense of increased empowerment and ownership from participation (Buchanan, 2000) with a sense of exploitation and irritation produced by inadequate and uninformative debriefings, studies that terminate in dead ends and "oversampling." The later concept refers to the resistance to responding within organizations to a request to complete another survey that eventually may spread to and through the Web (Stanton & Rogelberg, 2001). The benefit of empowering participants is that they may return and contribute to other studies in the future whereas the liability of irritating participants is that they will not return and may also discourage others from participation in online research in the future. It is important to note that the issue of participation in future online studies is quite different from the methodological concern widely discussed in the literature regarding participants who do the same study more than once (e.g., Buchanan, 2000; Reips, 2000).

The practical problem is how to make online participants proactive and encourage them to ask questions if they do not have adequate information and speak up if they feel exploited. Perhaps, there is a need for an online participants' bill of rights (Stanton & Rogelberg, 2001). According to these researchers, "This bill of rights would promote norms concerning what online research participants can expect and demand from researchers who seek their participation. These norms would pertain to the whole networked research experience—from receiving solicitation all the way to obtaining reports of the research results" (p. 213). Although Stanton and Rogelberg did not provide any details, Internet researchers might find a useful starting point in the bill of rights developed by Rogers (1996). Perhaps such a bill will garner support from an Internet counterpart to the Alliance for Human Research Participation (http://www.researchprotection.org/). This organization represents lay people and professionals dedicated to advancing responsible and ethical medical research practices, to ensuring protection of the human rights, dignity and welfare of human participants and to minimizing the risks associated with such endeavors. In preparing this chapter, our search revealed several universities that incorporate bills of rights into the process of face-to-face research. For example, the University of California at Davis posted its Experimental Subjects Bill of Rights online (http://ovcr.ucdavis.edu/Forms/hs/BillofRightsSocialBehaviorStudies.PDF). It is also noteworthy that this document states California law requires researchers to provide participants with a bill of rights and also to obtain a signature on both the bill of rights and the informed consent form. Future online researchers may have to provide a bill of rights to their online participants as well.

Internet Scientists

Our own results and reading of the literature lead us to forecast two trends with respect to Internet scientists or online researchers. One trend is that many Internet scientists will face much greater regulation and scrutiny with regard to all online research studies in the future. The second trend is that Internet scientists as a matter of necessity will become public relations agents.

Most Internet researchers in the future will have to deal with more regulation and scrutiny than the initial cohorts of online researchers did. In fact, the initial generations of Internet researchers have had it relatively easy because IRBs have had more questions than answers about online research. For example, we must remember that inquiries and uncertainty about research in cyberspace on the part of IRBs was one of the driving forces that led the AAAS to convene its panel in June 1999. Since that time, organizations such as the Association of Internet Researchers (2003) and institutions such as the University of New Hampshire have implemented specific guidelines for Internet research ("Guidelines," 2002). Other institutions will implement guidelines of their own that will increase the demands on Internet researchers. As an example noted before, the University of New Hampshire specifically requires Internet researchers to request the IRB to waive the requirement for obtaining a signed consent from each participant (i.e., clicking on "I Agree" as a way to document informed consent). In the previous section we described recent developments regarding bills of rights for research participants. Will it be long before IRBs require Internet researchers to distribute a bill of rights to participants? The common advice for Web researchers to keep their informed consent pages short to minimize putting off participants may no longer be an option. On the other hand, online researchers may be able to employ intrinsically more entertaining methods for their informed consent and debriefing procedures such as the use of video streams discussed earlier.

Internet researchers will also become public relations agents who must reconsider their views about participants. The emphasis here is both ethical in the sense of promoting and protecting the dignity of research participants as well as practical in the sense of recruiting new and experienced subjects to share among the growing number of Internet studies.

Stanton and Rogelberg (2001) argued that researchers must treat Internet research participants as a finite and depletable resource. Furthermore, they stated "the potential for overuse of participant resources argues for some type of networked research consortium. Such a consortium could provide a similar project registry function, but this could be paired with guidelines and assistance to help researchers avoid alienating potential research participants" (p. 213).

What we have here is an instance of the tragedy of the commons (Hardin, 1968). Hardin described the common as a grazing area that belongs to a community. Herders can graze a few cattle or sheep, and everyone in the community benefits from the common resource. The practical problem is that as soon as too many herders assert their individual interests, they will overgraze the common and render it unusable by anyone. In preparing this chapter, a quick search of the Internet revealed that others had applied the concept of the tragedy of the commons to other instances of behavior in cyberspace. For example, Howard Rheingold illustrated an online commons that was violated by lawyers who "spammed" every online newsgroup with advertising for their services (http://www.well.com/user/hlr/tomorrow/tomorrowcommons.html). Clearly, future Internet researchers must recognize that the population of online participants may be another instance of a commons that we must maintain and nurture rather than exploit for individual or scientific gain.

IRBs

The results of our content analysis and review of the contemporary literature have implications for IRBs. For example, our results provide norms regarding current online surveys and experiments and a baseline for evaluating future proposals for online research. We forecast two trends with regard to IRBs in the next decade. One trend is that IRBs will face more proposals for online research. As noted previously, there is a steady increase in the number of Internet surveys and experiments from year to year. Thus, IRBs will have more proposals to consider. The second trend is that IRBs will devote more attention to the various issues raised by this chapter and this volume. In the discussion above, we have identified a number of proposals and procedures that IRBs may need to consider as they evaluate online research proposals. For example, IRBs may decide to establish their own guidelines specific to Internet research such as those of the University of New Hampshire. In addition, IRBs may have to take a stand on specific practices such as clicking on "I Agree" as an acceptable alternative to a signature on the informed consent. Finally, IRBs may consider the wisdom of adopting guidelines pertaining to a bill of rights for participants in both face-to-face as well as online research.

Ideally, IRBs and researchers should be partners in the effort to protect the welfare of human research participants. Nonetheless, the prospect of greater regulation of Internet research is daunting to online researchers who may believe that bill of rights, longer instructions and informed consent documents with quizzes may turn off participants. In other words, procedures put in place to protect human participants may in fact deter them from participating in online surveys and experiments either at the moment or ever again. In sum, there may be a delicate balance between protecting and alienating online participants, both in the short term as well as the long term.

We opened the chapter with a quote from Jim Thomas (1999) that indicated online research requires a commitment to established principles rather than the invention of new ethical rules. We concur and hope that Internet researchers and IRBs can work together to this end.

ACKNOWLEDGMENTS

We thank the Office of Research and Sponsored Programs at the University of Wisconsin-Eau Claire for grants to support data collection and preliminary presentations of the results at the National Conference for Undergraduate Research and Midwestern Psychological Association in 2002.

We thank Christopher Gade for his help with data collection and Ruth Cronje, Mike Donnelly, Ryan Hanson, Allen Keniston and April Bleske-Rechek for helpful comments on drafts of this manuscript. Finally, thanks to Ping Zing, the West Highland white terrier, whose companionship and gentle snoring provided a calming influence during the preparation of this manuscript.

REFERENCES

American Psychological Association. (1992). Ethical principles of psychologists and code of conduct. *American Psychologist, 47,* 1597-1611.

American Psychological Association. (2003). *Ethical principles of psychologists and code of conduct 2002.* Retrieved Feb. 15, 2003 from: http://www.apa.org/ethics/.

Association of Internet Researchers. (2003). *Ethical decision-making and Internet research.* Retrieved Jan. 15, 2003 from: http://www.aoir.org/reports/ethics.pdf.

Azar, B. (2000a, April). A Web of research. *Monitor on Psychology, 31*(4), 42-45.

Azar, B. (2000b, April). A Web experiment sampler. *Monitor on Psychology, 31*(4), 46-47.

Azar, B. (2000c, April). Online experiments: Ethically fair or foul? *Monitor on Psychology, 31*(4), 50-52.

Baron, J. & Siepmann, M. (2000). Techniques for creating and using Web questionnaires in research and teaching. In M. H. Birnbaum (Ed.), *Psychological Experiments on the Internet* (pp. 235-265). New York: Academic Press.

Batinic, B., Reips, U.-D., & Bosnjak, M. (Eds.) (2002). *Online Social Sciences.* Seattle, WA: Hogrefe & Huber Publishing.

Beans, B. E. (2000, April). Free of charge, open all hours. *Monitor on Psychology, 31*(4), 48-49.

Bier, M. C., Sherblom, S. A., & Gallo, M. A. (1996). Ethical issues in a study of Internet use: Uncertainty, responsibility, and the spirit of research relationships. *Ethics & Behavior, 6,* 141-151.

Birnbaum, M. H. (ed.) (2000). *Psychological Experiments on the Internet.* New York: Academic Press.

Birnbaum, M. H. (2001). *Introduction to Behavioral Research on the Internet.* Upper Saddle River, NJ: Prentice-Hall.

Bourke, K. (1998, September). The APS Internet Connection-Now available on-line: Interactive Experiments. *APS Observer, 11*(5), 14-15.

Buchanan, T. (2000). Potential of the Internet for personality research. In M. H. Birnbaum (Ed.), *Psychological Experiments on the Internet* (pp. 121-140). New York: Academic Press.

Childress, C. A. & Asamen, J. K. (1998). The emerging relationship of psychology and the Internet: Proposed guidelines for conducting Internet intervention research. *Ethics & Behavior, 8,* 19-35.

Elgesem, D. (2002). What is special about the ethical issues in online research? *Ethics and Information Technology, 4,* 195-203.

Frankel, M. S. & Siang, S. (1999, November). *Ethical and legal aspects of human subjects research on the Internet.* Retrieved Jan. 2, 2002: from http://www.aaas.org/spp/dspp/SFRL/projects/intres/main.htm.

Guidelines for conducting Web-based survey research. (2002, June). Retrieved Jan. 19, 2003 from University of New Hampshire, Office of Sponsored Research-Regulatory Compliance website: http://www.unh.edu/osr/compliance/Internet%20Research.pdf.

Hardin, G. (1968). The tragedy of the commons [electronic version]. *Science, 162,* 1243-1248. Retrieved Feb. 21, 2003 from: http://dieoff.com/page95.htm.

Hewson, C. M., Laurent, D., & Vogel, C. M. (1996). Proper methodologies for psychological and sociological studies conducted via the Internet. *Behavior Research Methods, Instruments, & Computers, 28,* 186-191.

Jones, R. A. (1994). The ethics of research in cyberspace [electronic version]. *Internet Research, 4*(3), 30-35.

Jones, S. G. (ed.) (1999). *Doing Internet Research: Critical Issues and Methods for Examining the Net.* Thousand Oaks, CA: Sage Publications.

Krantz, J. H. & Dalal, R. (2000). Validity of Web-based psychological research. In M. H. Birnbaum (Ed.), *Psychological Experiments on the Internet* (pp. 35-60). New York: Academic Press.

Lotteries as participant remuneration. (2000, March). Retrieved Oct. 31, 2001 from the University of Calgary, Department of Psychology website: http://www.psych.ucalgary.ca/Research/ethics/lotteries.html.

Michalak, E. E. & Szabo, A. (1998). Guidelines for Internet research: An update. *European Psychologist, 3,* 70-75.

Mueller, J. (1997, October 13). *Research on-line: Human participants ethics issues.* Retrieved Dec. 30, 2001 from: University of Calgary, Department of Psychology website: http://www.psych.ucalgary.ca/research/ethics/online.html.

Mueller, J. H., Jacobsen, D. M., & Schwarzer, R. (2000). What are computing experiences good for? A case study in online research. In M. H. Birnbaum (Ed.), *Psychological Experiments on the Internet* (pp. 195-216). New York: Academic Press.

Musch, J. & Reips, U-D. (2000). A brief history of Web experimenting. In M. H. Birnbaum (Ed.), *Psychological Experiments on the Internet* (pp. 61-87). New York: Academic Press.

Nosek, B. A., Banaji, M. R., & Greenwald, A. G. (2002). E-research: Ethics, security, design and control in psychological research on the Internet. *Journal of Social Issues, 58,* 161-176.

Paasche-Orlow, M. K., Taylor, H. A., & Brancati, F. L. (2003). Readability standards for informed-consent forms as compared with actual readability. *The New England Journal of Medicine, 348,* 721-726.

Psychology and the Internet. (2000, April). [special issue]. *Monitor on Psychology, 31(4).*

Reips, U-D. (2000). The Web experiment method: Advantages, disadvantages, and solutions. In M. H. Birnbaum (Ed.), *Psychological Experiments on the Internet* (pp. 89-117). New York: Academic Press.

Reips, U-D. & Bosnjak, M. (eds.) (2001). *Dimensions of Internet Science.* Lengerich, Germany: Pabst Science Publishers.

Rogers, T. (1996, November 13). *Research participants' bill of rights.* Retrieved Dec. 30, 2001 from University of Calgary, Department of Psychology website: http://www.psych.ucalgary.ca/Research/ethics/bill/bill.html.

Stanton, J. M. & Rogelberg, S. G. (2001). Using Internet/Intranet Web pages to collect organizational research data. *Organizational Research Methods, 4,* 200-217.

Statement on corporate funding of academic research. (n.d.) Retrieved February 2003 from the American Association of University Professors website: http://www.aaup.org/statements/Redbook.repcorf.htm.

Thomas, J. (1999, Spring). Balancing the ethical conundrums of Internet research: An existentialist view from the trenches. *Iowa Journal of Communication, 31,* 8-20.

Chapter II

Ethical Decision-Making and Internet Research: Recommendations from the AoIR Ethics Working Committee[1]*

Charles Ess
Drury University, USA

Steven Jones
University of Illinois at Chicago, USA and
Association of Internet Researchers

ABSTRACT

The AoIR ethics statement, developed by ethicists and researchers from 11 countries, articulates guiding questions for online research appropriate to the many disciplines—both within the social sciences and the humanities—that undertake such research. These guidelines are characterized by an ethical pluralism—one that acknowledges the legitimacy of a range of possible ethical responses to a given problem, especially as viewed from the perspectives of the diverse national and cultural traditions represented on the Web and the Net as global media. This is an excerpt of the full working document available at http://www.aoir.org/reports/ethics.pdf.

PROLOGUE

The Internet has opened up a wide range of new ways to examine human actions and/or interactions (inter/actions[2]) in new contexts, and from a variety of disciplinary and interdisciplinary approaches. As in its offline counterpart, online research also raises critical issues of risk and safety to the human subject. Hence, online researchers may encounter conflicts between the requirements of research and its possible benefits, on the one hand, and human subjects' rights to and expectations of autonomy, privacy, informed consent, etc., on the other hand.

The many disciplines already long engaged in human subject research (sociology, anthropology, psychology, medicine, communication studies, etc.[3]) have established ethics statements intended to guide researchers and those charged with ensuring that research on human subjects follows both legal requirements and ethical practices. (At United States colleges and universities, these are characteristically called Institutional Review Boards or IRBs.) Researchers and those charged with research oversight are encouraged in the first instance to turn to the discipline-specific principles and practices of research (many of which are listed in Resources).

But as online research takes place in a range of new venues (e-mail, chatrooms, Web pages, various forms of "instant messaging," MUDs and MOOs, USENET newsgroups, audio/video exchanges, etc.)—researchers, research subjects and those charged with research oversight will often encounter ethical questions and dilemmas that are not directly addressed in extant statements and guidelines. In addition, both the great variety of human inter/actions observable online and the clear need to study these inter/actions in interdisciplinary ways have thus engaged researchers and scholars in disciplines beyond those traditionally involved in human subject research. For example, researching the multiple uses of texts and graphics images in diverse Internet venues often benefits from approaches drawn from art history, literary studies, etc. This interdisciplinary approach to research leads, however, to a central ethical difficulty: The primary assumptions and guiding metaphors and analogies—and thus the resulting ethical codes—can vary sharply from discipline to discipline, especially as we shift from the social sciences (which tend to rely on medical models and law for human subject's protection) to the humanities (which stress the agency and publicity of persons as artists and authors).

This array of ethical issues and possible (and sometimes conflicting) approaches to ethical decision making are daunting, if not overwhelming. Nonetheless, as we have worked through a wide range of issues, case studies and pertinent literature, we are convinced that it is possible—up to a point, at least—to clarify and resolve at least many of the more common ethical difficulties.

This chapter—as it synthesizes the results of our nearly two years of work together—is intended to aid both researchers from a variety of disciplines and those responsible for insuring that this research adheres to legal and ethical requirements during their work of clarifying and resolving ethical issues encountered in online research.

This chapter stresses:

Ethical Pluralism

Ethical concerns arise not only when we encounter apparent conflicts in values and interests—but also when we recognize that there is more than one ethical decision-making framework used to analyze and resolve those conflicts. In philosophical ethics, these frameworks are commonly classified in terms of deontology, consequentialism, virtue ethics, feminist ethics and several others.[4]

Researchers and their institutions, both within a given national tradition and across borders and cultures, take up these diverse frameworks in grappling with ethical conflicts. Our first goal in this document is to emphasize and represent this diversity of frameworks, not in order to pit one against another, but to help researchers and those charged with research oversight to understand how these frameworks operate in specific situations. On occasion, in fact, ethical conflicts can be resolved by recognizing that apparently opposing values represent different ethical frameworks. By shifting the debate from the conflict between specific values to a contrast between ethical frameworks, researchers and their colleagues may understand the conflict in a new light, and discern additional issues and considerations that help resolve the specific conflict.[5]

Cross-Cultural Awareness

Different nations and cultures enjoy diverse legal protections and traditions of ethical decision making. Especially as Internet research may entail a literally global scope, efforts to respond to ethical concerns and resolve ethical conflicts must take into account diverse national and cultural frameworks.[6]

Guidelines—Not "Recipes"

As noted in our Preliminary Report (AoIR Ethics Working Committee, 2001), given the range of possible ethical decision-making procedures (utilitarianism, deontology, feminist ethics, etc.), the multiple interpretations and applications of these procedures to specific cases and their refraction through culturally diverse emphases and values across the globe, the issues raised by Internet research are ethical problems precisely because they evoke more than one ethically defensible response to a specific dilemma or problem. Ambiguity, uncertainty and disagreement are inevitable.

In this light, it is a mistake to view our recommendations as providing general principles that can be applied without difficulty or ambiguity to a specific ethical problem so as to algorithmically deduce the correct answer.

At the same time, recognizing the possibility of a range of defensible ethical responses to a given dilemma does not commit us to ethical relativism ("anything goes").[7] On the contrary, the general values and guidelines endorsed here articulate parameters that entail significant restrictions on what may—and what may *not*—be defended as ethical behavior. In philosophical terms, then, like most philosophers and ethicists, we endorse here a middle ground between ethical relativism and an ethical dogmatism (a single set of ostensibly absolute and unquestionable values, applied through a single procedure, issuing in "the" only right answer, with all differing responses condemned as immoral).

To make this point a last way: Since Aristotle (in the West), ethicists have recognized that doing the right thing, for the right reason, in the right way, at the right time remains a matter of judgment or phronesis.[8] Again, such judgment cannot be reduced to a simple deduction from general rules to particular claims. Rather, it is part of the function of judgment to determine just what general rules apply to a particular context.

Developing and fostering such judgment, as Aristotle stressed, requires both guidance from those more experienced than ourselves and our own cumulative experience in seeking to reflect carefully on ethical matters and to discern what the right thing at the right time for the right reason and in the right way may be (cf. Dreyfus, 2001).

Our hope is that the materials collected here will serve Internet researchers and those who collaborate with them in attempting to resolve the ethical issues that emerge in their work—first of all, that these materials will foster precisely their own sense of phronesis or judgment.

QUESTIONS TO ASK WHEN UNDERTAKING INTERNET RESEARCH
Venue/Environment—Expectations—Authors/Subjects— Informed Consent

Where does the inter/action, communication, etc., under study take place?
Current venues include:
- Home pages,
  - Weblogs,
  - Google searches,
- E-mail (personal e-mail exchanges),
- Listservs (exchanges and archives),
- USENET newsgroups,
- ICQ/IM (text-based),
- CUSeeMe (and other audio-video exchanges),
- Chatrooms, including IRC,
- MUDs/MOOs,
- Gaming,
- Images and other forms of multimedia presentation (Webcams, etc.) and
- Computer-supported cooperative work systems (some forms).

What ethical expectations are established by the venue?
For example:

Is there is a posted site policy that establishes specific expectations—e.g., a statement notifying users that the site is public, the possible technical limits to privacy in specific areas or domains, etc.

Example: Sally Hambridge has developed an extensive set of "Netiquette Guidelines" that includes the following advice: Unless you are using an encryption device (hardware or software), you should assume that mail on the Internet is not secure. Never put in a mail message anything you would not put on a postcard. (See <http://www.pcplayer.dk/Netikette_reference.doc>.)

Is there a statement affiliated with the venue (chat room, listserv, MOO, MUD, etc.) indicating whether discussion, postings, etc., are ephemeral, logged for a specific time and/or archived in a private and/or publicly accessible location such as a website, etc.?

Are there mechanisms that users may choose to employ to indicate that their exchanges should be regarded as private—e.g., "moving" to a private chat room, using specific encryption software, etc.?—to indicate their desire to have their exchanges kept private?

One broad consideration: The greater the acknowledged publicity of the venue, the less obligation there may be to protect individual privacy, confidentiality, right to informed consent, etc.

Who are the subjects posters/authors/creators of the material and/or inter/actions under study?
While all persons have rights and researchers the obligation to protect those rights, the obligation—and attendant difficulties—of researchers to protect their subjects is heightened if the subjects are (a) children and/or (b) minors (between the ages of 12 and 18). In the United States, for example, children cannot give informed consent, according to the Code of Federal Regulations (Office for Protection from Research Risks, 1991; cf. Walther, 2002).

Minors also represent special difficulties, as they inhabit something of a middle ground—legally and ethically—between children and adults. For example, are Web pages created by minors—but often without much understanding of the possible harms some kinds of posted information might bring either to the author and/or others—to be treated as the same sort of document as those authored by adults who (presumably) are better informed about and sensitive to the dangers of posting personal information on the Web? Or are researchers rather required to exercise greater care in protecting the identity of minors—perhaps even to inform them when their materials may pose risks to themselves and/or others (see Ridderström, forthcoming).

A broad consideration: the greater the vulnerability of the author/subject, the greater the obligation of the researcher to protect the author/subject.

Informed Consent: Specific Considerations
Timing
Ideally, protecting human subjects' rights to privacy, confidentiality, autonomy and informed consent means approaching subjects at the very beginning of research to ask for consent, etc.

In some contexts, however, the goals of a research project may shift over time as emerging patterns suggest new questions, etc. Determining not only if, but when to ask for informed consent is thus somewhat context dependent and requires particular attention to the "fine-grained" details of the research project not only in its inception but also as it may change over its course.

Medium?

Researchers should determine which medium—e-mail? postal letter?—for both requesting and receiving informed consent best protects both the subject(s) and their project. (As is well known, compared with electronic records, paper records are less subject to erasure and corruption through power drops, operator error, etc.)

Addressees?

In studying groups with a high turnover rate, is obtaining permission from the moderator/facilitator/list owner, etc., sufficient?

How material is to be used?

Will the material be referred to by direct quotation or paraphrased?

Will the material be attributed to a specified person? Referred to by his/her real name? Pseudonym? "Double-pseudonym" (i.e, a pseudonym for a frequently used pseudonym)?

(Obviously, the more published research protects the confidentiality of persons involved as subjects, the less risk such publication entails for those persons. Such protections do not necessarily lessen the need for informed consent. Rather, researchers seeking informed consent need to make clear to their subjects how material about them and/or from them will be used—i.e., the specific uses of material and how their identities will be protected are part of what subjects are informed about and asked to consent to.)

Initial Ethical and Legal Considerations

How far do extant legal requirements and ethical guidelines in your discipline "cover" the research? (For the guidelines as published by a number of disciplines, see Resources, below. See as well the discussion of the ethical and legal contrasts between the United States and Europe, "VI. Addendum 2," (in the complete document online, <www.aoir.org/reports/ethics.pdf>), pp. 18f.)

How far do extant legal requirements and ethical guidelines in the countries implicated in the research apply?

For example: all persons who are citizens of the European Union enjoy strong privacy rights by law as established in the European Union Data Protection Directive (Directive 95/46/EC, 1995), according to which data subjects must:

- Unambiguously give consent for personal information to be gathered online;
- Be given notice as to why data is being collected about them;
- Be able to correct erroneous data;
- Be able to opt out of data collection and
- Be protected from having their data transferred to countries with less stringent privacy protections. (see http://www.privacy.org/pi)

US citizens, by contrast, enjoy somewhat less stringent privacy protections.

Obviously, research cannot violate the legal requirements for privacy protection enforced in the countries under whose jurisdiction the research and subjects find themselves.

What are the initial ethical expectations/assumptions of the authors/subjects being studied?

For example: Do participants in this environment assume/believe that their communication is private?[9] If so—and if this assumption is warranted—then there may be a greater obligation on the part of the researcher to protect individual privacy in the ways outlined in human subject research (i.e., protection of confidentiality, exercise of informed consent, assurance of anonymity—or at least pseudonymity—in any publication of the research, etc.).

If not—e.g., if the research focuses on publicly accessible archives, inter/actions intended by their authors/agents as public, performative (e.g., intended as a public act or performance that invites recognition for accomplishment), etc., and venues assigned the equivalent of a "public notice" that participants and their communications may be monitored for research purposes, then there may be less obligation to protect individual privacy.[10]

Alternatively: Are participants in this environment best understood as "subjects" (in the sense common in human subjects research in medicine and the social sciences)—or as authors whose texts/artifacts are intended as public?

If participants are best understood as subjects in the first sense (e.g., as they participate in small chat rooms, MUDs or MOOs intended to provide reasonably secure domains for private exchanges), then greater obligations to protect autonomy, privacy, confidentiality, etc., are likely to follow.

If, by contrast, subjects may be understood as authors intending for their work to be public (e.g., e-mail postings to large listservs and USENET groups; public Web pages such as home pages, Weblogs, etc., chat exchanges in publicly accessible chat rooms, etc.)—then fewer obligations to protect autonomy, privacy, confidentiality, etc., will likely follow.[11]

(The following three questions are interrelated. As will be seen, they reflect both prevailing approaches to ethical decision making—e.g., Johnson (2001)—as well as cultural/national differences in law and ethical traditions.)

What ethically significant risks does the research entail for the subject(s)?
Examples (form/content distinction):

If the content of a subject's communication were to become known beyond the confines of the venue being studied—would harm likely result?

For example: If a person is discussing intimate topics—psychological/medical/spiritual issues, sexual experience/fantasy/orientation, etc.—would the publication of this material result in shame, threats to material well being (denial of insurance, job loss, physical harassment, etc.), etc.?

A primary ethical obligation is to do no harm. Good research design, of course, seeks to minimize risk of harm to the subjects involved.

By contrast, if the form of communication is under study—for instance, the linguistic form of requests ("Open the door" vs. "I'd appreciate it if you'd open the door," etc.), not what is being requested—this shift of focus away from content may reduce the risk to the subject.

In either case (i.e., whether it is the form or content that is most important for the researcher), if the content is relatively trivial, doesn't address sensitive topics, etc., then clearly the risk to the subject is low.

What benefits might be gained from the research?
This question is obviously crucial when research may entail significant risk to the author(s)/agent(s) considered as subjects.

From a utilitarian standpoint, research can only be justified—especially if it risks harm to individuals—if the likely benefits arguably outweigh the real and possible costs (including potential harm).

From a deontological standpoint, even if significant benefits may be reasonably expected from the research, such research may remain ethically unjustified if it violates basic principles, rights, duties, etc., e.g., rights to autonomy, privacy, and so forth (cf. Elgesem, 2002).

What are the ethical traditions of the researchers' and the subjects' culture and country?
This question is crucial when facing the conflict between possible risks to subjects, including the violation of basic human rights to self–determination, privacy, informed consent, etc., and the benefits of research.

In the United States, for example, there may be a greater reliance on utilitarian approaches to deciding such conflicts—specifically in the form of "risk/benefit" analyses—as compared with other countries and cultures. Crudely, if the benefits promise to be large, and the risks/costs small, then the utilitarian calculus may find that the benefits outweigh the risks and costs.

By contrast (and as is illustrated in the differences in laws on privacy), at least on an ideal level, European approaches tend to emphasize more deontological approaches— i.e., approaches that take basic human rights (self-determination, privacy, informed consent, etc.) as so foundational that virtually no set of possible benefits that might be gained from violating these ethically justifies that violation.[12]

When considering conflicts between subjects' rights and benefits to be gained from research that compromises those rights—researchers and those charged with research oversight may well arrive at different decisions as to what is ethically acceptable and unacceptable, depending on which of these cultural/ethical approaches they utilize.

We hope this list is useful as a first effort to suggest a characteristic range of questions that Internet researchers and those responsible for oversight of such research should consider, and that it is further useful as it suggests an initial range of ethically defensible ways to respond to such questions.

But, of course, this list is neither complete nor final. Invariably, as Internet researchers encounter new venues, contexts, inter/actions, etc., additional questions and responses will inevitably arise (either as variations of these and/or as distinctively new). Perhaps this list will remain useful in those new contexts as it at least suggests starting points and possible analogies for raising new questions and developing new responses.

In any case, we hope this document will prove helpful, at least for a while, to researchers, ethicists and others concerned with the important ethical challenges of Internet research.

REFERENCES

Allen, C. (1996). What's wrong with the "Golden Rule"? Conundrums of conducting ethical research in cyberspace. *The Information Society, 12*(2), 175-187.

American Psychological Association. (2002). *Ethical principles of psychologists and codes of conduct.* Retrieved from: http://www.apa.org/ethics/homepage.html.

AoIR Ethics Working Committee. Retrieved June 9, 2003 from the AoIR Ethics Working Committee website: http://www.cddc.vt.edu/aoir/ethics/.

AoIR Ethics Working Committee. (2001) A preliminary report. Retrieved June 9, 2003 from: www.aoir.org/reports/ethics.html.

Association for Computing Machinery. (1992, October 16). *ACM code of ethics and professional conduct.* Retrieved June 9, 2003 from: http://www.acm.org/constitution/code.html.

Baird, R. M., Ramsower, R., & Rosenbaum, S. E. (eds.) (2000). *Cyberethics: Social and Moral Issues in the Computer Age.* Amherst, NY: Prometheus Books.

Bassett, E. H. & O'Riordan, K. (2002). Ethics of Internet research: Contesting the human subjects research model. *Ethics and Information Technology*, 4(3), pp. 233-247. Retrieved June 9, 2003 from: http://www.nyu.edu/projects/nissenbaum/ethics_bassett.html.

Boehlefeld, S. P. (1996). Doing the right thing: Ethical cyberspace research. *The Information Society,* 12(2), 141-152.

Bruckman, A. (2002a). *Ethical guidelines for research online.* Retrieved June 9, 2003 from: http://www.cc.gatech.edu/~asb/ethics/.

Bruckman, A. (personal communication, August 8, 2002b).

Bruckman, A. (2002c). Studying the amateur artist: A perspective on disguising data collected in human subjects research on the Internet. *Ethics and Information Technology,* 4(3), pp. 217-231. Retrieved June 9, 2003 from: http://www.nyu.edu/projects/nissenbaum/ethics_bruckman.html.

Buchanan, E. A. (2002). Internet research ethics and institutional review boards: New challenges, new opportunities. In E. D. Garten & D. Williams (Eds.), *Advances in Library Administration and Organization* (Vol. 19, pp. 85-99). Elsevier Science. Greenwich, CT: JAI Press.

Buchanan, E. A. (ed.) (2004). *Readings in Virtual Research Ethics: Issues and Controversies.* Hershey, PA: Idea Group Publishing.

Bynum, T. W. (1998). Global information ethics and the information revolution. In T. W. Bynum & J. H. Moor (Eds.), *The Digital Phoenix: How Computers are Changing Philosophy* (pp. 274-291). Oxford: Blackwell.

Danet, B. (2001). *Ethical aspects in CyberPl@y.* Retrieved June 9, 2003 from: http://www.cddc.vt.edu/aoir/ethics/case.html.

Directive 95/46/EC of the European Parliament and of the Council of 24 October 1995 on the protection of individuals with regard to the processing of personal data and on the free movement of such data. (1995). Retrieved June 9, 2003 from: http://europa.edu.int/comm/internal_market/privacy/law_en.htm.

Dreyfus, H. (2001). *On the Internet*. New York: Routledge.

Elgesem, D. (2002). What is special about the ethical issues in online research? *Ethics and Information Technology*, 4(3), pp. 195-203. Retrieved June 9, 2003 from: http://www.nyu.edu/projects/nissenbaum/ethics_elgesem.html.

Ermann, M. D, Williams, M. B., & Shauf, M. S. (1997). *Computers, Ethics, and Society*. New York: Oxford University Press.

Ess, C. (2002). Introduction. (Special Issue on Internet Research Ethics). *Ethics and Information Technology*, 4(3), pp. 177-188. Retrieved June 9, 2003 from: http://www.nyu.edu/projects/nissenbaum/ethics_ess.html.

European Commission. (n.d.) *Privacy on the Internet – an integrated EU approach to on-line data protection*. Retrieved June 9, 2003 from: http://europa.eu.int/comm/internal_market/en/dataprot/wpdocs/wpdocs_2k.htm.

Eysenbach, G. & Till, J. (2001, November 10). Ethical issues in qualitative research on Internet communities. *British Medical Journal 323*(7321), 1103-1105. Retrieved from: http://www.bmj.com/cgi/content/full/323/7321/1103.

Frankel, M. S. & Siang, S. (1999). *Ethical and legal aspects of human subjects research on the Internet*. Retrieved June 9, 2003 from the American Association for the Advancement of Science website: http://www.aaas.org/spp/dspp/sfrl/projects/intres/main.htm.

Hamelink, C. J. (2000). *The Ethics of Cyberspace*. London: Sage Publications.

Hine, C. Message posted to the AoIR ethics working group e-mail list. For a copy of this document, contact Charles Ess at cmess@drury.edu, pending permission of the author.

Jankowski, N. & van Selm, M. (2001). *Research ethics in a virtual world: Some guidelines and illustrations*. Retrieved June 9, 2003 from: http://www.brunel.ac.uk/depts/crict/vmpapers/nick.htm.

Johnson, D. G. (2001). *Computer Ethics* (3rd ed.). Upper Saddle River, NJ: Prentice-Hall.

King, S. (1996). Researching internet communities: proposed ethical guidelines for the reporting of results. *The Information Society*, *12*, 119-128.

Mann, C. & Stewart, F. (2000). *Internet Communication and Qualitative Research: A Handbook for Researching Online*. London: Sage.

Michelfelder, D. (2001). The moral value of information privacy in cyberspace. *Ethics and Information Technology, 3*(2), 129-135.

Nancarrow, C., Pallister J., & Brace, I. (2001). A new research medium, new research populations and seven deadly sins for Internet researchers. *Qualitative Market Research: An International Journal*, 4(3), 136-149.

National Committee for Research Ethics in the Social Sciences and the Humanities. (NESH – Norway) (2001). Guidelines for research ethics in the social sciences, law and the humanities. Retrieved June 9, 2003 from: http://www.etikkom.no/NESH/guidelines.htm.

Natural Sciences and Engineering Research Council of Canada. *Tri-Council policy statement: Ethical conduct for research involving humans*. Retrieved June 9, 2003 from: http://www.nserc.ca/programs/ethics/english/ policy.htm.

Office for Protection from Research Risks, National Institutes of Health, Department Of Health And Human Services. (1991). *Code of federal regulations: Protection of human subjects* (Title 45, Part 46). Protection of Human Subjects. Retrieved June 9, 2003 from: http://ohsr.od.nih.gov/mpa/45cfr46.php3.

O'Riordan, K. (personal communication, August 13, 2002).

Ridderström, H. (forthcoming). Ethical challenges in research on youths' personal homepages. In M. Thorseth (Ed.), *Internet and Research Ethics*. Trondheim, Norway: Programme for Applied Ethics, Norwegian University of Science and Technology, Trondheim.

Schrum, L. (1997). Ethical research in the information age: Beginning the dialog. *Computers in Human Behavior, 13*(2), 117-125.

Sharf, B. F. (1999). Beyond netiquette: the ethics of doing naturalistic discourse research on the Internet. In S. Jones (Ed.), *Doing Internet Research* (pp. 243-256). Thousand Oaks, CA: Sage.

Smith, K. C. (2003). 'Electronic eavesdropping': The ethical issues involved in conducting a virtual ethnography. In S. Chen & J. Hall (Eds.), *Online Social Research: Methods, Issues, and Ethics*. New York: Peter Lang.

Spinello, R. (2002). *Cyberethics: Morality and Law in Cyberspace* (2nd ed.). Sudbury, MA: Jones and Bartlett.

Suler, J. (2000). *Ethics in cyberspace research*. Retrieved from the Psychology of Cyberspace website: http://www.rider.edu/users/suler/psycyber/ethics.html.

Sussex Technology Group. (2001). The company of strangers. In S. R. Munt (Ed.), *Technospaces: Inside the New Media,* (pp. 205-223). London: Continuum.

Sveningsson, M. (2001). *Creating a sense of community: experiences from a Swedish Web chat.* Unpublished doctoral dissertation Linköping University, Sweden.

Sveningsson, M. (2002, September 25). Message posted to the AoIR ethics working group e-mail list. For a copy of this document, contact Charles Ess at cmess@drury.edu, pending permission of the author.

Swedish Council for Research in the Humanities and Social Sciences (HSFR) (1990). *Ethical principles for scientific research in the humanities and social sciences.* Retrieved June 9, 2003 from: http://www.cddc.vt.edu/aoir/ethics/private/ Swedish_HFSR_1990b.pdf.

University of Bristol. (n.d). *Self assessment questionnaire for researchers using personal data.* Retrieved June 9, 2003 from: http://www.bris.ac.uk/Depts/Secretary/ datapro.htm.

Waern, Y. (2001). Ethics in global Internet research. (Department of Communication Studies Rep. 2001:3). Linköping University, Sweden.

Walther, J.B. (2002). Research ethics in Internet-enabled research: Human subjects issues and methodological myopia. *Ethics and Information Technology, 4*(3), 205-216. Retrieved June 9, 2003 from: http://www.nyu.edu/projects/nissenbaum/ ethics_walther.html.

White, M. (2002). Representations or people? *Ethics and Information Technology, 4*(3), 249-266. Retrieved June 9, 2003 from: http://www.nyu.edu/projects/nissenbaum/ ethics_white.html.

ADDITIONAL WEB-BASED RESOURCES

For a discussion of legal and other aspects, see:
http://www.unet.brandeis.edu/~jacobson/Doing_Research.html.

Stuart Offenbach (Department of Psychological Sciences, Purdue University) offers the
following:
> If you are interested in codes of professional ethics/standards, I recommend the
> site at Illinois Institute of Technology. Vivial Weil has put together a very nice
> collection at:

http://csep.iit.edu/codes/.

Ethics in science: http://www.chem.vt.edu/ethics/ethics.html.

Office of Human Research Protection: http://ohrp.osophs.dhhs.gov/.

The Association for Practical and Professional Ethics: http://ezinfo.ucs.indiana.edu/
~appe/home.html.

The Online Resource for Instruction in Responsible Conduct of Research: http://
rcr.ucsd.edu/.

RESOURCES ON US/EU/ EUROPEAN DIFFERENCES

Aguilar, J. R. (1999/2000, Winter). Over the rainbow: European and American consumer
protection policy and remedy conflicts on the Internet and a possible solution.
International Journal of Communications of Law and Policy, 4, 1-57.

Nihoul, P. (1998/1999, Winter). Convergence in European telecommunications: A case
study on the relationship between regulation and competition (law). *International
Journal of Communications Law and Policy, 2,* 1-33.

Reidenberg, J. R. (2000). Resolving conflicting international data privacy rules in
cyberspace. *Stanford Law Review, 52,* 1315-1376.

RESOURCES IN PHILOSOPHICAL ETHICS

Birsch, D. (1999). *Ethical Insights: A Brief Introduction.* Mountain View, CA: Mayfield
Publishing.

Boss, J. (2001). *Ethics for Life: An Interdisciplinary and Multicultural Introduction* (2nd
Ed.). Mountain View, CA: Mayfield Publishing.

Rachels, J. (1999). *The Elements of Moral Philosophy* (3rd Ed.). Boston, MA: McGraw-
Hill.

Thomson, A. (1999). *Critical Reasoning in Ethics: A Practical Introduction.* London,
New York: Routledge.

Weston, A. (2001). *A 21st Century Ethical Toolbox.* New York: Oxford University Press.

Zeuschner, R. B. (2001). *Classical Ethics: East and West.* Boston, MA: McGraw-Hill.

For additional question lists and protocols, see:

Bruckman, A. (2002c). *Ethical guidelines for research online.* Retrieved June 9, 2002
from: http://www.cc.gatech.edu/~asb/ethics/.

Danet, B. (2001). *Suggested guidelines for discussion.* Retrieved June 9, 2003 from the
AoIR Ethics Working Committee website: http://www.aoir.or/reports/ethics.html.

University of Bristol. (n.d.). *Self assessment questionnaire for researchers using personal data.* Retrieved June 9, 2003 from: http://www.bris.ac.uk/Depts/Secretary/datapro.htm.

Suler, J. (2000). Ethics in cyberspace research. *Psychology of Cyberspace.* Retrieved from: http://www.rid110er.edu/users/suler/psycyber/ethics.html.

ENDNOTES[13]

[1] My profound thanks to the members of the committee who have generously shared their time, expertise, and care through discussion and critical evaluation of the issues raised in this document. The committee includes: Poline Bala (Malaysia); Amy Bruckman (USA); Sarina Chen (USA); Brenda Danet (Israel/USA); Dag Elgesem (Norway); Andrew Feenberg (USA); Stine Gotved (denmark); Christine M. Hine (UK); Soraj Hongladarom (Thailand); Jeremy Hunsinger (USA); Klaus Jensen (Denmark); Storm King (USA); Chris Mann (UK); Helen Nissenbaum (USA); Kate O'Riordan (UK); Paula Roberts (Australia); Wendy Robinson (USA); Leslie Shade (Canada); Malin Sveningson (Sweden); Leslie Tkach (Japan); and John Weckert (Australia).

[2] "Inter/action" is intended as a shorthand for "actions and/or interactions"—i.e., what humans do, whether or not our actions engage and/or are intended to engage with others. Part of the intention here is to avoid other terms, e.g., "behavior," that are too closely tied in the social sciences to specific approaches, schools of thought, etc. (By contrast, as the citations from Johnson (2001) make clear [note 4, below], "behavior" is used as a more neutral term in philosophical ethics.)

[3] In their project to collect all (English) literature pertinent to online research, the Committee on Scientific Freedom and Responsibility of the AAAS includes the following disciplines: anthropology, business, communications/media, computer science, economics, education, law, linguistics, medicine, nursing, pharmacology, philosophy, political science, psychology, public health, social work, sociology and statistics. (AAAS CSFR, "Categories.doc," quoted by permission.)

[4] Johnson (2001) provides excellent definitions of these (and other) basic terms in her classic introduction to computer ethics.

"*Utilitarianism* is an ethical theory claiming that what makes behavior right or wrong depends wholly on the consequences. … utilitarianism affirms that what is important about human behavior is the outcome or results of the behavior and not the intention a person has when he or she acts" (p. 36; emphasis added). When faced with competing possible actions or choices, utilitarian approaches apply an ethical sort of cost/benefit approach, in the effort to determine which act will lead to the greater benefit, usually couched in terms of happiness (a notoriously difficult and ambiguous concept—thus making utilitarian approaches often difficult to apply in *praxis*). As Johnson goes on to point out here, there are several species of utilitarianism (what some ethicists also call teleological or goal-oriented theories). Briefly, one can be concerned solely with maximizing benefit or happiness for oneself (*ethical egoism*) and/or maximizing benefit or happiness for a larger group (hence the utilitarian motto of seeking "the greatest good for the greatest number").

"By contrast, *deontological theories* put the emphasis on the internal character of the act itself," and thus focuses instead on the motives, intentions, principles, values, duties, etc., that may guide our choices" (Johnson, 2001, p. 42). For deontologists, at least some values, principles or duties require (near) absolute endorsement—*no matter* the consequences. As we will see in this document, deontologists are thus more likely to insist on protecting the fundamental rights and integrity of human subjects, no matter the consequences—e.g., including the possibility of curtailing research that might threaten such rights and integrity. Utilitarians, by contrast, might argue that the potential benefits of such research outweigh the possible harms to research subjects. In other words, the greatest good for the greatest number would justify overriding any such rights and integrity.

Virtue ethics derives in the Western tradition from Plato and Aristotle. The English word "virtue" in this context translates the Greek arete—better translated as "excellence." In this tradition, "... ethics was concerned with excellences of human character. A person possessing such qualities exhibited the excellences of human good. To have these qualities is to function well as a human being" (Johnson, 2001, p. 51).

Contemporary feminist ethics traces much of its development to Carol Gilligan's work on how women make ethical decisions—in ways that both parallel and often sharply contrast with the ethical developmental schema established by Lawrence Kohlberg. Briefly, Gilligan found that women as a group are more likely to include attention to the details of relationships and caring, choosing those acts that best sustain the web of relationships constituting an ethical community—in contrast with men who as a group tend to rely more on general principles and rules. For Gilligan, this basic contrast between an ethics of care and an ethics of justice is by no means an either/or choice. On the contrary, she finds that the highest stages of ethical development are marked by the ability to make use of both approaches. See Rachels (1999, pp. 162-74) for an overview and suggestions for further reading. Rachels also provides a more complete account of utilitarianism, deontology and still other ethical decision-making procedures. In addition, interested readers are encouraged to review Weston (2001), Thomson (1999), Birsch (1999) and Boss (2001) for both more extensive discussion and applications of ethical theory. (See note 6 for additional resources in cross-cultural ethics.)

Finally, while ethicists find that these distinctions between diverse theories and approaches are useful for clarifying discussion and resolving conflicts—they (largely) agree that a complete ethical framework requires a careful synthesis of several of these theories.

5   See Bruckman (2002c) and Walther (2002) for specific examples of an ethical pluralism that allows us to recognize a range of specific ethical positions as legitimate, rather than either insisting on a single ethical value (monolithic ethical dogmatism) or simply giving up on ethics altogether and embracing ethical relativism. The examples and models of such pluralism, as a middle ground between dogmatism and relativism, are consistent with the larger convergence that I suggest is taking place (Ess, 2002)—i.e., as these offer us specific instances and frameworks that encompass both agreement (e.g., on basic values or first prin-

ciples) and irreducible differences (e.g., in the specific application of those basic values, principles, etc.) (see also King, 1996; Smith, 2003).

6   Cross-cultural differences are addressed especially by an ethical pluralism that rests on a shared commitment to a fundamental norm, value or guideline: the interpretation or application of that norm, however, differs in different contexts. For example, a central issue for Internet researchers is whether, and, if so, under what circumstances informed consent is required—especially if recording activity is taking place. For US-based researcher Walther (2002), such recording is ethically unproblematic. For Norwegian ethicist Elgesem (2002), by contrast, such recording (audio and/or video) requires informed consent. In both cases, however, the issue is one of expectations. For Elgesem and the National Committee for Research Ethics in the Social Sciences and the Humanities (NESH) guidelines, people in public places do not expect to be recorded without their knowledge and consent. By contrast, Walther follows Jacobsen's argument that such expectations are misplaced. Hence, while Elgesem and Walther reach different conclusions regarding the ethical propriety of recording inter/actions in public spaces on the Net—they do so through a shared argument. In both cases, the expectations of the actors/agents involved are paramount. Hence, while the US and Norwegian positions differ on a first level—on a second (meta-ethical) level, they agree on the ethical importance of actors' expectations. This ethical pluralism thus conjoins both important shared norms or values (the importance of expectations in guiding our ethical responses) and differences (in the interpretation or application of those norms or values).

This same sort of pluralistic structure, finally, is at work with regard to the significant differences between US and European Union approaches to computer ethics, in general, and Internet research ethics, in particular. Broadly, the European Union Data Privacy Protection laws and ethical codes for research (primarily, the NESH guidelines) more fully endorse a deontological insistence on protecting the rights of individuals, no matter the consequences. By contrast, US law regarding data privacy appears to favor the utilitarian interests of economic efficiency (see Aguilar, 1999/2000, for an extensive comparison). This same contrast can be seen in research guidelines. For example, where US-based research guidelines focus on the protection solely of the individual participating in a research project, the NESH guidelines require researchers to respect not only the individual, but also "… his or her private life and close relations. …" (2001). But again, these large differences may again be seen as differences on a first level—i.e., with regard to interpretation, implementation, etc.—coupled with fundamental agreements on a second level, i.e., with regard to shared values, norms, commitments, etc. So Reidenberg discerns a global convergence on what he calls the First Principles of Data Protection. The differences we have noted result from differences in implementation, i.e., through "either [current US-style] liberal, market based governance or [current E.U.-style] socially-protective, rights-based governance" (Reidenberg, 2000, p. 1315). Similarly, Michelfelder (2001) traces the ways in which both US and European law are rooted in a shared conception of fundamental human rights—conceptions articulated both in the 1950 European Convention for the Protection of Human Rights and in the US Constitution itself (p. 132).

For cross-cultural approaches to ethics in addition to Boss (2001), see, for example Zeuschner (2001).

7   The term "ethical relativism" as used here is often—but unnecessarily—the occasion for considerable confusion, because philosophers usually use the term differently from their colleagues in the social sciences.

That is: ethicists distinguish between ethical relativism, on the one hand, and cultural relativism, on the other. The latter is a methodological starting point for anthropology and other human sciences, one that takes a morally neutral stance in the effort to simply describe, rather than judge, the morés, beliefs, habits and values of a particular culture or time. In this way, cultural relativism consists of descriptive "is" statements; it simply is the case, descriptively considered that values, beliefs, customs, habits, practices, etc., differ from culture to culture.

Ethical relativism, by contrast, is a normative position—i.e., one that prescribes a specific moral stance and in the language of "ought." Most briefly, ethical relativism begins with the claim that there are no universally valid values, and therefore, one ought not to feel any obligation to any claims to such universal values, and, in the absence of such universal values, one ought to do whatever seems best to the individual (whether as inspired by desire, reason, self-interest, altruism, dis/conformity with prevailing norms, etc.). Finally, because no universal values exist and one ought to do what seems best to the individual, one also ought to not impose one's own moral views on others, one ought not to judge others, etc. In sum, "anything goes."

Confusion between these two views often arises, in part, because ethical relativism usually supports the premise that there are no universally valid values with the descriptions developed from the perspective of cultural relativism. That is, given the simple description that values, etc., vary from culture to culture, ethical relativism draws the conclusion (erroneously, on both logical and empirical grounds) that this diversity must mean there are no universal values—valid for all times and places. From here, then, there is the move to the ought statements—e.g., one ought to do as it seems best to the individual, etc.

Most contemporary ethicists, to my knowledge, generally reject ethical relativism on a range of grounds (empirical and logical) as the last word in ethics, but it is recognized as an important position among a range of positions, one that is defensible at least up to a point (e.g., with regard to fashion, etc.). Hence, to identify someone as an ethical relativist does not automatically count as a statement of ethical condemnation. Rather, ethical relativism is to be examined seriously, along with its supporting and critical arguments and evidence, as part of a critical analysis of diverse ethical views.

Despite their overlap, cultural relativism—as a methodological principle and correlative descriptions within the social sciences—is not to be confused with ethical relativism as a particular normative theory. Specifically, when philosophers criticize ethical relativism, they thereby do not mean to attack cultural relativism as an important component of the social sciences—as if the philosophers were seeking to make ethical judgments that would restrict and undermine the disciplines and findings of the social sciences. Rather to the contrary, philosophers distinguish between ethical and cultural relativism, precisely in order to distinguish the (legitimate, if arguable) ethical position from the methodological starting point and (more or less) universally accepted description of diverse cultures.

[8] Aristotle defines *phronesis* as "…a truth-attaining rational quality, concerned with action in relation to things that are good and bad for human beings" (Nichomachean Ethics, VI.v.4, Rackham trans., 1926).

[9] Bruckman (2002b) points out that people's expectations regarding their online communication are often out of sync with the realities of online communication—e.g., BLOG authors' expectations as to who will read their material, etc.

[10] The NESH's "Guidelines for research ethics in the social sciences, law and the humanities" (2001) point out that "public persons" and people in public spaces have a reduced expectation of privacy, such that simple observation of such persons and people is not ethically problematic. By contrast, recording (e.g., using audio- or videotape) such persons and people does require their (informed) consent.

On the other hand, with reference, for example, to Benjamin's concept of the *flaneur* and the Sussex Technology Group (2001), O'Riordan (2002) observes that "some research/theory also points the other way, to the inversion of publics where the private-in-public space can be perceived to be more private than the spatially 'private.'"

[11] For discussion of participants as subjects—and thus subject to US Federal Codes—see Walther (2002). For discussion of participants as activists, authors and/or amateur authors whose work—especially as treated from the disciplines and ethical perspectives of the humanities—see Bassett and O'Riordan (2002), Bruckman (2002c) and White (2002).

As a middle ground between more public and more private domains, and between greater and lesser obligation to protect privacy, there is the correlative set of expectations as to what counts as polite or courteous behavior, sometimes called "Netiquette." For example, it is arguable that any listserv or e-mail is public because the Internet is technologically biased in favor of publicity; listserv archives are often made available publicly on the Web, etc. Insofar as this is true, there is no strict ethical obligation, say, to ask permission before quoting an e-mail in another context. Nonetheless, it seems a matter of simple courtesy, if not ethical obligation, to ask authors for permission to quote their words in other electronic domains.

If the request is for quoting an electronic document in print, then prevailing practice—and perhaps the requirements of copyright law?—strongly suggest that all such quotes require explicit permission from the author. (For arguments that everything posted on the Web is de facto subject to copyright law, see Bruckman (2002c) and Walther (2002).)

See also Allen (1996), who argues for a "ground-up" dialogical ethics—i.e., one developed over the course of the research project through ongoing communication with one's research authors (in contrast with the usual social science and medical approach that presumes these are subjects). The results of this approach are a concrete instance of the sort of middle ground described above.

[12] The point of the contrast sketched out here is simply to illustrate that ethical approaches and traditions vary among countries and cultures, and thus it is important to be aware of and take these larger contexts into account.

For its own part, of course, this particular example is open to criticism and further refinement. In particular, Malin Sveningsson (2002) has challenged this contrast as follows:

If we look at Sweden, for example, there *is* a difference between what is stated in the ethical guidelines and what is actually done. I guess you could say that the ethical guidelines draw up lines for what would be the *ideal* research design. At the same time, the Swedish Research Council acknowledges that it might not always be possible to strictly follow the guidelines. They also stress the importance of doing important research that will benefit society and its members, and state that ethical guidelines sometimes have to be measured against this. So, my point is: It is possible that ethical GUIDELINES are more strict and deontological, but in practice, researchers might not be stricter than in, for example, the US.

Sveningsson (2001) points to her own work as an example of research that is more utilitarian in its ethics, in contrast with Bruckman's guidelines (2002a) that are more deontological.

[13]   Annotations to many of these references may be found in the online version of the AoIR ethics working committee report, "Ethical Decision-Making and Internet Research" (2002, www.aoir.org/reports/ethics.pdf).

[*]   This chapter is based on "Ethical decision-making and Internet research: Recommendations from the aoir ethic working committee", copyright 2002 by Charles Ess and the Association of Internet Researchers, reprinted by permission.

Chapter III

Ethics in Internet Ethnography

Malin Sveningsson
Karlstad University, Sweden

ABSTRACT

Doing research and collecting data online is not the same as offline. This chapter discusses the wide range of possible ethical conflicts we are confronted with when we do Internet research, as well as how and in which cases existing ethical guidelines may be difficult to apply when our research field is online. It is also discusses how research ethics may be reconsidered: how we may think about, reason and make decisions when doing ethnographic Internet research. Above all, it illustrates the importance of reflecting and being conscious of our role as researchers and about the consequences that our research may have.

INTRODUCTION

The new environments that we find on the Internet have come to pose a number of questions and challenges. Not only have we been faced with new ways of looking at community and communication, we have also had to reconsider questions on how to do research on such phenomena. Notably, Internet research has actualized issues of research ethics. Research ethics on the Internet might mean several things. In this chapter, however, the focus will be on questions of what is ethically appropriate to do when research involves human subjects.

An increasing number of scholars are conducting research on phenomena referred to as Internet culture. The Internet communities that have evolved as cultures encourages the use of ethnographic method, and a growing number of articles within the field of Internet culture also address issues of what is known as online ethnography (e.g., Paccagnella, 1997) or virtual ethnography (Hine, 2000).

Within ethnographic research, issues of culture are central. The notion of culture has been defined in several ways (see, for example, Storey, 1993), but within ethnographically-oriented studies, researchers typically regard culture from a comprehensive view. They define culture as a specific way to live ("a whole way of life"), whether it is an ethnic group, a group in society or an organization that is under study. The assumption that guides ethnographic research is that each group of people who spend time together will create ways of organizing and making sense of the world. With culture, we then mean the mutual understandings and patterns of behaviors that structure the group's culture, or way of living. As a way to grasp the culture of a group, ethnographic research means studying members' thoughts and conceptions of the world, norms and values, as well as the practices that are attached to them (Sveningsson, Lövheim, & Bergquist, 2003).

As Sveningsson et al. (2003) acknowledge, ethnography should not really be seen as one method, but rather an approach, which often involves a combination of a variety of methods. However, the most widely used and with which the term ethnography is sometimes even used interchangeably is participant observation. Participant observation is often combined with other methods, for example, interviews. In its most characteristic form, ethnography means that researchers participate, openly or hidden, in people's daily life for an extended period of time (Hammersley & Atkinson, 1995). They observe what happens in the environment; they listen to what is said and they ask questions. Through the interaction with people and the participation in their activities, they learn about the local world with its traditions and value systems. The ethnographic researcher is concerned with notions, such as realism and subjectivity, and studies natural environments, as opposed to constructed experimental settings. The goal is to describe the environment under study in a way that corresponds to what it normally looks like. For ethnographic researchers, it is important to get rich material, and as a result the descriptions of environments are often referred to as "thick" (Geertz, 1973).

Within ethnographic research, the ideal for a long time was for the participant observer to be able to see, hear and document everything that happened without being noticed, or at least without people knowing that they were observed by a researcher. This thought was based on the ideal of the researcher being as neutral and unbiased as possible and on the challenges this was perceived to imply. A researcher who chooses to participate will inevitably influence the environment simply by being part of it. By actively contributing in shaping the social situation, s/he will actually come to take part in the shaping of the culture of the group that is under study. It is not only through participating that the researcher risks influencing the environment. The mere presence of an observer may affect the situation and the people that are under study. For a long time, this was seen as a dilemma in ethnographic research. Since the ambition was to study groups and cultures in their natural state, many researchers were occupied with what could be done in order to minimize their influence. For example, specific interview techniques were introduced that aimed at reducing the asymmetric character of the interview situation, while allowing informants to take on a more salient role within interviews.

As Sveningsson et al. (2003) note, today most researchers consider it impossible to completely avoid the researcher's influence over the situation. The researcher is present and must instead constantly reflect upon what his or her presence does to the situation. This is referred to as reflexivity and is considered an important quality in researchers. This is the reason why we, in ethnographic studies, often see how researchers dedicate relatively large parts of the text to telling the readers about themselves, their previous knowledge and their role in relation to the informants and the field of study.

The Internet makes it possible for us to collect data without being noticed. It is easy for researchers to gather and store material, not only from public documents, such as Webzines and the Web pages of organizations, but we can also document conversations and discussions between private persons without their knowing it, for example, in chat rooms and newsgroups. The opportunity of doing observations in online environments without informing the individuals who are under study decreases the risk that the presence of a researcher influences the natural flow of the environment, and, thus, it lets us observe cultures as they normally are. However, this opportunity evokes new questions of research ethics. What happens to the privacy and integrity of the people we study? How should we consider the opportunity of collecting data unobserved? In Sweden, there are ethical rules and guidelines for how research that involves human subjects should be conducted (e.g., Swedish Council for Research in the Humanities and Social Sciences (HSFR), 1990/1999; National Committee for Research Ethics in the Social Sciences and Humanities (NESH)[1], 1999), but can and should the rules that are used in research in offline environments really be applied on online environments? These are questions that will be discussed in this paper, using the framework of the Swedish Research Council's Ethics Committee for Research in the Humanities and Social Sciences.

PRESENT GUIDELINES

Different countries may sometimes have different policies for research ethics, and the kind of organizations that make sure that guidelines are actually followed may also differ. The typical American university structure, for example, includes an Institutional Review Board (IRB) that has oversight responsibility for university-based research, in particular, research that involves human subjects in some way. IRBs are to be consulted before each new research project and judge whether the project fulfills ethical requirements or not (Ess, 2002b). In Sweden, on the other hand, there is nothing equivalent to the U.S. university IRBs[2]. Instead, there are a few centralized national committees, such as the ones that the Swedish Research Council hosts, with responsibility for ethical oversight in the various branches of scholarship (medicine, humanities and social science, etc.). This committee does not take an active role in reviewing research projects: rather, it works out general guidelines that are used and referred to by researchers— regardless of the type of research question. Should a researcher be in doubt of how to act, the committee can also be directly consulted.

In 1990, the Swedish Council for Research in the Humanities and Social Sciences (HSFR) (which later became part of the Swedish Research Council) established a set of general guidelines for research ethics in the humanities and social sciences (HSFR, 1990/1999). The purpose was to establish norms and guidelines for how the relationship between researcher and individuals who participate in research should function. The guidelines can be summarized in the statement that people who participate in research must not be harmed, either physically or mentally, and they must not be humiliated or offended. This is called "the claim for individual protection," which HSFR regards as an evident point of departure for ethical considerations in research. Within this overarching claim, there are four main requirements:

- The informational requirement states that the researcher shall, at least in sensitive situations, inform those affected about his or her activity, and obtain their consent.
- The requirement of consent states that the participants should have the right to decide whether, for how long and on what conditions they will take part.
- The confidentiality requirement states that participants should be given the highest possible confidentiality, and that personal information should be stored in a way that keeps unauthorized persons from accessing part of its content. All information should also be registered, stored and reported confidentially and in forms where individuals cannot be identified. [3]
- The requirement of restricted use states that the data gathered must not be used for other purposes than research.

Guidelines for research are not the same as laws. The requirements above should be seen as recommendations and guidelines, rather than fixed rules. There may sometimes be reasons to make exceptions, and, in their guidelines, HSFR states that risks sometimes have to be measured against advantages of the research. Research is important and necessary for society and its development, and existing knowledge must be elaborated and developed. HSFR calls this the "claim of research," which may sometimes be measured against the claim for individual protection. According to the Norwegian equivalent of HSFR, the National Committee for Research Ethics in the Social Sciences and Humanities (NESH) (1999), the claim for individual protection is considered less vital in research where individuals cannot be identified, either directly or indirectly.

Ethical guidelines work by pointing to certain aspects of which all researchers should be aware, but can, in some instances, be outweighed by other important factors (NESH, 1999). The ethical guidelines for research are meant to guide the research community and help us to become aware of the different norms in research. Should norms be conflicting, they may help us to measure them against each other. In that way, ethical guidelines may improve our ability to make well-grounded decisions in ethical issues.

APPLYING PRESENT GUIDELINES ON INTERNET RESEARCH

The Internet has (especially in its early days) been depicted as something dramatically different from so called "real-life" environments. However, as Miller and Slater (2000) argue: "we need to treat Internet media as continuous with and embedded in other social spaces, that they happen within mundane social structures and relations that they may transform but that they cannot escape into a self-enclosed cyberian apartness" (p. 5). In other words, the environments that exist on the Internet should not be seen as a new, different form of reality, but rather as just a part of a reality that includes several different communication modes. Even if this is certainly true, the Internet as a space for communication and social interaction does have some characteristics that make conditions for research different. There are certain aspects of online environments that may complicate our work, and make it difficult to stay with the traditional ways of doing research. In this section, the guidelines of the Swedish Research Council will be taken as points of departure, and we will see how and in which aspects they may be difficult to apply when our research fields are online.

The Informational Requirement

As stated above, the informational requirement means that the researcher shall, at least in sensitive situations, inform those concerned about research being conducted, as well as about its purpose. Here, there are different approaches between which an ethnographic researcher may choose. Lieberg (1994) structures the different roles and approaches of a researcher doing observations into four categories: (1) the participant observer, who is openly observing and participating; (2) the reporter, who is openly observing but not participating; (3) the wallraff, or undercover researcher, who is a hidden participant observer and (4) the spy, who is a hidden, nonparticipant observer (p. 176). However, Lieberg's classification may be criticized as being too "dichotomizing"; there are indeed several differences in degree between the opposite poles above. Patton (1990), for example, gives a more nuanced description of the participant observer's role. These can be seen as two different variables: extent of participation and extent of openness. As researchers, we can be (1) participating; (2) partly participating; or (3) only observing. At the same time our observations can be (1) open observations where those observed are aware of being observed and who the researcher is; (2) observations where the researcher is known by some, but not all; and (3) hidden observations where none of the observed knows that observations are being made. The researcher who does observations online has many opportunities for not making her/himself visible, and, thus, becoming a "lurker"—one who watches what happens in the environment without being seen her/himself. Compared to Lieberg's classification above, this corresponds to the spy. Being a hidden observer has its advantages. When people in a certain environment know that a researcher is there observing them, they will likely change their behavior, changing the environment. Thus, it has been argued that hidden observers capture the situation as it normally looks better than open observers (cf. Paccagnella, 1997). By lurking, we can create a relationship with the field of study and the people who dwell in it in a way that is seldom or nearly possible to do in traditional observations. The researcher can now finally become the "fly on the wall" that for a long time corresponded to the dream of capturing a natural setting without influencing it.

Even if hidden observations could sometimes increase the quality of research, it is highly controversial. People have the right to know that they are participating in a research situation. In other words, we can agree that we should inform the people we study that we are there, watching them. On the Internet, however, this is not always an easy task. In most Internet environments, there are far too many people to allow us to inform them one by one, if it possible to get in touch with them at all (see also next section).

One alternative can be to ask permission to observe from the owners, moderators or Web masters, whether it is a chatroom, a newsgroup or a mailing list (cf. Correll, 1995; Sharf, 1999). However, can the owner's or moderator's opinions really be considered as representing all participants? In order to be certain that all participants in the environment we wish to study know that research is being conducted, we must find a way of reaching all of them. For example, a researcher could have the owner or Web master put up an "advertisement" at the entrance to the environment, where everybody who logs on will see it.

The Requirement of Consent

The requirement of consent states that participants in research should have the right to decide whether, for how long and on what conditions they will take part in the study. Issues of informed consent are, in most cases, self-evident when we do research in offline environments. For example, we would not like to go to the therapist and discuss our problems just to learn afterwards that someone has tape recorded our conversation, analyzed and quoted parts from it in a research report. This is also true in less sensitive situations. How, for example, would we react if someone had hidden a tape recorder under the table in a café where we sit talking with our friends? Here, it is clearly a public environment, where we are aware of that people might overhear or even eavesdrop on what we say, but we do not expect that what we say and do may also be documented and published in some way (although this is how authors of fiction often work). Even though the subjects of discussion may not be sensitive, we would probably like to have the right to decide for ourselves whether what we say should be recorded and used for research or not. In other words, we can also agree that we should ask for consent from the people we study.

Here, the Internet poses problems for us. How are we to proceed if there are no ways of contacting the people who have left tracks online? One example can be online guest books or bulletin boards, where people may have written a greeting or a message, without signing it. Is it appropriate to use such material? Here, most would say it is, and refer to the similarity with genres such as letters to the editors and graffiti. In general both letters to the editors and graffiti are public, and it can therefore be considered appropriate to use the material gathered in those contexts without getting consent. However, there are other types of Internet media where such a procedure may be more problematic, but where it is difficult for us to inform and ask for consent to collect data. In chatrooms, for example, there are often many users logged on at the same time, and they appear and disappear at a very fast pace. Therefore, the opportunities of informing and getting consent are very small. If we were to post messages where we asked for consent from each new individual who logged on, we would probably take up so much space ourselves that we would destroy the research situation. Furthermore, the users would probably classify us as spammers, get annoyed and treat us the way spammers are generally treated, i.e., filter us out or harass us to make us leave (Sveningsson, 2001a). As a last resort, they might even leave the chatroom themselves.

Researchers who wish to avoid a biased environment by participants knowing they are under observation can sometimes document phenomena and then inform and ask for consent afterwards. Even if both the Swedish Research Council and NESH advise researchers against it, such procedures are sometimes practiced. It can also be (especially in ethnographic research) that one has not specified the purpose of the research from the start, and that one does not know what the research questions will be or what parts of the data will be used (Danet, 2001). In such cases, it can be difficult to know who to ask for permission and what to ask for permission to do. In those cases it might be justifiable to wait and ask for permission after the data has been collected. This approach is acceptable only on the condition that such a procedure is really necessary and, of course, that one respects the decisions of the people under study. However, in several Internet environments, such as chatrooms, it may be difficult to track the users afterwards. Although some providers monitor and log all communication, this is far from always the case. Users seldom use their ordinary offline names, and there are no lists of telephone numbers or e-mail addresses where the users can be reached. These are aspects that make it very difficult to satisfy the informational requirement and the requirement of consent.

In some cases, as both HSFR and NESH indicate, there may be reasons to make exceptions to the requirements of informed consent. According to the Swedish Research Council's guidelines for research ethics, it is permissible to observe and analyze things that take place in public environments, such as streets and squares, without getting informed consent. It is also permissible to publish the results from such research, on the condition that no single individual is identifiable. If we regard the online environments we study as public places, we may thus conclude that it is justifiable to study them without obtaining informed consent. However, what methods for collecting data are allowed differ among countries. In Norway, it is not permissible to tape record or videotape material in public places, because this material could be used to create a personal register (NESH, 1999). Since such registers demand the consent of the involved, NESH states that in order to record material in public environments one must obtain informed consent. In Sweden, on the other hand, it is in principle permissible to record material, but it must not be possible to identify any individual persons in the published material. What kind of documentation is allowed in the researcher's home country may have consequences for whether and how s/he can proceed to collect data. In countries such as Sweden, where it (in general) is permissible to videotape public environments, we may conclude that it is also allowed to save screen dumps from public Internet environments. In countries where it is not allowed to videotape or make recordings in public environments, the researcher might perhaps instead have to work with field notes, as in traditional participant observation in offline environments.

The Confidentiality Requirement

The confidentiality requirement states that the participants should be given the highest possible confidentiality, and that personal information should be stored in a way so as to keep unauthorized persons from taking part of its content. All information should also be registered, stored and reported in such a way so that no individuals can be identified. The confidentiality requirement might seem easier to satisfy on the Internet, where even we as researchers know little about the people we study. There are two different aspects of this. The first concerns the fact that, due to the disembodied environment, we have few opportunities of actually recognizing people we might have interacted with before in the online environment. Taylor (1999), for example, mentions the fact that participants in the online environment she studied often changed names. During her fieldwork, she would get messages from users with unfamiliar names who told her that they had been talking before. Since then, they had changed names, which made it impossible for her to recognize them in their new online identities. Similarly, Folkman Curasi (2001) mentions the fact that people tend to change e-mail addresses quite often, which may make it difficult to contact them for follow up questions or, for that matter, to ask for informed consent.

The second aspect with which we are concerned here has to do with the long discussed fact that on the Internet we cannot know that people really are who they claim to be. This discussion has been held both in the public media as well as among scholars (see, for example, Sundén, 2002). To this, we can add that in many Internet media, such as chatrooms and MUD, it is praxis not to perform under one's given offline name, but instead come up with a more or less imaginative signature. This might perhaps be used as an argument for publishing data from online environments without changing usernames. The argument could then be that since people's offline identities are unknown, the confidentiality requirement is automatically satisfied. However, this assumption has to be called into question.

For many users, online interaction is perceived as just as real and important as their offline interactions. They may become acquainted with other users in a MUD, or a chatroom, and they will, in most cases, prefer to interact under the name they have made themselves known, rather than inventing new names (Bechar-Israeli, 1999). Even though all users are anonymous, in the sense that we do not know what physical person hides behind the name, it is a fact that individual's usernames are often identified by other users, which is especially true in small Internet environments with few users and a large proportion of regulars. So it follows that as researchers we cannot refer to the fact that users are anonymous or can change their names, since, in most cases, they will want to be recognized online by the other users in the group in which they are members, and in order to be recognized, they will have to retain their nicknames. As Donath (1999) argues, users are not anonymous; they are pseudonymous, because even if other users may not know much about the offline identities of other users, they recognize their online names.

Therefore, many researchers choose to change the usernames of individuals who occur in their material, as well as the name of the specific Internet arena. When juxtaposed to offline research, we see that this is how things are most often done. Changing the names of individuals who take part in research is a perfectly reasonable requirement, even when applied to Internet research. However, there are some differences between online and offline names, which might make the changing of names problematic. When people are online, they choose a nickname—an alias. Even though there are users who choose to use their offline names as nicknames, Myers (1987) points out an important difference that users themselves deliberately choose to use them in their presentations of self. The nickname one chooses is extremely important for how one is perceived by others, at least in the initial stage. It is the first and sometimes the only thing that other users see, and sometimes it may be used as a "merchandise description" in order to show what kind of person one is (or wants to appear to be). The nickname thus works as a "face"— something that gives the individual user an appearance and which others recognize the next time they meet him or her. The nickname may carry information about characteristics such as gender, age, interests, musical or political preferences, profession, ideals, civil status or even sexual orientation. Such information is not necessarily in accordance with the offline reality, but it can still reveal something about the users' ideals, and how they wish to be perceived by other users (for more about nicknames, see Bechar-Israeli, 1999). In many cases, the nicknames may reveal a lot about the culture within the environment. What are the norms and ideals? What characteristics are desirable within the culture? Such aspects can sometimes be grasped by observing what characteristics users try to display in their nicknames.

Usernames are an important part of the actual conversation data, and can sometimes provide a topic for conversation. Conversations are often started just because someone has chosen a name that relates to a certain subject. For example, it is likely that many of the conversations that are started with a user who calls himself "Beatles-fan23" will be about the Beatles or about music. Furthermore, if one looks at the conversations held, there are a lot of references, such as jokes, puns, allusions and associations, to the users' nicknames. Because of all of this, if we quote excerpts from chatroom discourse and change the users' names, much of the meaning will be lost or changed. Jokes and allusions will lose their meaning and the local color disappears (cf. Danet, 2001). Alternatively, we might misrepresent the environment. If we are interested in understanding the culture of a specific Internet environment, we will perhaps have to keep usernames the way they are. This is especially true if our research interests are in issues of presentation of self—how people act and how they wish to be perceived by others.

There are also other instances where changing of names might affect data. Danet (2001), for example, describes an occasion where changing usernames would have been fatal to her results. She conducted a study of ASCII-art (where the "artists" used the letters and symbols available on the keyboard in order to create pictures). Danet found that it was not as simple as calling it an analysis of art, where the artist's name could be removed without the work being changed. ASCII-art has similarities with graffiti, in the sense that the artist's nickname is often embedded in the picture. Here, removing the name would not be possible without altering the picture. In this specific case, one might consider the ASCII-images as art, and then regard the procedure of giving out names as a question of copyright, i.e., something that one must do. However, as we see, on the Internet it can sometimes be very difficult to draw boundaries between what is a piece of art and what is a contribution to a discussion. Nevertheless, the problem described above points to another perspective in research in the humanities and social sciences. In addition to the approaches to research ethics that emphasize protecting human subjects' rights to confidentiality, humanities-based approaches (such as art history and literature) begin with quite different assumptions about the originators of texts and interactions online. According to those perspectives, people online may not always be subjects, but can just as well be authors who seek publicity and for whom "protection" in the form of anonymity may not be ethical.

In this section, we have seen that the requirement of confidentiality can sometimes be difficult to satisfy, depending on what research question we have chosen. In some cases, it is not necessary to know what the users call themselves, and then usernames can and should be changed. In other cases, such a procedure would seriously affect the authenticity of data and thereby the quality of research. Here, we must measure advantages against risks in each specific case. On the other hand, what we can do is to make identification of users' offline identities difficult. Users' personal characteristics like offline names, cities of residence and appearances should be changed. It might still be possible for some to, by their knowledge of others' online names, identify offline persons, but the number of people who can do so decreases drastically. This is not to say that offline identities are always more "true" or more important to protect than online identities. Online identities are often important, and the general rule should be to protect both online and offline identities. However, should such a procedure damage data, it might be justifiable to keep the authentic online names, provided that certain conditions are fulfilled (see "Rethinking Research Ethics").

Out of the four requirements from HSFR, we see that it is only the requirement of restricted use that may be applied to online settings without any problems, i.e., the requirement that data collected must not be used for purposes other than research . All requirements that have to do with how to actually collect data are more troublesome, and it seems like we will have to rethink and reconsider them to do any Internet research naturalistically.

DIFFERING VIEWS

The problem of research ethics as applied to online environments has only recently begun to be discussed, and there is no consensus as to what recommendations should be given. As Paccagnella (1997) and Bruckman (1997) point out, Internet researchers often have divergent opinions of what ethical rules should be followed. There are examples of studies of online interaction where the researcher has stored and used material from newsgroups, BBSs, or chatrooms without getting informed consent from the participants in the group (cf. Paccagnella, 1997; O'Leary, 1996), as well as studies where the researcher explicitly asks for permission to use transcripts from the group in his/her research (cf. Sharf, 1999).

There may be several reasons why researchers have different approaches to ethics in Internet research. First, as Bruckman (1997) says, the attitude a researcher has to research ethics may depend on what discipline s/he comes; researchers in anthropology, journalism and political science often have different ethical requirements on their research. Since Internet research is a multidisciplinary project that involves researchers from a variety of scientific fields, there will also be a variety of ethical requirements.

A second reason why researchers have different opinions of ethics in Internet research is that different types of Internet environments actually are very different. Since they have different characteristics, it is impossible to set up any one fixed rule that can be applied to all Internet research. Here, one can get some help from the existing ethical guidelines and compare Internet media to their offline equivalents. For instance, if one would like to study a Webzine, one could find out what ethical guidelines are used for studies of offline newspapers and magazines. Likewise, if one wishes to study e-mail, one could compare it to studying private letters, and get valuable advice in the ethical guidelines that are used in such studies. However, what makes this procedure difficult is that the Internet has given rise to new hybrid media that have few analogies in the previous media structure. When it comes to chatrooms, MUD and personal Web pages, we must sometimes explore new guidelines that can show us which way to go.

Even if we can get some advice in looking at what type of Internet arena we are dealing with by comparing it to its offline equivalent, it is also a fact that different environments within a specific kind of Internet medium (e.g., chatrooms) differ from one another, depending on their purpose and target group. Thus, just as it would be impossible to create ethical rules that can be applied to all Internet media, so would it be impossible to create ethical rules that will work for all chatrooms or all newsgroups. Before we adopt a set of ethical guidelines, we must also take into account what kind of activities and conversations take place in the specific environment we want to study. It is self-evident that we will have to treat a newsgroup dedicated to support for people who suffer from bad health or are going through a life crisis differently than we treat a newsgroup dedicated to discussions on sports, cooking or fashion.

A third reason why ethical norms differ lies within the focus of our research questions. Research within the very same Internet environment may be considered appropriate or inappropriate, depending on what the research question is. There is, for example, an important difference between sorting out and following single individuals in a mailing list by analyzing the content of their postings to try to analyze their personalities, and simply looking at patterns in how people use the language when they converse through written text online. As Herring (1996) points out that in linguistic research, the focus is usually on form rather than content, and the users' individual identities are generally of less interest than their membership in a group of people whose language use is under study.

RETHINKING RESEARCH ETHICS

In 2000, the Association of Internet Researchers (AoIR), an international organization, established a working group to develop ethical guidelines for Internet research. In their statement (Ess, 2002a), they found that two useful variables for deciding whether and how to use material from online settings is how public the medium is and how sensitive the shared information is. This recommendation has also been given by King (2000).

In Figure 1, we see four different variations. If the medium is public and the information shared is not sensitive, we might conclude that it is acceptable to make exceptions as for ethical requirements. If, on the other hand, the medium is public and the information is sensitive, we might have to be more careful when making our decisions. Do people within the environment realize that they are observed and that they may be quoted? If the medium is private, one should probably respect people's right to integrity and not collect any data at all, even though the information is not sensitive. As was mentioned previously, there is no consensus among Internet researchers on what should be considered ethically correct to do in Internet research. However, most researchers would probably agree that the left lower field in the figure above is forbidden fruit, whereas the attitudes to the other three fields may vary.

Some researchers are careful to follow ethical guidelines as they look today (e.g., Bruckman, 2001). They state that no matter how public the medium is and how insensitive the material is, people still have the right to know that they are part of a scientific study. If it is not possible to inform participants and ask for their consent, one will have to abstain from doing the study. According to this view, the right thing to do will be to design studies in a way as to make it possible to get informed consent. This can be done, for example, in experimental settings. For some researchers, this approach works fine, but it depends on the research question. If the interest lies in linguistics or how people solve tasks in computer-mediated communication, conducting studies in experimental settings

Figure 1

	Non-sensitive information	
Private	? ?	Public
	— ?	
	Sensitive information	

would often be perfectly suited for the purpose. If, on the other hand, our research interest lies in studying culture, it becomes more difficult. Authentic cultures cannot be studied in constructed experimental environments. We might provide an environment where users are told that research will be done and then hope for a community and a culture to eventually evolve as a consequence of people spending time together. However, it is far from certain that this will ever happen. Even if a community should arise, we have to ask ourselves the question: What is it that we are studying? Can we really do an ethnographic study of a culture that we ourselves have created?

Other researchers (e.g., Danet, 2001; Sveningsson, 2001a, 2001b) have a more utilitarian approach and state that the purpose of research will have to be measured against existing guidelines. NESH (1999) states that exceptions from the requirement of informed consent may be considered in cases where the research has little or no risk for the participants, and is necessary to get insights that are beneficial for the society (p. 10). Here, it is the requirement of research (HSFR, 1990/1999) that is referred to. There might be a value in studying the new environments and cultures that have evolved on the Internet, and this implies that there may be reasons to make exceptions from certain ethical guidelines, especially if the information is not sensitive. If one decides to make such exceptions, one must of course make careful considerations as to what actions, utterances and conversations are studied and reported on. Can individuals be identified in their online and/or offline identities? If so, can they be harmed in any way as a consequence of research being done? A summarizing principle that all researchers will probably agree on is that people must not be harmed as a consequence of taking part in research.

Even if the variables of sensitive information and public/private can guide us in some sense, they are problematic. Who, for example, decides whether a specific material is sensitive or not? In some cases, the answer is a given. For example, we would not quote conversations in an online support group for HIV victims without permission, especially if it is possible to identify the individuals in question. In other cases it may be more difficult to draw the line because what is considered sensitive can be an individual matter. Another difficulty lies in deciding whether a specific Internet environment is public or if it is private. One aspect that may sometimes blur our conceptions of public and private on the Internet is that both private and public spaces can exist within the same Internet arena (Allen, 1996). For example, Web communities typically offer various arenas and communication modes to its members, with some that are public while others are private. In chatrooms, a large proportion of conversations are held in a public room, where anyone with Internet access can log on and watch what happens. Simultaneously, it is possible to send private messages to other users: messages that will not be visible in the public room. However, now and then users make typing errors, resulting in private messages being sent to the public room, visible to all logged-on users. How should we attend to this? The user had intended to keep the message private. Should we as researchers respect that or should we conclude that since it turned out public it is acceptable to use it?

Another problem is that an Internet arena is public, but may not be perceived as such by its users. If the medium is accessible to the public, we might perhaps assume that it is also perceived as a public place (Sudweeks & Rafaeli, 1995). However, it can sometimes be that even if a certain Internet medium admittedly is public, it doesn't feel public to its users. For many users, the anonymity in terms of lack of social and biological cues that CMC provides may encourage a less restricted, more intimate communication than would be the case in offline contexts (Lövheim, 1999). Writing an e-mail or a message to a newsgroup or chatroom feels like a more private act than sending the same message to other kinds of public forums, and it is easy to forget that the message may sometimes be stored and retrievable for a long time afterwards. Since we cannot know whether users perceive a specific Internet environment as public or not, we must at least think it over and see if the information we quote and publish in our research papers can safely be put forward without the risk of harming any of those involved. Here, too, it can be difficult to know what will harm people. As pointed out by NESH (1999): the mere fact that one's actions and motives are described and evaluated by strangers may in itself be offensive (p. 9). Here, Ess (2002b) provides some useful intellectual experiments to be used before each study: "Never treat a person who participates in research in a way you would not be comfortable explaining to that person face to face" and "before you decide on how to conduct your research, ask yourself: If I was the person who take part in research, how would I like to be treated?"

CONCLUSION

The ethical concerns brought up in this chapter and the examples given show that when we are doing Internet research, the two principles for research (the claim of research and the claim for individual protection) may sometimes be in opposition. On the one hand, we have the responsibility to perform research of high quality that is beneficial to society. Ethnographic research in natural online settings may very well fit into that definition, in that it increases our understanding of community and culture in the relatively new social environments of the Internet. On the other hand, we have the responsibility to protect the privacy and integrity of individuals.

In this chapter, we looked at the ethical guidelines provided by the Swedish Research Council and how they apply to ethnographic research in online environments. We have looked at the specific problems that occur, especially in terms of informed consent. It is difficult, and sometimes impossible, to obtain informed consent from everyone in the arenas we wish to study. Does this mean that we have to abstain from doing the research? Here, there are both those who would answer "yes" and those who would answer "no."

As Lövheim (1999) states, the arguments that can be given for gathering data without obtaining informed consent are often based on a principle of protecting certain values that are considered important for the research quality. Such values may be objectivity, neutrality and a desire not to affect the natural flow of events in the environments that are under study. Arguments for studying people and environments without informing them may sometimes also be based upon the potential value of the knowledge we obtain by our studies. An important premise here is that the environment is public and that the information gathered is not sensitive.

On the other hand, Lövheim (1999) continues, researchers who stress the importance of always obtaining informed consent usually base their arguments on a principle where individuals' privacy and integrity are seen as fundamental and inviolable, whatever the circumstances may be. An additional ethical argument that takes the consequences of research into account is that research that sets aside the privacy and integrity of the individuals studied might harm the possibility of conducting further research and might even destroy the object of study. If participants begin to fear the misuse of their confidence and commitment to each other online, they might refrain from engaging in such interaction (c.f. Sharf, 1999).

It is not possible to answer the question of how we are to proceed in our ethical considerations in an unambiguous way. In certain cases, the claim of research may make the case for making exceptions to the ethical guidelines, while other cases do not. It is a question of whether the research is considered important and valuable to society. An important aspect is whether the research can be done without harming participants. In some cases, research can be considered harmless, while not so in other cases. Between these opposite poles, we find a gray area.

As we have seen throughout this chapter, we are confronted with a wide range of possible ethical conflicts when we do Internet research. What they illustrate is the importance of reflecting and being conscious about our role as researchers and about the consequences that our research may have. The first duty we have as researchers is to do no harm to the people we study, but we also have duties to society to do important research of high quality. How these goals are negotiated and attained can vary and, ultimately, is a matter of the characteristics of our diverse disciplines, research questions and research fields. As researchers, we must constantly reflect upon our choices, and balance our duties to our participants and to society: the claim for individual protection against the claim of research. While being reflexive, we must thus also be flexible.

REFERENCES

Allen, C. (1996). What's wrong with the "Golden Rule"? Conundrums of conducting ethical research in cyberspace. *Information Society, 12,* 175-187.

Bechar-Israeli, H. (1999). From <Bonehead> to <cLoNehEAd>: Nicknames, play and identity on Internet Relay Chat [electronic version]. *Journal of Computer-Mediated Communication, 1*(2). Retrieved April 26, 2001 from: http://jcmc.huji.ac.il/vol1/issue2/bechar.html.

Bruckman, A. (1997, January). *MediaMOO Symposium: The ethics of research in virtual communities.* Retrieved Feb. 12, 2002 from: http://www.cc.gatech.edu/fac/asb/MediaMOO/ethics-symposium-97.html.

Correll, S. (1995). The ethnography of an electronic bar. The Lesbian Cafe. *Journal of Contemporary Ethnography, 24,* 270-298.

Danet, B. (2001). *Studies of Cyberpl@y: Ethical and methodological aspects.* Retrieved Jan. 15, 2002 from the Ethics Working Committee, Association of Internet Researchers website: http://www.cddc.vt.edu/aoir/ethics/case.html.

Donath, J. S. (1999). Identity and deception in the virtual community. In M. A. Smith & P. Kollock (Eds.), *Communities in Cyberspace* (pp. 29-59). London: Routledge.

Ess, C. (2002a). *Ethical decision-making and Internet research. Recommendations from the AoIR ethics working committee.* Retrieved Aug. 1, 2002 from the AoIR website: http://www.cddc.vt.edu/aoir/ethics/public/draftthree.html.

Ess, C. (2002b, June). *Internet studies and new ethical challenges – making common ground in the international researcher society?* Keynote speech presented at the conference: Making common ground: Methodological and ethical challenges in Internet research. Nordic interdisciplinary workshop at NTNU, Trondheim, Norway.

Folkman Curasi, C. (2001). A critical exploration of face-to-face interviewing vs. computer-mediated interviewing. *International Journal of Market Research, 43*(4), 361.

Geertz, C. (1973). *The Interpretation of Cultures.* New York: Basic Books.

Hammersley, M. & Atkinson, P. (1995). *Ethnography: Principles in Practice* (2nd ed.). London: Routledge.

Herring, S. (1996). Linguistic and critical analysis of computer-mediated communication: Some ethical and scholarly considerations. *The Information Society, 12*(2), 153-168.

Hine, C. (2000). *Virtual Ethnography.* London: SAGE.

King, S. (2000, September). The state of the interdiscipline. Panel presentation at the first conference of the Association of Internet Researchers, University of Kansas, Lawrence.

Lieberg, M. (1994). Att forska om ungdom: om kunskapssökande och reflexivitet bland deltagande ungdomsforskare (Researching on youth. On the search for knowledge and reflexivity among participant youth researchers). In J. Fornäs, U. Boéthius, M. Forsman, H. Ganetz, & B. Reimer (Eds.), *Ungdomskultur i Sverige* (*Youth culture in Sweden*) (FUS-rapport nr 6; pp. 171-201). Stockholm/Stehag: Symposion.

Lövheim, M. (1999, November). *Making meaning of virtual religion: Methodological and ethical concerns.* Paper presented at the annual meeting of the Society for the Scientific Study of Religion, and the Religious Research Association, Boston, Massachusetts, USA.

Miller, D. & Slater, D. (2000). *The Internet: An Ethnographic Approach.* Oxford: Berg.

Myers, D. (1987). A new environment for communication play: On-line play. In G. A. Fine (Ed.), *Meaningful Play, Playful Meaning* (pp. 231-245). *Proceedings of the 11th Annual Meeting of the Association for the Anthropological Study of Play (TAASP) held at Washington D.C.* (March 14-17, 1985). Champaign: Human Kinetics Publishers.

National Committee for Research Ethics in the Social Sciences and Humanities (NESH). (1999). *Forskningsetiske retningslinjer for samfunnsvitenskap, jus og humaniora.* (Guidelines for research ethics in the social sciences, law and the humanities). Retrieved Feb. 11, 2002 from: http://www.etikkom.no/NESH/nesh.htm.

O'Leary, S. D. (1996, Winter). Cyberspace as sacred space: Communicating religion on computer networks. *Journal of the American Academy of Religion, 64*(4), 781-808.

Paccagnella L. (1997). Getting the seats of your pants dirty: Strategies for ethnographic research on virtual communities [electronic version]. *Journal of Computer-Mediated Communication 3*(1). Retrieved April 26, 2001 from: http://www.ascusc.org/jcmc/vol3/issue1/paccagnella.html.

Patton, M. Q. (1990). *Qualitative Evaluation and Research Methods.* Newbury Park: SAGE.

Sharf, B. F. (1999). Beyond netiquette: The ethics of doing naturalistic discourse research on the Internet. In S. G. Jones (Ed.), *Doing Internet Research. Critical Issues and Methods for Examining the Net* (pp. 243-256). Thousand Oaks, CA: SAGE

Storey, J. (1993). *An Introductory Guide to Cultural Theory and Popular Culture.* New York: Harvester Wheatsheaf.

Sudweeks, F. & Rafaeli, S. (1995). How do you get a hundred strangers to agree? Computer-mediated communication and collaboration. In T. M. Harrison & T. D. Stephen (Eds.), *Computer Networking and Scholarship in the 21st Century University* (pp. 115-137). New York: SUNY Press.

Sundén, J. (2002). 'I'm still not sure she's a she': Textual talk and typed bodies in online interaction. In P. McIlvenny (Ed.), *Talking Gender & Sexuality: Conversation, Performativity and Discourse in Interaction.* Amsterdam: John Benjamins.

Sveningsson, M. (2001a). Creating a sense of community. Experiences from a Swedish Web chat. *Linköping Studies in Art and Science, 233.*

Sveningsson, M. (2001b). *Ethical aspects of research in a Web chat community.* Retrieved Jan. 15, 2002 from the Ethics Working Committee, Association of Internet Researchers website: http://www.cddc.vt.edu/aoir/ethics/case.html.

Sveningsson, M., Lövheim, M., & Bergquist, M. (2003). *Att fånga Nätet: Kvalitativa Metoder för Internetforskning.* Lund: Studentlitteratur. (To Catch the Net: Qualitative Methods for Internet Research.

Swedish Council for Research in the Humanities and Social Sciences (HSFR). (1990/1999). *Forskningsetiska principer i humanistisk-samhällsvetenskaplig forskning. Antagna av Humanistisk-samhällsvetenskapliga forskningsrådet i mars 1990, reviderad version april 1999. (Ethical principles for scientific research in the humanities and social sciences adopted by the Swedish Council for Research in the Humanities and Social Sciences (HSFR)).* Retrieved Feb. 11, 2002 from: http://www.hsfr.se/humsam/index.asp?id=24&dok_id=838.

Taylor, T. L. (1999). Life in virtual worlds: plural existence, multimodalities, and other online research challenges. *American Behavioral Scientist, 43*(3), 436-449.

ENDNOTES

[1]   Den nasjonale forskningsetiske komité for samfunnsvitenskap og humaniora (The National Committee for Research Ethics in the Social Sciences and the Humanities), The Research Council of Norway.

[2]   Nonetheless, an official report was done during 2002, where it was proposed that such authorities be established in Swedish universities as well (Etikprövning av forskning som avser människor, Ds 2001, p. 62).

[3]   In the United States, most IRBs distinguish between confidential data and anonymous data. In Sweden this distinction is seldom or never made. The guiding principle instead seems to be that no matter if data are anonymous or not, they should be handled and presented in a way that protects the privacy of subjects, i.e., they should be confidential.

Chapter IV

Conducting Congruent, Ethical, Qualitative Research in Internet-Mediated Research Environments

M. Maczewski
University of Victoria, Canada

M.-A. Storey
University of Victoria, Canada

M. Hoskins
University of Victoria, Canada

ABSTRACT

Research practices in Internet-mediated environments are influenced by the dynamic interplay of online, onground and technical research spheres. This chapter illuminates the different ways in which studies can be located within these spheres and explores the resulting implications for researcher-participant relationships. Issues of participant recruitment, data collection, data use and ownership, trust and voice are discussed. The authors suggest that to conduct ethical qualitative research online, the researcher is required to develop and demonstrate awareness of the specific Internet-mediated research contexts, knowledge of technologies used and of research practices congruent with the situatedness of the study.

INTRODUCTION

The rapid adoption of the Internet has resulted in many recent changes in economic, political, social and psychological spheres of human and social interactions (e.g., Castells, 1996; Gergen, 1991; Surratt, 2001; Turkle, 1995). From conducting e-business to debating politics to exploring multiple identities online, many people using the Internet are experiencing human interactions in very different ways than they would in onground[1] communities. The medium used, in this case the Internet, both shapes and forms human and social interactions and is shaped by human and social interactions (McLuhan, 1964). Therefore, it is important to recognize how technical and social realms are connected and inform each other; and, more specifically, how research practices are shaped and being shaped by technologies used.

Denzin and Lincoln (2000) define qualitative research as:

"... a situated activity that locates the observer in the world. It consists of a set of interpretive, material practices that make the world visible. These practices transform the world. They turn the world into a series of representations, including field notes, interviews, conversations, photographs, recordings, and memos to the self. At this level qualitative research involves an interpretive, naturalistic approach to the world. This means that qualitative researchers study things in their natural settings, attempting to make sense of or interpret phenomena in terms of the meanings people bring to them" (p. 3).

But in an Internet-mediated research setting what is the "natural setting" that Denzin and Lincoln refer to? The natural setting could be conceptualized as being located in the interplays of online, onground and technical research spheres. We suggest that in order to conduct online research, awareness of the interplay of these three spheres is important for the development of ethical, virtual research practices. Researchers need to expand their own traditional onground knowledge of research ethics to include the understanding of technologies used and an awareness of their impact on human and social interactions.

From this interplay, new conceptualizations of research practices may arise that go beyond traditional research methods and ethics, creating research practices that are congruent[2] within innovative Internet-mediated research environments. The intent of this chapter is to add to the discussion of what constitutes ethical online qualitative research by illuminating how the situatedness of both researchers and participants in technically-mediated environments actively shapes research processes. When conducting qualitative research online, it is important to ask the following questions: How are the technical characteristics of the Internet enabling research interactions? What are the human and social implications of using this new medium? Extended into the contexts of conducting qualitative research online, the questions become: How do technical characteristics of the Internet influence qualitative research? What social and ethical implications do Internet-mediated forms of human and social interactions have on qualitative research practices, specifically researcher-participant relationships?

First, the social and technical contexts of Internet-mediated research are illuminated and the implications of the interplay of three research spheres, online, onground and technical, for human and social interactions are discussed. How these changed cultural contexts impact qualitative research practices is then illustrated by exploring issues of participant recruitment, data collection, trust and voice. Later sections will provide guidelines for congruent, ethical online qualitative research practices. All explorations are grounded in cyberculture, virtual and traditional research methods literature as well as many professional conversations and research experiences.

INTERNET-MEDIATED RESEARCH CONTEXTS

When conducting research using virtual space, three spheres of interactions inform the research process: online, onground and technical (see Figure 1).

The online sphere encompasses the virtual space and all forms of actions that are completed within it, for example, a conversation in a chatroom. The onground sphere encompasses the material world and all actions grounded in physical realities, for example, the institution that employs the researcher. The technical sphere is grounded in the onground world and enables the virtual—it connects the onground and online worlds, forming the latter. The technical contexts in which the online research is embedded consist of many parts. For example: hardware, software, infrastructure, bandwidth as well as local, institutional, national and global information and communication laws and policies. In Internet-mediated research both researcher and participants are located in onground and online communities within their specific cultural parameters and their technologically-mediated interactions are influenced by the interplay of all three spheres.

When considering the growing field of Internet research, one can observe that it has been conducted in diverse quantitative and qualitative ways. Given the methodological variety seen in Internet research, the relevance of online, onground and technical spheres differs in relevance to the study. Ethical implications need to be considered

Figure 1: Interplay of Online, Onground and Technical Research Spheres in Internet-Mediated Research

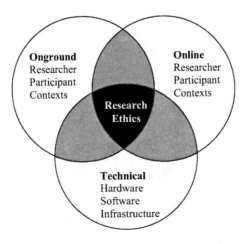

within their unique contexts and primary locations within the three spheres. For example, online surveys have been conducted (e.g., Tapscott, 1998; Wellman, Quan-Haase, Witte, & Hampton, 2001), psychological experiments undertaken (e.g., Buchanan & Smith, 1999), ethnographic studies of online communities conducted (e.g., Baym, 2000; Markham, 1998; Smith & Kollock, 1999; Turkle, 1995) and Web content analyzed and archived (e.g., Schneider & Larsen, 2000). In these studies, the spaces in which the research is conducted, the location of researchers and participants, their relationship to each other and the form of data collected, varies tremendously.

For example, in an ethnographic study of a virtual community, the researcher and participants interact directly with each other and the virtual community is the actual research focus (e.g., Baym, 1999; Markham, 1998). In this form of Internet-mediated research, the research field is primarily located online. Research findings are interpreted within the contexts of virtual communities. They are primarily written referring to online identities, actions and language use without necessarily connecting these identities with onground realities. They are located within the technical parameters that enable cyberspace.

A survey posted online, however, locates the researcher and participants primarily in their onground communities. Both parties asynchronously post and reply to the survey (e.g., Bampton & Cowton, 2002). In these surveys the virtual sphere is used as a space in which data is collected. It is not the virtual space itself that is studied but primarily people's ideas and opinions in their onground lives about a specific topic. In this kind of research, people's onground realities are important and the Internet is used as a technology that enables this particular study to be conducted in a specific way— very similar to research surveys conducted via telephone.

In yet other studies, the integration of the Internet into people's lives is the research focus (e.g., Kiesler, Kraut, Lundmark, Patterson, Mukopadhyay, & Scherlis, 1998; Hampton & Wellman, 1999; Wellman et al., 2001). It is explored primarily through onground contacts and inclusion of the analysis of the use of Internet-mediated interactions (e.g., e-mail, listserv, Web). Again the researcher and participants are primarily situated in onground settings, but this time the use of the Internet itself and its relevance for people's onground lives is studied.

Electronic data collection from listserv archives or from an archived website (e.g., Schneider & Larsen, 2000) represents other forms of primarily technologically-mediated research. In this research methodology, there is usually no direct interaction between the researcher and participant (listserv member or website designer)—the analysis of technologically-mediated texts and images is the focus of the study. All methodologies and spheres can overlap and are in dynamic interaction with each other. This can be seen in studies where researcher and participants initially meet in virtual space and follow up with meetings in person.

In the early years of Internet research, it seemed that traditional research methodology (e.g., ethnography, survey, discourse analysis) and research methods (e.g., interviews, participant observation) used for conducting studies in physical environments were applied in more or less the same form to study virtual interactions. As stated in the "Tri-Council Policy Statement: Ethical Conduct for Research Involving Humans," ethical principles guiding traditional research are based on the following principles: respect for human dignity, respect for free and informed consent, respect for vulnerable persons, respect for privacy and confidentiality, respect for justice and inclusiveness, balancing of harms and benefits, minimizing of harm and maximizing of benefits (National Sciences and Engineering Research Council of Canada, 1999). In general, these remain applicable when conducting online research; however an expansion of these concepts is necessary to include human interactions in Internet-mediated environments. Existing ethical guidelines for researchers do not yet address the interplay of research spheres sufficiently. Changes in research methods are accepted and discussed, but the technical underpinnings that influence human and social interactions and create different cultural contexts are ignored.

Hine (2000) points out that "using the Internet meaningfully is about acquiring the cultural competences within which it makes sense" (p. 152). As part of understanding the "natural setting" that Denzin and Lincoln (2000) refer to, it is not only necessary for the researcher to understand the cultural codes within virtual communities but also to be able to cross the boundaries of virtual environments into the technical sphere located in digital onground realities. For ethical research to be conducted online, this would mean considering the effects of the research on participants from their online, onground and technical situatedness. For example, when a study that is conducted primarily in the virtual environment and a member of this community is quoted in the research text—whose identity needs to be protected? The online persona? The onground person? And how much does the researcher need to alter the text quoted in a document for it to become unrecognizable by search engines? The previous practice of quoting a participant's words by using a synonym may not be sufficient anymore, when considering the interplay of online, onground and technical contexts of this research. What are the specific characteristics of the Internet that create different forms of human and social interactions and innovative research spaces and forms?

As one of the author's experience lies within research conducted primarily through virtual spaces (interviews, survey and ethnographic observations) and researcher-participant interactions, which were conducted primarily online, the following section will highlight the unique characteristics of the Internet that enable different forms of researcher-participant interactions within primarily online research contexts.

INTERNET CHARACTERISTICS AND CHANGES IN HUMAN INTERACTIONS

One of the issues most challenging in writing this chapter was to be conscious of the technical sphere informing human interactions as well as human interactions informing the technical sphere—to demonstrate the dynamic interplay of spheres instead of easily falling into technologically-deterministic language. For the purposes of this section, however, we only focus on what characterizes the virtual space and how this technologically-mediated space enables different forms of human interactions within this space.

De Kerckhove (1997) points out that the three characteristics of the Internet, "connectivity, interactivity and hypertextuality," build the basis for a sense of "webbedness" among users, which is characterized by the "mental linking of people" or the "industries of networks" (p. xxv). Technical features, such as digital data transfer, networked environments and hypertext, enable a sense of connectivity and interactivity among frequent users. These characteristics are crucial for the Internet "... to have multiple spatial and temporal orderings" (Hine, 2000, p. 114), which in turn impact forms of human and social interactions online.

Interactivity and connectivity involve information that is moved in many ways: simultaneously, quickly and in a distributed manner. In networked environments, the pattern of power is described as being less hierarchical than onground and more distributed than linear. The power does not lie primarily within hierarchical institutions but is distributed among networked dynamic local and global interactions with new emerging organizational structures (Castells, 1996, 1997; Dobell & Neufeld, 1994). Hyperlinks and electronic mail, for example, enable people to link to each other immediately, locally and globally, asynchronously and synchronously. Consequently, time and place shift in relevance: people begin expecting quick answers to e-mail, to reach anybody at anytime and to be able to access online information 24 hours a day. Digital data transfers enable a quicker and more immediate transfer of information than previous forms of mail or fax. In comparison to traditional data storage possibilities, digital data information is easily stored and replicated. Records of all interactions are easily kept and traced. This differs from onground access to information where linearity of communication patterns is common. Convenience, accessibility, speed and interactivity are dynamics of online interactions that are commonly expected by online users (Storey, Philips, Maczewski, & Wang, 2002).

In addition, text-based environments have taken away some cues of physical interactions on which many initial judgments and assumptions are made in onground worlds. Missed physical cues, for example, gender, age and ethnicity, mean that people explore their identities and experience themselves in different ways. A different sense of identity and embodiment is facilitated, which promotes a shifting in power structures among people interacting (e.g., O'Brien, 1999; Turkle, 1995).

These Internet characteristics and resulting changes in human interaction patterns play out in research contexts and have implications for ethical research conduct as well. Important issues, such as access, privacy, informed consent, intellectual property and confidentiality, are discussed by other authors (e.g., Buchanan, 2000; Eysenbach & Till, 2001; Nosek, Banaji & Greenwald, 2002; Sharf, 1999; Suler, 2000). This chapter focuses more specifically on aspects of researcher-participant relationships in online qualitative research: participant recruitment, data collection, voice and trust[3].

IMPLICATIONS FOR RESEARCHER-PARTICIPANT RELATIONSHIPS

In qualitative studies "researchers stress the socially constructed nature of reality, the intimate relationship between the researcher and what is studied, and the situational constraints that shape inquiry. ... They seek answers to questions that stress how social experience is created and given meaning" (Denzin & Lincoln, 2000, p. 8). To do so, the researcher-participant relationships are of central importance in qualitative inquiries. As described above, the cultural, Internet-mediated contexts of researcher-participant relationships have expanded and now include issues located in technical and online spheres as well.

Recruitment of Participants

The researcher is initially faced with the task of understanding how participant recruitment is changed within Internet-mediated environments. Using the Internet to recruit participants enables the researcher to use new forms of accessing and recruiting, leading to both successes and frustrations (e.g., Bampton & Cowton, 2002; Holge-Hazelton, 2002).

In Maczewski's (1999) study with young people, the impact of hyperlinks on the recruitment of participants became clear early on and quickly alerted the researcher to the implications of interactivity and connectivity. Maczewski's aim was to recruit frequent Internet users between the ages of 13 and 19 with an active presence on the Web (e.g., youth who have designed a personal website, acted as a chathost, etc.). After having become aware of their online involvement, the question became: How did the researcher interact with them and interest them in becoming participants? In accordance with de Kerckhove's (1997) three characteristics, Maczewski recognized that the shift from onground to online participant recruitment also meant a shift from linear distribution and control over information to an environment of immediately accessible information sources that enabled potential participants to gain access to information at their time and leisure. She had initially planned to contact participants linearly through engaging in an asynchronous e-mail dialogue (as compared to a person-to-person environment), and revealing information step-by-step depending on the participant and his/her expressed interest. Upon entering the online environment, having information about the research project available to participants 24 hours a day now seemed appropriate. (All relevant information about the research project and researcher was placed on a Web information page as a resource for participants.) This enabled participants, after the researcher's initial contact by e-mail that included the information website's URL, to access the project information 24/7, to follow hyperlinks to more background information on the researcher and research project, depending on their interest, and to gain an understanding of the project without directly engaging with the researcher. Using a website as a primary information source allowed potential participants to respond in their own time, allowing for individual reflection on whether to participate or not, without the added pressure of engaging directly with the researcher. The environment of hypertextuality, interactivity and connectivity had now shifted control over what parts of information to access at what time from the researcher toward the participant.

Even prior to this step, however, the website design became an important factor in the recruitment of participants. Instead of a voice on the phone, the website now provided the first impression of the project and the researcher for the participants. Information design through text and images now conveyed the research project without personal contact and raised questions of inclusion and exclusion. Although information was accessible 24/7, what information and in what form did the researcher choose to present online? For example, if the researcher only chose clip art that represented males, it would be possible that females felt excluded. The website color choices may appeal to specific groups of people. The text style may attract or exclude certain groups of young people. Information design guidelines (Mullet & Sano, 1995) were a powerful tool in not only recruiting participants but also in establishing a respectful relationship with the participant. This was taken into account when considering the websites' design, text and structure and the presentation of information on the Web in appropriate and respectful ways. Technical knowledge of website design, knowledge of website conventions, as well as awareness of onground assumptions and online styles of interaction all played out in this initial research step. Mann and Stewart (2000) point out that the action of researchers and participants referring each other to their respective websites is part of creating a trusting relationship. The website design becomes a "social action which has meaning to them [the designers] and which they consider will have meaning for its recipients" (Hine, 2000, p. 148). As Hine continues:

"... this competence involves the conceptualization of the Web page as a means of communicating with an audience, the ability to read the temporal collage of the Web and to negotiate the space of flows, and the ability to produce appropriate displays of authenticity" (p. 148).

Understanding the Web page as a form of social action is one aspect of demonstrating cultural competence in Internet-mediated relations within the interplay of the technical, online and onground.

Data Collection

Data collection in online qualitative research presents issues for reflection that are located primarily in the technical sphere. A significant issue to be considered by the researcher is the "agency" of the technology used and how this can affect researcher-participant relations. What capabilities does the technology being used have? Although data collection tools are programmed and controlled by researchers and technicians, not all capabilities of the tool may be initially transparent to the users. Moor (2000) suggests that:

"The invisibility factor [of computer technology] presents us with a dilemma. We are happy in one sense that the operations of a computer are invisible. We don't want to inspect every computerized transaction or program every step for ourselves or watch every computer calculation. In terms of efficiency the invisibility factors is a blessing. But it is just this invisibility that makes us vulnerable. We are open to invisible abuse or invisible programming or inappropriate values or invisible miscalculation" (p. 33).

This invisibility of technological features is discussed in Storey, Philips and Maczewski's (2001) study of Web-based learning tools in which students were asked to evaluate the tools by completing three online surveys. In the signed consent form, students agreed to provide information by completing these three surveys. However, during the course of the study they discovered that the tool had also collected information on student's tool use as well as the date and time of use. This information would have been useful in relating the students' opinion of the tool to the amount of time they had spent using the tool. The information was discarded as no consent had been obtained to gather this information. In this case the time to learn all of the technical capabilities of the new tool had been limited and this tool's capability was missed. Theoretically, these kinds of capabilities could also be employed purposefully without knowledge of the participants.

Invisibility also plays a significant role in issues arising from data storage. Traditionally, the human subjects research approval form may only say that data is stored in a "locked filing cabinet." How does this apply to electronic data? Electronic data is stored on at least one computer, a server may automatically conduct backups and e-mails may be read by institutional observers, trying to hinder misuse of their system. As part of ethical research, it would be important to address appropriate ways of designing data collection tools, storing electronic data and monitoring the pathways it takes. This kind of invisibility and its possibilities of collecting data without users' knowledge are very problematic and raise ethical issues. Whose responsibility is it to ensure this doesn't happen? The tool designers or the tool users?

The Association for Computing Machinery (ACM) Code of Ethics and Professional Conduct (1992) presents some guidance for computing professionals, but what can be expected of social scientists and their institutional affiliations in this respect? What institutional policies are being developed to address these issues? What do participants need to know about how electronic data is kept safe and confidential? What is safe and confidential in a digital, networked environment? These issues need to be further discussed and reflected in ethical research guidelines for technologically-mediated research studies.

Data Use and Ownership

Data use and ownership are further important issues to consider. Digitalization of data allows for simple manufacturing and distribution of multiple data copies. For example, when Maczewski (1999) conducted interviews on ICQ[4], she realized that both the researcher and participant could save a copy of the interview transcript. This was an interesting dilemma for the researcher, as the consent form had only specified how the researcher would use and protect the data. What were the participants' responsibilities in regards to data use? Would the participant consider posting the data on her personal website? Would she post parts of it on a bulletin board? How would this influence the research study? In this case, the researcher negotiated with the participant to not use the data in any form before the completion of the researcher's thesis. This was based on a trusting relationship, not on any consent form signed prior to the research process.

The technical possibilities of easy duplication, the online cultural contexts of interactivity and connectivity enabling many people to access this information once posted as well as researcher's and participants' onground interests needed to be recognized and negotiated within these contexts. Ideally, having recognized the interplay of the three research spheres and their implications for data collection, ownership, use, storage and accessibility would be negotiated prior to the research being conducted. Consent forms need to address the above issues and reflect the technological influences on data collection and storage.

It can be seen how the technology used adds further ethical dimensions into the research process. We consider the researchers' knowledge of tools and further Internet technical capabilities as crucial in conducting ethical research with participants and again an important element in building a trusting relationship with research participants. Many technical features of the Internet and of the tools used may initially be invisible to the researcher and/or the participants but need to be transparent in order for all research members to consent fully to the research process. So far, technologies used in qualitative research, such as tape recorders and video cameras, seem to have been more transparent to the participant and the researcher than computer-mediated technologies.

With digital technologies and their "invisibility factor," the handling of technologies used becomes a significant part of the conduct of ethical online qualitative research[5].

Trust and Voice

Trust

As can be seen from the above sections, researcher-participant relations in Internet-mediated environments are altered and influenced by changed parameters of interaction. The interplay of the three research spheres also has implications for the concepts of trust, voice and power within these relations. For example, technological mediation removes the traditionally present physical cues of onground personal identity, such as age, race and gender. Turkle (1995) elaborately describes how virtual spaces allow for the experience of and play with multiple identities. The possibility of multiple identities online introduces new complexities into the building of trusting relationships. As Lincoln (1985) points out:

"The building of trust is a developmental task; trust is not something that suddenly appears after certain matters have been accomplished, but something to be worked on day to day. Moreover, trust is not established once and for all; it is fragile and even trust that has been a long time building can be destroyed overnight in the face of an ill-advised action" (p. 257).

How does this apply within online contexts when multiple identities are in play and physical identity markers are lacking? Several authors describe how trusting relationships are built online, for example, by replacing onground identity markers by relational processes, such as being open about the research project, disclosing information about oneself and using humor and tone of written text to convey personality and empathy (Baym, 2000; Mann & Stewart, 2000; Markham, 1998; Holge-Hazelton, 2002). These processes promote the building of a trusting relationship with participants—but how does the researcher "really" know with which participant identities they are interacting? Is this important and does it matter? For example, when Maczewski (1999) interviewed young people online and felt that a relationship had been built through their continuous interaction, the researcher was sure that in their physical lives they were actually young people. The different cues and dynamics of their conversations that led her to believe that these were young people still remain somewhat unclear to her. It leaves her to wonder whether it would have been possible for a 65 year old to play such a fantastic youth online and whether she could have been convincingly deceived. What implications for their relationship and the research project would this have had, if the participant's portrayed online age was different from their real age?

The concept of trust within online relationships is tightly interwoven among online and onground spheres. Researchers' and participants' identities onground, the focus of the research study (onground youth) and interactions in virtual spaces with chosen online identities made for a complex set of characteristics influencing the relation to each other.

Nosek, Banaji and Greenwald (2002) point out how the researcher's presence may hinder participants from withdrawing from the study. Online the researcher's presence is less immediate and barriers to ending the relationship therefore are perceived as lower. As with participant recruitment, a shift of power from researcher to participant can be seen.

Hine (2000) points out that researchers have to familiarize themselves with the cultural contexts into which they are entering when conducting research online. This local cultural knowledge should be acquired by the researcher to promote the building of trusting and respectful relationships with participants. If this is not done, there are many examples of how participants react negatively if a researcher does not understand the cultural codes of the research environment. For example, virtual community members may feel that their privacy has been invaded, when a researcher has not made her or his presence and intent known (Eysenbach & Till, 2001). Mann and Stewart (2000) describe how netiquette or "standards of politeness and courtesy" (p. 59) appropriate to the specific online environment are expected by users and present a beginning of an ethical framework for conducting online qualitative research.

Voice

Issues of trust are also linked with issues of voice. Within different parameters of building trusting relationships, participants' voices also need to be recognized within these same parameters. Hertz (1997) describes voice as "a struggle to figure out how to present the author's self while simultaneously writing the respondents' accounts and representing their selves" (p. xi). The question arises of which voices are presented when multiple identities are experienced online and onground by both researcher and participants. For example, participants in Maczewski's study expressed that it was easier to voice their opinions online, because they did not have to face the threat of rejection as severely as onground or of people judging them by external appearances alone:

<M>   so what is it about online, that makes you be more open?

<Ky>   well, it varies from person to person, reasons for opening up…

<Ky>   a lot of people are shy IRL, and not having to look someone in the eye really benefits them, makes them feel more self-assured.

<Ky>   with me, it's more of my deep-rooted poetic love… I read into things a lot more, I like to be able to express myself.

<Ky>   Also, it's not that split-second judgment thing… I tend to get a few gawks IRL…hehe

<Ky>   whereas online, it's all about the message, and not about the image…
(Maczewski, 1999, p. 143)

In this example, Ky's onground voice is different from her online voice, as she is more open online. This is an example of how respondents' voices are negotiated among researcher, participants and technology within the interplay of all three spheres. Joinson (2002) concurs that sometimes a higher level of self-disclosure is experienced in online than in person-to-person interviews.

Returning to the example of interacting with youth online, if a 65 year old could have a convincing youth voice online and his onground age was discovered later on, which voice would the researcher then have prioritized in this context? The physical reality? The youth voice online? In recognition of multiple voices that people own, would acknowledging the youthful voice of a 65 year old be credible in research contexts researching youth experiences? Who has voice, what is voice and how voice(s) can be represented in technologically-mediated contexts are critical questions that require further research.

Representing multiple voices in linear texts is challenging. Perhaps technologically-mediated environments could offer new opportunities for representing multiple, simultaneous voices. If the research medium allows for direct connectivity and interactivity through hypertexts[6], perhaps it would be possible to more directly include participants in presenting research findings and to illuminate multiple voices more easily than traditionally has been the case. Would it be a future role of the researcher to connect people with each other, if further knowledge would emerge from these connections? For example, with participants' consent, presenting research findings on a Web page with contact links to participants, allowing readers to directly ask further questions of research participants, could be considered. Perhaps more advanced visualization tools will be developed to assist representation of networks of research findings. Whether these changed parameters of interaction in text-based environments will be lost and missed physical cues for interaction reappear with the emergence of newer technologies, such as Voice over Internet Protocol[7], video data or digital pictures, remains to be seen.

Trust, Voice and Confidentiality

Issues of trust and voice online are further intertwined with notions of "confidentiality" and "anonymity," yet the understanding of these notions within the cultural contexts of Internet-mediated research is a complex issue. Some research participants may already have a diary of their personal life online with much of the same information as presented in a research interview. Using a synonym, for example, would not protect a participant from harm, if the reader could search the Web for interview excerpts and easily identify the page. Similar to young people using the Web to express their personal opinions as a means of empowerment and exploration of identities (Chu, 1997; Maczewski, 2002), a sense of power could perhaps be experienced by participants in acknowledging participation in a research setting. This could be achieved, for example, by transcripts being published online on participants' websites, on a common project website or the researchers' website, or by creating links among participants' websites. In networked, technologically mediated environments, there is the potential to build a different form of researcher-participant interactions in which connectivity assists the efforts of the researcher in more immediate collaboration with the participant and through different conceptualizations of confidentiality. A different form of coming to know research findings may emerge by readers exploring linked data, rather than reading text the researcher has composed (Brewer & Maczewski, 2001). How and if this would be appropriate, what form of understanding "confidentiality" and "anonymity" in contexts of interactivity, connectivity and the dynamic interaction of online and onground identities are important ethical issues for further discussion.

DEVELOPING GUIDELINES FOR CONDUCTING ETHICAL ONLINE QUALITATIVE RESEARCH

As has been demonstrated, the ethics of Internet-mediated research are located in the intersection of the online, onground and technical spheres. This intersection is characterized by interactivity, connectivity and hypertextuality and changed researcher-participant relationships. Within this interplay, the researcher is faced with the question of how to ethically conduct research that is congruent within these parameters.

Oberg (2001) suggests that in congruent research, the researcher is connected to the research topic, assessment criteria, methodology choice and epistemological assumptions. According to Oberg, continuous researcher reflexivity and mindfulness are important aspects of enabling researchers' awareness of their own assumptions and facilitating congruent research practices. When conducting Internet-mediated research, we believe these practices of congruent research to be applicable and relevant for enabling ethical research practices. Congruent, ethical online research would not depend on the researcher using onground methods online, but the researcher showing awareness of changes in cultural contexts and the implications for researcher-participant interactions. An entry point for a researcher to conduct qualitative research online would be for him/her to reflect on and answer the following questions about the research study:

1. What are the cultural contexts of the research project?
2. What kinds of technologies are used?
3. How will the interplay of online, onground and technical spheres impact the research project?
4. What are the changes in human and social interactions that occur through the specific technologies used?
5. Are my assumptions about research processes applicable within the technologically mediated research contexts?
6. Do research concepts need to be redefined to fit within new cultural contexts?
7. What changes in ethical implications arise?

These questions aim to make visible the connectedness of the online, onground and virtual research spheres. Congruent research can then be conducted when the researcher understands the complex levels of interplay of the three research spheres and adjusts the research practices used in accordance with the defining characteristics of interactivity, connectivity and hypertextuality.

As general principles for researchers, we would suggest that before conducting Internet-mediated research:

1. The researcher develops and demonstrates awareness of the specific Internet-mediated research contexts—how human and social online interactions are shaped by the medium of the Internet, differ from onground interactions and how this impacts online research processes.
2. The researcher develops and demonstrates awareness of required technological skills for operating hard- and software, including data analysis tools, to adequately conduct the research project.
3. The researcher develops and demonstrates research practices (e.g., building trusting relationships) that are congruent with the medium in which research is conducted.

In addition to the researcher personally reflecting on the above questions and gaining appropriate skills, some ethical guidelines exist that address issues raised. For example, the ACM Code of Ethics and Professional Conduct (1992) is an example of ethical guidelines that take computing technology into account. Boehlefeld (1996) discusses how ACM guidelines can be useful for social science researchers, for example, by considering computer professionals' responsibility to share their understanding of the technology with the public. This may address concerns of privacy and anonymity. For the social sciences ethical guidelines for conducting Internet research are in the process of being discussed and established (e.g., Ess, 2002; Eysenbach & Till, 2001; Jones, 1999a; Mann & Stewart, 2000).

THE FUTURE?

The processes of conducting Internet-mediated research have been discussed within today's contexts of western information societies and recognition of the novelty of Internet research for social scientists. As new technologies are rapidly developing, what different research conceptualizations and methodologies will emerge in the future? New technological media enhance processes as well as render others obsolete (McLuhan & McLuhan, 1988), for example, electronic mail reduces the need for surface mail. This dynamic leaves researchers to ponder not only which new research practices emerge but also which research practices are lost. For example, if ethnographic studies moved to explore the connections of linkages instead of in-depth field research (Wittel, 2000), what insights would be gained or lost? Qualitative research in virtual reality caves will also prove to be fascinating and yet again leave us with further complex ethical issues and show different nuances of researcher-participant relations. For example, if human physical processes, such as excitement, sadness or joy, could be externalized and projected onto screens, what research practices need to be reconceptualized in order to conduct ethical research? To ensure that technologically-mediated qualitative research is conducted in ethical ways, research practices will continually need to be critically evaluated within their unique contexts.

REFERENCES

Association for Computing Machinery (ACM) (1992). *ACM code of ethics and professional conduct.* Retrieved Jan. 27, 2003 from: http://www.acm.org/constitution/code.html.

Bampton, R. & Cowton, C. J. (2002, May). The e-interview. *Forum Qualitative Sozialforschung/Forum:Qualitative Social Research, 3*(2). Retrieved Jan. 27, 2003 from: http://www.qualitative-research.net/fqs/fqs-eng.htm.

Baym, N. (2000). *Tune In, Log On. Soaps, Fandom and Online Community.* Thousand Oaks, CA: Sage.

Boehlefeld, S. P. (1996). Doing the right thing: Ethical cyberspace research. *The Information Society, 12*(2), 119-127.

Brewer, K. & Maczewski, M. (2001, April). *Knowing in Internet-mediated-interactions: What do we know and how do we know it?* Paper presented at the 82nd Annual Meeting of the American Educational Research Association, Seattle, Washington, USA.

Buchanan, E. (2000, Fall). Ethics, qualitative research, and ethnography in virtual space. *Journal of Information Ethics, 9*(2), 82-87.

Buchanan, T. & Smith, J. L. (1999). Using the Internet for psychological research: personality testing on the World Wide Web. *British Journal of Psychology, 90,* 125-144.

Castells, M. (1996). *The Rise of the Network Society.* Cambridge, MA: Blackwell Publishers.

Castells, M. (1997). *The Power of Identity.* Cambridge, MA: Blackwell Publishers.

Chu, J. (1997). Navigating the media environment: How youth claim a place through zines. *Social Justice, 24*(3), 71-84.

De Kerckhove, D. (1997). *Connected Intelligence: The Arrival of the Web Society.* Toronto, Canada: Somerville House Publishing.

Denzin, N. K. & Lincoln, Y. S. (2000). Introduction: The discipline and practice of qualitative research. In N. K. Denzin & Y. S. Lincoln (Eds.), *Handbook of Qualitative Research* (2nd ed.) (pp. 1-17). Thousand Oaks, CA: Sage.

Dobell, R. & Neufeld, M. (1994). *Transborder Citizens. Networks and New Institutions in North America.* Lantzville, Canada: Oolichan Books.

Ess, C. (2002, October 7). Re: Draft SIX, that's it. Message posted to the Association of Internet Researchers Air-l electronic mailing list, archived at: http://www.aoir.org/pipermail/air-l/2002-October/002463.html.

Eysenbach, G. & Till, J. (2001, November). Ethical issues in qualitative research on Internet communities. *British Medical Journal, 323*(7321), 1103-1105. Retrieved Jan. 27, 2003 from: http://bmj.com/cgi/content/full/323/7321/1103.

Gergen, K. (1991). *The Saturated Self. Dilemmas of Identity in Contemporary Life.* New York, NY: Basic Books.

Gibbs, G., Friese, S., & Mangabeira, W. C. (2002, May). The use of new technology in qualitative research. *Forum Qualitative Sozialforschung/Forum:Qualitative Social Research, 3*(2). Retrieved Jan. 27, 2003 from: http://www.qualitative-research.net/fqs/fqs-eng.htm.

Hampton, K. & Wellman, B. (1999, November). Netville on-line and off-line. Observing and surveying a wired suburb. *American Behavioural Scientist, 43*(3), 475-492.

Hertz, R. (1997). *Reflexivity and Voice.* Thousand Oaks, CA: Sage.

Hine, C. (2000). *Virtual Ethnography.* Thousand Oaks, CA: Sage.

Holge-Hazelton, B. (2002, May). The Internet: a new field for qualitative inquiry? *Forum Qualitative Sozialforschung/Forum:Qualitative Social Research, 3*(2). Retrieved Jan. 27, 2003 from: http://www.qualitative-research.net/fqs/fqs-eng.htm.

Joinson, A. (2002, April). *Self-disclosure in on-line research: Media effects, motivated choices and the design of virtual methodologies.* PowerPoint presentation presented at ESRC Virtual Methods Series conducted at CRICT, Brunel University, Uxbridge, Middlesex, UK. Retrieved Jan. 27, 2003 from: http://www.joinson.com.

Jones, S. (1999a). *Doing Internet Research: Critical Issues and Methods for Examining the Net.* Thousand Oaks, CA: Sage.

Kiesler, S., Kraut, R., Lundmark, V., Patterson, M., Mukopadhyay, T., & Scherlis, W. (1998). A social technology that reduces social involvement and psychological well-being? *American Psychologist, 53*(9), 1017-1031.

Lincoln, Y. (1985). *Naturalistic Inquiry.* Thousand Oaks, CA: Sage.

Maczewski, M. (1999). *Interplay of online and onground realities: Internet research on youth experiences online.* Unpublished master's thesis, University of Victoria, Victoria, British Columbia, Canada.

Maczewski, M. (2002). Exploring identities through the Internet: Youth experiences online. *Child and Youth Care Forum, 31*(2), 111-129.

Mann, C. & Stewart, F. (2000). *Internet Communication and Qualitative Research. A Handbook for Researching Online.* Thousand Oaks, CA: Sage.

Markham, A. (1998). *Life Online: Researching Real Experience in Virtual Space.* London: Altamira Press.

McLuhan, M. (1964). *Understanding Media.* Cambridge, MA: MIT Press.

McLuhan, M. & McLuhan, E. (1988). *Laws of Media: The New Science.* Toronto, Canada: University of Toronto Press.

Moes, J. (2000, January). Von der Text-zur Hypertextanalyse: Konsequenzen fuer die qualitative Sozialforschung. *Forum Qualitative Sozialforschung/ Forum:Qualitative Social Research, 1*(1). Retrieved Jan. 27, 2003 from: http:// qualitative-research.net/fqws.

Moor, J. (2000). What is computer ethics? In R. M. Baird, R. Ramsower, & S. E. Rosenbaum (Eds.), *Cyberethics: Social and Moral Issues in the Computer Age* (pp. 23-33). Amherst, NY: Prometheus Books.

Mullet, K. & Sano, D. (1995). *Designing Visual Interfaces: Communication Oriented Techniques.* New York, NY: Prentice-Hall.

National Sciences and Engineering Research Council of Canada (1999). *Tri-council policy statement: Ethical conduct for research involving humans.* Retrieved Jan. 27, 2003 from: http://www.nserc.ca/programs/ethics/english/intro03.htm#C.

Nosek, B. A., Banaji, M. R., & Greenwald, A. G. (2002). E-research: Ethics, security, design, and control in psychological research on the Internet. *Journal of Social Issues, 58*(1), 161-176.

Oberg, A. (in press). Paying attention and not knowing. Presented at the Annual Meeting of the American Educational Research Association, Seattle, Washington, USA. In E. Hasebe-Ludt & W. Hurren (Eds.), *Curriculum Intertext.* New York: Peter Lang.

O'Brien, J. (1999). Writing in the body: Gender (re)production in online interaction. In M. Smith & P. Kollock (Eds.), *Communities in Cyberspace* (pp. 76-106). London: Routledge.

Schneider, S. & Larsen, E. (2000, September). *Campaign 2000: What's on congressional candidate Web sites? A preliminary analysis.* Paper presented at Association of Internet Researchers 1st Annual Conference, Lawrence, Kansas, USA.

Sharf, B. F. (1999). Beyond netiquette: The ethics of doing naturalistic discourse research on the Internet. In S. Jones (Ed.), *Doing Internet Research* (pp. 243-256). Thousand Oaks, CA: Sage.

Smith, M. & Kollock, P. (eds.). (1999). *Communities in Cyberspace.* London: Routledge.

Storey, M.-A., Philips, B., & Maczewski, M. (2001). Is it ethical to evaluate Web-based learning tools using students? *Empirical Software Engineering, 6*(4), 343-348.

Storey, M.-A., Philips, B., Maczewski, M., & Wang, M. (2002). Evaluating the usability of Web-based learning tool. *Educational Technology & Society, 5*(3). Retrieved Jan. 27, 2003 from: http://ifets.ieee.org/periodical/vol_3_2002/storey.html.

Suler, J. (2000). *Ethics in cyberspace research.* Retrieved Jan. 27, 2003 from: http:// www.rider.edu/users/suler/psycyber/ethics.html.

Surratt, G. C. (2001). *The Internet and Social Change.* Jefferson, NC: McFarland & Company.

Tapscott, D. (1998). *Growing up Digital.* New York, NY: McGraw-Hill.

Turkle, S. (1995). *Life on the Screen*. New York, NY: Touchstone.

Wellman, B., Quan-Haase, A., Witte, J., & Hampton, K. (2001, November). Does the Internet increase, decrease or supplement social capital? Social networks, participation and community commitment. *American Behavioral Scientist, 45*(3), 437-456.

Wittel, A. (2000, January). Ethnography on the move: From field to net to Internet. *Forum Qualitative Sozialforschung/Forum:Qualitative Social Research, 1*(1). Retrieved Jan. 27, 2003 from: http://qualitative-research.net/fqws.

ENDNOTES

1   The term "onground" is used instead of "in real life" to convey physical, material communities as the authors consider both online and onground events as part of "real life."

2   Oberg (2001) observed students engaged in qualitative research and found that their research process excelled when "the [research] topic becomes the method through which the topic is pursued." For example, when studying mindfulness, mindfulness became an integral research method for the research process. This occurrence Oberg named "congruence." Similarly, we believe, in online qualitative research, technological capabilities and their interactions become important aspects of research methods and are integral parts of conducting ethical research. Although absolute congruency is not necessary to conduct ethical research, expanding the scope of ethical research practices to reflect characteristics of human interactions within Internet-mediated environments is necessary.

3   We realize that given the wide range of topics described here, each topic is addressed relatively briefly. More in-depth reflection and analysis of each point raised are important issues for further research.

4   ICQ is a widely accessible software that enables chats. For more information, see http://www.icq.com.

5   For further reading on the process of data analysis with computer software, see Gibbs, Friese & Mangabeira (2002) as a starting point.

6   For a further discussion on the implications of a shift to hypertext analysis, see Moes (2000).

7   VoiP is a means of transmitting voice using the Internet protocol, rather than the telephone network.

Section II

Media, Messages and Ethics?

Chapter V

Blurring the Boundaries: Ethical Considerations for Online Research Using Synchronous CMC Forums

Danielle Lawson
Queensland University of Technology, Australia

ABSTRACT

As use of the Internet has grown, so to has the amount of research concerning various aspects of computer-mediated communication (CMC). In recent years, there has been an increase in the number of research projects dealing with Internet-based, synchronous chat programs. Although timely, this increased research interest in synchronous chat media is problematic due to potential ethical dilemmas regarding data gathering and research publication. This paper examines the ethical problems related to subject identity, privacy and "chat copyright" in synchronous online research. Additionally, it addresses possible strategies for minimizing ethical conflict, while maintaining research integrity.

INTRODUCTION

In the last two decades, as use of the Internet for business as well as artistic and social expression has grown, so too has the amount of research focussing on various aspects of the burgeoning Internet culture. Researchers from many social science fields, such as education (Tu & Corry, 2001; Beller, 1998; Chester & Gwynne, 1998), psychology (Nosek, Mahzarin, & Greenwald, 2002; Wallace, 1999; Turkle, 1995), communication (Rafaeli, Sudweeks, Konstan, & Mabry, 1998; Riva & Galimberti, 1998; Sudweeks & Rafaeli, 1995; Walther, Anderson, & Park, 1994) and gender studies (Witmer & Katzman, 1997; Herring, 1996a; Saviki, Lingenfelter, & Kelly, 1996; Allen, 1995; We, 1993), have gravitated toward the Internet as a research medium and source of data. An extensive amount of Internet research has examined asynchronous computer-mediated communication (CMC) forums, such as news groups and e-mail lists, where additions to conversations are not instantaneously posted to other members, rather they can take anywhere from several minutes to several days (Rafaeli et al., 1998; Saviki et al., 1996; Sudweeks & Rafaeli, 1995; Sproull & Kiesler, 1986; Kiesler, Siegel, & McGuire, 1984; Kerr & Hiltz, 1982). However, in recent years researchers have begun to take an interest in synchronous, "real-time" chat environments such as Multi-User Domains[1] (MUDs) and Internet Relay Chat (IRC), where conversational texts are posted to others in the forum almost instantaneously (Cherny, 1999; Paolillo, 1999; Hentschel, 1998; Rodino, 1997; Reid, 1991).

Despite the increasing numbers of researchers utilizing synchronous CMC programs as a research medium, to date very little has been written specifically concerning the ethical issues facing "synchronous CMC" (SCMC) researchers. The ethical issues SCMC researchers are faced with are similar to those presented to asynchronous CMC and face-to-face (FTF) researchers: whether to gain informed consent and how to handle the issue of copyright while protecting participant anonymity. However, Reid (1996) suggests that SCMC research is more ethically complex than asynchronous CMC research.

This chapter will broadly discuss the ethical issues of informed consent and copyright as they relate to both asynchronous and synchronous media, while discussing SCMC's specific concerns, including: personal identity creation and maintenance in SCMC, when and why consent for research is needed and the question of whether SCMC chat should be treated as casual speech or written text for the purposes of copyright. It will also discuss several strategies for reducing ethical conflict while retaining research integrity.

WHO ARE YOU?—THE NATURE OF IDENTITY IN SCMC

"When we step through the screen into virtual communities, we reconstruct our identities on the other side of the looking glass" (Turkle, 1995, p. 117).

Identity as a term has many different meanings depending upon the academic field and theoretical perspective from which one is working. Although it has been acknowledged that a user's psychological identity (both for their "real" persona and their online persona) does play a part in the creation and maintenance of online identity (Wallace, 1999; Turkle, 1995), the present chapter is concerned with "identity" as the online presence/persona a user creates specifically for a SCMC forum.

SCMC participants use text to create/recreate reality, which includes creating and recreating their identities within the context of the chat forum. Unlike our "real-life" identity that is shown to others through our actions, appearance and words, our online identity is constructed purely through written text. As such, our online identity is fluid—it can be changed in a myriad of ways with just a few keystrokes. This forms a key concept in the work of Danet, Rudenberg-Wright and Rosenbaum-Tamari (1998), which examined Internet chat as a form of "play," where participants used the anonymous nature of chat to play with situations, reality and their identities. Wallace (1999) expands upon this research, remarking upon the potential of Internet chat to serve as an "identity laboratory," where participants are free to experiment with different personality traits and attributes. Each time a person logs into a SCMC medium they are given the chance to create their identity anew, or use a previously established persona. The choice is theirs, but it starts with the innocuous question "Who are you?" Perhaps a better question is "Who do you want to be today?"

SCMC users play a very active role in the creation, change and/or maintenance of their online persona, spending an extensive amount of time and energy in developing their online identity. Although the effort that goes into creating/maintaining an online identity has prompted several researchers to suggest that a person's online identity is an "extension of the self" (Troest, 1998; Bechar-Israeli, 1995; Reid, 1991), which suggests that the online identity is not a separate self, but rather an online version of the self, or perhaps an idealized version. These researchers maintain that even in the anonymous medium of SCMC, users still incorporate aspects of themselves into their online identity, evidence of which is seen by examining the nicknames used.

At first glance, online nicknames seem to be a minor aspect of communicating in the CMC milieu. However, upon closer examination, it is a SCMC user's nickname that gives other users their "first impression" of the person behind the screen. SCMC lacks many of the subtle sensory cues people normally use to categorize others, generally referred to as "Cues-Filtered-Out" theory, thus nicknames become a particularly important means of identifying each other. Cues-Filtered-Out is a collective term for those CMC theories that maintain CMC is limited in its socioemotional and relational possibilities in comparison to FTF communication (Sproull & Kiesler, 1986; Kiesler et al., 1984; Short, Williams, & Christie, 1976). However, Behchar-Israeli (1995) found that most users manage to give social cues despite the lack of visual and aural stimuli. Bechar-Israeli surveyed 278 IRC users about their nickname choice and found that while only 7 percent used a version/part of their legal name, almost half (45 percent) used a nickname that related to themselves in some way. This research concluded that SCMC users frequently used identifiers such as their age, gender and location as part of their name, for example, tiger-18, LoudMale or NYCdude.[2] Bechar-Israeli (1995) further maintains that "… [real life] names become an integral part of the self, the way people perceive themselves and the way they are perceived by others" (¶ 24). The same can be said of online nicknames; they influence how SCMC users see themselves and how others see them. Therefore, it can be argued that one's online nickname is more than a simple identifier for the person behind the screen, it is a vital part of our "cyberself."

Despite the potential for identity play in SCMC (Wallace, 1999; Turkle, 1995), Bechar-Israeli (1995) maintains that most SCMC users create one persona and use it consistently, becoming deeply attached to it—"… people usually prefer the social attributes of a permanent, recognized identity" (¶ 11).[3] The sustained use of one nickname by a person not only encourages them to become attached to it, but also allows for the creation and maintenance of a "reputation" associated with the name. Thus, a nickname is not merely an identifier of the individual who uses it. The nickname also develops an associated reputation in chat forums regular SCMC frequent, thereby indicating to those users familiar with the name and reputation, what interactions are acceptable and what behaviors to expect from the "nickname."

For example, I have been chatting regularly in two rooms on two different IRC networks for more than six years using the same nickname—destiny^. Many online friends and "real-life" friends of mine recognize this nickname as "belonging" to me. They are familiar with the way I "act" online, as such the name "destiny^" has a particular reputation associated with it. Not only do others view the nickname "destiny^" as belonging to me, but I view it as "mine" and have spent time and effort building the reputation now associated with it. This feeling of ownership/possessiveness is supported by the research of Bechar-Israeli (1995) and Wallace (1999), who maintain that online people have very few possessions, thus they feel very possessive toward the few they have—one of which is their online nickname. "In effect, then, nicks [nicknames] are treated as a form of intellectual property, created and maintained in cyberspace" (Bechar-Israeli, 1995, ¶103). The possessiveness SCMC users feel toward their nicknames has even prompted the programmers of the IRC networks to create a "nickserv" database where users can register their nicknames, so they cannot be used by others. If a nickname is not protected through registration, then it can essentially be "hijacked" by another user, who may then act in ways contrary to what others expect of the person behind the nickname. Other forms of SCMC have also adopted some form of protective technology to guard nicknames for users. This type of SCMC identity hijacking causes frustration and turmoil for both the user who has had the nickname "stolen" and the user's online friends (Bechar-Israeli, 1995).

INFORMED CONSENT:
PUBLIC VERSUS PRIVATE CHAT

"... privacy is a condition that allows the individual freedom to choose when to establish a relationship and when not" (Katsh, 1995, p. 234).

Ethical practice guidelines for several of the world's leading social science research organizations stress the need to protect participants from harm. This includes maintaining confidentiality and participant anonymity, as well as respecting the right to privacy, to dignity and whether or not to participate in research (British Psychological Society, 2002; British Sociological Association, 2002; International Sociological Association, 2001; American Sociological Association, 1997; American Psychological Association, 1992). According to the American Sociological Association (1997), social science researchers should:

"... obtain consent from research participants or their legally authorized representatives (1) when data are collected from research participants through any form of

communication, interaction or intervention; or (2) when behavior of research participants occurs in a private context where an individual can reasonably expect that no observation or reporting is taking place" (12.01a).

However, this same code of ethics maintains that researchers can conduct research freely in public places and through the use of public records or archives. Therefore, for a researcher to determine whether or not informed consent is necessary when conducting research using SCMC mediums, they must determine whether or not communication via the medium in question is public or private. Recent articles exploring issues of ethical CMC research, while failing to agree on the development of guidelines for researchers, manage to agree that the key factor in ethical CMC research centers around whether the nature of the CMC is public or private (Eysenbach & Till, 2001; Sixsmith & Murray, 2001; Sudweeks & Rafaeli, 1995). As noted by Waskul and Douglass (1996), "The blurring of public and private experience is particularly characteristic of online communication, and comprises a source of much of the ethical controversy of online research" (p. 131).

Early CMC researchers whose work primarily examined asynchronous CMC mediums, such as e-mail discussion lists and newsgroups, maintained that since people were already posting anonymously to public forums, gaining consent for using their discourse as part of a data set was moot since their identity was hidden (Rafaeli et al., 1998; Jones, 1994). In fact Jones (1994) states: "If the research does not involve identifiable subjects, there is no risk to subjects, and therefore the protection of these rights and interests no longer applies" (p. 33). [4]

The concept of people online as being "unidentifiable" is short sighted, considering the myriad of ways people can be identified online (e-mail address, username, nickname, etc.). Viewing all Internet communication as inherently anonymous does not take into account the fact that, particularly with regard to asynchronous mediums like newsgroups, participants are not always hidden behind an anonymous pseudonym or e-mail address. For example, people using work e-mail addresses often are required to use their real name as their Internet "username"[5] when accessing e-mail and online programs. In newsgroups and some synchronous chat programs, this username (and in some cases their full e-mail address) is displayed to other readers/participants. Thus, researchers cannot always assume that users are not going to be identifiable via their username, e-mail address or online nickname.

This view is shared by Liu (1999) who maintains that, "Conversations in publicly accessible IRC channels ... are public acts deliberately intended for public consumption" (¶98). Additionally, Liu suggests that analyzing logs of such conversations and reporting the results "is not subject to 'Human Subject' constraints" (1999, ¶98) because individual identities via IRC are hidden through the use of pseudonyms. This is flawed since it has been shown that many synchronous users incorporate aspects of their real-life (RL) identity into their online nickname choice and the identity they create (discussed in the previous section). In addition, albeit rare, some SCMC users use their real name as their online nickname, therefore assuming that all SCMC participants are truly anonymous is unsubstantiated.

Although various researchers maintain that CMC is inherently public (Liu, 1999; Rafaeli et al., 1998; Jones, 1994), very few researchers have promoted the view that it is private in nature. Rather, the widely promoted perspective is that CMC is neither inherently public nor private, instead it depends upon the individual participant's perceptions of the communication context (Sixsmith & Murray, 2001; Eysenbach & Till, 2001; Binik, Mah, & Kiesler, 1999; Herring, 1996a). Waskul and Douglass (1996) suggest that the simplistic dichotomy of public/private is often misused to refer to the accessibility of communication, rather than the experience of the individual participants. They maintain that assuming CMC is public because it is easily accessible is "an ethically dangerous misconception" (Waskul & Douglass, 1999, p. 132), a view shared by Reid (1996) who asserts that easy access to archives and online conversations does not mean it is meant for the general consumption of the wider public. She suggests that when individuals create Usenet postings (and other online communication texts), while publicly accessible, "…it is doubtful whether each author intends his or her words to be placed in the public domain" (Reid, 1996, p. 170).

Various researchers maintain that there is a degree of blurring between public and private spaces online. Stefik (1999) maintains that while in "real" life we define private spaces through physical cues like closed doors and locked filing cabinets, online "… the physical cues are lost, and distinctions between public and private space are blurred" (p. 200). Since cyberspace is a "place" only in the mental sense, the labels "public" and "private" as metaphors for cyberspace interaction will always disintegrate when applied to the individual experiences of participants, thus there exists the potential for two participants to view the same situation differently (Waskul & Douglass, 1996). For example, a participant chatting in an "invite-only"[6] IRC channel can reasonably assume that the conversations taking place within the channel are private and for channel participants only. CMC also allows participants to interact in a public forum from the privacy of their own home, a situation that encourages the perception that the communication is private (King, 1996; Waskul & Douglass, 1996). This is supported by Stefik (1999) who maintains that in private "… with close friends, we feel differently, act differently, and are less on guard than we are in public" (p. 199). He further suggests that "private time" can be time spent in solitude or in intimate contexts with family and friends. Additionally, many mailing lists and SCMC forums state in their rules that forum posts are to remain in that forum only and are not to be copied to other lists or forums. This indicates that the owners who set the rules and guidelines view forum communication as private for channel participants only. Thus, it can be argued that the difference between private and public communication via SCMC mediums is determined in part by the individuals involved, who interpret this through the established purposes and procedures of the particular SCMC forum.

Researchers such as Waskul and Douglass (1996), King (1996) and Herring (1996a) maintain that online participants may act according to their personal perception of privacy, even in seemingly public areas of SCMC, such as IRC channels, although these perceptions may not be consistent depending upon the personal situation and/or the context of the situation in general. According to Binik et al. (1999), "Legally, the boundary between public and private life is based on people's expectations…" (p. 3)—a perspective supported by Cherny (1999). This view is further substantiated by the British Psychological Society's (2002) "Code of conduct, ethical principles and guidelines," which suggests that due care must be taken by researchers as their data collection in a seemingly public place may be "… intruding upon the privacy of individuals who, even while in a normally public space, may believe they are unobserved" (sect. 9.1).

Cho and LaRose (1999) attribute this gray area concerning the public or private nature of online communication to the "intimate relationships" between online users and their computers, as well as the relationship between users and the communities in which they participate online (both asynchronous and synchronous). This is a view examined earlier by We (1993), who found that online users become strongly involved emotionally in their online interactions. Additionally, Cho and LaRose (1999) maintain that these online relationships "... create new privacy boundaries that are easily transgressed by researchers" (p. 9).

Several researchers maintain that the relationship between users and their computers leads to the lowering of inhibitions (Wallace, 1999; Sproull & Kiesler, 1986; Kiesler et al., 1984; Kerr & Hiltz, 1982; Hiltz & Turoff, 1978). The isolation of CMC allows users to communicate with less sense of restriction, due to the lack of immediate criticism and social control. Sproull and Kiesler (1991) state that the feeling of privacy that CMC users develop "... makes them feel less inhibited in their relations with others" (p. 48). Additionally, due to the reduction of inhibition found in CMC, users have been found to use a higher level of profanity and other emotionally charged language. In addition they divulge more intimate and sensitive details of their lives to others in their online communities compared to FTF interactions (Walther et al., 1994; Lea & Spears, 1992; Hiltz, Johnson, & Agle, 1978), particularly if they perceive the situation in which information is divulged as private.

Furthermore, Sixsmith and Murray (2001) suggest that social presence theory (Short et al., 1976), or a Cues-Filtered-Out theory, indicates that in the absence of visual, aural and other social cues, CMC users would be less aware of their audience, and therefore "... more likely to treat their posts as private communications" (¶ 17). The Cues-Filtered-Out[7] approach to CMC research suggested that the medium is limited in its socioemotional and relational possibilities when compared FTF communication. However, this work has been made passé by the work of various researchers who have shown that CMC users have adapted to the lack of visual, aural and other social cues through creative use of text, such as emoticons[8] (Witmer & Katzman, 1997; Walther, 1992). Yet this does not negate the possibility that the reduced awareness of others when participating in online communication (both asynchronous and synchronous) allows users to feel as if the communication is private, even when posted to a public forum such as an IRC chatroom. Therefore, with the public or private nature of SCMC being dependent upon the individual participant's expectations and perceptions (as discussed earlier), seeking informed consent is one way to determine how participants view their communication in a given CMC situation. This view is supported by various researchers who criticize those who use online conversations (both synchronous and asynchronous) without gaining informed consent from the conversants (King, 1996; Waskul & Douglass, 1996). Thus, taking for granted, the seemingly public context of many online chat forums fails to consider the frequent emergence of private interaction among the participants and "is not a sufficient license to invade the privacy of others, and does not relieve the researcher from ethical commitments of informing participants of research intent" (Waskul & Douglass, 1996, p. 133).

For example, in SCMC mediums where participants are identified only by a nickname, failing to gain prior informed consent to record a participant's conversation makes it possible for a researcher to log and publish text along with a nickname, recorded during a time when the name was "hijacked" by someone other than the usual owner of the nickname. Publication such as this has the potential to injure the nickname's reputation, which was developed by the usual owner, particularly if the conversation exhibited by the "hijacker," and consequently published by the researcher, contains inflammatory remarks (i.e., racist, sexist or a lie about the real owner of the name). Thus, not seeking consent before recording and publishing a person's text and nickname could injure her personally or the reputation associated with her nickname.

However, this is not to say that gaining informed consent is easily achieved. Several researchers have found that CMC users are wary of researchers wishing to analyze their communication (Lindlif & Shatzer, 1998; Paccagnella, 1997). Cherny (1999), writing about her experiences studying the synchronous medium of MUDs, notes: "The "natives" in MUDs are increasingly cognizant and wary of outsiders "research agendas" (p. 301). Cherny attributes this reticence to CMC participants having been misrepresented in publication by journalists and casual researchers, who did not fully understand the particular nuances of the medium.

In an effort to increase the number of SCMC participants granting consent for the recording, analyzing and publication of their chat, researchers could disguise participants further by removing identifiers, such as their nickname, or assigning them a pseudonymous nickname (Sixsmith & Murray, 2001; Liu, 1999; Paccagnella, 1997). Yet, researchers are then faced with the question of whether to protect the anonymity and privacy of participants or give them credit as authors of their conversational text, thus leading to the question to whom does CMC copyright belong?

COPYRIGHT AND SCMC

"[T]he institution of copyright stands squarely on the boundary between private and public" (Rose, 1993, p. 2).

As noted by Rose (1993), copyright is intimately linked to the concepts of public and private discussed in the previous section, a view supported by Katsh (1995) who suggests that: "It should not be surprising that privacy and copyright are linked by an intriguing focus on and concern for individual choice" (p. 235). It is just this concern for individual choice and privacy that makes use of participant text and copyright an ethical concern for CMC researchers.

In the past 10 years, much has been written about copyright and the Internet, although a majority of the copyright discussion regarding the Internet deals with fair use as it applies to standard forms of intellectual property, such as artworks, books, articles, and musical works (Stefik, 1999; Godwin, 1998; Katsh, 1995; Rose, 1993), and their use/ abuse on Web pages. Very little of the existing literature examines copyright as it relates to asynchronous CMC, and even less discusses the specific copyright issues facing SCMC researchers (see Cherny, 1999; Reid, 1996). When studying SCMC, researchers must decide who owns the copyright on SCMC interactions.

From a legal perspective, copyright belongs to either (or jointly) the author or publisher of an item of intellectual property (U.S. Copyright Office, 2001, sect. 201), where intellectual property as it relates to copyright "… includes literary and artistic works such as novels, poems and plays, films, musical works, artistic works such as drawings, paintings, photographs and sculptures, and architectural designs" (World Intellectual Property Organisation, n.d.). The World Intellectual Property Organisation (WIPO) also maintains that copyright provisions apply to performances of artists as well as recordings and broadcasters of radio and television programs. This interlinking of intellectual property and copyright has several implications for SCMC: (1) if all participants in CMC environments are essentially authors (Katsh, 1995), then the text falls under copyright protections; (2) if participation in a synchronous medium is "performance" (Danet, Rudenberg & Rosenbaum-TAmari, 1998), then the performance falls under copyright protections; (3) if, although presented in a textual form, we take the stance that SCMC is ephemeral like speech (it scrolls off the screen unless saved to a file), then unless it is recorded, it does not qualify as intellectual property and, therefore, does not fall under copyright protections.

Therefore taking the view that when participants enter their conversation text into a synchronous medium they are in essence both the author and the publisher, then from a legal perspective they own the copyright to their words. The same holds true if we support the view that synchronous chat is "performance," such as Danet et al. (1998) suggest in their work "Hmmm ... where's that smoke coming from?: writing, play and performance on Internet relay chat," as performance falls under copyright provisions. Although with regard to performance, researchers must then consider whether the individual speakers hold the copyright to their words, or whether the group of speakers holds the copyright. The idea of group ownership of chat presents difficulties, as the very nature of synchronous media facilitates a fluid group membership, with participants arriving and leaving at will. Thus, determining who the owners of a particular section of chat are would be difficult if not impossible.

Implications one and two suggest that SCMC is a distinct textual or performed expression of an idea, therefore falling under the provisions of copyright.[9] However, the third implication suggests that SCMC is neither textual nor oral, thus the existing copyright guidelines are difficult to apply.

Several CMC researchers have been interested in the fact that CMC, particularly synchronous forms of CMC, display elements of both standard written expression and orality (Turkle, 1995; December, 1993; Ferrara, Brunner, & Whitmore, 1991). Alternately, I suggest that SCMC falls into a third form of communication, *textoral,* whereby the communication exhibits characteristics of both speech (formal and/or casual) and text. Although it is difficult to comprehensively define the characteristics of spoken and written language, as they are complex concepts (Finnegan, 1988), various researchers (Hughes, 1996; Chafe, 1982) have shown that speech and text have distinct features: (1) speech involves more audience interaction, whereas text has little or no audience interaction; (2) speech is often simple in construction (e.g., use of sentence fragments as stand alone clauses), whereas text uses more formal, complex sentence structures; (3) speech tends to include more personal references (e.g., I went out), whereas text does not; (4) speech is ephemeral unless recorded, whereas text is relatively permanent and can be revisited and (5) speech utilizes more tag-questions, interruptions, unfinished clauses and other interpersonal dynamic indicators than text.

Sample IRC Text[10]

1<P1>	That's true. ... so is that enough?
2<P2>	yeah. should be plenty
3<P3>	Ok. ... HUGS ... how is XXXX doing?

4<P2>	hmm ... okay from what I can tell
5<P2>	will probably be very glad to get home from work tonight ... it's been raining all day ... so I'm sure the shop was pretty quiet
6<P1>	nodnods
7<P2>	hmm ... sounds like the bottom just dropped out.
8<P3>	Ahhh, isn't he home yet?
9<P1>	How was Your day?
10<P2>	No, he'll get home around 6pm. I'll have to get ready so we can go out.
11<P3>	Ok .... boring with the writing
12<P2>	He wants to get me out of the house for a bit, which I don't mind. Although, going out in this rain doesn't really appeal to me very much.
13<P1>	I agree you should go out. ... Take a break XXXXX!
14<P2>	yeah ... problem is, with this rain, where do we go?
15<P2>	Hmmm
16<P1>	it's really pouring here now.
17<P3>	Anywhere. .... get some food somewhere
18<P1>	yeah
19<P3>	It will stop soon. ... It's not raining here right now
20<P2>	I guess we could do that *nods*
21<P2>	I hope it doesn't stop, as we really need the rain.

As shown in the excerpt above, SCMC involves the rapid exchange of ideas via text, thus facilitating audience interaction through the potential for instantaneous audience feedback. The sample shows three people involved in an IRC interaction, at times with two different conversations happening simultaneously. SCMC also exhibits both complex and simplistic sentence structures. For example, lines 10, 12 and 21 are formal in nature, starting with a capital letter and ending with proper punctuation. Additionally, there are quite a few sentences in the sample that show simple structure, including the use of sentence fragments. Other sentences show a combination of simplistic and formal structure, for instance, line 17 starts formally with a capital, something that is missing in most of the informal statements of the sample, but the punctuation takes an informal turn with the use of ellipses in the middle of the line and the lack of punctuation at the end. Furthermore, the sample text displays frequent use of personal references, and other interpersonal dynamic indicators, including action descriptors (see line 3—HUGS; and line 20—*nods*).

SCMC is also essentially ephemeral, lasting only as long as it takes to scroll off the computer screen. The sample text shown above was purposely logged so it could be revisited. However if it was not logged, it would eventually be deleted from the network buffer as newer text is generated and temporarily[11] stored.

Thus, as illustrated above, SCMC does not fit neatly within the speech or text characteristics suggested by Hughes (1996) and Chafe (1982), rather it may exhibit characteristics of either or both at any given moment in time depending upon the participant's SCMC style. Attempting to categorize SCMC as either speech or text fails because it does not take into account the unique nature of SCMC. The question now becomes how to deal with textoral communication where copyright issues are concerned, as this communication type is not adequately represented in current copyright legislation.

For the moment, researchers exploring SCMC mediums must determine for themselves whether the communication they are "overhearing" is like casual speech (e.g., in a coffee shop), a written text or performance that falls under copyright protection or is textoral and thus does not fall under current copyright legislation. The primary way researchers can resolve this particular ethical dilemma is by "speaking" to the participants about their perceptions regarding the public or private nature of the communication situation, which relates to the previous issue of informed consent.

Additionally, some researchers suggest that utilizing extensive passages of CMC text without attributing the work to the "author" may infringe on another's intellectual property rights (Eysenbach & Till, 2001; Cavazos, 1994; Boehlefeld, 1991). However, Cherny (1999) notes that: "Research rigor usually demands that the researcher provide a trail of supporting evidence sufficient for another researcher to duplicate her [sic] efforts" (p. 312). She goes on to state that protecting the privacy of research participants "means thwarting just such a research duplication" (Cherny, 1999, p. 312). Given the nature of the research, strict research duplication (as in a scientific experiment) is probably not practical or possible, therefore casting doubt upon Cherny's assertions. However, crediting CMC texts used in academic publications to the participants who authored the texts raises another ethical dilemma for researchers, who must now decide which is more important, giving participants credit for their intellectual property in the form of CMC written communication or protecting their identities and anonymity as participants of the research in question.

STRATEGIES FOR MAINTAINING THE ETHICAL INTEGRITY OF SCMC RESEARCH

"The ease of covert observation, the occasional blurry distinction between public and private venues, and the difficulty of obtaining the informed consent of subjects make cyberresearch [sic] particularly vulnerable to ethical breaches by even the most scrupulous scholars" (Thomas, 1996, p. 108).

As discussed in the previous sections, CMC researchers, particularly those examining SCMC mediums, face various ethical questions that must be considered in all stages of CMC research, from project development to publication. Although many of the issues raised in this chapter do not have concrete answers and must be decided by the individual researcher, various researchers offer strategies for maintaining the ethical integrity of CMC research in the face of such problematic ethical concerns. This section will discuss strategies for dealing with the ethical concerns central to this chapter: protection of participant identity, informed consent and copyright.

Protection of Participant Identity Strategies

Social science research is governed by various principles depending upon the particular field in which the research lies; however, all social science fields share a common concern over protecting the welfare and privacy of participants, as mentioned in previous sections. The American Sociological Association's (1997, sect. 11.04a) ethical guidelines state that before publication, all participant identifiers must be deleted from the work—a strategy supported by Waskul and Douglass (1996) with regard to online research. An alternative to removing all identifiers that has been used by several CMC researchers is the practice of changing the names of participants, essentially giving them a pseudonym for their online pseudonym. Finn and Lavitt (1994) used this strategy, however they chose not to disguise the names of the bulletin boards on which the messages appeared, in addition to publishing the dates and times the posts appeared. They maintained that participant anonymity was protected by changing the names. This view was contradicted in 1996 by Waskul and Douglass who argue that merely changing a user's pseudonym is not enough. They maintain that this perspective not only misinterprets online anonymity as a feature of the individual, rather than a condition of the online social environment, but it also "confuses online [sic] anonymity with the ethical standards of anonymity, and ... is neglectful and potentially harmful to the participants' experience" (Waskul & Douglass, 1996, p. 134). Simply changing a participant's pseudonym while publishing additional information (date, time, bulletin board name) would allow someone to track down and identify the individual who posted, as many bulletin boards (as well as some mailing lists and newsgroups) archive messages for a set period of time.[12]

Additionally, several researchers suggest that identifying an online participant, even by their online pseudonym, could have damaging consequences for the person and/or chat forum (King, 1996; Reid, 1996; Waskul & Douglass, 1996).

Although she published the name of the synchronous chat programs where she recorded her data set, Cherny (1999) changed the names of all participants who appeared in the work, as well as changing the nicknames/characters discussed in articles and posts she referenced from other sources. As an added precaution, she "broke up" characters/nicknames that might be too easy for participants to identify into two or more nicknames, thus protecting participants further. According to Paccagnella (1997), this sort of attention to detail, "Changing not only real names, but also aliases or pseudonyms (where used) proves the respect of the researchers for the *social reality* [sic] of cyberspace" (p. 8).

Cherny (1999) suggests four ways researchers can protect the privacy of their CMC research participants: (1) use disguises for names and online communities; (2) delete or mask compromising details; (3) create composite characters; and (4) break characters, who might be identifiable when described "whole," into multiple characters in the final publication. However, changing and omitting participant nicknames or creating composites for complex characters in published work may lead to problems regarding validity, replicatability and research reliability (Sixsmith & Murray, 2001; Cherny, 1999), by not providing the information needed to replicate work, such as gender, age and other social characteristics. Additionally, eliminating all identifying information from research to protect participant anonymity could also result in a loss of research detail that is provided by thick description.

Consent Strategies: Nondisclosure Versus Disclosure

When discussing CMC research, "There is increasing evidence that researchers posting or "lurking" on such communities may be perceived as intruders and may damage the communities" (Eysenbach & Till, 2001, p. 2), resulting in members being reluctant to chat and/or leaving the community entirely. This assertion supports the beliefs of CMC researchers, such as Cherny (1999), Lindlif and Shatzer, (1998) and Paccagnella (1997), who maintain that CMC participants, both in asynchronous and synchronous CMC communities, are wary of researchers.

However, Cho and LaRose (1999) assert that:

"The flexible nature of personal identity and frequent abuse of privacy norms on the Internet mean that the authenticity of online researchers, the purposes of their research and the credibility of the anonymity and confidentiality guarantees they offer always are open to question" (p. 9).

Thus, it stands to reason that CMC participants would be reluctant to consent to being yet another "guinea pig" in the flood of CMC research.

Despite this, there are ways in which researchers can build confidence and rapport, while hopefully increasing the potential that CMC participants will consent to being part of CMC research. For instance, Waskul and Douglass (1996) suggest that researchers should gain entry to CMC communities starting with the "owner" of the group. Although this suggestion was made concerning asynchronous CMC mediums, particularly e-mail discussion lists, it can be applied to synchronous forums like IRC or AOL chat, where registered channels on the network are "owned" by the person(s) who registered them. However, Cherny (1999) cautions that merely seeking the permission of medium administrators (e.g., MUD wizards or IRC channel owners) "does not seem a sufficiently nuanced approach to obtaining informed consent" (p. 302), particularly since channel administrators do not have the authority to give informed consent on behalf of the members/participants in their channel. It should be noted that Cherny used e-mail to obtain consent from the speakers she quotes in her work, but this is not always possible or practical as people change e-mail addresses, change Internet providers or possibly drift away from Internet usage altogether. Thus, it would be more practical to obtain before or at the time of data collection.

In addition, researchers such as Cherny (1999) and Reid (1991) support the perspective that CMC researchers, who are participants in the synchronous communities (or asynchronous for that matter) they are seeking to examine, will have more success gaining consent to participate from the members. However, Lindlif and Shatzer (1998) suggest that it does matter to online participants whether other users are sincere users there to participate or "a person whose goal is to cast a long-term analytic eye on their activities and publish the result" (p. 181). Although active participation in a research setting is not always practical or desirable, it is another way in which researchers can, over time, gain consent and, in some cases, understanding from group members. Unfortunately, this may have negative implications for researchers hoping to set up an experimental chat situation, as participants may be reluctant to chat merely for "research purposes."[13] Additionally, gaining informed consent of participants in some types of online research may be detrimental to the research. For instance, Reid (1996) found that some participants, on learning of her research objectives through informed consent, "set about to deliberately manufacture quotable quotes" (p. 171), which she says strengthened her belief that nondisclosure at times is "both justified and necessary" (p. 171).

Furthermore, as privacy is based on choice (Katsh, 1995; Rose, 1993), then giving potential participants in online research more choice about how their participation is used may increase the consent rate. Reid (1996) attempted this by giving participants a choice regarding how they were identified in the published text of her research. Surprisingly, some participants wanted their real names and/or e-mail addresses used in the publication. Although she complied with participant wishes at the time, Reid (1996) is ambivalent about this decision now, suggesting that the disinhibition seen in online participant interactions "could conceivably lead people to agreeing to or even insisting upon a kind of public exposure by which they may eventually be harmed" (p. 172).

However, I believe that offering potential participants the ability to choose their level of consent should increase their feeling of control over the situation, while demonstrating that the researcher respects the "social reality" of the virtual community (Paccagnella, 1997). When negotiating informed consent with potential research participants, researchers could allow the participant to choose to: (1) consent to having their nickname and communicative text used for data analysis only (no publication of name or text); (2) consent to having either their nickname or text published in an academic work, but never together (i.e., no identifiers); (3) consent to having either their nickname or text published in an academic work, but never together (i.e., no identifiers) and providing they get to see the "write up" prior to publication; (4) consent to having both their nickname and text published in academic work, thereby being credited as the authors of their own words or (5) consent to having both their nickname and text published in academic work, thereby being credited as the authors of their own words, providing they get to see the "write up" prior to publication. The last two options deal directly with the issue of CMC copyright.

Copyright Strategies

With regard to copyright, Liu (1999) suggests that researchers can err on the side of caution and guard data confidentiality "by avoiding direct quotation of postings, by not referring to any particular IRC participants" (¶ 95). In cases of linguistic or sociological study, discussion of language in the context of the particular conversation or a portion of the conversation, as well as publishing excerpts of text "in situ" may be necessary for clarity and demonstration[14]. An alternative to Liu's suggestion would be to limit the number of lines used and/or remove all text not related to the particular conversation.[15] Alternatively, researchers could follow the lead of the ProjectH team (Rafaeli et al., 1998) who supported the view that online communication in publicly accessible newsgroups, mailing lists and chatrooms is public and, therefore, open to use as research data. The ProjectH team was instructed to use only communications that were posted to publicly accessible archives (such as newsgroups), with the caveat that no individuals would be identified by name in the database or in publication unless they had been contacted and written consent was given (Rafaeli et al., 1998). As stated earlier, removing all identifiers and/or not using any data samples in the final publication does not allow for the thick description that makes academic research useful and informative.

Yet, using excerpts of text for demonstration within a publication and not crediting the speaker fails to credit the individual with the "authorship" of their text. Boehlefeld (1991) argues for seeking participants permission to use quotes and their name (nickname) to protect their privacy as much as possible, while also respecting their copyright over their written words. This strategy is used by several SCMC researchers, including Reid (1991) and Cherny (1999). This strategy would also allow attribution to the author of the CMC text, but may compromise participant privacy unknowingly (e.g., they are recognized in the publication), as well as not being an option if the researcher cannot contact the individuals involved.

A possible solution to both issues would be to change participants' nicknames and notify the participants of what their "pseudonym" is as well as keeping a record of it in case needed. This option credits the participant with ownership, while protecting their privacy and allowing for the "paper trail" expected in academic research. Alternately, researchers could allow participants to review transcripts of communication logs and/or drafts of the paper before publication. This strategy has benefits in that it would give participants some control over the final product, particularly how they are represented in it. However, this strategy also has potentially negative aspects, as noted by Cherny (1999) who suggests that processing participant criticism of research text is difficult as "they are responding to a text not intended for them as primary audience, and a text potentially confusing in its rhetorical style" (p. 315). Herring (1996b) suggests that critical theorizing cannot take place when the study population has the final say over the analysis published. Thus, it is up to the researcher to determine how much influence participants' criticisms will have over the final product.

CONCLUSION

"Determination of whether a research approach is ethical should not be based on whether informed consent is sought from research participants, but rather whether the researcher makes his or her best effort to protect the research participants" (Liu, 1999, p. 102).

This chapter has discussed identity creation and maintenance via SCMC, as well as the two fundamental ethical issues concerning SCMC research: informed consent and its relationship to the public/private nature of SCMC; and SCMC copyright versus protection of participant privacy. It has been noted that researchers must make several decisions regarding their Internet research: (1) Is informed consent needed? and (2) Does SCMC fall under current copyright provisions, or is it textoral and, therefore, does not fit within current legislation?

It has been discussed that due to a desire to protect participants from harm, informed consent is a key consideration of social research. However, the need for informed participant consent is dependent upon the public or private nature of the communication being studied. This is further complicated in SCMC forums as participants may view a seemingly public situation as private. Thus, to determine whether informed consent is required, researchers must first discover how the study population views the communication situation, whether it is private or public.

Furthermore, researchers must decide if the SCMC data recorded falls under copyright provisions and should therefore be credited to the source, or if they should protect participant anonymity by not crediting the "speaker." This is further complicated by the blurred boundary between speech and text exhibited in SCMC. It has been suggested that SCMC is neither casual speech and therefore not covered by copyright legislation, nor text, which does fall under copyright provisions. Rather, I maintain that SCMC falls into a third communication category, "textoral," which is defined as communication that exhibits characteristics of both speech and text simultaneously.

In addition to examining the ethical issues raised in SCMC research, several strategies for increasing the ethical integrity of SCMC research have been discussed, including the concept of giving participants the choice of "levels" of consent. Allowing participants the chance to choose their level of consent addresses all of the primary issues discussed in this chapter. It would give participants control over how much of their online identity they wish to have published, while potentially increasing the number of participants consenting to participate in research. However, future research is needed to test whether giving participants a choice over their level of consent actually increases the rate of consent in Internet-based research.

Ethical Internet research is not merely a matter of following a series of guidelines, but of individual researchers' ongoing commitment to protect CMC participants/research subjects from harm, factors that also govern non-CMC social research. SCMC researchers are faced with the responsibility to decide for themselves how to answer the ethical questions of gaining informed consent, whether SCMC is public or private and whether to protect copyright or protect participant privacy. Reid (1996) suggests that the disinhibition seen online may encourage participants to "flock toward the chance to be immortalized in research can also cause the researcher of online [sic] communities to distance him—or herself from the humanity of subjects" (p. 173). Thus, it is up to individual researchers to determine the ethical standards that apply to their research, while upholding the protection and humanity of their research participants. As synchronous Internet technology advances, researchers will have to continually reevaluate the way in which they conduct research to ensure they protect the research participants from harm, as well as determining how to answer the various ethical questions raised regarding SCMC, all while striving to maintain the integrity of their research.

REFERENCES

Allen, B. J. (1995). Gender and computer-mediated communication. *Sex Roles: A Journal of Research, 32*(7-8), 557-564.

American Psychological Association. (1992). *Ethical principles of psychologists and code of conduct.* Retrieved Sept. 30, 2002 from: http://www.apa.org/ethics/code.html.

American Sociological Association. (1997). *American Sociological Association code of ethics.* Retrieved Sept. 30, 2002 from: http://www.asanet.org/members/ecoderev.html.

Bechar-Israeli, H. (1995). From <Bonehead> to <cLoNehEAd>: Nicknames, play and identity on Internet Relay Chat. *Journal of Computer Mediated Communication 1*(2). Retrieved July 10, 2002 from: http://www.ascusc.org/jmc/vol1/issue2/bechar.html.

Beller, M. (1998). The crossroads between lifelong learning and information technology: A challenge facing leading universities. *The Journal of Computer-Mediated Communication, 4*(2). Retrieved Sept. 2, 2002 from: http://www.ascusc.org/jcmc/vol4/issue2/beller.html.

Binik, Y. M., Mah, K., & Kiesler, S. (1999). Ethical issues in conducting sex research on the Internet. *The Journal of Sex Research, 36*(1), 82-90.

Boehlefeld, S. P. (1991). Doing the right thing: Ethical cyberspace research. *The Information Society, 12*(2), 141-152.

British Psychological Society. (2002). *Code of conduct, ethical principles and guide-lines*. Retrieved Sept. 30, 2002 from: http://www.bps.org.uk/documents/Code.pdf.

British Sociological Association. (2002). *Statement of ethical practice*. Retrieved Sept. 30, 2002 from: http://www.britsoc.org.uk/about/ethic.htm.

Cavazos, E. A. (1994). Intellectual property. In E. A. Cavazos & G. Morin (Eds.), *Cyberspace and the Law: Your Rights and Duties in the On-Line World* (pp. 44-66). Cambridge, MA: MIT Press.

Chafe, W. L. (1982). Integration and involvement in speaking, writing and oral literature. In D. Tannen (Ed.), *Spoken and Written Language: Exploring Orality and Literacy* (pp. 35-54). Norwood, NJ: ABLEX.

Cherny, L. (1999). *Conversation and Community: Chat in a Virtual World*. Stanford, CA: CSLI Publications.

Chester, A. & Gwynne, G. (1998). Online teaching: Encouraging collaboration through anonymity. *The Journal of Computer-Mediated Communication, 4*(2). Retrieved Sept. 2, 2002 from: http://www.ascusc.org/jcmc/vol4/issue2/chester.html.

Cho, H. & LaRose, R. (1999). Privacy issues in Internet surveys. *Social Science Computer Review, 17*(4), 421-434.

Danet, B., Rudenberg, L., & Rosenbaum-Tamari, Y. (1998). Hmmm...where's that smoke coming from?: Writing, play and performance on Internet relay chat. In F. Sudweeks, M. McLaughlin, & S. Rafaeli (Eds.), *Network and Netplay: Virtual Groups on the Internet* (pp. 41-76). Menlo Park, NJ: AAAI Press.

December, J. (1993). *Characteristics of oral culture in discourse on the Net*. Paper presented at the 12th Annual Pennsylvania State Conference on Rhetoric and Communication, University Park, PA.

Eysenbach, G. & Till, J. E. (2001). Ethical issues in qualitative research on Internet communities. *British Medical Journal, 323*(7321), 1103-1105.

Ferrara, K., Brunner, H., & Whitmore, G. (1991). Interactive written discourse as an emergent register. *Written Communication, 8*(1), 8-34.

Finn, J. & Lavitt, M. (1994). Computer based self help groups for sexual abuse survivors. *Social Work With Groups, 17*, 21-46.

Finnegan, R. (1988). *Literacy and Orality: Studies in the Technology of Communication*. London: Basil Blackwell.

Godwin, M. (1998). *CyberRights: Defending Free Speech in the Digital Age*. New York: Times Books.

Hentschel, E. (1998). Communication on IRC. *Linguistik Online, 1*. Retrieved July 17, 2001 from: http://viadrina.euv-frankfurt-o.de/~wjournal/irc.htm.

Herring, S. (1996a). Posting in a different voice: Gender and ethics in computer-mediated communication. In C. Ess (Ed.), *Philosophical Perspectives on Computer-Mediated Communication* (pp. 115-145). Albany, NY: State University of New York Press.

Herring, S. (1996b). Linguistic and critical analysis of computer-mediated communication: Some ethical and scholarly considerations. *The Information Society 12*, 153-168.

Hiltz, S. R. & Turoff, M. (1978). *The Network Nation: Human Connection via Computer*. Reading, MA: Addison Wesley.

Hiltz, S. R., Johnson, K., & Agle, G. (1978). *Replicating Bales Problem Solving Experiments on a Computer Conference: A Pilot Study* (Research Rep. No. 8). Newark,

NJ: Newark Computerized Conferencing and Communication Center, New Jersey Institute of Technology.

Hughes, R. (1996). *English in Speech and Writing: Investigating Language and Literature*. London: Routledge.

International Sociological Association. (2001). *Code of ethics*. Retrieved Sept. 30, 2002 from: http://www.ucm.es/info/isa/codeofethics.htm.

Jones, R. A. (1994). The ethics of research in cyberspace. *Internet Research, 4*(3), 30-35.

Katsh, M. E. (1995). *Law in a Digital World*. New York: Oxford University Press.

Kerr, E. B. & Hiltz, S. R. (1982). *Computer-mediated Communication Systems: Status and Evaluation*. New York: Academic Press.

Kiesler, S., Siegel, J., & McGuire, T. W. (1984). Social psychological aspects of computer-mediated communication. *American Psychologist, 39,* 1123-1134.

King, S. (1996). Researching Internet communities: Proposed ethical guidelines for the reporting of results. *The Information Society, 12*(2), 119-127.

Lea, M. & Spears, R. (1992). Paralanguage and social perception in computer-mediated communication. *Journal of Organizational Computing, 2*(3-4), 321-341.

Lindlif, T. R. & Shatzer, M. J. (1998). Media ethnography in virtual space: Strategies, limits, and possibilities. *Journal of Broadcasting and Electronic Media, 42*(2), 170-190.

Liu, G. Z. (1999). Virtual community presence in Internet relay chatting. *Journal of Computer-Mediated Communication, 5*(1). Retrieved Sept. 5, 2002 from: http://www.ascusc.org/jcmc/vol5/issue1/liu.html.

Nosek, B. A., Mahzarin, R. B., & Greenwald, A. G. (2002). E-research: Ethics, security, design, and control in psychological research on the Internet. *The Journal of Social Issues, 58*(1), 161-176.

Paccagnella, L. (1997). Getting the seats of your pants dirty: Strategies for ethnographic research on virtual communities. *Journal of Computer-Mediated-Communication, 3*(1). Retrieved June 15, 2002 from: http://www.ascusc.org/jcmc/vol3/issue1/paccagnella.html.

Paolillo, J. (1999). The virtual speech community: Social network and language variation on IRC. *Journal of Computer-Mediated Communication, 4*(4). Retrieved Aug. 10, 1999 from: http://www.ascusc.org/jcmc/vol4/issue4/paolillo.html.

Rafaeli, S., Sudweeks, F., Konstan, J., & Mabry, E. (1998). ProjectH: A collaborative quantitative study of computer-mediated communication. In F. Sudweeks, M. McLaughlin, & S. Rafaeli (Eds.), *Network and Netplay: Virtual Groups on the Internet* (pp. 265-281). Cambridge, MA: MIT Press.

Reid, E. M. (1991). *Electropolis: Communication and community on Internet relay chat.* Retrieved July 12, 2000 from: http://home.earthlink.net/~aluluei/electropolis.htm.

Reid, E. M. (1996). Informed consent in the study of on-line communities: A reflection on the effects of computer-mediated social research. *The Information Society, 12*(2), 169-174.

Riva, G. & Galimberti, C. (1998). Computer-mediated communication: Identity and social interaction in an electronic environment. *Genetic, Social, and General Psychology Monographs, 124,* 434-464.

Rodino, M. (1997). Breaking out of binaries: Reconceptualizing gender and its relationship to language in computer-mediated communication. *Journal of Computer-*

Mediated Communication, 3(3). Retrieved Jan. 22, 2002 from: http://www.ascusc.org/jcmc/vol3/issue3/rodino.html.

Rose, M. (1993). *Authors and Owners: The Invention of Copyright.* Cambridge, MA: Harvard University Press.

Saviki, V., Lingenfelter, D., & Kelly, M. (1996). Gender language style and group composition in Internet discussion groups. *The Journal of Computer-Mediated Communication, 2*(3). Retrieved Dec. 6, 2001 from: http://www.ascusc.org/jcmc/vol2/issue3/savicki.html.

Short, J., Williams, E., & Christie, B. (1976). *The Social Psychology of Telecommunications.* London: John Wiley & Sons.

Sixsmith, J. & Murray, C. D. (2001). Ethical issues in the documentary data analysis of Internet posts and archives. *Qualitative Health Research, 11*(3), 423-432.

Sproull, L. & Kiesler, S. (1986). Reducing social context cues: Electronic mail in organisational communication. *Management Science, 32,* 1492-1512.

Sproull, L. & Kiesler, S. (1991). *Connections: New ways of working in the networked organization.* Cambridge, MA: MIT Press.

Stefik, M. (1999). *The Internet edge: Social, Legal and Technological Challenges for a Networked World.* Cambridge, MA: MIT Press.

Sudweeks, F. & Rafaeli, S. (1995). How do you get a hundred strangers to agree? Computer-mediated communication and collaboration. In T. M. Harrison & T. D. Stephen (Eds.), *Computer Networking and Scholarship in the 21ˢᵗ Century University* (pp. 115-136). New York: SUNY Press.

Thomas, J. (1996). Introduction: A debate about the ethics of fair practices for collecting social science data in cyberspace. *The Information Society, 12,* 107-108.

Troest, M. O. (1998). *Computer-mediated communication: lingua ex machina.* Retrieved Aug. 15, 2000 from: http://www.sprog.auc.dk/~motr96/marvin/www/library/uni/papers/cmc/cmc.htm.

Tu, C. & Corry, M. (2001). A paradigm shift for online community research. *Distance Education, 22*(2), 245-263.

Turkle, S. (1995). *Life on the Screen: Identity in the Age of the Internet.* London: Phoenix.

U.S. Copyright Office. (2001). *Copyright law of the United States of America.* Retrieved Sept. 27, 2002 from: http://www.copyright.gov/title17/chapter02.pdf.

Wallace, P. M. (1999). *The Psychology of the Internet.* Cambridge, UK: Cambridge University Press.

Walther, J. B. (1992). Interpersonal effects in computer-mediated interaction: A relational perspective. *Communication Research, 19*(1), 50-88.

Walther, J. B., Anderson, R., & Park, D. W. (1994). Interpersonal effects in computer-mediated interaction: A meta-analysis of social and antisocial communication. *Communication Research, 21*(4), 460-487.

Waskul, D. & Douglass, M. (1996). Considering the electronic participant: Some polemical observations on the ethics of on-line research. *The Information Society, 12*(2), 129-139.

We, G. (1993). Cross-gender communication in Cyberspace. Retrieved June 4, 2000 from http://www.mith2.umd.edu/womensstudies/computing/articles+researchpapers/cross-gender-communication.

Witmer, D. F. & Katzman, S. L. (1997). On-line smiles: Does gender make a difference in the use of graphic accents. *Journal of Computer-Mediated Communication, 2*(4). Retrieved June 2, 2002 from: http://www.ascusc.org/jcmc/vol2/issue4/witmer1.html.

World Intellectual Property Organisation. (n.d.). *World Intellectual Property Organisation, Intellectual Property information page*. Retrieved Oct. 2, 2002 from: www.wipo.org/about-ip/en/.

ENDNOTES

[1]   MUD is an acronym for "Multi-User-Dungeon," a SCMC forum that gained popularity through a number of MUDs set up as fantasy role-playing games.

[2]   All examples given here are fictitious. Any resemblance to nicknames currently being used in SCMC mediums is purely coincidental.

[3]   As a participant in SCMC chat for many years, I would dispute Bechar-Israeli's (1995) assertion regarding the creation and maintenance of only one nickname. Although I have no empirical evidence to support this, I believe that most SCMC users use more than one nickname, although they may feel a greater sense of "loyalty" to one particular nickname and use it most often.

[4]   It should be noted at this point, in a personal survey of 30 Internet studies from a variety of social science fields, only seven stated they had gained prior permission either from the channel manager, the group owner or the individual participants; three specifically stated they did not seek permission and the rest failed to account for the issue of consent either way

[5]   A username is the first part of an e-mail address. For example, destiny@email.org, where 'destiny' is the username and e-mail.org is the host name.

[6]   IRC channels can be public (open to any IRC users), restricted (open to IRC users who are entered in the channel's database as members) or invite-only (open only to IRC users who are invited to join).

[7]   Cues-Filtered-Out is a collective term for those CMC theories that maintain CMC is limited in its socioemotional and relational possibilities in comparison to FTF communication.

[8]   Emoticons are textual graphics used to enhance CMC and SCMC chat. For example, :) , which is called a smiley.

[9]   As stated in "Copyright Law of the United States of American" (U.S, Copyright Office, 2001), a thought or idea does not fall under the copyright act until it has been expressed. Then, it is the particular expression of the idea that can be copyrighted, not the idea itself.

[10]   The log excerpt printed here is used with the full permission of all participants involved. I was asked to remove their pseudonyms and any other identifying characteristics within the text as a condition of publication. It was recorded using the "log" function in mIRC, an IRC software client.

[11]   "Temporary storage buffers" in IRC and other SCMC forums generally store data for a matter of minutes, deleting older data as newer data is generated.

[12]   Archives of mailing lists, bulletin boards and newsgroups, as well as other primarily asynchronous CMC mediums may be kept for as little as several days up to several years, depending upon the wishes of the group host.

[13]   This was the finding in my doctoral design. The original design called for the creation of a basic, "random chat" IRC channel with no particular topic. Very few people volunteered despite numerous efforts to attract more participants. When feedback was asked for, the reason often quoted for not wanting to participate was the lack of "focus" or reason to chat in the channel. Additionally, I feel the fact that I made it clear I was going to be watching, but not participating, put off many potential participants.

[14]   For a further discussion of this, see Herring (1996b).

[15]   As synchronous chat participants quickly learn, at any given time in a channel there may be more than one conversation going on. Thus, it would be possible for 20 lines of text to have references to two or more conversations, making it possible for a researcher to remove the extraneous conversation portions, so long as doing so would not damage the content they wish to discuss.

Chapter VI

When the Ethic is Functional to the Method: The Case of E-Mail Qualitative Interviews

Nadia Olivero
University of Milan - Bicocca, Italy

Peter Lunt
University College London, UK

ABSTRACT

This chapter explores the methodological implications of using e-mail for qualitative interviews. It draws on computer-mediated communication (CMC) literature to remark that, contrary to generalized assumptions, technological-based anonymity does not always correspond to increased self-disclosure. Conversely, it is shown that e-mail interviews make the interviewer effect unavoidable, stimulate reflexivity and must rely on trust and equal participation more than face-to-face interviews. To address the interviewee's resistance and avoid unwanted phenomena of strategic self-presentation, a model of interview based on a feminist ethic is proposed.

INTRODUCTION

For many social scientists the Internet has become a time saving and cost effective medium for conducting empirical research. The use of the Internet for data collection raises, however, a number of methodological and ethical issues. Although at first the issue appeared to be whether the Internet transformed research practices, more recently there is developing consensus on the need to identify guidelines that are specific to electronic communication.

Quantitative researchers have answered the call for studies on Internet methodology promptly. Several papers investigated issues of questionnaire design and distribution (e.g., Batinic, 1997; Kaplan; 1992; Kiesler & Sproull, 1986; Swoboda, Muehlberger, Weitkunat, & Schneeweiss, 1997; Witmer, Colman, & Katzman, 1999), compared content and response rate of e-mail surveys to mail-based surveys (Kittleson, 1995; Metha & Sivadas, 1995; Paolo, Bonaminio, Gibson, Partridge, & Kallail, 2000) and identified strategies to increase the response rates in electronic media (Kittleson, 1997; Schaefer & Dillman, 1998). On the other hand, ethical considerations are often a main concern for qualitative researchers. Studies adopting participant observation and discourse analysis to investigate spontaneous communication over the Internet raise awareness of the need to conform to principles of research ethics. The ease of access to Internet users' discourses, together with the increased opportunity for the researcher to copy, store and quickly disseminate data, emphasize to a greater extent than ever before issues of privacy, informed consent and narrative appropriation (e.g., Glaser, Dixit, & Green, 2002; Sharf, 1999).

However, qualitative methods that involve interaction between the participant and the researcher introduce additional issues for the design of research guidelines. For instance, the conduct of qualitative interviews over the Internet requires taking into account dynamics of interpersonal communication and processes of meaning construction that are computer-mediated, and, therefore, dependent on the way people interact with the technology. In this chapter we focus on the use of e-mail for qualitative interviews, and in particular on the implications of establishing interview relationships based on written, asynchronous computer-mediated communication (CMC).

The existing literature on e-mail interviews assesses practical advantages and disadvantages by observing differences between face-to-face (FTF) and e-mail communication. Among the advantages, authors pointed out overcoming time and geographical constraints (Foster, 1994), easily eluding transcriptions and related errors (Olivero & Lunt, 2001; Selwyn & Robson, 1998) and avoiding interviewer effects or problems with shy participants. The main limitation appears to be the lack of non-verbal cues, such as body language, physical appearance, and voice qualities (cf. Bampton & Cowton, 2002; Fontana & Frey, 2000; Selwyn & Robson, 1998).

If the lack of non-verbal cues reduces the interview material that is normally available for interpretation, then the sense of protection that results from physical anonymity seems to increase the willingness to disclose. In an e-mail interview study on diabetes sufferers, it was noted that rapport was easily established and that, compared to face-to-face interviews, respondents were less inhibited and willing to talk about highly personal topics (Holge-Hazelton, 2002). Nevertheless, previous research also pointed to the potential lack of spontaneity, which might be fostered by asynchronous communication, and generally to difficulties due to the lack of control over the participation of the interviewee (Olivero, 2001; Olivero & Lunt, 2001). In these studies it was found that, for retaining the interviewee and maintaining participation, the adoption of an interview style oriented to constructing a gratifying rapport was more effective than the use of financial incentives alone (Olivero, 2001; Olivero & Lunt, 2001).

With the aim to extend on these findings, we propose that the analysis of the social psychological literature on CMC helps to clarify the key factors for managing technologically-mediated interview relationships. In this chapter we integrate literature on CMC with observations from our research practice to indicate a theoretical framework for a model of interview adapted to e-mail communication. Drawing on CMC literature, we challenge generalized assumptions about the effects of anonymity, showing the limitations of those approaches that, moving from information theory perspectives, have pointed to the advantage of avoiding the interviewer effect. Conversely it is shown that e-mail interviews make the interviewer effect unavoidable, stimulate reflexivity and must rely on trust and equal participation more than FTF interviews. We note that to address the interviewee's resistance and avoid unwanted phenomena of strategic self-presentation, ethical considerations, such as those put forward by feminist researchers should become central to the e-mail interview model.

The chapter is structured as follows: First, assumptions about the effects of anonymity in terms of its influence on decreased sociality, antinormative behavior and increased self-disclosure are discussed; second, the analysis of the literature is combined with examples from empirical data to indicate new research guidelines.

BACKGROUND

Decreased Sociality

The existing literature on the use of the Internet for the conduct of qualitative interviews and of Internet-based research, in general, has pointed to advantages and disadvantages by drawing on generalized, although not necessarily accurate, beliefs on the effects of electronically-mediated communication. One of these assumptions is about the advantage of avoiding the interviewer's effect (cf. Fontana & Frey, 2000; Nosek & Banaji, 2002; Selwyn & Robson, 1998). According to this idea, the lack of non-verbal cues in conditions of technologically-supported anonymity eliminates or reduces "attributional" processes through which the interviewee adapts his or her disclosure as a result of perceived power inequalities in the interview relationship. Interviewees are believed to disclose more as a result of anonymity, feeling less pressured by the physical presence of the interviewer and less likely to attempt self-presentation strategies to manage impressions. Conversely, the same literature emphasizes that a main limitation of the lack of non-verbal cues is that it eliminates the possibility for the researcher to monitor body language and use it as an integral part of the interview data (cf. Fontana & Frey, 2000; Selwyn & Robson, 1998).

These arguments seem to imply that in CMC the interaction between interviewer-interviewee takes place in a socially neutral space, where an interviewee's disclosure could be more truthful because it is not influenced by status asymmetries, whereas reduced channels of communication effects the richness of the data. Information theory perspectives that used communication bandwidth as a criterion to quantify the efficiency of a communication medium, and adopted the same principle to evaluate its sociality, contributed significantly to diffuse this viewpoint. For instance, communication theories such as Social Presence Theory (Short, Williams & Christie, 1976) and Media Richness Theory (Daft & Lengel, 1986) evaluated CMC in terms of information processing capacity, emphasizing the limitations of reduced interpersonal contact in comparison to FTF communication. Similar assumptions underpin Social Context Cues Theory (Sproull & Kiesler, 1991), which posits that a lack of information for framing and interpreting the other effects the sensitivity between participants in computer-mediated interactions. For this theory, the condition of reduced opportunities for social categorization has the advantage of emancipating communication from social influences, including those of status and power inequalities.

There is, however, extensive evidence that contradicts the thesis of decreased sociality in CMC. Studies that emphasized the growth of online interpersonal relationships show that the absence of non-verbal cues has only a relative impact on the effectiveness and sociality of online communication (Finholt & Sproull, 1990; Parks & Floyd, 1996; Stafford et al. 1999; Wilkins, 1991). Analysis of relationship formation over the Internet indicates that the lack of non-verbal cues can be overcome by adaptation to the textual format of the exchanges (Parks & Floyd, 1996; Wilkins, 1991). People make social attributions on the basis of metacommunicative contents expressed in the text (e.g., style of writing, choice of language, use of punctuation and emoticons) and other paralinguistic cues conveyed through the use of the technology. For instance, the time between e-mail exchanges can be used to convey relational meanings. Walther and Tidwell (1995) found that both the time in which e-mails are sent and the answering time can deliver specific meanings according to the aim of the message. The speed of response to e-mail messages interacts with message content. For example, a prompt reply to a task request will indicate a positive attitude toward the sender (Walther & Tidwell, 1995). For the purposes of a qualitative interview, the metacommunicative contents expressed in the text and the paralinguistic use of the technology could then assume the same significance carried by body language and voice qualities in FTF interviews.

Antinormative Behavior

Those who have argued for decreased sociality in CMC also pointed to a relation between anonymity, loss of identity and antinormative behaviors, such as the use of flaming (e.g., Siegel, Dubrovsky, Kiesler & McGuire,. 1986; Sproull & Kiesler, 1991). This thesis, however, which is based on de-individuation theories that propose behavior as socially deregulated in conditions of anonymity (e.g., Diener, 1980; Zimbardo, 1969), overlooks the psychological mechanism originally advocated to explain the impact of anonymity on de-individuation. Diener (1980) postulated that anonymity would produce de-individuation through the mediating effect of decreased self-awareness. This conceptualization was then further elaborated on by Prentice-Dunn and Rogers (1982; 1989) who indicated that only reduced private self-awareness caused by a shift in attention to external cues (as opposed to public self-awareness caused by accountability cues) was associated with a state of internal de-individuation. Anonymity was not described as a cause of de-individuation but rather as a condition of antinormative behavior that reducing accountability could explain. Experimental manipulations aimed at increasing private self-awareness were conducted by isolating subjects and asking them to perform individual tasks. In this experimental condition, self-focused subjects reported less de-individuation effects than the subjects exposed to a condition of external attention cues (Prentice-Dunn & Rodgers, 1982). The condition of external attention cues as a criterion for reducing self-awareness and causing de-individuation not only challenges the generalized assumption about the effects of anonymity, but also supports the opposite argument in which reduced social context cues and technological-induced anonymity can increase self-awareness.

Moreover, in the specific example of e-mail, asynchronous communication can have an additional influence on individual self-awareness. The opportunity to reexamine the content of messages previously delivered and the time available to elaborate on thoughts before sending a new message are both conditions for increasing self-focus (Olivero, 2001; Olivero & Lunt, 2001). As we will discuss further, this feature of e-mail communication suggests the potential for the interviewee's reflexivity, which has epistemological and, hence, methodological implications for qualitative interviews. Furthermore, the idea that technological features of e-mail might encourage self-awareness and reflexivity raises an additional counter-argument against the supposed relationship between CMC and loss of social influence. Increased self-focus might make impression management salient, resulting in communication that reflects greater social regulation.

These effects of CMC are explained by Social Identity De-individuation Effects (SIDE) theory in terms of strategic self-expression, depending on the culturally salient identities and on the relationships of power within the audience (Reicher, Spears, & Postmes, 1995; Spears & Lea, 1994). Under this perspective, dissimulation over the Internet might reflect strategic interaction goals, which take advantage of anonymity to elude the constraints of social categorization and stereotyping or for the negotiation of power (Lea & Spears, 1995, see Spears Postmes, Lea, & Wolbert, 2002). Therefore, increased self-awareness in conditions of power inequalities, such as those that are typically in play in the researcher-subject relationship, might stimulate impression formation and deceptive behavior. On the other hand, anonymity could weaken the effects of power asymmetries favoring more spontaneous disclosure.

Self-Disclosure

A third generalized assumption is that anonymity over the Internet leads to increased depth and breadth of self-disclosure (e.g., McKenna & Bargh, 2000). In recent years, many practitioners have pointed to the advantage of developing Internet-based services for psychological advice, personal counselling and therapy (cf. Barak, 1999; Murphy & Mitchell, 1998). However, visual anonymity might not always correspond to lack of accountability. Although observed phenomena of increased self-disclosure in online relationships suggest that the Internet provide a particularly suitable setting for the development of intimacy and for the expression of the true self (Bargh, McKenna, & Fitzsimons, 2002; McKenna, Green, & Gleason,. 2002; McKenna & Bargh, 2000), these results are found in contexts of anonymous interactions between strangers that are not defined by social roles or issues of status differentials. Conversely, CMC often takes place between individuals who, although visually anonymous, are interacting on the basis of established social norms, involving the assumption of roles and the use of strategies for self-presentation in the attempt to reach specific aims. In a research interview setting, even if the sense of relative anonymity provided by CMC might encourage self-disclosure, perceived status asymmetries might represent a barrier to disclosure.

IMPLICATIONS FOR
E-MAIL QUALITATIVE INTERVIEWS

The above review of the potential effects of anonymity suggests that in e-mail interviews, the interviewer effect could be even stronger if, in conditions of anonymity and private self-awareness, the asymmetry of a power relation between interviewer-interviewee is made salient. Conversely, the risk of self-presentation to a powerful audience may, however, be reduced with an interview style oriented to minimize asymmetries. In this respect the language adopted by the interviewer has an important impact on the perception of power differentials. As remarked by Spears, Lea and Postmes (2001), the text-based nature of CMC makes linguistic factors even more influential, because the written language used to carry the message also represents the main channel for conveying relational affiliation and social influence. In the absence of other social cues, the language adopted strongly affects the stance of the interaction, providing indications of the situational definition of roles and influencing the contextual salience of social determinants, such as power asymmetries. The interviewer's language might then attempt to reduce status inequality cues, reinforcing the sense of equal participation and underlining the role of the interviewee's individual contribution, to increase the salience of personal identity (as opposed to group identity salience, see Spears, Lea, & Lee, 1990).

Complementary to this issue, there are the potential advantages of anonymity on self-disclosure, and, in particular, of the increased self-awareness and reflexivity on self-investigation, which is normally a main objective in qualitative in-depth interviewing. These advantages can be pursued by means of linguistic and paralinguistic practices aimed at implementing a relational approach that aims to develop a sense of equal participation, in order to stimulate trust and self-disclosure. In our previous research, we pursued these goals by adopting a friendly style of communication (also with the use of emoticons, such as "J"), expressing thanks for the interviewee's answers, treating him or her as a peer, answering any questions, even when unrelated to the topic of study, and providing personal opinions, that is, by transforming the interview in a positive and gratifying interpersonal exchange.

Moreover, as discussed earlier, in order to overcome the limits of the lack of non-verbal information and establish effective communication, the interviewer should look for meanings conveyed through the use of the technology. For instance, changes in latency between the exchanges can be very expressive. Questions that are considered difficult or too sensitive can lead to a delay in answering or be avoided in the next reply. The interviewer should then maintain a high level of flexibility in order to interpret interviewee's feelings and constantly renegotiate participation (Olivero & Lunt, 2001).

FEMINIST ETHIC FOR A RELATIONAL
AND INTERPRETATIVE MODEL
OF E-MAIL INTERVIEW

The above methodological guidelines emphasize the importance of the rapport between interviewer and interviewee. Feminist researchers have advocated the need to develop a potentially long relationship, based on equal participation and trust, with the aim of fostering genuine disclosure. Such a relational approach involves restructuring the epistemological assumptions of objectivity that present interview data as detached from the social situation in which they develop. Efforts to neutralize the interviewer stimulus are abandoned in favor of an understanding of the processes that can explain the construction of shared meanings, while a rule of reciprocity is adopted to transform the interview into a real conversation (cf. Oakley, 1981; Reinharz, 1992; Smith, 1987).

This approach moves from an ethical standpoint aiming at decreasing interviewer control over the interviewee and with it the masculine, paternalistic, asymmetric balance of power implicit in the interview relationship. Feminist researchers provide a model of the interview, where participation results from the kind of emotional involvement that is required for relationship formation and not from the interviewer's control, legitimized by means of a research contract and, as such limited to the research setting. It is important to note that, in e-mail interviews, interviewee participation is not constrained by the immediacy and co-presence of the researcher. Conversely, the interviewees are asked for a high level of active involvement, while the mediated nature of the exchange provides them with the possibility to abandon the interview at any time. E-mail interviews require, then, a degree of active participation that must rely on motivational components, rather than initial agreements on a research contract and that can only exist within the gratifying, trusted, reciprocal exchange indicated by the feminist perspective.

Moving away from objectivistic approaches (according to which the interviewer should adhere to a rigor of neutrality, disregarding questions posed by the participant, as well as issues related to the study in order to preserve the objectivity of the data, cf. Fontana & Frey, 2000), a growing number of qualitative researchers define the interview as a negotiated text, or a conversation where social identities intersect and that produces situated understandings of meaningful interactions instead of neutral discoveries (cf. Denzin & Lincoln, 2000; Fontana & Frey, 2000).

The asynchronous text-based nature of e-mail exchanges seems to create prototypical conditions for a negotiated, as well as reflexive, construction of meanings. Following the philosophical hermeneutic of Gadamer (1986, 1989), the meaning of a text results from the mediated process of interpretation established between the text and the reader/inquirer. Remarkably, in the e-mail context, both the interviewer and the interviewee, at the same time writers and readers, enter the reflexive circle of interpretation that the ontological hermeneutic described as basic to human science enquiry. The opportunity to access previous disclosure fosters reflexive processes of self-investigation. Through the negotiation and the elaboration of emerging meanings, the interviewee becomes at once the object of inquiry and inquirer, and by so doing makes himself/herself subject to change (cf. Schwandt, 1998). Verbatim extracts from one of our e-mail interview studies show the interviewees' tendency to elaborate on the exteriorized material[1]:

L: I have been thinking about what I said in answer 2 (...) I am not sure about it. It's something I have never really paid much attention before. I wrote that I am not concerned about privacy, but this is not exactly true. Very often I feel uncomfortable (...)

C: I would like to add something to the third answer, I admit that reading it again one week later (...) well I don't know if it makes so much sense ... it may seems contradictory but (...)

A: Why would you believe that these people are really working to improve things? Sorry, I am not convinced at all. I think there is still a long way to go before (....). I tend to be cautious more then necessary, perhaps, (...) but I would like it to be true. Don't take my previous message as such, I mean, I am not so cynical! (...) I guess it is that these things worry me a lot (...).

Processes of self-investigation often result from the elaboration of the interviewer's messages and relate to the meanings that are jointly constructed in the exchange between interviewer-interviewee. Based on our experiences, it is notable that interviewees generally attempt to establish a reciprocal exchange with the interviewer. When the interviewer's approach was limited to an empathic interview style (cf. King, 1996), without establishing a real conversation, interviewees looked for confirmation about the adequacy of their contributions and asked directly for the interviewer's opinion. Failures to respond to this need for reciprocity resulted in the erection of barriers on the part of the interviewee or even in withdrawals. The following example relates the reaction of an interviewee after his/her question about the interviewer's view was not adequately addressed.

S: Is this answer the sort of thing you are looking for? What do You think about these issues?

Interviewer: Thanks very much S, your answer is absolutely fine. It is your point of view that interests me and that is important for the research.

S: I am not quite sure of the point of the question—it all seems quite simple to me and innocuous. I really don't know what more you want me to say on the subject. I feel I have already said most of this. Perhaps you could devise a specific questionnaire for me to elicit what you truly are after.

Interviewees' reactions indicate that in e-mail interviews the adoption of an interview model based on reciprocity and equal participation is particularly crucial for the development of trust. Follow up FTF interviews confirmed this thesis. Participants who were invited to discuss their e-mail interview reported experiencing a lack of trust when they couldn't relate to the interviewer as an equal in a reciprocal exchange. One interviewee observes:

"the good things are that you can take your time to answer and you don't get biased but ... sometimes I didn't know if you were laughing or ... e-mail is impersonal, but then your feedback, I found, was useful, I guess I asked what did you think about my answer. At the beginning I was wondering if this would be a questionnaire or ... a more personal style ... probably because in e-mail there is no personal interaction. I didn't expect to get to know you but it was good to see that you were actually reading my answers, I thought the interview could have been like an exchange not a survey. Sometimes, when you did not reply to my jokes, I admit having felt uncomfortable and wary, I thought you had to follow some sort of structure for your questions (...)."

FUTURE TRENDS

The uncertainty that some of our interviewees have experienced and the difficulties we have encountered in managing interview relationships testify that in e-mail communication, the asynchronous and text nature of the exchange makes the quality of the rapport even more crucial than in FTF interviews.

The relevance of issues of trust and willingness to disclose is also likely to increase as research participants become aware of risks of privacy invasions over the Internet. Although these problems exist in any kind of research settings in virtual reality, research participants assume more risks for the lack of control on the identity of the interviewer and the potential uses of their private information. On the other hand, they can exercise complete control over their participation, which will be dependent on the kind of interpersonal involvement with the interviewer. For qualitative interviews, the ethics of online research is a matter of establishing rapport, giving voice to the participants and substituting criteria of objectivity with principles of reciprocity.

As the use of the Internet for empirical research continues to expand, ethical considerations become increasingly important for the design of methodological guidelines. In the attempt to develop methods that are specific to electronic communication, researchers might discover that the first challenge involves adapting to principles of virtual research ethics.

CONCLUSION

With this chapter we illustrated the main implications of using e-mail for qualitative interviews. Drawing on CMC literature, we pointed out that in e-mail interviews the effects of asymmetric power relationships, such as strategic self-presentation, could be even stronger than in FTF interviews. Reduced social context cues and anonymity were described as factors leading to an increased self-focus, which together with text-based asynchronous communication create the conditions for the reflexive processes of self-investigation. Besides this advantage, it was noted how increased self-awareness can result in strategic self-presentation, when power asymmetries are made salient.

The model of the proposed e-mail interview aims at avoiding deceptive behavior and self-presentation, by minimizing power asymmetries in the interview relationship. Following feminist ethical concerns, we suggest establishing a trustful and reciprocal exchange to foster equal participation and genuine disclosure. Concurrently this model responds to the need to stimulate the interviewee's active participation, providing relational gratifications in the place of interviewer control, which is traditionally exercised by means of a research contract. Finally, since the asynchrony of e-mail messages predispose prototypical conditions for a negotiated construction of meanings, it should be noted that e-mail interviewing, above all, challenges old objectivist epistemologies, making salient the occurrence of reflexivity and showing the unavoidability of the interviewer's effect.

REFERENCES

Bampton, R. & Cowton, C. (2002). The e-interview. *Forum: Qualitative Social Research, 3*(2). Retrieved from: http://www.qualitative-research.net/fqs/.

Barak, A. (1999). Psychological applications on the Internet: A discipline on the threshold of a new millennium. *Applied and Preventive Psychology, 8,* 231-246.

Bargh, J. A., McKenna, K.Y., & Fitzsimons, G. M. (2002). Can you see the real me? Activation and expression of the "true self" on the Internet. *Journal of Social Issues, 58*(1), 33-48.

Batinic, B. (1997). How to make an Internet based survey? In W. Bandilla & F. Faulbaum (Eds.), *SoftStat '97 Advances in Statistical Software 6* (pp. 125-132). Stuttgart, Germany: Lucius & Lucius.

Daft, R. & Lengel, R. (1986, May). Organizational information requirements, media richness and structural design. *Management Science, 32*(5), 554-571.

Denzin, N & Lincoln, Y. (2002). *Handbook of Qualitative Research.* Thousand Oaks, CA: Sage.

Diener, E. (1980). Deindividuation: The absence of self-awareness and self-regulation in group members. In P. B. Paulus (Ed.), *Psychology of Group Influence* (pp. 209-242). Hillsdale, NJ: Erlbaum.

Finholt, T. & Sproull, L. S. (1990). Electronic mail and weak ties in organizations. *Office Technology and People, 3,* 83-101.

Fontana, A. & Frey, J. H. (1994). Interviewing: The art of science. In N. K. Denzin & Y. S. Lincoln (Eds.), *Handbook of Qualitative Research* (pp. 47-78). Thousand Oaks, CA: Sage.

Fontana, A. & Frey, J. H. (2000). The interview. From structured questions to negotiated text. In N. Denzin & Y. Lincoln (Eds.), *Handbook of Qualitative Research* (pp. 645-673). Thousand Oaks, CA: Sage.

Gadamer, H. G. (1986). Text and interpretation. In B. R. Wachterhauser (Ed.), *Hermeneutics and Modern Philosophy* (pp. 377-398). Albany, NY: Albany State University of New York Press.

Gadamer, H. G. (1989). *Truth and Method* (2nd rev. ed.; J. Weinsheimer & D. G. Marshall, trans.). New York: Crossroads. (Original work published in).

Glaser, J., Dixit, J., & Green, D. P. (2002). Studying hate crime with the Internet: What makes racists advocate racial violence? *Journal of Social Issues, 58*(1), 177-193.

Hewson, C. M., Laurent, D., & Vogel, C. M. (1996). Proper methodologies for psychological and sociological studies conducted via the Internet. *Behaviour Research Methods, Instrument and Computers, 28,* 186-191.

Holge-Hazelton, B. (2002). The Internet: A new field for qualitative inquiry? *Forum Qualitative Social Research, 3*(2). Retrieved Sept. 10, 2002 from: http://www.qualitative-research.net/fqs/fqs-eng.htm.

Kaplan, H. L (1992). Representation of on-line questionnaires in an editable, auditable database. *Behaviour Research Methods, Instruments and Computers, 24,* 373-384.

Kiesler, S. & Sproull, L. S. (1986). Response effects in the electronic survey. *Public-Opinion-Quarterly, 50*(3), 402-413.

King, E. (1996). The use of the self in qualitative research. In J. T. E. Richardson (Ed.), *Handbook of Qualitative Research Methods for Psychology and the Social Sciences* (pp. 175-188). Leicester, UK: BPS Books.

Kittleson, M. J. (1995). An assessment of the response rate via the postal service and e-mail. *Health Values: The Journal of Health Behavior, Education and Promotion, 19*(2), 27-39.

Kittleson, M. J. (1997). Determining effective follow-up of e-mail surveys. *American Journal of Health Behaviour, 21*(3), 193-196.

Lea, M. & Spears, R. (1995). Love at first byte? Building personal relationships over computer networks. In J. T. Wood & S. Duck. (Eds.), *Understudied Relationships: Off the Beaten Track* (pp. 107-233). Thousand Oaks, CA: Sage.

McKenna, K. Y., Green, A. S., & Gleason, M. E. (2002). Relationship formation on the Internet: What's the big attraction? *Journal of Social Issues, 58*(1), 9-31.

McKenna, K. Y. A. & Bargh, J. A. (2000). Plan 9 from cyberspace: The implications of the Internet for personality and social psychology. *Personality and Social Psychology Review, 4,* 57-75.

Metha, R. & Sivadas, E. (1995). Comparing response rates and response content in mail versus electronic mail surveys. *Journal of the Market Research Society, 37*(4), 429-439.

Murphy, L. & Mitchell, D. L. (1998). When writing helps to heal: E-mail as therapy. *British Journal of Guidance and Counselling, 26*(1), 21-32.

Nosek, B. A. & Banaji, R. M. (2002). E-research: Ethics, security, design, and control in psychological research on the Internet. *Journal of Social Issues, 58*(1), 161-176.

Oakley, A. (1981). Interviewing women: A contradiction in terms. In H. Roberts (Ed.), *Doing Feminist Research* (pp. 30-61). London: Routledge & Kegan Paul.

Olivero, N. (2001, June). *Internet as a research tool, implications for methodology and epistemology.* Paper presented at the Seminar on Internet Research, London Business School, Department of Organizational Behavior, UK.

Olivero, N. & Lunt, P. (2001, November). *E-mail repeated interviews: Adapting qualitative research to computer mediated communication.* Paper presented at the European Conference on Psychology and the Internet, British Psychological Society, Farnborough, UK.

Olivero, N. & Lunt, P. (in press). Privacy versus willingness to disclose in e-commerce exchanges: The effect of risk awareness on the relative role of trust and control. *Journal of Economic Psychology.*

Paolo, A. M., Bonaminio, G. A., Gibson, C., Partridge, T., & Kallail, K. (2000). Response rate comparisons of e-mail and mail-distributed student evaluations. *Teaching and Learning in Medicine, 12*(2), 81-84.

Parks, M. R. & Floyd, K. (1996). Making friends in cyberspace. *Journal of Communication, 46*(1), 80-97.

Postmes, T. & Spears, R. (1998). Deindividuation and antinormative behavior: A meta-analysis. *Psychological Bulletin, 123*(3), 238-259.

Prentice-Dunn, S. & Rogers, R. W. (1982). Effects of public and private self-awareness on deindividuation and aggression. *Journal of Personality and Social Psychology, 43,* 503-513.

Prentice-Dunn, S. & Rogers, R. W. (1989). Deindividuation and the self-regulation of behavior. In P. B. Paulus (Ed.), *The Psychology of Group Influence* (2nd ed., pp. 86-109). Hillsdale, NJ: Erlbaum.

Reicher, S. D., Spears, R., & Postmes, T. (1995). A social identity model of deindividuation phenomena. *European Review of Social Psychology, 6,* 161-198.

Reinharz, S. (1992). *Feminist methods in social research.* New York: Oxford University Press.

Schaefer, D. R. & Dillman, D. A. (1998). Development of a standard e-mail methodology: Results of an experiment. *Public Opinion Quarterly, 62*(3), 378-397.

Schwandt, T. A. (1998). Constructivist, interpretivist approaches to human inquiry. In N. K. Denzin & Y. S. Lincoln (Eds.), *The Landscape of Qualitative Research* (pp. 221-259). Thousand Oak, CA: Sage.

Selwyn, N. & Robson, K. (1998). *Using E-Mail as a Research Tool* (Update no. 21). University of Surrey, Department of Sociology, Guilford, UK.

Sharf, B. F. (1999). Beyond Netiquette: The ethics of doing naturalistic discourse research on the Internet. In S. Jones (Ed.), *Doing Internet Research Critical Issues and Methods for Examining the Net* (pp. 243-257). Thousand Oaks, CA: Sage.

Short, J., Williams, E., & Christie, B. (1976). *The Social Psychology of Telecommunications*. London: John Wiley & Sons.

Siegel, J., Dubrovsky, V., Kiesler, S., & McGuire, T. W. (1986). Group processes in computer-mediated communication. *Organizational Behavior and Human Decision Processes, 37,* 157-187.

Smith, D. E. (1987). *The everyday world as problematic: A feminist sociology*. Boston, MA: Northeastern University Press.

Spears, R. & Lea, M. (1994). Panacea or panopticon? The hidden power in computer-mediated communication. *Communication Research, 21,* 427-459.

Spears, R., Lea, M., & Lee, S. (1990). De-individuation and group polarisation in computer-mediated-communication. *British Journal of Social Psychology, 29,* 121-134.

Spears, R., Lea, M., & Postmes, T. (2001). Social psychological theories of computer-mediated communication: Social gain or social pain? In H. Giles & P. Robinson (Eds.), *New Handbook of Language and Social Psychology* (pp. 601-624). New York: John Wiley & Sons.

Spears, R., Postmes, T., Lea, M., & Wolbert, A. (2002). When are Net effect gross products? The power of influence and the influence of power in computer-mediated communication. *Journal of Social Issues, 58*(1), 91-107.

Sproull, L. & Kiesler, S. (1991). *Connections: New Ways of Working in the Networked Organisation*. Cambridge: MA: MIT Press.

Stiles, W. B. (1993). Quality control in qualitative research. *Clinical Psychology Review, 13,* 593-618.

Strauss, A. L. & Corbin, B. (1998). Grounded theory methodology: An overview. In N. K. Denzin & Y.S. Lincoln (Eds.), *Strategies of Qualitative Inquiry* (pp. 158-183). Thousands Oaks, CA: Sage.

Swoboda, W. J., Muehlberger, N., Weitkunat, R., & Schneeweiss, S. (1997). Internet surveys by direct mailing: An innovative way of collecting data. *Social Science Computer Review, 15*(3), 242-255.

Walther, J. B. & Tidwell, L. C. (1995). Nonverbal cues in computer-mediated communication, and the effects of chronemics on relational communication. *Journal of Organizational Computing, 5*(4), 355+.

Wilkins, H. (1991). Computer talk: Long-distance conversations by computer. *Written Communication, 8,* 56-78.

Witmer, D. F., Colman, R. W., & Katzman, S. L. (1999). From paper-and-pencil to screen-and-keyboard: Toward a methodology for survey research on the Internet. In S. Jones (Eds.), *Doing Internet Research: Critical Issues and Methods for Examining the Net.* (pp. 145-161). Thousand Oaks, CA: Sage.

Woolgar, S, (ed.) (1988). *Knowledge and Reflexivity*. London: Sage.

Zimbardo, P. G. (1969). The human choice: Individuation, reason, and order vs. deindividuation, impulse, and chaos. In W. J. Arnold & D. Levine (Eds.), *Nebraska Symposium on Motivation* (pp. 237-307). Lincoln: University of Nebraska Press.

ENDNOTES

[1]   In this study of 23 e-mail interviews on privacy concerns in e-commerce (Olivero & Lunt, in press), participants were sent an introductory e-mail explaining the aim of the research and the interview procedure. The first topic was prompted and the participant was asked to reply with a brief paragraph. None of the participants met the interviewer before or during the interview. Interviews were semi-structured in order to ensure that a standard list of topics was covered in all interviews. However, interviewees' disclosure was allowed to flow freely, without imposing any limit on the amount, the timing or the content of the information provided. Also the topics prompted did not follow a pre-established order but were introduced by the interviewer whenever the developing meanings offered the possibility of connection. Since interviewees could control the answering time, the length of exchanges varied considerably; three interviews were protracted for more than six weeks. The number of exchanges per interview varied from 17 to 24 messages. As an incentive, we offered £20 to be paid at the conclusion of the interview and an additional incentive of £10 if e-mails were answered within 24 hours. Nine participants responded to all of their questions within this time.

Chapter VII

The Ethics of Conducting E-Mail Surveys

Sandeep Krishnamurthy
University of Washington, Bothell, USA

ABSTRACT

E-mail is a low-cost and highly effective form of individual contact for primary research. However, researchers who contact strangers for their survey research through e-mail are, in essence, sending them Spam. Some academic researchers might argue that due to the low volume and infrequent nature of their surveys and the general positive perception of academia, their e-mail surveys do not add to the Spam problem. However, this is an insufficient resolution of the ethical problem. This chapter examines one solution to avoid this problem—the use of respondent permission prior to contact. Obtaining respondent permission is tricky and can be costly. But, it may be the only long-term solution. Importantly, using this approach could lead to a loss of randomness in the sampling procedure due to self-selection. Ideas for implementation of a permission-based contact system at the individual researcher and academic field level are provided at the end.

INTRODUCTION

E-mail is an integral part of online survey research. For any survey research, there is a need to contact informants and e-mail is the most effective form of contact. Other methods of online contact (e.g., pop-ups, website registration) are seen as ways of building a database—once an entry is made in a database, future online contact is almost entirely through e-mail.

Academic researchers have shown great enthusiasm about using e-mail because of its promise as an effective method of contact. A meta-analysis of academic studies conducted from 1986 to 2000, found the average response rate to be 39.77% (Sheehan & Hoy, 1999), a number that is dramatically higher than the figure for postal mail surveys which rarely exceeds 25%[1]. Moreover, e-mail surveys are cheaper, responses are received rapidly and the data is collected in electronic form facilitating quicker analysis (Goree & Marsalek, III, 1995).

Many academic papers have compared e-mail surveys with other modes of respondent contact (Sheehan, 2001). Early studies reported both high (Anderson & Gansneder, 1995) and low (Kittleson, 1995) response rates. Clearly, audience characteristics were at play here. It is possible that Kittleson (1995) may have attracted a sample that was less familiar with e-mail. That would be consistent with Ranchhod and Zhou (2001) who report that e-mail surveys yield better results when the target audience has high technology awareness and are extensive e-mail users. It is also the case that conducting surveys in a certain way leads to better results. Many researchers have pointed out that pre-notification and multiple follow-ups lead to better results. Kittleson (1997) found that follow-up memos led to a doubling in the response rate. In a meta-analysis, Sheehan (2001) concluded that pre-notification was perhaps the most useful tool in improving response rate. Moreover, Schafer and Dillman (1998) argue that e-mail surveys work very well when there is a multi-mode form of contact, i.e., where individuals are contacted in multiple ways (e.g., through e-mail, a reminder phone call and a reminder card). The bottom line is that academic researchers currently feel that, if done correctly with the right audience, e-mail surveys can lead to phenomenal results.

E-mail is a virtually costless communication mechanism for the sender. The marginal cost of contacting an additional person is nearly zero (Shiman, 1996). This creates an incentive to overload consumers with messages. Survey researchers are tempted to pre-notify their participants and then send multiple reminders. As a result, the multiple instances of contact contribute to the transactional burden on the recipient.

Using e-mail in survey research is particularly troublesome when the researcher is contacting a stranger (i.e., prospect) for the very first time. Such solicitations to participate in surveys are Spam or unsolicited e-mail[2] (Sheehan & Hoy, 1999; Krishnamurthy, 2000). Spam is an unethical communication practice from the standpoint of consumers due to six reasons—privacy violation, volume, irrelevance, deceptiveness, message offensiveness and targeting vulnerable consumers[3] (Krishnamurthy, 2000). At the same time, Spam affects multiple stakeholders—e.g., Internet Service Providers bear significantly higher costs as a result of Spam. America Online, the leading Internet Service Provider (ISP) testified in court, in 1998, that up to 30% of the e-mail it processed was Spam (Alexander, 1998). In some weeks, this proportion was as high as 50% of all messages (Patch & Smalley, 1998).

Thus, if everybody used unsolicited e-mail to contact respondents for survey research, several negative consequences result—consumers are over-burdened and researchers add to the Spam problem described above. Formally speaking, unsolicited e-mail as a method of contact fails the deontological principles of universality and reversibility[4].

This is not a problem limited to survey research, of course. Commercial firms with huge consumer databases are struggling to find effective ways to contact customers. E-mail is virtually the only online vehicle for customer contact for promotion and market research for these large companies. These corporations have suggested obtaining customer permission prior to contacting them (Krishnamurthy, 2001; Petty, 2000). Interestingly, academic researchers have not followed this approach to this point (Sheehan, 2001). Also, the market research conducted by companies has the implication of an ongoing relationship. Companies have increasingly moved from a one-time transaction perspective to a relational perspective (Sheth & Parvatiyar, 1995). On the other hand, academic survey research tends more often to focus on one-time individual contact[5]. Therefore, due to these two factors (low volume and one-time contact), there has not been a big backlash to the Spamming of academic surveys. However, as the legal, ethical and cultural landscapes change, this comfort may not be afforded to academic researchers in the future. Therefore, it is no wonder that obtaining respondent permission prior to contact is currently being touted as an ethical form of contact (Yun & Trumbo, 2000).

In this chapter, I carefully examine the implications of taking this approach. I start by studying the different types of online market research. Next, I look at the impact of the Internet and the Web on market research. I then introduce the notion of respondent permission and investigate the application of permission to all forms of online market research. I then turn to the problems in applying permission to e-mail survey research.

CLASSIFYING TYPES OF ONLINE MARKET RESEARCH

Even though computers have been extensively used in survey research for a long time (e.g., Computer-Assisted-Telephone-Interview or CATI), the Internet has opened up completely new avenues for market research. I classify online techniques on two dimensions, Qualitative/Quantitative and Requiring/Not Requiring direct respondent contact (for research purposes). The resulting four quadrants are shown in Figure 1[6].

The Qualitative/Quantitative distinction is well known to academic researchers. Qualitative research involves getting rich and textured information about individuals. The focus is on getting deep insights and a rich understanding into what the informant thinks. Instead of placing the respondents into predetermined categories, the idea is to understand the categories respondents use to think of a problem. On the other hand, the focus of quantitative research is to quantify the magnitude of effects and draw inferences about the statistical validity of the inferences. Survey research is mostly quantitative. Of course, one could have open-ended questions in surveys. But, the overriding focus of surveys tends to be generalizability and statistical inference. Surveys are typically used when the nature of the problem is already understood whereas qualitative research is frequently used to identify the structural characteristics of the problem.

Figure 1: Types of Online Market Research

	Respondent contact	No respondent contact
Qualitative	*Quadrant I* Online Focus Groups In-depth Interviews Lab Studies	*Quadrant II* Search log analysis

Quantitative	*Quadrant III*
	Surveys
	  -E-mail
	  -Pop-ups
	Lab Studies
		Quadrant IV
		Click-stream
		analysis
		Profiling

Online research can either involve direct respondent contact or not. Survey research is an example where there is direct contact. On the other hand, indirect methods involving tracking the imprint of individuals as they browse and shop over the Internet. These imprints (or clickstreams[7]) are stored in logs that can either be studied qualitatively or mined for relationships among different actions[8]. The respondent does not have to be bothered again. Rather, the behavior of the respondent is used to draw inferences about how he or she thinks. It is possible to contact respondents directly to ask them what they think about a topic of interest.

Quadrant I represents research that is qualitative and requires direct contact. Examples of this type of research are online focus groups or in-depth interviews. In this case, the interviewer can ask a single respondent or a group of respondents about their opinions of a product/service/experience. The data collected is usually in the form of a transcript.

Quadrant II is for research that is qualitative, but does not require contacting the respondent directly. An example of this is search-log analysis. Whenever respondents visit a website and search for something, it is recorded in a search log. This log can be studied to identify patterns of behavior. For instance, if visitors are persistently and unsuccessfully searching for something at a site, that may be a clue that the content for the site needs to be revisited.

Quadrant III stands for research that is quantitative and requires respondent contact. A prime exemplar of this category is survey research. Individuals are contacted either by e-mail or a pop-up ad and asked to participate in an online survey. The survey is typically available on a website. The data is captured in a text file that can be directly analyzed using a statistical package.

Quadrant IV is for research that is quantitative and requires no respondent contact. Clickstream analysis and profiling are examples of this. As the respondent passes through the website, data is recorded about his or her behavior. This can be analyzed using data mining models to identify relationships among variables (e.g., does greater time spent on a sub-page increase the likelihood of buying a product?).

The role of respondent permission is different in each quadrant. Whenever there is direct contact, only individuals who have provided permission may be contacted. Hence, this holds for survey research and online focus groups. In many cases, it may be possible to contact a customer a few times to achieve efficiency based on the terms of the original permission. When there is no direct contact, the issue of permission continues to be important. However, here, the permission may be obtained prior to conducting the research (e.g., when a user signs to be on a panel or registers for a website). The ethical issue of maintaining the privacy of respondent records is an important one and is discussed later.

IMPACT OF THE INTERNET
ON SURVEY RESEARCH

There are four steps in the market research process—data collection, data storage and sharing, data analysis and result reporting/action. The Internet has affected all four steps significantly and has generated new ethical dilemmas. Let us look at its impact on each step.

Data Collection

The Internet has impacted the first step, data collection, in five ways.

1. *Multiple modes of information gathering*
    Organizations now have detailed databases about their respondents. Each respondent has a profile that includes clickstream, behavioral and demographic data. By linking these data elements with survey data, organizations are able to gain a deep understanding into the respondent. This leads to an ability to target the respondent better.

2. *Efficient, quick and low-cost respondent contact for surveys*
    All companies survey their respondents from time to time to gather information about perceptions, attitudes, etc. In general, this is a cumbersome and drawn-out process. Respondents may be sent surveys by mail or contacted at their local shopping mall by interviewers. The answers then need to be manually entered into a computer. This is usually the step that takes the longest time and is prone to human error. In general, it is not uncommon for a company to have to wait for three to six months to get the results from a survey. Using e-mail and pop-up ads, marketers are now able to survey respondents quickly and obtain the data in electronic form in a fraction of that time. This approach also allows for low cost per contact.

3. *Large-scale information gathering*
    Partly driven by the arguments in point two (i.e., efficient, quick and low-cost), using online market research it is possible to gather information from consumers on an unprecedented scale. For example, every 24 hours America Online (AOL) subscribers are invited to participate in a short survey. The company was able to

collect about two million responses from consumers over a period of 18 months and use this for detailed evaluations of its respondent support.

4.   *Contacting respondent groups that were previously hard to access*
Some respondent groups have traditionally been hard to access. For example, companies pay a lot of money to survey working professionals who are strapped for time and thus, may not be willing to participate in a mail or telephone survey. Similarly, respondents in remote locations and those who are place-bound are usually very hard to survey. Now, these types of groups can be contacted easily using Web technology easily leading to more representative samples.

Data Storage and Sharing

The Internet has enabled complete digitization of the market research process. Rather than worrying about paper surveys, researchers can store all research data digitally on computers. As a result, much more data can be stored effectively for a longer period of time. This also allows for more efficient sharing of information. Using the Internet for market research also changes the sheer scale of information collected. It is possible to collect millions of records about individual behavior on a daily basis.

Data Analysis

Generally, the data is subjected to statistical analysis to make proper inferences. The data may be analyzed using statistical packages such as SAS and SPSS. Typically, the analysis starts with the descriptive statistics (e.g., mean, standard deviation) and then progresses to more advanced modeling techniques such as regression and clustering. The nature of data analysis changes substantially when the Internet is used to conduct market research. Specifically, the changes are:

Data Mining

Traditional statistical techniques were built for the days when there was a scarcity of data. Now, there is an abundance of data. In many cases, it is no longer necessary to sample a subset of the population, a census can be done, i.e., data on the entire respondent base of an organization can be made available. New variables are being measured for the first time. Data mining is the new label for a set of techniques that companies can use to work on large datasets. It incorporates learnings from statistics, pattern recognition, machine learning and database technology. It can be defined as the process of inductive computer analysis of large datasets aimed at finding unsuspecting relationships among variables. Since it is inductive, the researcher does not start the process with a set of hypotheses. Rather, he or she starts with a large dataset and a set of objectives (e.g., to maximize sales).

Analysis of Data in Real-Time

Generally, there is a gap between measurement and the availability of data. With the Internet, researchers can access information in real time. This creates the opportunity for new types of academic research.

Individual-Level Data

It is possible now to build a complicated database that includes disparate data elements. This changes the nature of academic research where typically not much is known about the respondent prior to contact. Having deep knowledge about our informants prior to contact allows us to tailor our questions appropriately leading to better responses.

Reporting/Action

With the Internet, the gap between information gathering and action has diminished. The Internet now allows for real-time decision making using fresh market research. This is best illustrated using an example from the corporate world.

Consider Internet advertising. Systems now capture fresh respondent response information in real-time. As a result, it is possible for a company to simultaneously release (say) 20 banner ads with creatives which vary on dimensions such as colors, fonts etc. on a subset of the market. Then, the response to each ad can be monitored in real-time. Based on the click-through and then, the conversion rate, managers can quickly decide to discard the ones that lead to poor results and can focus all resources on the ones that have performed well.

This sort of quick-strike capability is provided by the melding of fresh market information with quick marketing action. As a result, marketing objectives are met more effectively in shorter time and with lower cost. In short, with the advent of the Internet, market research is not an activity that is conducted periodically with tenuous links to action. Rather, its value lies in providing fresh market data to managers who can act quickly to maximize the return on marketing investments.

The implications of this shrinking distance between information gathering and action on market research are yet to be fully explored.

PERMISSION

Academic researchers are now slowly, but surely, turning to e-mail lists that have been collected with the permission of the individual (e.g., Yun & Trumbo, 2000). For example, Jackson and DeCormier (1999) demonstrated the use of targeted lists using respondent permission leads to dramatically better results. By targeting people who had indicated an interest in financial matters, they reported a response rate as high as 85%.

Many survey research organizations have developed a code of ethics that includes a reference to permission. For instance, the code of ethics for Internet research of the Council of American Survey Research Organizations (Appendix) says in part four: "When receiving e-mail lists from clients or list owners, research organizations are required to have the client or list provider verify that individuals listed have a reasonable expectation that they will receive e-mail contact."

Market research is an asymmetric activity—the agency conducting the market research activity needs information from an individual and hence, initiates the contact. One way to overcome this intrinsic asymmetry is to compensate survey participants. Financial compensation turns market research into a transaction and makes it less asymmetric. Consumers provide information about themselves in exchange for financial

Figure 2a: Spam Targets Indiscriminately

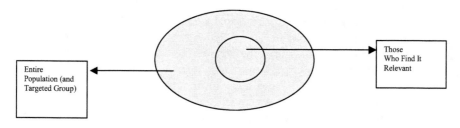

Figure 2b: Permission Marketing Leads to Targeting

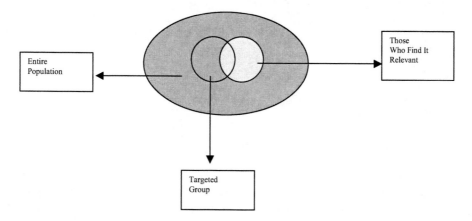

gain. However, it may not be a sufficient motivator for people who do not care about the topic of the survey. Permission marketing proposes grouping individuals by their interests and then targeting them based on these interests. The idea is that consumers may be more receptive to surveys in areas that interest them.

The key difference between Spam and permission marketing is the extent of targeting. As shown in Figure 2a, Spam targets indiscriminately. Large numbers of people are targeted and therefore, a great proportion of recipients find the message to be irrelevant. On the other hand, as shown in Figure 2b, permission-based targeting is focused only on those who have expressed an interest in a certain topic or activity. As a result, it is likely to receive a better response.

Clearly, from a statistical point of view, Spam may represent an ideal. By targeting the population, Spam can be thought of as maximizing the chances of attracting a random sample[9]. At the other extreme, permission marketing can be thought of as introducing a self-selecting respondent bias making it less attractive statistically. This is where the statistical and ethical perspectives collide. While the statistician may cheer for Spam, the ethicist is much more comfortable with permission-based targeting.

How to obtain respondent permission is still a matter of some ethical controversy. Three methods have emerged—opt-out, opt-in and double opt-in. Opt-out refers to the case when the agent sends an unsolicited e-mail and then provides individuals an option of not receiving future messages[10]. Each message includes a statement to the effect of—"If you do not wish to receive such e-mails in the future, just click here." Typically, the consumer has provided personal information to the sender for some other purpose—e.g., purchasing a product, registering for a newsletter. Opt-in requires the consumer to explicitly tell the corporation that it has the permission to send messages to him or her. For instance, when an individual may shop at an online retailer she could provide it with permission to send her promotional messages from time to time. But, opt-in leaves out one problem. Consumer A can sign up a friend, consumer B, for a service that B has no interest in. All of a sudden, B starts to receive e-mails for products that she does not care for. In order to avoid this loophole, double opt-in calls for a stricter standard in building e-mail lists. It requires that senders include a confirmation e-mail to all individuals who have opted in. When an individual confirms, the loop is complete and the sender can be doubly sure that the right person is on the list.

Researchers who use e-mail lists must pay careful attention to how those lists were put together. I propose that the following elements must be part of any well-designed permission-based program[11]:
1.   Explicit Permission Seeking Process
2.   Verification Process
3.   Recognition of Relationship
4.   Access to Personal Information
5.   Communication Control
6.   Frictionless Exit Ability

First, the permission must be obtained in an explicit rather than an implicit manner. This means that the sender must first assume that it does not have the respondent's permission to send out promotional e-mails. Then, the respondent must be presented with a real choice of granting permission to the firm or not. The respondent's right to be left alone must be honored. The permission-seeking process must be clear and devoid of deceptive tactics.

Second, the firm must verify the identity of each consumer. This is necessary to disallow consumers deceptively signing on others without their knowledge. For example, consumers may sign up their friends and associates indiscriminately thus placing undue transactional burden on them. Permission-based services that offer this are referred to as "double opt-in"—e.g., yesmail.com. This is easily accomplished by sending an e-mail immediately after an individual registers.

Third, the consumer must understand that he or she is entering an on-going two-way relationship that is mutually beneficial. The consumer must understand that he or she is a willing partner of equal stature who stands to benefit from this alliance. A well-designed permission-based campaign will create well-defined expectations in the mind of the consumer about the nature and volume of messages. Moreover, the consumer's perception of the level of permission will be aligned with the sender's perception of the permission level.

Fourth, the consumer must know exactly what the sender knows about him or her. Moreover, the consumer must be able to modify this information suitably at any point in time. This is the "access" part of the FTC's fair information practice list (Culnan 2000). The argument is that such continuous access to one's personal information would be empowering and reassuring to the consumer. Moreover, this is beneficial to a firm or corporation because consumers who update their profiles more often are more likely to receive relevant ads and hence, have higher response rates.

Fifth, the consumer must be able to control the nature and volume of messages being sent to him or her. The true promise of permission marketing is that consumers can control the flow of promotional messages to them. They can dictate the types of categories they will see ads for by filling out forms on interests and product preferences. This is being done routinely by many firms today. Some firms also allow consumers to control the volume of e-mail in any category. This sort of control over promotional communication underscores the true promise of permission marketing.

Finally, the consumer must be able to effortlessly exit from a permission marketing relationship at any point. Not letting consumers exit at any point equates to assuming one has the permission to market to them when, in fact, one does not. Moreover, frustrated consumers will no longer attend to the messages leading to low response rates.

THE APPLICATION OF PERMISSION TO ALL MARKET RESEARCH

Permission is typically discussed in the context of e-mail based survey research. The issue then becomes if permission can be an over-arching test of ethical respondent contact. Questions such as these come up in this context: Should respondent permission be a pre-requisite for click-stream or search log analysis? Should e-mail-based respondent contact be held to a higher standard or should pop-ups (for example) also require prior respondent consent?

The Federal Trade Commission (FTC) identified five fair information practices in their 1998 report that are now widely accepted. These principles are:

1. **Notice.** Data collectors must disclose their information practices before collecting personal information from consumers.
2. **Choice.** Consumers must be given options with respect to whether and how personal information collected from them may be used for purposes beyond which they were collected.
3. **Access.** Consumers must be able to view and contest the accuracy and completeness of data collected about them.
4. **Security.** Data collectors must take reasonable steps to assure that the information collected from consumers is accurate and secure from unauthorized use.
5. **Redress.** Consumers must have a way to complain if these practices are not being followed.

Notice and Choice taken together come close to the permission standard—but fall short of it. However, the consistent application of these principles is likely to lead to more ethical practice. Annoyance (e.g., pop-up ads), in and of itself, is not sufficient to label something as unethical. Rather, the violation of one or more of these principles is a necessary condition for the judgment of ethical practice.

Table 1: Content Analysis of Spam Messages

Categories	No. of Messages	% of Total
Pornography	29884	30.2
Money Making/Get Rich/Work from Home	29365	29.6
Other Direct Product or Service/Misc	23326	23.5
Become a Spammer	4200	4.2
Gambling/Sweepstakes	3279	3.3
Health/Cures/Weight Loss (including Viagra)	9804	9.9
Totals	**99858**	**100.7**

ISSUES AND OBSTACLES WITH USE OF PERMISSION IN SURVEY RESEARCH

Issues

Low Volume

Spam is unsolicited e-mail. Large commercial Spammers send out messages in huge volumes, whereas academic researchers tend to send a fairly low volume. However, high volume is not a requirement for labeling a message as Spam. From the individual's perspective, an unsolicited message is an unsolicited message. Hence, using low volume of messages as an excuse to justify sending out unsolicited messages is not appropriate, nor ethical. Similarly, a low volume of messages does not justify the use of opt-out as a strategy for respondent contact.

Source Characteristics of Spam

Some have argued that the main problem with Spam is the nature of the message. Consider, for example, the result of a content analysis of about 100,000 messages by the Spam Recycling Center shown in Table 1. The categories are unsavory and are likely to irritate and offend many people.

The argument, therefore, is that it is fine if academics and non-profit organizations send Spam—but not if unsavory marketers do so. This is not an ethical argument. Once again, taking the recipient's perspective, an unknown sender is just that. It is possible to spoof the names of senders (i.e., act as if the sender is someone that he/she is not)—this is considered an unethical practice by all (e.g., see the code of ethics in the Appendix). Due to this, unless a recipient instantly recognizes the sender, it is unlikely that an e-mail from an .edu address will be treated more favorably.

Length of Survey

Many researchers have pointed out that a long survey is likely to add to the transactional burden of the recipient making it harder to process. Some studies have found that a shorter survey is likely to lead to a higher response rate. From a consumer perspective, it is not easy to prejudge the length of an electronic survey—especially if multiple screens are used in the delivery of the survey. Hence, it is hard to conclude that the length of the survey contributes to the transactional burden.

Obstacles

There are several obstacles to the implementation of permission while conducting survey research. Some of these obstacles are due to the structure of academic institutions and how academic research is conducted and published. Others have to do with resource constraints.

Self-Selection of Respondents

Perhaps the most serious problem with using permission in survey research is that there could be serious self-selection problems. Consider the case of a surveyor trying to assess interest in a new financial software. Targeting respondents who have indicated an interest in financial matters may mean focusing on those who already know the basics of financial management. This may not provide an accurate account of perceptions towards the software in question.

In other words, permission may lead to a sample that skews towards those with a greater level of awareness and knowledge about a topic. This is not always what the researcher is looking for and consequently, it may create problems in generalizations.

Of course, there is the usual self-selection problem of respondents who are "career" survey participants. In other words, respondents who want to participate in surveys may not be the ones that researchers want to reach.

Resources to Obtain and Maintain Permission

Academic researchers do not have the resources to obtain and maintain permission. As a result, they may be tempted to send Spam. Unless there is a community-wide effort to create disincentives for this, researchers will not stop. For instance, journals must start requiring that the respondents provided permission before accepting the results of survey-based papers. Code of Ethics must incorporate language about permission-based respondent contact. One of the problems is that the organizational structure of academic research is inefficient. Recruiting a sample for each study by a lone researcher leads to an inefficient process. A cooperative effort to build a large sample that could than be shared among researchers could be more resource-efficient. Already, the Time-Sharing Experiments for the Social Sciences (TESS) project at http://

www.experimentcentral.org has been set up along these lines. More such projects need to be initiated.

Permission and Privacy

Permission is not tradable—not even if a company has gone bankrupt. Academic researchers, especially, must be careful about what is being told to respondents when they fill out surveys. If the respondents are aware that the raw data will be shared with other researchers, then it is legitimate to do so.

CONCLUSION

The prospect of using e-mail in survey research can be very exciting to academic researchers. However, it raises many ethical concerns. While many people have started to say that obtaining consumer permission is important, there is no clarity on how to obtain and maintain permission. Some academic researchers might argue that due to the low volume and infrequent nature of their surveys and the general positive perception of academia, their e-mail surveys do not add to the Spam problem. However, this is problematic from an ethical perspective since it changes the definition of what Spam is from any unsolicited e-mail to a subset of these e-mails which have certain predefined characteristics. There are ways to implement permission-based respondent contact if the academic community wants to. The only negative to keep in mind will be the statistical problem of self-selection and the "loss of complete randomness" to some degree. Regardless, the future legal landscape may force academic researchers to adopt permission as the standard.

If the academic community buys into respondent permission as the appropriate approach to contacting consumers, it must put its money where its mouth is. Journals must ask researchers to use permission when compiling databases and scrutinize for this in the review process. For starters, there needs to be a serious conversation about this problem in the community and the hope is that this paper is a solid start in that direction.

Researchers can start implementing a permission-based approach in many ways. First, researchers can adopt a multi-mode approach to individual contact. Then, permission can be gathered through an offline approach before online contact. Second, frequently researchers have direct access to the audience- the infamous student subject pool comes to mind. In this case, obtaining permission for online contact may be relatively straightforward and may require a simple announcement in class. Third, as academic researchers, we must seriously think of approaching e-mail list brokers and asking them to donate lists for academic use. The lists can be updated every year to avoid repetition and over-exposure. Fourth, academic researchers must rethink their approach of recruiting individuals from scratch for each study. Reusing existing mail lists is likely to lead to a more efficient approach. Finally, sharing of e-mail lists can be considered on a limited basis.

The number of e-mail accounts per person has exploded in recent times due to free e-mail services. The number of messages sent out is increasing at a rapid pace. Over time, the scarce resource will be the attention of the consumer and using respondent permission gives us a fighting chance of getting high-quality data from individuals.

REFERENCES

Alexander, S. (1998). A spam hating man with a spam stamping plan. *Computerworld, 32*(25), 69-70.

Anderson, S. & Gansneder, B. (1995). Using electronic mail surveys and computer monitored data for studying computer mediated communication systems. *Social Science Computer Review, 13*(1), 33-46.

Churchill, G. (1996). *Marketing Research.* Fort Worth: The Dryden Press.

Culnan, M. J. (2002). Protecting privacy online: Is self-regulation working? *Journal of Public Policy and Marketing, 19*(1), 20-26.

Federal Trade Commission. (1998). *Privacy online: A Report to Congress.* Retrieved June 2003 from: http://www.ftc.gov/reports/privacy3/toc.htm.

Goree, C. T. & Marszalek III, J.F. (1995). Electronic surveys: Ethical issues for researchers. *College Student Affairs Journal, 15*(1), 75-79.

Jackson, A. & DeCormier, R. (1999). E-mail survey response rates: Targeting increases response. *Marketing Intelligence and Planning, 17*(3), 135-139.

Kittleson, M. (1995). An assessment of the response rate via the postal service and e-mail. *Health Values: The Journal of Health Behavior, Education and Promotion, 19*(2), 27-39.

Kittleson, M. (1997). Determining effective follow-up of e-mail surveys. *American Journal of Health Behavior, 21*(3), 193-196.

Krishnamurthy, S. (2000). Spam revisited. *Quarterly Journal of Electronic Commerce, 1*(4), 305-321.

Krishnamurthy, S. (2001). A comprehensive analysis of permission marketing. *Journal of Computer Mediated Communication, 6*(2). Retrieved from: http://www.ascusc.org/jcmc/vol6/issue2/krishnamurthy.html.

Patch, K. & Smalley, E. (1998). E-mail overload. *Network World, 15*(43), 1-46.

Petty, R. D. (2000). Marketing without consent: Consumer choice and costs, privacy and public policy. *Journal of Public Policy and Marketing, 19*(1), 42-54.

Ranchhod, A. & Zhou, F. (2001). Comparing respondents of e-mail and mail surveys: Understanding the implications of technology. *Marketing Intelligence and Planning, 19*(4), 254-262.

Schaefer, D. R. & Dillman, D. (1998). Development of a standard e-mail methodology: Results of an experiment. *Public Opinion Quarterly, 62*(3), 378-397.

Sheehan, K. (2001). E-mail survey response rates: A review. *Journal of Computer Mediated Communication, 6*(2). Retrieved June 6, 2003 from: http://www.ascusc.org/jcmc/vol6/issue2/sheehan.html.

Sheehan, K. & Hoy, M. G. (1999). Using e-mail to survey Internet users in the United States: Methodology and assessment. *Journal of Computer Mediated Communication, 4*(3). Retrieved June 6, 2003 from: http://www.ascusc.org/jcmc/vol4/issue3/sheehan.html.

Sheth, J.N. & Parvatiyar, A. (1995). Relationship marketing in consumer marketing: Antecedents and consequences. *Journal of the Academy of Marketing Science*, 23, 255-271.

Shiman, D. R. (1996). When e-mail becomes junk mail: The welfare implications of the advancement of communications technology. *Review of Industrial Organization, 11*(1), 35-48.

Yun, G.W. & Trumbo, C. (2000, September). Comparative response to a survey executed by post, e-mail, & Web form. *Journal of Computer Mediated Communication, 6*(1). Retrieved from: http://www.ascusc.org/jcmc/vol6/issue1/yun.html.

ENDNOTES

1   Using response rates as the metric to evaluate a mode of individual contact is problematic on many counts. An x% response rate does not tell us anything about the attitudes of (1-x)% of the audience. Moreover, a low response rate may only indicate the lack of a clear targeting approach—which may or may not be "bad." I mention this only because many published studies almost exclusively use this to evaluate effectiveness.

2   There is some inconsistency in the definition of Spam as noted in Krishnamurthy (2000). Some researchers have defined Spam as unsolicited *commercial* e-mail. Similarly, some have argued that only unsolicited e-mail sent out in huge volumes should count. For the purposes of this chapter, I am thinking of Spam as any unsolicited e-mail.

3   All these characteristics need not apply to all Spam messages. For instance, academic surveys may not be particularly offensive—but may contribute to the transactional burden of the consumer due to their volume and irrelevance.

4   Universality is the ethical principle that "every act should be based on principles that everyone could act on" and reversibility is the principle that "every act should be based on reasons that the actor would be willing to have all others use" (Churchill, 1996, p. 65).

5   Studies which involve a customer panel providing information over a predefined time period may be an exception, for example.

6   I discuss the role of permission for each quadrant at the end of this section.

7   A clickstream is an imprint of a visitor's path on a website. It includes information such as time spent on a page and the number of pages visited in a session. Behavioral data could include information about actions such as clicking on a link. Demographic data is the usual information about individual characteristics.

8   Collecting and analyzing consumer clickstreams can create many ethical concerns. Perhaps, the main concern is if consumers are aware that this process is going on. To some, this may sound like somebody is watching them as they shop or browse and create a sense of paranoia. The FTC principles of Notice, Choice, Access, Security and Redress might apply in this context as well.

9   The author is grateful to one of the reviewers of this chapter, Maxmillan Forte, for this observation.

10   There are other problems with opt-out. In many cases, Spammers masquerading as legitimate senders introduce false opt-out links. Clicking on an opt-out link then merely alerts these Spammers to the legitimacy of the e-mail address leading to further messages in the future.

11   A previous version of this appeared in Krishnamurthy (2000).

APPENDIX

Internet Research Ethics from the Council of American Survey Research Organizations (source: http://www.casro.org/codeofstandards.cfm, excerpt)

The unique characteristics of Internet research require specific notice that the principle of respondent privacy applies to this new technology and data collection methodology. The general principle of this section of the Code is that survey research organizations will not use unsolicited e-mails to recruit respondents for surveys.

1. Research organizations are required to verify that individuals contacted for research by e-mail have a reasonable expectation that they will receive e-mail contact for research. Such agreement can be assumed when ALL of the following conditions exist.

   a. A substantive pre-existing relationship exists between the individuals con tacted and the research organization, the client or the list owners contracting the research (the latter being so identified);

   b. Individuals have a reasonable expectation, based on the pre-existing relationship, that they may be contacted for research;

   c. Individuals are offered the choice to be removed from future e-mail contact in each invitation; and

   d. The invitation list excludes all individuals who have previously taken the appropriate and timely steps to request the list owner to remove them.

2. Research organizations are prohibited from using any subterfuge in obtaining e-mail addresses of potential respondents, such as collecting e-mail addresses from public domains, using technologies or techniques to collect e-mail addresses without individuals' awareness, and collecting e-mail addresses under the guise of some other activity.

3. Research organizations are prohibited from using false or misleading return e-mail addresses when recruiting respondents over the Internet.

4. When receiving e-mail lists from clients or list owners, research organizations are required to have the client or list provider verify that individuals listed have a reasonable expectation that they will receive e-mail contact, as defined, in (1) above.

Chapter VIII

Organizational Research Over the Internet: Ethical Challenges and Opportunities

W. Benjamin Porr
George Mason University, USA

Robert E. Ployhart
George Mason University, USA

ABSTRACT

This chapter presents a framework through which ethical Internet-based organizational research can be conducted. Organizational constraints that promote the use of the Internet for applied research are identified, followed by potential benefits and drawbacks. The chapter then discusses the ethical issues that must be considered when conducting Internet-based organizational research; these include concerns about privacy, confidentiality, anonymity, informed consent and providing a debriefing. A case study illustrates these issues, and the chapter concludes with directions for future research. Numerous tables and figures are used to serve as a quick reference for the key points of the chapter.

INTRODUCTION

The Internet and the World Wide Web (WWW) have affected nearly every aspect of our everyday lives. It has spawned a new method of communicating and expressing oneself, whether it is an individual, a group of individuals or an organization. It should therefore come as no surprise that the Internet has also become a growing and increasingly important medium for conducting research. There are many reasons for this, but perhaps the most important ones are the Internet's use as a more effective and efficient research tool over traditional methods, such as face-to-face or paper-and-pencil research methods.

One area where the Internet could dramatically improve research methodology is in the domain of organizational research. Organizational research is a broad domain that is concerned with studying the behavior and activities of organizations, which includes the employees, shareholders and customers of these organizations. When conducting applied research in organizations, the Internet offers many advantages over traditional methods, such as a greater ability to reach geographically dispersed samples that may work at different times (e.g., day or night), lowering costs (no proctor present, no paper, etc.), reducing missing or erroneous data and reducing the time from data collection to data analysis (e.g., Baron & Austin, 2000; Smith & Leigh, 1997; Mehta & Sivadas, 1995; Sproull, 1986; Yost & Homer, 1998). Given that many organizations operate or cooperate with branch offices in multiple states and, even, countries, the savings in terms of time, paper and mail costs can be substantial for Internet assessments (Church, 2001). As we discuss below, two of the biggest factors limiting organizations when conducting research are time and money. The potential advantages of Web-based data collection, thus make organizational research more frequent and potentially useful.

Although use of the Internet in conducting organizational research is becoming more popular, one issue that has been largely neglected is the new and different ethical concerns. Clearly they are at the forefront of any research enterprise, and there are many guidelines for ensuring ethical standards in research. However, problems arise when a methodology for conducting research is so novel that there are no universally accepted standards or guidelines for its ethical use. The Internet has been around more than 20 years; organizational researchers have been conducting research over the Internet for more than 10 of those years, and yet there is still no common standard researchers use to assess whether their study is ethically sound. For example, the "Publication Manual of the American Psychological Association" (American Psychological Association (APA), 2001) includes a chapter on ethical behavior in research, but has no reference to Web-based research. Likewise the "Standards for Educational and Psychological Testing" (APA, 1999) and the "Ethical Principles In the Conduct of Research with Human Participants" (APA, 1982) have no specific focus, suggestions or guidelines for conducting Web-based research or testing.

Unfortunately, conducting ethical research in organizations is often difficult, because organizations are constrained by money, time and resources. As will be discussed, the Internet offers many benefits over traditional research methods for conducting organizational research, but also raises new ethical issues not previously encountered. For example, ensuring participant anonymity (and perceptions of anonymity) can be difficult with Web-based data collection. As many employers consider any information sent over the company's computers to be the property of the organization, there may be concerns about how anonymous and confidential responses actually are. For instance, a case in California, in which employees were fired for poking fun at the manager over email, sided with the organization. The judge ruled that the company had the right to read the email because it owned and operated the equipment (McMorris, 1995). Likewise, many Institutional Review Boards (IRBs) believe there is no such thing as anonymity on the Internet. This raises issues regarding Web-based research because respondents might not participate, if they are identifiable. Similarly, obtaining informed consent becomes difficult when consent requires participants to read and physically sign an informed consent form. When research is conducted over the Internet, there is no guarantee that participants have actually read the consent form, or that they completely understand the nature of their consent. Finally, providing an adequate debriefing or even answering questions during the data collection can be difficult if not impossible with Web-based assessment. When data collection is conducted via paper-and-pencil surveys, these concerns are more easily addressed.

These are just a few examples of the kinds of ethical issues we have frequently encountered in our Web-based organizational research. We have at times found the existing human subjects guidelines difficult to translate into practice. As a result, we have developed some protocols and procedures that may help others who are interested in conducting Web-based research in an ethical manner. Thus, the purpose of this chapter is to (a) identify the major ethical challenges that result from conducting Web-based research in organizations; (b) discuss how one may ensure the ethical treatment of participants in Web-based research and (c) provide suggestions and guidelines for the design and conduct of Web-based research in organizations. Note that we do not offer a comprehensive treatment of research ethics, but rather focus on how the Internet affects the ethical conduct of research in organizations.

An overview of the balancing act the applied researcher must perform is shown in Figure 1. This figure illustrates that the researcher must balance three often competing concerns: research issues, organizational constraints and research ethics. As we discuss throughout this chapter, there are many instances where two or even all three of these issues are incompatible with the others, and the applied researcher must find a way to strike a balance between all three. Understanding the Web-based ethical concerns in such guidelines as the "APA Ethical Principles" and the "Code of Federal Regulations" can certainly help researchers better design and conduct ethical research. However, the current state of these guidelines is in some ways out of date, and at times does not reflect the reality of current Web research practice. By delineating the key ethical issues and how one might address them, we hope to increase the application of Web-based research in organizations.

In the following sections, this chapter will review these issues in detail. First, we discuss the major issues foreshadowed by Figure 1, including organizational constraints, research issues and ethics. The constraints section describes how organizational research is typically enacted; the research issues section focuses primarily on the benefits and drawbacks of Web-based research and the ethics section will focus on how the Internet both presents opportunities and challenges for organizational research. We then substantiate these issues by providing a case study, describing the challenges and solutions for conducting Web-based organizational research, and conclude by discussing important areas for future research on ethics and the Internet in organizational research.

Figure 1: The Intersection of Ethics, Organizational Constraints, and Theoretical Advancement

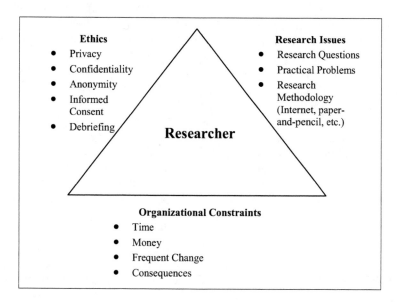

Please note that in the following sections, many of the issues intersect each other and to a certain degree overlap. This is to be expected, given that ethical issues are interrelated issues with overlapping boundaries. Therefore, to facilitate readers' identification of the key underlying issues, we suggest they pay careful attention to the tables interspersed throughout the chapter. We have structured our paper around these tables, so they can provide a quick summary of the key ethical issues in organizational Web-based research.

ORGANIZATIONAL CONSTRAINTS: THE REALITY OF RESEARCH IN ORGANIZATIONS

Organizational research, whether traditional or Web-based, is conducted in a manner very different from the typical lab study. Sometimes the researcher contacts members from the organization and requests the opportunity to conduct the study; other times members from the organization contact the researcher for help with an important practical problem (yet one the researcher also finds intriguing and potentially publishable). In either instance, the researcher must comply with IRB guidelines before conducting the study, while also identifying and developing a research question to address (Bickman, Rog, & Hedrick, 1998). Unfortunately, the reality of research in organizations makes applying these guidelines very difficult. This is because organizational research is characterized by many constraints, such as time, money, frequent change and the potential for negative or unintended consequences.

First, nearly all organizational research occurs on a timeline set by members within the organization (Bickman et al., 1998; Cascio, 1998). In our experience, the typical field research study is marked by long periods of inactivity interrupted at various times by high-pitched, intense activity. Precisely when such activity takes place is usually dictated by the organization. In most organizations, there is an intense pressure for projects to start and end quickly, and there is often little advance notice for when a project may start. For example, it is not uncommon to have only a one-month window from the start of a project to its completion. Clearly this condensed and unpredictable timeline makes it difficult to obtain IRB approval in sufficient time to start the study. Organizations ultimately exist to survive and profit, and few mangers realize that research can help improve an organization's profitability. Researchers thus get very little time to conduct their studies, and this makes ensuring IRB approval quickly an important part of the research process. Designing ethical research from the outset increases the speed through which approval will be granted and can mean the difference between projects that are completed and those that are never started.

Second, organizations are constrained by money. This is becoming even more true in the 21st century (Cascio, 1995). Again, organizational research is usually something that is not seen as central to the organization, and, therefore, few resources will be devoted to it. Web-based research actually increases the likelihood of organizational research being conducted because it costs the organization practically nothing (e.g., no mailing costs, photocopying costs, etc.).

Third, organizational research is marked by frequent change, and adapting to these changes is a necessity (Hammer & Champy, 1996). For example, it is not uncommon for a researcher to have a survey approved by one manager in an organization, only to have a more senior manager make additional changes to the survey. As another example, organizational members may look at a survey, and then suddenly decide they want to survey all of their employees instead of a smaller sample. If IRB approval was already obtained, the study must be resubmitted and a request for approval of the changes from the IRB must be made. Changes that occur within a split second in the organization can take weeks to be approved by IRB panels. Thus, organizational research is a very fluid process, where there is constant change of varying degrees of magnitude. Adapting to these changes is challenging, and complying with ethical principles and IRB guidelines can be particularly difficult.

Finally, organizational research carries important consequences that may not be as present in traditional lab-based research. Perhaps the most important difference is that the participants in the organizational study are people working in their real jobs; they are often suspicious of research, may feel their jobs are at jeopardy or that the organization is trying to obtain personal information to use against them. For example, one of the most important parts of conducting organizational research is the informed consent portion of the study, where the researcher must ensure the trust and commitment from respondents. In contrast to the lab study where participants may have little concern over whether their responses will in some way be used against them, organizational employees are highly concerned with this issue. If the researcher cannot ensure the trust of respondents, the data collection is usually derailed before it ever begins. It is therefore critical that organizational research be conducted in an ethical manner that is sensitive to these issues.

Thus, organizational research is characterized by short timelines, little monetary resources, frequent change and important personal consequences. Addressing these challenges is difficult, and many organizational decision makers do not care about such things as obtaining IRB approval. For example, many such decision makers are shocked to learn the researcher cannot start a project when they want because the researcher is waiting for IRB approval. Problems arise when the organization wants the researcher to do things he or she cannot ethically do [e.g., failing to provide informed consent (Sieber, 1998)]. We find these situations difficult because there is enormous pressure to get the project started, and, in fact, the project will often proceed with or without the involvement of the researcher. This leads to a lack of scientific research findings from field settings, a loss of potential opportunities for the researchers and an organization that will most likely not work with the researchers again. We have lost opportunities because of this issue and have learned that, to the extent all ethical issues can be adequately addressed up front in an IRB application, the more likelihood that the applied research study will occur. Thus, applied organizational research must balance two often competing demands: the IRB and the organization.

RESEARCH ISSUES: BENEFITS AND DRAWBACKS TO INTERNET RESEARCH

The previous section described the many constraints of organizational research. In this section we briefly examine the second part of Figure 1—the research issues posed by conducting organizational research. Opportunities include a chance to test theories in a naturalistic environment, expand the generalizability of lab studies and solve important, immediate, practical problems. Addressing these issues also involves how the research will be conducted, and it is on this point that Web-based research moves ahead of more traditional approaches, such as paper-and-pencil surveys and interviewing participants. Therefore the Internet essentially helps reduce organizational constraints and may make organizational research more frequent and productive. However, it may also have some drawbacks, and we present the major benefits and drawbacks to using the Internet in organizational research in Table 1. We do not go into great detail about these benefits and drawbacks in this section because the various issues are discussed in conjunction with the ethical issues in the following section and in the case study presented later. Further, these issues have been well-documented and comprehensively described in previous research (e.g., Church, 2001; Lievens & Harris, 2003; Stanton, 1998).

As shown by the table, most benefits include an emphasis on saving time, money and/or availability for the organization to conduct research. Of course, these help reduce the impact of organizational constraints described above and help make organizational research more likely. The drawbacks described in Table 1 mainly deal with the ethical concerns of researchers when conducting Web-based organizational research, as discussed next. By examining Table 1, one can further understand the dilemma faced by organizational researchers in Figure 1.

Table 1: The Benefits and Drawbacks of Using Web-Based Research

Benefits	Drawbacks
• Less time to distribute and collect measures • No data entry phase • No mistakes in data entry • Participants can take assessment anytime, anywhere • Less money spent on administration • Almost no limit to the number of people that can complete the measure simultaneously • Fast turnaround from administration to results • More honest responses have been shown	• Anonymity can never be assured • No *signed* informed consent • Usually, no investigator to describe research and provide debriefing • Concerns of invasiveness/loss of privacy • Questions about who owns the data • Less honest responses have been shown • May discriminate against people who do not have access to a computer • May discriminate against people who do not know how to use a computer or feel uncomfortable with them

ETHICAL ISSUES AND SOLUTIONS FOR INTERNET RESEARCH IN ORGANIZATIONS

The following section describes the ethical concerns that are encountered in organizational research over the Internet and potential solutions to these concerns are suggested. Table 2 provides an overview of these concerns and solutions. The issues discussed are concerns of privacy, confidentiality, anonymity, informed consent and debriefing in the research process. Each individual issue is important in considering how to go about implementing ethical organizational research over the Internet. It is important to understand that some points may be important in some instances but may be less important in other situations. This section is a summary of what to address and how to solve issues when conducting organizational research, but does not attempt to suggest when particular issues are more important then others. That will be dictated by the interaction between the three parts in Figure 1, and ultimately comes down to the researcher's decision on how to implement the research.

Privacy Concerns

A major topic in ethical Web research is the invasion of the respondents' privacy. Before understanding the steps taken to ensure ethical Internet research in organiza-

Table 2: Comparing Ethical Issues and Solutions Between Traditional and Internet Research

Issues	Concerns of Internet Research	How Traditional Research Handles Concerns	Potential Solutions for Internet Research
Privacy	• Gathering information through direct and indirect methods • Tracking people through *Internet cookies* • Speed and amount of data-exchanging between companies	• Indirect methods of gathering information are expensive • Data-exchanging is slow and laborious	• Explain privacy issues and what they entail • Ability to turn *Internet cookies* off • Post a privacy seal and explain steps taken to ensure privacy of results
Confidentiality	• Results can be traced back to an individual by the organization • Unauthorized sources could gain access to results from a computer	• Data collection in bulk, so unable to trace back to individual person • Access to results only if person views hard copy	• Take assessment on alternate computers • The use of firewalls and data encryption to secure individual results
Anonymity	• Never have full anonymity?	• Can have full anonymity	• Take assessment on alternate computers • Use of non-identifying information
Informed Consent	• No signature • No proof that it was read • All information must be written or told beforehand because nobody is there to answer questions	• Easy to get a signature • More proof that it was read • Respondents are told all information during session and the investigator is there to answer questions	• Have a multiple step process to gain informed consent through checkboxes • Phone number and email of the investigator are provided for any questions before person participates
Debriefing	• Never sure participant read debriefing • All information pertaining to study must be written because nobody is there to answer questions during the session	• Respondents are told all information during session and the investigator is there to answer any questions the person has	• Have check boxes at the end of debriefing to make sure respondent understands information • Phone number and email of the investigator are provided for any further questions

tions, we need to first understand the privacy issues the Internet raises and how potential respondents feel about these issues.

Privacy is seen as "either a presumed or stipulated interest that individuals have with respect to protecting personal information, personal property, or personal space" (Tavani, 2000, p. 65). This is not a trivial issue as Wright and Kakalik (1997) report that 70 percent of respondents are more concerned about Internet privacy than with any other media. Benassi (1999) found privacy to be the number one issue concerning consumers in a Business Week/Harris survey. Some people feel that taking an assessment over a computer is an invasion of privacy known as the Big Brother Syndrome (Rosenfeld & Booth-Kewley, 1996), a belief that computers are monitoring and controlling our lives in ways we can't directly determine. For example, every time a person goes to a website, the individual computer the person uses has a number called the Internet protocol (IP) address. This number is like a telephone number or street address, because it is specific to the computer. By using your IP address, it is possible for someone to find out websites you visit or when you are online.

The age of information technology has enabled the collection of information pertaining to individuals on a scale much larger than anything preceding it (mass emails, electronic searches, etc.). Consider the amount and speed at which information can be gathered as opposed to more traditional and laborious methods, such as paper surveys. Therefore, privacy concerns did not originate with the Internet, but have intensified because of the speed at which information is transferred. Such privacy issues show why we need guidelines for Internet research. By understanding the privacy issues, a researcher will better understand the steps necessary to ensure the ethical conduct of organizational research over the Internet. We now discuss specific privacy issues in Web-based research.

Information gathering. There are two main ways organizations gather information over the Internet. The first involves a direct method of gathering information through the use of Web forms. This data-gathering mechanism requires Web users to enter information online (Nissenbaum, 1997) and is a form of survey research. An example would be someone answering a few questions about their preferences on a website. This method is relatively uncontroversial, because the online users willingly share their information. A second and more controversial way online users can be tracked is by using an indirect method for gathering information on Internet server log files (Kotz, 1998). Each person's Web browser transmits certain information to Web servers, such as the IP address of the user's computer system as well as the brand name and version number of the user's Web browser and operating system software. For example, when people visit a website, their information is automatically sent to the website server in order to identify how often a person has visited the website, or to gain information pertaining to which Web browser or operating system people typically use. Thus, the indirect methods constitute a more serious form of invasion of privacy. Unfortunately, when respondents think about Web-based research, the potential invasion of privacy caused by these indirect methods may be the reason they are unwilling to participate in the research.

There is no solution to prevent this latter type of invasion of privacy, because it is not illegal for organizations to use the methodology (Tavani, 2000). Fortunately, indirect methods of gathering information are expensive and are not frequently used in traditional research. In general, researchers should explain how they are collecting data and steps taken to protect privacy. For instance, an IP address does not identify an individual, unless the person identifies himself or herself as the user (Im & Chee, 2002). In this case the IP address is unknown unless the user allows access for other users to obtain his/her IP address. Therefore the organization (or other user) receives the data, but the person's name is unidentifiable, which allows a higher level of privacy. Researchers should make it a point to explain this to the examinee, in case the person is concerned about being identified.

Internet cookies. Private online businesses can monitor the activities of people who visit their websites, determine how frequently these people visit each site and draw conclusions about the preferences of those visitors when accessing their sites through the use of Internet cookies (Tavani, 2000). Internet cookies are ways in which online businesses can store and retrieve information about a user who visits their websites, typically without the user's knowledge or consent. An example of cookies is when you connect to the Internet or go to a specific website and certain pop-up screens appear. These screens are different Web pages that suddenly open up on your desktop when you visit a particular website, and are based on the preferences located by your cookies. Cookies have generated a large controversy (Tavani, 2000), because a person's browsing preferences can be stored on the individual's computer hard drive and retrieved by the organization whenever the person visits their website. Defenders of cookies maintain they are performing a service for repeat customers, by providing the user with a list of preferences for future visits to that website. Some may see this as an invasion of privacy because these organizations are saving information on the computer without the person's knowledge.

A solution to this issue is that more current versions of website browsers allow a user to disable cookies (Tavani, 2000). This way the website needs to ask a person whether the cookies can be downloaded onto the computer. In this situation the person could refuse to ever receive cookies from websites, and therefore be private in their browsing preferences. It is also a good way for a person to track which websites they give permission to install cookies, and gives the person control over which preferences they wish to emit to websites.

Data exchanging. Although an organization can only access cookie-related information from their individual website, it can exchange this data with other companies to access more information about a particular user. This ethical concern is known as data exchanging (Tavani, 2000). The exchange of online personal information often involves the sale of such data to third parties, which has resulted in commercial profits for certain online entrepreneurs—often without the knowledge and consent of the individuals whose information has been exchanged. Organizations can sell or trade information about people with other companies to gain a larger audience. An example would be when a person visits a particular website, and then gets a barrage of emails from multiple companies' websites he/she has never visited. Many people object to having their information used this way. For instance, Cranor, Reagle and Ackerman (1999) examined this phenomenon and found that, although people wanted to have a tailored and quicker experience while on the Internet, they did not want this speed, if it meant that information would be shared between companies without the person's consent. Participants in Internet research should be aware of the degree of privacy an organizational researcher will provide them. If participants feel the organization exchanges information with other companies, that person may not want to participate in any research.

A solution to this issue is to let the respondent know that the researcher views personal privacy as an important issue and has taken steps to ensure it. Sites that post a privacy policy, privacy seal of approval and whether they disclose a data retention program are viewed as important to respondents (Cranor et al., 1999). These terms are ways in which companies can express how they protect personal information about the participant. For instance, a researcher in an organization may explain his/her privacy policy as one in which no information is transferred to other organizations or people. The researcher can post an official privacy stamp to further corroborate privacy intentions. Finally, the researcher can explain how he/she retains the data and who has access to it through a data retention program (i.e., not participating in data-exchanging). Respondents view this as important because the company is showing concern for the person's data (Cranor et al., 1999).

Confidentiality

An issue closely related to privacy is confidentiality. Confidentiality, as stated in the APA guidelines principle 9-J (APA, 1982), is as follows:

Information obtained about a research participant during the course of an investigation is confidential unless otherwise agreed upon in advance. When the possibility exists that others may obtain access to such information, this possibility, together with the plans for protecting confidentiality, is explained to the participant as part of the procedure for obtaining informed consent (p. 7).

Thus, confidentiality refers to who should have access to data. The researcher must assure the participant that the data collected from them will be safeguarded. That is, the information collected from the participant will not be disclosed to the public in a way that could identify the participant's results. The respondent should be told what the results will be used for and who will have access to them. Confidentiality is very important among respondents pertaining to Internet surveys (Homer & Saari, 1997), as opposed to traditional paper-and-pencil based surveys. In turn, these concerns have been found to lead to lower response rates among electronic respondents (Sproull, 1986; Kiesler & Sproull, 1986). There is a need to set and establish unambiguous rules of access and security to prevent the data from falling into inappropriate hands (Baron & Austin, 2000). The next few paragraphs discuss issues pertaining to confidentiality in Web research.

Tracing results. Many people feel the computer can monitor and identify specific individuals' responses. This is known as the Big Brother Syndrome (Rosenfeld & Booth-Kewley, 1996). That is, individuals believe there is no confidentiality on the Internet, because they believe organizations can keep track of anything that is sent to the organization's server. For instance, a person may not feel safe taking an Internet survey from home, because he/she feels the organization can identify individual responses through the computer or collect personal information. These people also feel someone can always gain access to personal information through the computer, even without the consent of the person. This is an important issue; a person may not participate in research, because he/she feels the answers are not confidential and the organization will use these results against him/her.

A solution is difficult in this scenario. If a person is convinced that, no matter what, his/her personal information will not be confidential, then it is difficult to convince him/

her otherwise. These people will most likely self-select themselves out of the experiment. This may be seen as a benefit to an organization, because, if people are concerned about these issues and they participate in the research, they may answer questions in a socially desirable manner. By self-selecting themselves out of the experiment, their socially-desirable responses will not contaminate the data and meaningful results will have a better chance of being found. This is a problem for organizational research, because it might not be reflective how the person feels and therefore adds no constructive data to the results. Socially-desirable responding has been shown to occur in organizational research and influences the validity of the results (Douglas, McDaniel, & Snell, 1996). A possible solution for convincing participants of their confidentiality is to suggest they take the Web-based survey on a computer other than their own. The researcher could set aside a few computers people could use within the organization, or the researcher could suggest places like a library or an Internet café where the respondent could participate. This is so the person understands that the computer being used is not able to identify the individual. By offering these suggestions, the person may feel his/her responses to the Web-based research are more confidential. However, other researchers suggest that Web responses may actually be more honest, presumably because the Web is more anonymous (particularly on personal or sensitive topics (Levine, Ancill, & Roberts, 1989). For example, Ployhart, Weekley, Holtz and Kemp (2002) found Web responses by applicants were much less extreme than paper-and-pencil responses by applicants. We consider this discrepancy later in this chapter.

Unauthorized access. Another concern in Web research is to maintain the confidentiality of results by preventing access from unauthorized sources, such as a hacker. This problem takes the previous issue into account and broadens it to the rest of the Internet community. As opposed to the organization gaining access to results, this issue deals with anyone who is unauthorized to view the results. This is again a problem in Web research because a person may not participate in Web-based research, if he/she feels other people can access his/her information.

A solution to this problem is to make sure certain steps are taken to ensure the confidentiality of the results. For instance, companies should set up a firewall, encrypt data and fully explain precautions taken to ensure confidentiality. Researchers should consider using a firewall and explain to the respondent that this is in place to protect information and eliminate unauthorized access to proprietary and confidential information. Another possible step is to encrypt the data, ensuring an individual's response is kept anonymous. Encryption is the coding of information so that only those who know the code will be able to decipher it. This will not stop an unauthorized person from gaining information, but it discourages them from investigating the data and they are more likely to make a mistake in decoding the information. The uses of firewalls and data encryption are ways for the researcher to keep the results of the organizational research confidential, but they are not foolproof. Thus, the first step is to set up these precautionary measures to protect the data (i.e., firewalls and data encryption). The second step is to explain to participants the steps taken in securing their information (i.e., how firewalls and data encryption will protect their information). This will hopefully make it more likely more likely for participants to answer honestly.

Anonymity

Anonymity is the condition of being unidentifiable, as opposed to confidentiality, which pertains to the protection of a person's data. Research has suggested that it is impossible to gain complete anonymity over the Internet because of technologies such as cookies, IP addresses and Internet server log files (Weckert, 2000). Some describe anonymity with respect to a certain audience as a key factor in Internet research (Weckert, 2000). For example, in organizational research, the researcher may be able to identify the individual respondent, but when reporting the overall results to management, no individual is identified. In this example, the respondent is anonymous with respect to the organization and anyone else for that matter, but not with respect to the researcher.

From the perspective of IRBs, if there is any possibility of identifying a person, the data collection is not anonymous. We have found it difficult to obtain complete anonymity through any research method. Let us take two examples to understand the discrepancy; one is based on a paper-and-pencil survey and the other on a Web-based survey. Say a person is filling out an unidentifiable paper-and-pencil survey in a room; he or she is considered anonymous if no identifying information is collected. But, if the same survey is filled out over the Internet, many believe this is no longer anonymous, because there are ways to track which person completed which survey.

We offer two solutions to maximize anonymity of participants. The first, as suggested in the confidentiality section, is to suggest the person participates in the Web-based research on a computer other than his/her own. The researcher should explain to the participant that he/she is not interested in identifying their individual results. If the person is still concerned about anonymity, he/she can take the assessment on an alternate computer (i.e., in the company, in the library or at an Internet café). The other suggestion is to use non-identifying questions, which is used in organizational research as a way to track responses over multiple assessments. In this scenario, the survey asks respondents to generate an anonymous code number. This way the person's data can be linked across time, but no two people would have the exact same code number, and no person could be identified. The more non-identifying questions asked, the more anonymous the person is.

Informed Consent

Informed consent happens prior to participation, when the researcher and the participant enter into an agreement that clarifies the obligation and responsibilities of each. This is an important part of ethical research, because the participant trusts that the researcher has reasonably explained everything that will occur to him/her during the experiment. This way the participant can make an informed decision, pertaining to whether they would still like to participate in the study. The informed consent process involves two components: (a) relating the purpose of the study and the subject's role and (b) ensuring the information is comprehended and obtained voluntarily from participants.

The first component essentially involves the issue of disclosure of information. Disclosure involves the researcher explaining why the research is being conducted and what the respondent's involvement will be. The disclosure portion also answers any questions a respondent might have about the research, and specifically what his/her role will be.

The second component focuses on the actual informed consent form. This form explains what will be asked of the participants during the study, and gives them the option of not participating. After reading all information pertaining to the study, the person must sign the form to give informed consent. Sometimes when in the presence of the researcher, it is difficult for organizational participants to truly feel the research is optional. For example, supervisors may be responsible for the actual collection of data, and participants may feel considerable pressure to participate in the research, because they feel there will be negative consequences if they do not. The Internet allows power imbalances such as this to be reduced, because there is no supervisor or researcher physically present when the decision must be made to participate.

Informed consent is a major problem in Web-based organizational research, because the researcher is not present, as opposed to traditional methods in which the researcher is present. This absence of the researcher brings up many issues.

No physical signature. The researcher is not able to collect a signed informed consent from the participants, because the person is taking the assessment online. When dealing with paper-and-pencil research, the person is able to sign the informed consent form and hand it in. But when dealing with Internet research, there is no form to sign. As stated in the "Code of Federal Regulations" (Title 45, Part 46.117), the individual must physically sign the documentation of informed consent. The use of Internet transmissions makes it virtually impossible to receive a signed informed consent form, so steps need to be taken to ensure that an equivalent form of signed consent is provided.

A solution to this problem can be the use of a multistep consent process. In the first step, explicitly state in the body of the informed consent form that by completing the survey/test online, the person is giving informed consent for the researchers to collect and analyze the information. Following the reading of the informed consent, we propose there should be a check box, which states the person understands all the information required of him/her during the session. Check boxes are the same as an inventory sheet in which a mark is placed in a box to show that a person has read the statement. So, the person clicks on the box to mark it and the computer can check whether this box has been marked or not. If this box is not checked, the person cannot move forward in the survey. Only when the box is checked will the person be allowed to participate. The phone number and email of the main researcher should also be provided on the informed consent page, and the person will be told that he/she will not able to move forward in the session until he/she checks that he/she understands the contact information and will use it if need be.

Proof. Since the informed consent is provided over the Internet, there is no clear proof that the person actually read all the relevant information. This is an ethical concern, because without the researcher there to explain important issues, one can never be sure the person actually understands these issues and makes an informed decision when giving consent.

A solution to this problem is again through the use of check boxes. Though the informed consent may be a couple of pages long explaining all the details of the study and the rights of the participant, by using check boxes a researcher can make sure the participant at least read the line that was checked. For instance, a researcher can add a check box at the end of the informed consent that states, "I understand why this research is being conducted, and I still want to participate." If the participant does not mark this check box, that person cannot move forward in the session until contacting the main researcher. Again, the main researcher's phone number and email should be provided in the informed consent.

Conveying information. A third issue with informed consent over the Internet involves how consent information is conveyed. In traditional methods, the researcher is present to explain the study and clear up any misconceptions people may have. When conducting traditional research, before the session begins the investigator is there to disclose as much information as possible to the respondent, as well as answer any questions that may arise due to concerns about the study. This is not as easy in Internet research, because the information is written and the researcher is not physically present. A problem occurs when conducting Internet research because the investigator is not present to answer any questions the respondent might have before giving his/her informed consent to participate. This may violate the APA ethical principle 9-D (APA, 1982), which is as follows:

The investigator must inform the participants of all aspects of the research that might reasonably be expected to influence willingness to participate and explain all other aspects of the research about which the participants inquire (pp. 5-6).

Since the researcher is not actually present, he/she is unable to explain all aspects about which the participants inquire. This is an ethical problem because the person must understand all information pertaining to the study in order to give his/her informed consent.

A solution to this situation would be to not let people continue on in the study, until they communicate to the main researcher any questions or concerns they may have and convey their understanding through the use of check boxes. Schmidt (1997) agrees with this stance and feels the person should not be allowed to submit results until he/she has read and agreed with the informed consent. The main difference in our particular solution is to not let the person see the survey until all the participants' questions have been answered and he/she gives informed consent. Then the person must check a box explaining that he/she has no further questions about the study, because he/she understands what is asked and gives informed consent to be a research participant.

Debriefing

The debriefing occurs after the research session is over. This involves explaining any deception used in the session and answering any questions the respondent might have pertaining to the study. The debriefing is critical because the respondent needs to leave the session understanding why the research was important, how it adds to scientific understanding and to clarify any misconceptions the person may have pertaining to the study. An ethical problem arises in Internet research, because the researcher is not there to explain any deception, nor is the researcher there to answer any questions the participant might have about the study.

Do participants read the debriefing? Since the debriefing is provided over the Internet, there is no physical way to know if the person actually read all the relevant information to understand the purpose of the study. Thus a key purpose for the debriefing is to clear up misconceptions the person may have had during the study or explain any deception used. For instance, say the organizational research involved telling people the company was changing its business practices, and the researcher was interested in the adaptability of the employees. Adaptability is the ability to change work habits given the situation encountered (Pulakos, Arad, Donovan, & Plamondon, 2000), so the more adaptable a person is the more likely he/she would succeed, if the business changed its practices. During the debriefing, let's say the researcher explicitly states that results show specific skills as being deficient throughout the company and training sessions are required for everyone to learn these skills. If the debriefing is written and the researcher is not present to explain that everyone, no matter how they scored on the specific skills, will need training in deficient areas, the person may feel he/she scored low. This person may withdraw from learning these new skills because he/she is embarrassed or upset with being singled out, and the person may not participate in any future research because of this misunderstanding.

A solution to this problem would be to again use check boxes to highlight any concerns the researcher must address. For instance, in the above situation, the debriefing may state the purpose of training sessions and then at the end of the debriefing would be a line that says, "I understand that training sessions will be required for deficient skill sets in the overall organization and not because of individual scores," followed by a check box. Or a generic statement could be used, such as "I understand the purpose of this study, and I understand how my responses will be protected and used," followed by a check box. If the person does not check the box, he/she will be prompted to contact the main researcher to answer any further questions, and then submit results. These check boxes are used to highlight the important areas of the debriefing, so if the person does not read the whole debriefing, he/she will at least have to pay attention to the statements with the check boxes. If questions arise in these one-sentence statements, the person can go back and read the debriefing to clarify any misconceptions. If his/her concerns are not completely addressed, the main researcher's phone number and email are provided.

Summary of Ethical Issues

As shown in Table 2, there are many ethical issues when using the Internet for research in an organizational setting. Each section has provided suggestions to increase the likelihood that research will be conducted as ethically as possible, and reviews of the study by the IRB will go as quickly as possible. This is clearly important for organizational research because of the time, money and availability constraints we noted earlier. The following case study describes different ways we have addressed some of the main issues in Internet research, as well as the challenges of working with both IRBs and organizations.

CASE STUDY

A university was in the process of undergoing a changeover to a new accounting system. The employees were to be given a training session to explain why the new system was being implemented and how to use it. We were asked by the university to administer a survey, before and after the training session, to measure the employee's adaptability, readiness for change and how they coped with change. They asked us to administer it over the Internet, because participants were geographically dispersed, the university was constrained by expense and training occurred at different times. They also did not want employees feeling they were coerced into participating; this way the research could remain truly voluntary. To make matters more interesting, the first training session was occurring within two weeks of when they notified us about the survey. We were not surprised at the short notice because, in our experience, a company usually asks for research when a problem occurs, and management wants the problem fixed immediately. Thus, we found many of the issues raised in Table 1 present in this instance, making the Internet an attractive research methodology.

Survey. The Web survey used was located on a remote server and contained self-report measures and demographic questions. The completed surveys were sent to a spreadsheet file on the remote server and were only accessible by the primary researcher.

The employees were sent an email with a link to an Internet survey on a remote server, separate from the company. At the beginning of the survey, the main researcher's name, telephone number and email address were presented. To alleviate ethical concerns about informed consent and debriefing, the participants were told that if they did not understand any part of the research study, they were to call or email the main researcher before moving forward with the study.

The first page explained the purpose of the research, why they were asked to complete the survey and how we were going to report the results. In the opening paragraphs, we stressed that by filling out this survey, employees could convey their thoughts about the university, whether positive or negative. This was their chance to have their voice heard, but heard in the context of a group, not individually. They were told that if they did not want to participate in the survey, all they had to do was press cancel on the screen and the survey would not be used. By clicking the cancel button, all information that had previously been recorded was lost because none of the information was saved until the person submitted the survey. They were also told the steps taken to ensure confidentiality (results placed on a remote server in no way connected to the organization, no identifying information asked, data only reported at group level not individual, etc.). At the end the respondents were told to email or call the main researcher if they had any questions pertaining to the research and/or survey.

Two months later, the same employees were sent the post-training survey regardless of whether they participated in the first survey. The same nonidentifying information questions were used, and nobody was excluded from participating in the second collection. Respondents were told that even if they had not participated before, their responses were still valued.

Ethical concerns and solutions. The first ethical dilemma we faced was the ability to connect people from time 1 to time 2 without having identifying information to link up responses. We considered just assigning random ID numbers to each person, but thought people would not remember their ID number from time one to time two. We decided, with suggestions from the organization, on using a question block of nonidentifying information to generate individual code numbers, based on the month and day of one's birth, followed by one's mother's maiden name.

The IRB felt that people would be too easily identified using this information, so we needed to change it. Working jointly with the IRB, we agreed on using a block of four nonidentifying questions that included: year you received your highest degree (four digits), number of years employed at the university (two digits), day of the month of your birthday (two digits) and favorite color. We figured it would be virtually impossible to identify individuals through these questions, and no two responses would be completely identical.

Besides the nonidentifying information, the ethical concerns raised by the IRB involved the need to explain to the participants that even though steps had been taken to ensure confidentiality (e.g., no identifying information, organization did not have access, etc.), we could not guarantee full confidentiality or anonymity. So, in response to the IRB requests, we wrote in the explanation of the study "While it is understood that no computer transmission can be perfectly secure, reasonable efforts will be made to protect the confidentiality of your transmission."

Another ethical concern from the IRB was the issue of obtaining informed consent. As per their request, we stated in the informed consent form that by continuing on with the survey, the person was giving the researchers consent to collect and analyze his/her results.

We found the IRB's comments to be valuable and constructive. However, the major problem we encountered was that the IRB had a policy that any information that was not completely anonymous (including all information sent over the Internet) had to go through a full review. This was a major concern for us, because with the training session being conducted the next week, the study would not get approved in time. This happens a great deal in organizational research because the investigator is at the mercy of when the organization is ready to survey its participants. But, if the IRB takes longer than expected to review the proposal, the researcher loses the opportunity because the organization cannot wait. As it turned out, we were lucky that the IRB was able to meet and discuss the study earlier than expected. It was, however, approved two days after the study was supposed to start. We were again lucky because the organization was willing to wait. This is not usually the case and we sometimes lose great opportunities for that reason.

At the conclusion of the study, the debriefing was provided to address any ethical concerns the participant might have had. The phone number and email of the main researcher was provided, and any questions the person had were to be addressed directly by him.

IMPROVEMENTS OVER TRADITIONAL RESEARCH

At this point one might wonder whether Web research in organizations is worth all of the practical and ethical difficulties. Beyond general benefits listed in Table 1, we have identified three improvements of Web-based research over traditional research, which may make such efforts worthwhile. The first benefit deals with the freedom of the respondent to decline to participate; the second is finding that Internet research may improve the truthfulness of participant's responses and the third is the ease of giving individual feedback.

The first improvement deals with the pressure to participate in a research experiment. The use of Internet research is an improvement over traditional methods with respect to APA ethical principle 9-F (APA, 1982), which states:

"The investigator respects the individual's freedom to decline to participate in or to withdraw from the research at any time. The obligation to protect this freedom requires careful thought and consideration when the investigator is in a position of authority or influence over the participant."

This principle was created so that people who are not comfortable participating in an experiment are free to leave whenever they wish. Forcing a person to participate in research is unethical and may corrupt the results because the person will probably not answer truthfully. In traditional research the participant is usually in a room with a number of other participants, and it may be difficult to decline to participate as the classic Asch (1955) studies on conformity demonstrate. The improvement in Internet research is that the participant is not participating in a group setting. Instead, the person is alone at a computer, so no outside influences are coercing him/her to continue with the research. This is important for organizational research because, as stated earlier, the organization usually wants to fix a problem; and if a person does not feel comfortable participating in the study, they might not answer the questions in an appropriate manner.

The second improvement involves the amount of self-disclosure participants are willing to do over the Internet. Studies have found increased levels of self-disclosure, when tests are administered through a computer as opposed to an actual person— particularly assessments on personal or sensitive topics (Levine, Ancill, & Roberts, 1988; Locke & Gilbert, 1995). This means that individuals are more open about their feelings when answering questions on a computer.

As stated earlier, companies mainly conduct research after a problem has already occurred. By finding out the best way to get true responses (how the employee actually feels) as opposed to socially desirable responses (how the employee feels the organization wants him/her to answer), the organization can focus on what areas need to be changed. If people are more self-disclosing over the Internet, then participants will rate a higher level of negative responses, and the organization will be better able to identify problem areas. However, we discussed in earlier sections how other research suggests people may respond more/less honestly when answering questions over the Web. We acknowledge this discrepancy as an important area for future research in the next section.

The third improvement involves the ease of sending participants individual feedback. Many times in organizational research, the respondent fills out an assessment tool, the investigator analyzes the data, sends overall results to the management in the organization and the respondent never hears about the study again. One consequence is that the respondent has no motivation to participate in the research, except for the fact that someone is telling him/her to do so. This goes back to the argument that if the person does not want to participate, he/she will not answer honestly, which in turn does not add to the research. For example, an employee in a company is asked to fill out a survey about the culture in the workplace and how his/her values fit with the overall organization's culture. He/she may fill out the survey because it was mandatory, but knowing that he/she will never receive results, he/she may not look at the experience as constructive or beneficial.

Of course, with traditional research, the investigator could give individual feedback to each employee, but this would cost time and money. With Web-based research individual feedback could be given through email, which may show overall results, or even how the person ranked in comparison to the average scores. An important requirement of this is to prepare a couple of generic statements explaining what the results mean, so the respondent understands the scores. A way to implement this method would be to add a question that asks whether the person would like individual feedback and, if so, include his/her email address. This gives the individual a reason to answer truthfully, which in turn helps the company receive constructive results. Of course, one must use caution with this approach and be sure to comply with the APA standards (1999).

UNANSWERED QUESTIONS
FOR FUTURE RESEARCH

This final section of the chapter raises some ethical questions that need to be researched to better understand the ethical use of Web-based organizational research. Such issues include the disclosure-reciprocity effect, a pattern of distrust on the Internet and differences in on-site v. off-site assessments. An overview of these issues is shown in Table 3.

Table 3: Implications and Suggestions for Future Research

Focus of Future Research	Questions to Address
• Disclosure reciprocity effect	• Do people answer more honestly when they feel everything has been disclosed to them about the security of their information over the Internet? • Do more people self-select themselves out of the study when they are alone as opposed to being in a group?
• Curvilinear pattern of distrust for the Internet	• Are people who know a large amount or a very little amount of information about the Internet less likely to feel their data is anonymous and confidential online?
• On-site v. off-site assessment	• Are there score differences between people who take assessment tools over the Internet within the organization as opposed to outside of the organization? • Are there more negative responses on survey's completed from home as opposed to on the job?

Disclosure-Reciprocity Effect

As we noted above, people unsure about what can happen with their information over the Internet may not participate in Web-based research, or if they do, they may not answer truthfully. This phenomenon may be explained by the disclosure-reciprocity effect (Berg, 1987; Miller, 1990; Reis & Shaver, 1988), which is the tendency for one person's intimacy of self-disclosure to match that of a conversational partner (Berg, 1987). In other words, we reveal more to those who have been open to us. If ethical concerns and safeguards of Internet research are not explained to the respondent by the investigator, then that person may be unwilling to fully disclose him/herself in the research, as opposed to the respondent who feels the investigator is being totally honest, by explaining the negative and positive points of the research. In this case, the person might either drop out because he/she feels the negative effects outweigh the positive effects, or answer honestly because everything has been explained to them. Ethical research requires full disclosure and future research should test whether people answer more honestly when the information about the security of responses over the Internet is fully disclosed, or whether they are more likely to decline to participate.

Curvilinear Pattern of Distrust

Another important issue for research is whether there is a curvilinear pattern of distrust for the Internet. First, people who have a lot of knowledge about the Internet understand how unsecure most information sent online really is. These people may be very distrustful because of this knowledge. Therefore, are people who have considerable knowledge about the Internet and understand the security issues more distrusting about research on the Internet, than people who have only a moderate understanding? Second, people who have practically no knowledge about the Internet may have overexaggerated preconceptions about what information can be accessed via the Internet, such as the Big Brother Syndrome (Rosenfeld & Booth-Kewley, 1996). Therefore, are people who have very little knowledge about the Internet more distrustful than people who have an average amount of knowledge? This proposed relationship is displayed in Figure 2. As shown, the people who are at the high or low end of "Knowledge of the Internet" would be at the high end of "Distrust for the Internet," but people who have an average or moderate level of "Knowledge of the Internet" would be at the low end of "Distrust for the Internet."

Research has found that as people become more familiar with computers, their lack of distrust with using it grows smaller (Dwight & Feigelson, 2000). However, research has also found that the computer might serve as a bogus pipeline (Jones & Sigall, 1971), in which the participant has the perception that the computer can identify response distortion (Kantor, 1991; Martin & Nagao, 1989; Rosenfeld & Booth-Kewley, 1996). Therefore, there might be less socially desirable responding for individuals with less computer experience or knowledge about the computer's actual capabilities. Although this has been proposed as a possibility, we know of no research that has directly tested this proposition.

Figure 2: The Curvilinear Relationship Between Knowledge of the Internet and Distrust for the Internet

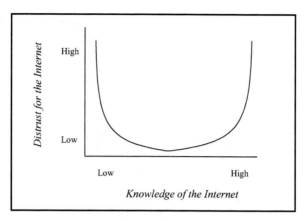

On-Site v. Off-Site

A major issue in organizational Internet research involves the place where the assessment occurs. For this discussion we will use on-site for within the company and off-site for anywhere outside of the organization.

One major problem with on-site Web-based research is that different sites have more/less access to computers, which could cause a problem in test space and time (Cowan, 2001). Tavani (2000) points out that people who fill out survey research in the office are more concerned that responses will be identified. This is mainly because the computers used are office property and therefore legally organizational property as shown in recent court cases (e.g., McMorris, 1995). A controversial issue dealing with off-site Web-based assessment is 24-hour access. A person can take the assessment from home, work, school or even a cyber net café (Baron & Austin, 2000). This is beneficial for the applicant because he/she can take the assessment in a comfortable environment and does not have to work his/her schedule around a specific test time. From an organizational perspective, this has many benefits because the participant is comfortable in his/her environment and may be more likely to respond truthfully. The drawbacks are that the person may not be paying as much attention to the survey because he/she is not at work taking it.

There has yet to be research on whether people feel more secure or anonymous when filling out survey information on-site versus off-site. Future research should look into the whether this effects survey research in an organization. Specifically, are people who take a survey within the organization more likely to respond in a positive light because of the fear of results being traced back to them, as opposed to people who complete the survey from home?

CONCLUSION

The preceding paper describes challenges and solutions we have developed to ensure our organizational research abides by ethical standards. In working with the IRB, issues arose that are not explicitly explained in the APA "Ethical Principles" or the "Code of Federal Regulations." The relevant issues were adapted to fit with organizational Internet research that is currently being conducted in the field.

It is important in organizational research to have involvement from the respondents on ways to improve upon the steps taken. As stressed throughout this chapter, the more comfortable and understanding the respondent is to the purpose of research, the more willing he/she is to participate. The more involved and informed the participants are in the process, the more constructive and meaningful the research and results will be.

We hope these guidelines help other researchers conduct ethical research in organizations, when using the Internet as an assessment tool. Taking Figure 1 into account, if the researcher can at least ensure the ethical treatment of participants through using the Internet, he/she can work better with organizational constraints and ultimately add to the scientific knowledge of human behavior in organizations.

REFERENCES

American Psychological Association. (1982). *Ethical Principles: In the Conduct of Research with Human Participants.* Washington, DC: American Psychological Association.

American Psychological Association. (1999). Ethical principles of psychologists and code of conduct. *American Psychologist, 47,* 1597-1611.

American Psychological Association. (2001). *Publication Manual of the American Psychological Association* (5 ed.). Washington, DC: American Psychological Association.

Asch, S.E. (1955, November). Opinions and social pressure. *Scientific American,* 192, 31-35.

Baron, H. & Austin, J. (2000). *Measuring ability over the Internet: opportunities and issues.* Paper presented at the 16th annual conference of the Society of Industrial and Organizational Psychology, New Orleans, Louisiana, USA.

Benassi, P. (1999). TRUSTe: An online privacy seal program. *Communications of the ACM, 42,* 56-59.

Berg, J. H. (1987). Responsiveness and self-disclosure. In V. J. Derlega & J. H. Berg (Eds.), *Self-Disclosure: Theory, Research, and Therapy* (pp. 3-35). New York: Plenum.

Bickman, L., Rog, D. J., & Hedrick, T. E. (1998). Applied research design: A practical approach. In L. Bickman & D. J. Rog (Eds.), *Handbook of Applied Social Research Methods* (pp. 26-55). Thousand Oaks, CA: Sage Publications.

Cascio, W. F. (1995). Whither industrial and organizational psychology in a changing world of work? *American Psychologist, 50,* 928-939.

Cascio, W. F. (ed.). (1998). *Applied Psychology in Human Resource Management* (5th ed.). Upper Saddle River, NJ: Prentice Hall.

Church, A. H. (2001). Is there a method to our madness? The impact of data collection methodology on organizational survey results. *Personnel Psychology, 54,* 937-969.

Cowan, R. (2001). Tests, but no papers: Following a trial in Northern Ireland could all exams soon be taken online. *The Guardian,* 3-4.

Cranor, L. F., Reagle, J., & Ackerman, M. (1999 March 25). *Beyond Concern: Understanding Net Users' Attitudes about Online Privacy* (Tech. Rep. TR 99.4.1). Florham Park, NJ: AT&T Labs-Research.

Douglas, E. F., McDaniel, M. A., & Snell, E. F. (1996). *The validity of non-cognitive measures decays when applicants fake.* Paper presented at the annual conference of the Academy of Management, Cincinnati, Ohio, USA.

Dwight, S. A. & Feigelson, M. E. (2000). A quantitative review of the effort of computerized testing on the measurement of social desirability. *Educational and Psychological Measurement, 60,* 340-360.

Hammer, M. & Champy, J. (1996). Reengineering the corporation: The enabling role of information technology. In J. M. Shafritz & J. S. Ott (Eds.), *Classics of Organization Theory* (4th ed., pp. 607-617). Fort Worth, TX: Harcourt Brace College Publishers.

Homer, L. E. & Saari, L. M. (1997). *So many techniques: So many issues.* Paper presented at the Society for Industrial and Organizational Psychology, St. Louis, Missouri, USA.

Im, E. & Chee, W. (2002). Issues in protection of human subjects in Internet research. *Nursing Research, 51,* 266-269.

Jones, E. E. & Sigall, H. (1971). The bogus pipeline: A new paradigm for measuring affect and attitude. *Psychological Bulletin, 76,* 349-364.

Kantor, J. (1991). The effects of computer administration and identification on the Job Descriptive Index (JDI). *Journal of Business and Psychology, 5,* 309-323.

Kiesler, S. & Sproull, L. S. (1986). Response effects in the electronic survey. *Public Opinion Quarterly, 50,* 402-413.

Kotz, D. (1998). Technological implications for privacy. In J. H. Moor (Ed.), *Proceedings of the Conference on the Tangled Web: Ethical Dilemmas of the Internet.*

Levine, S., Ancill, R. J., & Roberts, A. (1989). Assessment of suicide risk by computer-delivered self-rating questionnaire: Preliminary findings. *Acta Psychiatrica Scandinavica, 80,* 216-220.

Lievens, F. & Harris, M. M. (2003). Research on Internet recruitment and testing: Current status and future directions. In C. L. Cooper & I. T. Robertson (Eds.), *International Review of Industrial and Organizational Psychology,* Vol. 18 (pp.131-165). Chicester, UK: John Wiley & Sons.

Martin, C. L. & Nagao, D. H. (1989). Some effects of computerized interviewing on job applicant responses. *Journal of Applied Psychology, 74,* 72-80.

McMorris, F. A. (1995, February 28). Is office voice mail private? Don't bet on it. *The Wall Street Journal,* p. B1.

Mehta, R. & Sivadas, E. (1995). Comparing response rates and response content in mail versus electronic mail surveys. *Journal of the Market Research Society, 37,* 428-439.

Miller, L. C. (1990). Intimacy and liking: mutual influence and the role of unique relationships. *Journal of Personality and Social Psychology, 59,* 50-60.

Nissenbaum, H. (1997). Can we protect privacy in public. In M. J. Van den Hoven (Ed.), *Proceedings of the Conference on Computer Ethics: Philosophical Enquiry: CEPE 97* (pp. 191-204). Rotterdam: Erasmus University Press.

Ployhart, R. E., Weekley, J., Holtz, B., & Kemp, C. (2002). *Web-based vs. paper-and-pencil testing: Are test scores comparable across applicants and incumbents?* Paper presented at the 17ᵗʰ annual conference of the Society of Industrial and Organizational Psychology, Toronto, Canada.

Pulakos, E. D., Arad, S., Donovan, M. A., & Plamondon, K. E. (2000). Adaptability in the workplace: Development of a taxonomy of adaptive performance. *Journal of Applied Psychology, 85,* 612-624.

Reis, H. T. & Shaver, P. (1988). Intimacy as an interpersonal process. In S. Duck (Ed.), *Handbook of Personal Relationships: Theory, Relationships and Interventions* (pp. 469-486). Chichester, UK: John Wiley & Sons.

Rosenfeld, P. & Booth-Kewley, S. (1996). Impression management and computer surveys in organizations. In J. W. Beard (Ed.), *Impression Management and Information Technology* (pp. 119-131). Westport, CT: Quorum Books.

Schmidt, W. C. (1997). World-Wide Web survey research: Benefits, potential problems, and solutions. *Behavior Research Methods, Instruments, & Computers, 29,* 274-279.

Sieber, J. E. (1998). Planning ethically responsible research. In L. Bickman & D. J. Rog (Eds.), *Handbook of Applied Social Research Methods* (pp.127-156). Thousand Oaks, CA: Sage Publications.

Smith, M. A. & Leigh, B. (1997). Virtual subjects: Using the Internet as an alternative source of subjects and research environment. *Behavior Research Methods, Instruments, & Computers, 29,* 496-505.

Sproull, L. S. (1986). Using electronic mail for data collection in organizational research. *Academy of Management Journal, 29,* 159-169.

Standards for Educational and Psychological Testing. (1999). Washington, DC: American Educational Research Association.

Stanton, J. M. (1998). An empirical assessment of data collection using the Internet. *Personnel Psychology, 51,* 709-725.

Tavani, H. T. (2000). Privacy and security. In D. Langford (Ed.), *Internet Ethics* (pp. 65-95). New York: St. Martin's Press.

Weckert, J. (2000). What is new or unique about Internet activities? In D. Langford (Ed.), *Internet Ethics* (pp. 47-64). New York: St. Martin's Press.

Wright, M. & Kakalik, J. (1997). The erosion of privacy. *Computers and Society, 27,* 22-25.

Yost, P. R. & Homer, L. E. (April, 1998). *Electronic versus paper surveys: Does the medium affect the response?* Presented at the 13ᵗʰ annual conference of the Society of Industrial and Organizational Psychology, Dallas, Texas, USA.

ENDNOTE

[1]   Note that our primary focus in this chapter is on situations where the primary researcher is not directly affiliated with the organization or an employee of the organization, but is rather somebody external to the company (e.g., academic researcher, consultant. This is in contrast to research conducted by members who are internal employees of an organization (e.g., managers). There are some important differences between these two contexts, and while our chapter is relevant to both, it is most directly applicable to external individuals conducting research for organizations.

Section III

Researchers/Researched?
Research Ethics in Practice

Chapter IX

Conducting Ethical Research Online: Respect for Individuals, Identities and the Ownership of Words

Lynne Roberts
University of Western Australia, Australia

Leigh Smith
Curtin University of Technology, Australia

Clare Pollock
Curtin University of Technology, Australia

ABSTRACT

Online research introduces new ethical issues inherent to the medium. In this chapter we provide a case study of online research in action, focusing on the ethical issues of conducting qualitative research within virtual environments. The case study provides an example of how research can be conducted within virtual environments with the consent of research participants and their community, without compromising their confidentiality, violating their assumptions of privacy or infringing upon their copyright entitlements.

INTRODUCTION

Online research introduces new ethical issues inherent to the medium. As Jones (1994) noted, ethical dilemmas arise when attempts are made to translate existing ethical guidelines to online research. In this chapter we present a case study of online research, focusing on the ethical issues of conducting qualitative research within text-based virtual environments. The research described is a Grounded Theory study (Glaser & Strauss, 1967) of social interaction in multi-user dimensions, object oriented (MOOs), Internet-chat environments, with the researcher as participant observer. The focus is on the process, rather than the results of the research. Research findings from this study have been published and presented elsewhere (Roberts, Smith, & Pollock, 1996, 2000, 2002).

The chapter begins with a brief overview of the research conducted and the research setting. This is followed by an exploration of the ethical issues encountered during the research process. Issues addressed include the blurred distinction between public and private space in virtual environments, the identification of researchers within virtual communities, processes for obtaining informed consent, protecting the confidentiality of research participants and their online personae and maintaining the security of data collected. A further issue to be addressed is how to respond to research participants who indicate they are suffering from or exhibit psychological problems.

Researching ethically within virtual environments requires a familiarity with, and adherence to, the netiquette and social norms of the environments of interest. Through this case study, we highlight the conduct of ethical research within virtual environments with the consent of the individuals and their community, without compromising their confidentiality, violating their assumptions of privacy or infringing upon their copyright entitlements.

OVERVIEW OF RESEARCH

The case study presented here is based on a Grounded Theory (Glaser & Strauss, 1967) study of social interaction in MOOs. This study was part of a larger research project examining how characteristics of the individual interact with characteristics of computer-mediated communication (CMC) to enable socio-emotional communication and behavior in text-based virtual environments (Roberts, 2001). A research proposal was submitted to Curtin University of Technology's Human Research Ethics Committee[1] prior to the research commencing[2].

THE RESEARCH SETTING

The study examined social interaction in MOOs, and was also conducted largely within them. MOOs are socially oriented text-based virtual environments. Individuals from disparate geographic locations can connect simultaneously to a social MOO to engage in synchronous ("real time") text-based (typed) communication with one another.

A MOO consists of a database of rooms, characters and objects (Curtis, 1992; Curtis & Nichols, 1993). All MOO users have access to object-oriented programming to create and modify the virtual environment. MOO users can create descriptions of buildings and objects and write computer programs for use within the environment. MOO users "own" the objects they create and can allow or deny other MOO users access to these objects. Characters, buildings, objects and written programs modify the database, meaning the items continue to "exist" even while the user is not logged in.

MOOs vary in their purpose, size and requirements for identifying information. Allen (1996a) identified four genres of MOOs: social, adventure, professional and special interest. Most MOOs have a stated theme that newcomers are encouraged to read and are expected to adhere to. The number of individuals using a MOO varies widely. MOOs range from private ones set up for the use of owners and their invited friends to large public MOOs that are accessible to anyone with an Internet connection. While most MOOs are accessible by the general public, some have particular requirements for membership. For example, Media MOO is for media researchers only (Bruckman & Resnick, 1995) and MOOSE Crossing is specifically for children (Bruckman, 1997). The MOOs selected for this research were all publicly accessible social MOOs.

Upon connecting to a MOO, an individual is greeted with a welcome screen that provides an introduction to the MOO and details for obtaining guest and permanent characters for use on the MOO. Typically, a newcomer is provided with a temporary character for use during the session that identifies them to other MOO users as a "guest." Guest characters are by default assigned the gender "neuter" and have only basic descriptions. Upon connecting as a guest, the individual is invited to complete a tutorial that provides information on using MOOs and covers basic commands. A guest may request a permanent character on a MOO by providing their e-mail address, and the name they wish to use for their character.

Once a permanent character has been assigned, the character can be modified to suit the individual's requirement. Character names, descriptions and gender can be changed at will. In addition to the primary character, many MOOs support the creation of "morphs," alternative characters that also can be gendered and described. A "home" can be "built" and "furnished" (programmed) for the character and "possessions" (objects) can be created.

Commands are used to communicate and move around within the MOO. Basic commands are used to "walk," "teleport" and "look" at rooms, objects and characters. "Say" and "whisper" commands allow users to communicate with other characters present in the same "room," while the "emote" command can be used for expressing actions and feelings. "Paging" and "remote emoting" are used to communicate with characters, who are currently logged into the MOO but are not in the same "room." These text-based MOO worlds where all communication takes place in ASCII text provide the context for this study.

THE STUDY

As noted, this research was conducted with MOOs as not only the object of study, but also as the context in which the study was conducted. Active data collection within the communities of interest is consistent with recommendations by community researchers (Fernback, 1999; Thompsen, Straubhaar, & Bolyard, 1998) to conduct research within, rather than on, virtual environments. The "wizards" (administrators) of the MOOs where research was conducted were contacted and permission sought and obtained, to approach and interview users within the MOO environment prior to the research commencing. A character called "Questioner" and a virtual interviewing room called "Questioner's Retreat" were set up on each MOO.

A combination of passive and active data collection was used in this research. MOOs support synchronous CMC, enabling the use of online interviewing and participant observation. Sources of data for this research included online interviews, face-to-face interviews, participant observation, MOO documentation and postings to MOO mailing lists. The combination of active (participant-observation and interviewing) and passive (collection of postings to MOO mailing lists and MOO documentation) data collection techniques were used to strengthen the research. The use of multiple sources of data and methods is referred to as "triangulation" and increases the reliability and validity of Grounded Theory research (Glaser, 1992).

The role of participant-observer was adopted for this research. Jorgensen (1989) recommended the use of participant-observation when a phenomenon is relatively unknown, when insiders' views differ from outsiders and when the phenomenon is not easily accessible by outsiders. Very limited psychological research had been conducted in MOOs prior to this research beginning. Anecdotal reports from users suggested that they had difficulty explaining their online lives to outsiders, and they felt that someone outside of the environment "just can't understand" what they are experiencing. In addition, frequent sensationalist media attention to pornography and sexual activity on the Internet made users wary of outsiders' motives in conducting research.

An insider's viewpoint is also important in gaining an understanding of the culture, language and reality of the participants. One way of achieving this is for the researcher to experience the phenomenon directly. Participant-observation decreases the likelihood of miscomprehension and inaccurate observations resulting from failure to understand the culture (Jorgensen, 1989). As MOOs have developed their own specific cultures, immersion in these cultures was essential to understanding the nuances of behavior.

In accordance with Grounded Theory methodology, theoretical sampling was used to select the MOO users interviewed. The first MOO users interviewed were selected for their availability. Categories that emerged from the coding of early interviews guided the selection of further research participants. In total, 58 individuals were interviewed about their MOO-ing experiences. Fifty-four interviews were conducted on eight social MOOs, using typed CMC. MOO users were contacted individually and asked if they would like to be interviewed about their MOO-ing experiences. Interviews were conducted in the "Questioner's Retreat" or the research participant's MOO room. Interviews were semi-structured and lasted between one and three hours. Each interview was logged with the permission of the research participant. A further four interviews were conducted face-to-face with local MOO users, audio recorded and later transcribed.[3]

Data collection, data coding and analysis were conducted on an ongoing basis. The Non-numerical Unstructured Data Indexing Searching and Theorising (NUD*IST) program (NUD*IST, 1995) was used as a data management tool. Data were coded based on the constant comparison of data. Data collection and coding continued until saturation was achieved.

The outcome of the study was a substantive Grounded Theory of social interaction in MOOs. The theory provided a thick description of how individuals represented by virtual personae engage in social interaction within the MOO environment, and the effect this has on their offline lives. A stage model of social interaction in MOOs was developed. It details the stages an individual passes through in the process of integrating MOO use into their lives, as they come to terms with what initially appears to be an alternative reality (Roberts, 2001; Roberts et al., 1996).

ETHICAL ISSUES

Many professional associations provide ethical guidelines for the conduct of research. As researchers working within a psychological framework, we are guided by psychological codes of ethics for research. The Australian Psychological Society (APS) provides a code of ethics for member psychologists within Australia (APS, 1999). The three general principles guiding the code are responsibility, competence and propriety. Section E of the code details guidelines for the conduct of research. Similarly, the American Psychological Association (APA) provides a code of ethics covering research and practice for member psychologists in the United States. In August 2002, the APA adopted a new ethics code that will be published shortly[4]. The five general principles guiding the code of ethics, as outlined in Draft 7 of the new APA "Ethical principles of psychologists and code of conduct" (hereafter referred to as the APA code) are those of beneficence and non-maleficence, fidelity and responsibility, integrity, justice and respect for people's rights and dignity. More specifically, ethical standards for research and publication are outlined in Section 8 of the APA code (APA, 2002). These codes will be referred to, where appropriate, when discussing ethical issues that arose during this research process.

The APS and APA both recognize the emergence of the Internet as a new medium of relevance to members. The APA code specifically states that it applies "across a variety of contexts, such as in person, postal, telephone, Internet, and other electronic transmissions" (2002, p. 2). In 1999, the APS produced "Considerations for psychologists providing services on the Internet." Despite this, the APS has not specifically referred to the Internet in its code, nor has it released statements relating to ethics in conducting research online. While the codes contain guiding principles for research, the translation of these principles into actions for conducting research in virtual environments is open to interpretation.

Our approach to the conduct of ethical research in virtual environments is based on the premise that all research should comply with the principles of ethical research as outlined in professional associations' codes of ethics. When developing the research plan for this study, the question of how to translate ethical guidelines into ethical practice in virtual research became paramount. From initial explorations in virtual environments, a number of questions relating to the ethics of research online arose. Further issues were identified in the process of conducting the research.

For each ethical issue identified, the process of translating ethical guidelines into ethical practice involved a deliberation of the options available to the researcher and the likely impact on research participants, their communities and the research process. Central concerns in this process were maintaining respect for individuals, their online and offline identities, and their ownership of words.

Assumption of Privacy (Public vs. Private Space)

A major issue in developing ethical research procedures for use in virtual environment is determining the private versus public nature of the cyberspaces within which the research is conducted. The issue of assumption of privacy revolves around the blurred distinction between public and private space in virtual environments. Various attempts have been made to distinguish between the public and the private in virtual environments. For example, Lessig (1995) formed a typology of forms of association in cyberspace: association in public (newsgroups and bulletin boards), association in private (private chats) and association in construction (multiuser dimensions (MUDs)). However, there currently exists no general agreement over what constitutes public and private space in online environments.

Waskul and Douglass (1996) described the private/public distinction in virtual environments in terms of "publicly private" and "privately public," noting that public and private are metaphorical labels based on the assumption that cyberspaces are like physical places (p. 131). In cyberspace, the defining of public versus private "space" may be reduced to a matter of accessibility. A cyberspace may be viewed as a public space as it is publicly accessible, yet interactions that occur within that space may be deemed by the participants to be private. Waskul and Douglass (1996) argued that researchers do not have the right to define spaces as public or private to meet their own research needs. Rather, account should be taken of the size and nature of the online forum and the intrusiveness of the study.

The most public form of communication on the Internet occurs in newsgroups, as anyone with Internet access can read these. Despite this, newsgroup postings can be, and frequently are, high in self-disclosure (e.g., Salem, Bogat, & Reid, 1997). Posters to newsgroups have varying expectations as to the privacy of their communication. In a survey of posters to sex-related newsgroups, nearly half of the respondents (47 percent) believed the medium to be private, while only 35.3 percent perceived their postings to be public or extremely public (Witmer, 1997). Similarly Reid (1996) argued that while Usenet postings are publicly accessible, it is "doubtful whether each author intends his or her words to be placed in the public domain" (p. 170).

Despite the varying perceptions of privacy by users of newsgroups, Bordia (1996) claimed the advantage of online research is that it can "allow unobtrusive observation in a setting that is ethically defensible" (p. 149) on the basis that "presumably the participants were aware that their verbalisations were public domain" (p. 150). In direct contrast, Duncan (1996) argued that obtaining data without the express permission of the individuals involved is an invasion of their privacy.

Allen (1996b) differentiated between public and private spaces in MOOs. She defined public spaces as public rooms in the MOO that are accessible by all. In contrast, private spaces consist of private rooms created by users and that are only publicly accessible when and if the creator chooses to make them so. Based on this differentiation, she made the decision that public words and actions were available for analysis without the need for informed consent.

The presumption that online communication occurs in public space results is an anomaly in how research participants may be treated in equivalent settings in online and offline research. One pertinent example is psychological research on communication in support groups. Obtaining informed consent from research participants in offline support groups prior to the collection of data is required under current ethical guidelines. In contrast, where newsgroups are set up as support groups, individuals may neither be advised that their communication is being studied, nor may informed consent be obtained, on the grounds that all postings are public documents (see, for example, Salem et al.'s (1997) study of a depression support group).

There are currently no clear guidelines for psychological researchers on what constitutes private versus public space in virtual environments, yet the distinction is important as it affects the rights of participants to be advised of the nature of the research, and to give or withhold their informed consent. This is an issue we struggled with prior to our research commencing. For the purposes of our research, we accepted the distinction of private and public spaces in MOOs proposed by Allen (1996b), but also recognized that even within MOO public spaces, private interactions occur (Waskul & Douglass, 1996). In our view, the public nature of some MOO spaces was over-ridden in importance by respect for the expectation of privacy by MOO users.

Informed Consent

Given our stance that respect for the expectation of privacy over-rides the distinction between public and private spaces, the question arose whether there was a need in our research for informed consent for both active and passive data collection. Both ethical codes state that informed consent should be (except in specified circumstances) obtained from research participants. The APA code (2002) specifically states in standard 3(10) that "When psychologists conduct research ... in person or *via electronic transmission or other forms of communication*, they obtain the informed consent of the individual or individuals" (emphasis added) (p. 7).

The need for us to obtain informed consent from people to be interviewed in virtual environments (active data collection) was straightforward. However, the method of obtaining this consent was more contentious. Obtaining informed consent in virtual environments is more problematic than in offline settings. Obtaining informed consent in offline settings usually involves providing potential research participants with an information sheet (including information on the research, the researchers, participants rights, including the right to withdraw, and confidentiality), discussing the research and answering any questions and obtaining a signature on a consent form. In online research, these procedures cannot easily be followed, as the researcher and research participants are frequently geographically dispersed. In addition, research participants may be reluctant to divulge details of offline identities necessary for the posting of information and consent forms.

Jacobson (1999) outlined three methods for obtaining informed consent for online research where the completion of documentation offline is not possible. The first method involves obtaining informed consent by e-mail. Signatures in a digitalized form can now be transmitted by e-mail, although many research participants may not have access to the technology required to do this. A further disadvantage of this method is that research participants are required to provide their e-mail address, constituting a link to their offline identity. The second method involves obtaining implied consent. Implied consent is inferred when an individual takes part in a research activity, after reading information about it. For example, surveys on the WWW can be set up so that the gateway to a survey is an information page that requires interested individuals to click on a button to indicate they have read the information and consent to taking part in the research. The third method involves the creation of an electronic document through a computer, logging the information supplied by the researcher and the consent of the research participant.

Selection of a method for obtaining informed consent from both the community and individuals will necessarily be dependent upon the virtual environment used, the level of anonymity required by research participants and their access to high-level computing facilities.

In our research, the wizards of the selected MOOs were contacted and permission sought and obtained to approach and interview users within the MOO environment. Obtaining signed consent forms was not feasible as most research participants resided overseas and signatures cannot be easily transmitted electronically. Research participants interviewed on MOOs were provided with an information sheet sent via MOO-mail when their participation in the study was requested. Informed consent was obtained in text, prior to the interview, and the opportunity was provided for individuals to "ask" (type) questions about the research. This procedure was logged (similar to the third method described by Jacobson, 1999). Research participants interviewed face-to-face were given an information sheet and signed consent forms were obtained. We recommend that, regardless of the method used, the information about the research be presented in a format that the research participants can keep and refer back to at any time before, during or after their research participation.

In our research, where an individual was identified through questioning as under the age of 18 years, parental consent was obtained by e-mail before the interview commenced. Nosek, Banaji and Greenwald (2002) noted the difficulty in controlling children's access to research as children can self-present as adults online. No additional measures were taken to verify the age of research participants in our research. This is an area that needs to be addressed in future research.

The issue of whether to obtain informed consent for passive data collection was more contentious. The APA code exempts naturalistic observations and archival research from requiring informed consent, where no harm or distress is likely to come to those researched and where their confidentiality is protected. On the surface, the use of archived newsgroup and MOO group postings would seem to fall within these boundaries. However, research is emerging that questions this assumption.

King (1996) highlighted the potential for psychological harm to members of online groups, where research is conducted and published without the prior knowledge and informed consent of participants. Where there has been the expectation of privacy within a group (however misinformed that expectation may be), the individual may feel violated upon hearing of, or reading the results of, that research. Interpersonal dynamics of the group may change as the expectation of anonymity is removed. King (1996) cited the example of Finn and Lavitt's (1994) journal article on a self-help group with sexual abuse survivors. In the article the group was identified and postings by group members were used verbatim with only the names changed.

An alternative view was expressed by Sixsmith and Murray (2001). They argued that through the actual process of requesting consent to use archived material, researchers may alter group dynamics. However, they also question the ethics of researchers using material without consent, when the author of that material may be opposed to the purposes of that research.

Reid (1996) argued that even where informed consent is obtained in virtual environments, care needs to be taken to fully inform potential research participants of the possible consequences of their research involvement. Reid (1996) noted the possibility that her research into a MUD for survivors of sexual abuse contributed to the social disintegration of the MUD through "public scrutiny and personal exposure" resulting from participation in the research (p. 172).

Robinson (2001) developed a model that goes some way towards addressing the issue of whether to obtain informed consent for passive data collection. The model provides steps for deciding whether or not existing online data requires consent before use. The model is based on three pieces of information: whether the data is publicly accessible, whether data has a gatekeeper (e.g., moderated forum or password protected data) and the expectation of privacy by users. Where data is asynchronous, publicly accessible and does not have a gatekeeper (e.g., newsgroups), informed consent for use is not required. Where there is a gatekeeper, data is not publicly accessible (e.g., e-mail groups) or there is the expectation of privacy, consent should be obtained from respondents prior to use.

The wishes of the community also need to be considered when addressing this issue. The APA code (2002) states that, "Before deciding that research does not require informed written consent of research participants, members must consult with colleagues or gatekeepers and ethics committees as appropriate" (p. 6). In MOOs, the wizards are the gatekeepers. Some MOOs explicitly request researchers obtain permission for the use of material. For example, the first screen seen when logging on to LambdaMOO states:

NOTICE FOR JOURNALISTS AND RESEARCHERS
The citizens of LambdaMOO request that you ask for permission from all direct participants before quoting any material collected here.

Given the potential for harm, when informed consent is not obtained, and the stated preference for obtaining consent in some MOOs, in our research we adopted an approach to the use of MOO mailing list postings, based on respect for individual's right to say how their "work" is used. Permission was requested and obtained from individuals for the use of all postings included in the analysis. Quotes from postings have been used anonymously in all publications resulting from this research, except where individuals have requested that identifying information be included.

Identification of Researchers in Virtual Communities

The data collection methods used in this research included participant observation by the first author. The role of participant-observer can vary according to the degree and type of participation in the community studied, and the covert/overt nature of the participation (Spradley, 1980). For this research the role of "participant as observer" (Gold, 1969) was adopted where the researcher was clearly identified to research participants. The researcher's presence on MOOs as a researcher was overt. Characters were clearly identified as research characters by the pseudonym "Questioner." When a MOO user used the "look" command to look at "Questioner" they saw:

Questioner
Questioner raises her head from the keyboard to smile at you. She is probably going to ask you lots of questions about your MOO-ing experiences ...
She is awake and looks alert.

Other researchers have also used the ability to create and describe characters and objects in MUDs and MOOs to alert people to the presence of a researcher. Allen (1996b) identified herself as a researcher in her character description. Reid (1996, p. 170) used a "virtual approximation of a visible tape recorder" to alert MUD participants that sessions were being logged.

The degree of participation in MOOs was "complete participation" as categorized by Spradley (1980). That is, the researcher was researching in situations in which she was already accepted as an "ordinary participant." The roles of participant and observer are potentially conflicting. Conflict between the roles can result in research that lacks objectivity, is subjective and influenced by personal feelings (Jorgensen, 1989). To maintain a level of objectivity and to further separate the roles of participant and researcher, personal involvement in the virtual communities studied was limited for the duration of the research. Separate research identities were created, clearly identified and used for research purposes only.

Given the identity deception possible on MOOs and the strong negative reaction many MOO users have when they feel they have been deceived, a decision was made prior to the research commencing to adopt an open approach, linking social ("ordinary participant") and research identities. Where a social character already existed on a MOO, the research identity was created as a "morph" for that character. This meant that social and research identities were listed as "aliases" on the character and the connection between the two was overt. When requesting interviews with MOO users that had previously interacted with one of the researcher's social MOO identities, the MOO user was directly advised of the researcher's social identities. New characters (with research identities only) were set up on MOOs where no social character existed. The open approach and linking of identities demonstrated respect for individuals, increasing the information they had in terms of giving informed consent to participate in the research.

Protecting Anonymity

Many online users adopt a pseudonym (or pseudonyms) for use in virtual environments, which on the surface appears to provide a high level of anonymity to the individual. It can be argued that research involving pseudonymous characters is exempt from regulations governing human subjects as "true" or offline identities are not known (Jacobson, 1999). However, many factors act to decrease the level of anonymity a pseudonym provides. First, some individuals chose not to use a pseudonym and use their own name. In some cases, individuals use pseudonyms that are nicknames and may be recognizable by others who know them offline. In online settings identifying information about offline identities may be self-disclosed or actively sought (Allen, 1996b; Jacobson, 1996). The same pseudonym may be used in a range of online environments that vary in their requirements for offline identification details (Jacobson, 1999). The combination of these factors means that researchers cannot assume that pseudonyms provide adequate protection for offline identities.

Attempts to verify the offline identities of online pseudonymous characters are hindered by the use of some pseudonyms by more than one individual, and the possibility that more than one person may have access to, and use, a single pseudonymous character (the "typist problem," Jacobson, 1999). However, as Waskul and Douglass (1996) argued, the degree of anonymity conferred in these virtual environments does not reduce the ethical requirements for researchers to protect the anonymity of research participants and virtual interaction settings.

Consideration should be given to protecting the anonymity of online pseudonyms, not only for their possible linkages to offline identities but also in their own right. Pseudonyms themselves gain reputations over time. To maintain the anonymity of research participants, Sixsmith and Murray (2001) recommended all identifying information (including pseudonyms) in messages used in research publications be removed, in addition to information identifying the source of the message (e.g., newsgroup names). However, the practice of replacing existing pseudonyms with other pseudonyms in research materials confers little additional protection to the existing pseudonym, when text searches can be used to identify source documents (Allen, 1996b).

Given the need to protect both pseudonyms and offline identities, and the possible linkages between pseudonymous online and offline identities, the greatest protection to the identity of research participants is afforded by keeping both "real-life" names and online pseudonyms confidential. For our research the anonymity and confidentiality of research participants was maintained. The desire for anonymity of both individuals and their MOO characters were respected. Virtual research participants were not asked for their offline ("real-life") name, address or contact number. Neither MOO nor offline names have been used in any presentations or publications resulting from this study. There were two exceptions to this. First, some individuals specifically requested their postings were to be used with identifying information. Second, one individual, when approached for permission to use a quote from their interview as a heading in a conference paper, requested that the quote be attributed to their MOO name. For both these exceptions, the preferences of the research participants to have their words attributed to themselves were respected.

To provide protection for members of lists from which postings (whether used anonymously or identified) were used in this research, excerpts from postings included in all forms of written reports identified neither the name of the mailing list nor the MOO on which the mailing list was located. While it is still possible that a determined individual could track down the source of a quote from a posting, the ease of which this may be done is greatly hindered by excluding the mailing lists and MOO identifiers.

Ownership of Words

In trying to determine the ownership of electronic messages, we are entering murky legal waters. It is still unclear whether the individual who authored a message, the community to which it was sent or anyone who has access to the message is the owner of the electronic message (Sixsmith & Murray, 2001). Electronic postings may be considered original works protected by copyright, although this has not yet been legally tested (Ardito, 1996; Sixsmith & Murray, 2001). If informed consent is not obtained to use electronic messages, copyright provisions suggest that they should be referenced in the same way as paper documents. Researchers who neither obtain informed consent nor reference the material they use risk violating both ethical and copyright standards.

We concur with Sixsmith and Murray (2001) that "Seeking permission empowers people to choose whether they want their words used within a research publication and whether they would like to be credited" (p. 430). In our research, we sought permission for the use of all electronic postings. Most individuals chose to have their postings used anonymously, but some, as described above, chose to have the material attributed to either their pseudonym or offline name. We respected the right of individuals to make this choice and complied with their wishes.

In allowing the author of the posting the decision over the use of their posting, we have privileged the author, rather than the community or reader, as the "owner" of the message. However, we recognize that the community also has a stake in the ownership of the message, and their preference may be to not be identified. Out of respect for this, the source of postings (name of the mailing list and name of the MOO on which the mailing list is located) was not included in research publications. We deemed our potential ownership of messages as readers to be less important than that of the individual author or the community.

Responding to Psychological Problems or Distress

The researchers for this study are psychological researchers. Humphreys, Winzelberg and Klaw (2000) outlined the issues involved in psychology professionals' involvement in online settings, noting the absence of ethical guidelines covering psychologists' behavior in online groups. The major issues they identified were establishing and maintaining role definitions. Identifying oneself as a researcher once within an online group does not mean that absent or future members of the group are also informed of the researcher's role. For example, notification of research being conducted by posting to a group does not alert new group participants that research is being conducted (Sixsmith & Murray, 2001). There is a need to identify the researcher and restate and clarify the role of the researcher on an ongoing basis.

When research is conducted in areas that require individuals to introspect upon their behavior, there is the potential for research participants to confuse the role of the researcher with that of a therapist. An example of work where the line between research and therapy created role confusion is a study by Holge-Hazelton (2002). This study involved free association narrative interviews of young people with diabetes. Holge-Hazelton (2002) noted the problem that arose with one research participant when clear boundaries were not set on the duration of the contact between researcher and research participant.

In our research we delimited our role in the MOOs to research only. Prior to the research beginning, the first author consulted with a senior staff member, who is both an academic and a counseling psychologist, about the most appropriate action to take if a research participant raised concerns about their own Internet-related behavior or expressed other forms of psychological distress. The decision was made to advise any such individual to contact a registered psychologist or counselor in their local area to discuss the issue, but not to make referrals to specific professionals. We recognize that this course of action was not ideal, as it placed the onus on the individual to seek help. In offline research, where research participants live within a discrete geographical area, it is possible to set up specific referral arrangements. In online research such as this, the diversity of locations of research participants (both within and across countries) makes it impossible.

No attempt was made to offer counseling online by the researchers or other parties. Although we are psychological researchers, we are not clinical or counseling psychologists and are not qualified to provide therapeutic services. Even if we were, the provision of online psychological services is in its infancy and has yet to prove its efficacy. Furthermore, while the APS code (1999) states that: "Members must anticipate the subsequent effects of research participation and provide information on services available for participants to alleviate any unnecessary distress that follows from their participation" (p. 7), it specifically states that "Members must not engage in other professional relationships with research participants in relation to resolving any such distress" (p. 7).

Returning the Research Findings to the Community

The APS code (1999) states "Members must provide an opportunity for participants to obtain appropriate information about the nature, results, and conclusion of the research" (p. 7). This can be a difficult process in virtual research unless contact details (either e-mail address or name and physical mailing address) for research participants are collected. In our research, we recorded the MOO pseudonyms used by research participants. Following the initial analyses and write up of research findings, all MOO users who had participated in the research were sent a MOO-mail that contained the WWW address of a site containing a summary of the research findings. The Web-site address was also posted to mailing lists on MOOs. Participants and other interested MOO users were invited to provide feedback on the research findings. The feedback obtained was incorporated into the research findings. This process not only meets the ethical requirement to provide research participants with information about the outcome of the study, it also demonstrates respect for the individuals who participated in the research. In addition, the feedback obtained also strengthens the validity of research findings.

Maintaining the Security of Data Collected

The APS code (1999) states "Members must make provisions for maintaining confidentiality in the access, storage and disposal of research data" (p. 7). Maintaining confidentiality and security of data collected in computer-mediated research poses unique difficulties. In online research, confidentiality relies upon data security. Confidentiality may be breached at the site of data collection, during transmission of data or in the storage of data. Sites at which data is collected may not be secure. For example, wizards on MOOs can monitor all activity and access data stored within their MOO. This can include "listening in" on interviews conducted online. The use of surveillance tools on MOOs by users others than wizards is also possible. Confidentiality of data may be breached during data transmission, where another party intercepts data (Nosek et al., 2002). Possible interceptors include, but are not restricted to, the service provider of the research participant or researcher. Employers may also monitor employees' e-mail and Internet usage (Sipior & Ward, 1995; Weisband & Reinig, 1995). Confidentiality of data may be breached during storage of data, where hackers may access files stored on unprotected or poorly protected computer systems.

In our research in MOOs, we took several steps to increase the security of data collected. The biggest risks to breach of confidentiality were at the data collection stage. In MOOs, commands exist to "lock" rooms and to sweep for surveillance tools. The need to lock the room during interviewing soon became apparent, when another MOO user chose to teleport in uninvited during one interview. Before all future interviews were conducted in the researcher's room, it was swept for bugs and locked. While it was possible to take precautionary measures when interviews were conducted within the researcher's room, this was not possible where research participants requested that interviews be conducted in their own rooms. In these circumstances, the research participant had control over access to the room and interviews were suspended upon the arrival of any third party.

All data collected (including interview logs) were stored on a password protected site on a university server. While a copy of the information sheet for the research was created as an "object" on the MOO and located on the research character in the research room, no actual research data was held on the MOO itself. This was a decision made in recognition of the potential for breaches of confidentiality inherent in the MOO environment. Online researchers need to provide the most secure forms of data collection, transmission and storage possible, aiming to minimize the risks of unauthorized persons gaining access to research data at any stage of the research process. The procedures used to obtain this will differ according to the virtual medium used.

CONCLUSION

Our approach to the conduct of ethical research in virtual environments is based on the premise that all research should comply with the principles of ethical research as outlined in professional associations' codes of ethics. In the absence of specific guidelines for online research, we recommend researchers be guided by the principles outlined in the code, adapting guidelines for use in virtual environments as necessary.

Useful sources of information in identifying ethical issues specific to virtual environments are current researchers in the field, human research ethics committees and IRBs. We acknowledge that members of human research ethic committees and IRBs may have limited knowledge of the nature of online research, but their level of knowledge is increasing as the use of virtual environments as the object of and/or method of research increases. The prior identification of ethical issues and the development of strategies for addressing them is aided by researchers' familiarity with, and adherence to, the netiquette and social norms of the virtual environments that they are studying.

The adaptation of existing ethical frameworks for use in online environments requires careful consideration of the likely impact of adaptations on both research participants and the communities in which the research is conducted. The three stated areas of emphasis in this chapter—respecting individuals, their online and offline identities and their ownership of words—are not always complementary and provide a potential source of conflict between the optimal ethical treatment of individual research participants and their communities. For example, a decision to fully cite electronic sources, such as newsgroup postings, provides respect for the ownership of words of individuals and their copyright entitlements. However, such a decision may impact negatively upon other community members, who may feel exposed and experience a loss of privacy. Ethical dilemmas such as this highlight the need to develop ethically defensible strategies that balance the needs and offer protection to both research participants and their online communities.

In this chapter we have highlighted the need to identify and address ethical issues prior to research commencing, but also the necessity to adopt additional measures if new issues are identified during the research process. Allen (1996b) argued that research ethics for virtual environments "should be situated, dialogic agreements that develop over time between researchers and the participants of the research study" (p. 186). This leaves little protection for research participants unless these agreements are based on the principles of ethical research and are encompassed within an overarching ethical research framework.

All research conducted in virtual environments should be guided by ethical principles, with strategies adopted to ensure respect for individuals, identities and their ownership of words. In this case study we have attempted to provide an example of how research can be conducted within virtual environments with the consent of the individuals and their community, without compromising research participants' confidentiality, violating their assumptions of privacy or infringing upon their copyright entitlements. While the strategies adopted to conduct research may vary according to the type of research and virtual environment, research conducted online must not be exempt from ethical considerations.

REFERENCES

Allen, C. L. (1996a). Virtual identities: The social construction of cybered selves. *Dissertation Abstracts International,* DAI-A, *57*(6), 2268.

Allen, C. L. (1996b). What's wrong with the "golden rule"? Conundrums of conducting ethical research in cyberspace. *The Information Society, 12,* 175-187.

American Psychological Association (APA). (2002). *Ethical principles of psychologists and code of conduct,* (Draft 7). Retrieved Sept. 27, 2002 from: http://anastasi.apa.org/draftethicscode/.

Ardito, S. C. (1996). Electronic Copyright under siege. *Online Magazine,* (March), 83-88.

Australian Psychological Society (APS). (1999). *Code of ethics.* Retrieved Sept. 27, 2002 from: http://www.psychsociety.com.au/aps/ethics/default.asp.

Australian Psychological Society (APS). (1999). *Considerations for Psychologists Providing Services on the Internet.* Melbourne, VIC, Australia: Australian Psychological Society, Ltd.

Bordia, P. (1996). Studying verbal interaction on the Internet: The case of rumor transmission research. *Behavior Research Methods, Instruments & Computers, 28,* 149-151.

Bruckman, A. S. (1997). MOOSE Crossing: Construction, community and learning in networked virtual world for kids. *Dissertation Abstracts International*, DAI-A, *58*(11), 4241.

Bruckman, A. S. & Resnick, M. (1995). The MediaMOO project: Constructionism and professional community. *Convergence, 1*(1), 94-109.

Curtis, P. (1992). MUDding: Social phenomenon in text-based virtual realities. *Intertrek, 3*(3), 26-34.

Curtis, P. & Nichols, D. A. (1993). MUDs grow up: Social virtual reality in the real world. Retrieved May 2, 1996 from: ftp:parcftp.xerox.com:/pub/MOO/papers/MUDS growup.ps.txt.

Duncan, G. T. (1996). Is my research ethical? *Communications of the ACM, 39*(12), 67-68.

Fernback, J. (1999). There is a there there: Notes toward a definition of cybercommunity. In S. Jones (Ed.), *Doing Internet Research: Critical Issues and Methods for Examining the Net* (pp. 203-220). Thousand Oaks, CA: Sage.

Finn, J. & Lavitt, M. (1994). Computer based self-help groups for sexual abuse survivors. *Social Work with Groups, 17,* 21-46.

Glaser, B. G. (1992). *Emergence vs Forcing. Basics of Grounded Theory Analysis*. Mill Valley, CA: Sociology Press.

Glaser, B. G. & Strauss, A. (1967). *The Discovery of Grounded Theory: Strategies for Qualitative Research*. Chicago, IL: Aldine Publishing Company.

Gold, R. L. (1969). Roles in sociological field observation. In G. J. McCall & J. L. Simmons (Eds.), *Issues in Participant Observation: A Text and Reader* (pp. 30-39). Reading, MA: Addison-Wesley.

Holge-Hazelton, B. (2002). The Internet: A new field for qualitative inquiry? *Forum Qualitative Social Research, 3*(2). Retrieved Sept. 27, 2002 from: http://www.qualitative-research.net/fqs/fqs-eng.htm.

Humphreys, K., Winzelberg, A., & Klaw, E. (2000). Psychologists' ethical responsibilities in Internet-based groups: Issues, strategies, and a call for dialogue. *Professional Psychology: Research and Practice, 31*(5), 493-496.

Jacobson, D. (1996). Contexts and cues in cyberspace: The pragmatics of names in text-based virtual realities. *Journal of Anthropological Research, 52,* 461-479.

Jacobson, D. (1999). Doing research in cyberspace. *Field Methods, 11*(2), 127-145.

Jones, R. A. (1994). The ethics of research in cyberspace. *Internet Research, 4*(3), 30-35.

Jorgensen, D. L. (1989). Participant observation: A methodology for human studies. *Applied Social Research Methods Series* (Vol. 15). Newbury Park, CA: Sage.

King, S. (1996). Researching Internet communities: Proposed ethical guidelines for the reporting of the results. *The Information Society, 12*(2), 119-127.

Lessig, L. (1995). The path of cyberlaw. *Yale Law Journal, 104,* 1743-1755.

Nosek, B. A., Banaji, M. R., & Greenwald, A. G. (2002). E-research: Ethics, security, design, and control in psychological research on the Internet. *Journal of Social Issues, 58*(1), 161-176.

NUD*IST (Non-numerical Unstructured Data Indexing Searching and Theorizing) (1995). Qualitative Data Analysis Program. Melbourne, Australia: Qualitative Solutions and Research International Pty. Ltd.

Reid, E. (1996). Informed consent in the study of online communities: A reflection on the effects of computer-mediated social research. *The Information Society, 12,* 169-174.

Roberts, L. D. (2001). *Social interaction in virtual environments.* Unpublished doctoral dissertation, Curtin University of Technology, Perth, Western Australia. Available online at: http//adt.curtin.edu.au/theses/available/adt-WCU20030602.140704/.

Roberts, L. D., Smith, L. M., & Pollock, C. (1996, September). *A model of social interaction via computer-mediated communication in real-time text-based virtual environments.* Paper presented at the 31ˢᵗ Annual Conference of the Australian Psychological Society, Sydney, Australia.

Roberts, L. D., Smith, L. M., & Pollock, C. M. (2000). "u r a lot bolder on the net": Shyness and Internet use. In W. R. Crozier (Ed.), *Routledge Progress in Psychology: Shyness: Development, Consolidation & Change* (Vol. 5, pp. 121-138). London: Routledge.

Roberts, L. D., Smith, L. M., & Pollock, C. M. (2002). MOOing till the cows come home: The search for sense of community in virtual environments. In A. T. Fisher, C. C. Sonn, & B. J. Bishop (Eds.), *Psychological Sense of Community: Research, Applications, and Implications* (pp. 223-245). New York: Kluwer Academic/ Plenum Publishers.

Robinson, K. M. (2001). Unsolicited narratives from the Internet: A rich source of qualitative data. *Qualitative Health Research, 11*(5), 706-714.

Salem, D. A., Bogat, G. A., & Reid, C. (1997). Mutual help goes on-line. *Journal of Community Psychology*, 25, 189-207.

Sipior, J. C. & Ward, B. T. (1995). The ethical and legal quandary of email privacy. *Communications of the ACM, 38*(12), 48-54.

Sixsmith, J. & Murray, C. D. (2001). Ethical issues in the documentary data analysis of Internet posts and archives. *Qualitative-Health-Research, 11*(3), 423-432.

Spradley, J. R. (1980). *Participant observation.* New York: Holt, Reinhart, and Winston.

Thompsen, S. R., Straubhaar, J. D., & Bolyard, D. M. (1998, March). *Ethnomethodology and the study of online communities: Exploring the cyber streets.* Paper presented at IRISS '98, Bristol, UK.

Waskul, D. & Douglass, M. (1996). Considering the electronic participant: Some polemical observations on the ethics of on-line research. *The Information Society, 12,* 129-139.

Weisband, S. P. & Reinig, B. A. (1995). Managing user perceptions of email privacy. *Communications of the ACM, 38*(12), 40-47.

Witmer, D. F. (1997). Risky business: Why people feel safe in sexually explicit on-line communication. *JCMC, 2*(4), Article 8. Retrieved March 19, 1997 from: http: jcmc.huji.ac.il/vol2/issue4/witmer2.html.

ENDNOTES

[1]   Human research ethics committees are the Australian equivalent of institutional review boards.

[2]   The human research ethics committee approved the research, but raised two areas of concern requiring clarification prior to the research commencing. These were (a) how informed consent could be gained via the Internet given that "Normally, legally, a signature is required for consent" and (b) consideration of whether data collected should be coded.

[3]   There were insufficient face-to-face interviews to be able to assess the equivalence of interviews conducted on MOOs and face-to-face. The equivalence of online and face-to-face interviews is explored further in Roberts (2001).

[4]   This was published in the December 2002 issue of the American Psychologist.

Chapter X

Ethics and Engagement in Communication Scholarship: Analyzing Public, Online Support Groups as Researcher/ Participant-Experiencer

Mary K. Walstrom
Santa Rosa Junior College, USA

ABSTRACT

This chapter asserts an engaged research approach that aims to meet the ethical challenges of public, online support group studies. First, the intrinsic ethical orientation of the theoretical framework undergirding this approach is detailed. Second, how this approach may guide qualitative-interpretive analyses of public, online support groups is explored. This section features two excerpts from a larger study conducted of one such group. Third, three additional features of engaged research that bolsters its capacity to address the ethical concerns of public, online support group studies are presented. The chapter with a call and rationale for future engaged research of such sites, stressing the benefits to research and support group communities alike.

INTRODUCTION

Innovative uses of the Internet are transforming social structures worldwide. For example, healthcare systems have been challenged and improved as medical advice has flourished online (Ferguson, 1997; Kassirer, 1995). The Internet has also come to serve an important therapeutic role in housing support groups for those struggling with various physical and psychological afflictions (Barak, 1999; Ferguson, 1996; Grohol, 1999). The recent proliferation of these groups is likely due to their many advantages. Some of these advantages include relatively inexpensive, 24-hour access to discussions (and their archives) with others coping with rare or stigmatized conditions; increased self-disclosure, intimacy, a sense of autonomy and a recognition of oneself as an expert over time; decreased dependency on caretakers; communication apprehension (e.g., pressure for immediate response); access to social status markers (e.g., gender, race, socioeconomic status and age); and mobility barriers to group participation (Finn, 1996; Miller & Gergen, 1998; Murphy & Mitchell, 1998; Winzelberg, 1997). The continued growth of these online forums suggest that group participants view their disadvantages—such as, possible isolation, misinformation and promotion of problematic behavior (Finn, 1996; Fox, 1998; Grohol, 1999)—as tolerable.

A prime attraction of online support groups is their ability to provide participants access to practical information and emotional support for coping with various afflictions (Colon, 1996; Sharf, 1997; Walstrom, 1999, 2000b; Winter & Huff, 1996).[1] Such groups are also seen as safe environments for openly sharing problems and for finding relief from social stigma. However, perceptions of the safety of online support groups have diminished, as researchers unfamiliar with group culture have begun joining and studying group interactions (Eysenbach & Till, 2001). With this trend, controversy has ensued over the need for ethical guidelines for online support group research. Attempts to address this need are challenging, for appropriate guidelines are seen differently across global cultures and academic disciplines (Waern, 2001; Jankowski & van Selm, 2001). Creating ethical guidelines for online support group studies is seen as imperative, given the highly emotional and sensitive issues that participants discuss. That is, the group participants in these high-risk research contexts are regarded as requiring special protections from harm (Chen, Hall, & Johns, in press; Wearn, 2001). Thus, global and cross-disciplinary efforts are being made to establish ethical guidelines for such types of research (Ess & Association of Internet Researchers, 2002; Frankel & Siang, 1999).

Here I propose and aim to demonstrate an ethical approach to communication study of online support groups that are publicly accessible (e.g., USENET groups). This engaged research approach features two interlaced interpretive positions. The first position, *participant-experiencer*, entails the role of active contributor to the group being studied. This role specifically refers to a researcher who has personal experience with the central problem being discussed by group participants. The second interpretive position, *analyst*, involves the role of a skilled examiner of support group interactional processes and practices. Each position contributes distinct, valuable perspectives to an engaged research process. A participant-experiencer stance supplies historical and emotional understanding of the discussions, drawing both on one's background as a cultural member (or "native") of the local support group and of the larger social community that group represents.[2] An analyst viewpoint brings empirical insight to the systematic patterns occurring within support group exchanges, drawing on theoretical and methodological tools.

A primary advantage of the dual positionality of engaged research lies in the prospect of mapping under-explored terrains of social interaction. For example, communication research, as Shotter (1989) notes, has disproportionately focused on analyses by investigators socially detached from study participants. Such a research emphasis, Shotter (1989) claims, neglects important realms of interaction:

"And thus, in our researches, we have concentrated all our attention upon what is supposed to occur 'inside' isolated individuals studied 'externally,' from the point of view of third-person observers, socially uninvolved with them. We have failed to study what goes on 'between' people as first- and second-persons, the sense-making practices, procedures or methods made available to us as resources within the social orders into which we have been socialized" (p. 143).

Following Shotter (1989), I contend that as engaged researchers merge these *second-* and *third-person* positions—of participant-experiencer and analyst, respectively—untapped meanings that emerge between interlocutors may be richly shown. For example, as participant-experiencers, researchers gain access to the sense-making practices and (practical) procedures emerging "between" themselves and group participants (as second- and first-persons). Researchers (as third-persons) may then use their analytical proficiencies to illuminate these spontaneous, indeterminate and potentially transformative realms of unfolding interaction. The importance of mining these fleeting opportunity spaces in online talk is noted by Mann and Stewart (2000). These researchers observe that computer-mediated communication (CMC), perhaps even more than face-to-face conversation, "loses part of its sense and meaning when reread afterward by those who had not been involved" (Mann & Stewart, 2000, p. 87). Bridging the insights gained from participant-experiencer perspectives with those of analyst, I contend that researchers may innovatively capture and reveal online interactional processes, cultivating fertile new frontiers in communication scholarship.

The purpose of the forthcoming discussion is to present the nature and ethical foundation of an engaged research approach. I specifically seek to show how it may be employed to meet the ethical challenges of studying public, online support groups. Below, I first explain the theoretical framework that supports an engaged approach, highlighting its intrinsic ethical orientation. This framework, based in social constructionism, is characterized by the forming of dialogical relations with support group participants, while navigating between participant-experiencer and researcher positions. I detail the Bakhtinian roots of this theoretical framework to further demonstrate the ethical grounding it affords engaged research.

Second, I elaborate how the theoretical framework may inform qualitative-interpretive analyses of public, online support groups. This section features two excerpts from a recent study that I conducted of one such group of individuals struggling with eating disorders (i.e., anorexia and bulimia). A central finding of the analysis entailed a local narrative that participants routinely and resourcefully employed to achieve support group purposes (Walstrom, 1997, 1999).[3] These excerpts are presented to demonstrate how engaged research may evolve out of participant-experiencer and analyst perspectives, attending to "seen" and "sensed" dimensions of interaction (Katz & Shotter, 1996), respectively.

Third, I present three additional features of engaged research that bolster its capacity to meet the ethical concerns of studying public, online support groups. I conclude with a call and rationale for future engaged research of such sites. Here I contend and aim to show that engaged research may benefit research and support group communities alike.

THEORETICAL FOUNDATIONS OF ENGAGED RESEARCH

Social Constructionism

Engaged research is theoretically based in social constructionism (Edwards & Potter, 1992; Gergen, 1982, 1985; Harré, 1983; Shotter, 1984, 1993a; 1993b, Shotter & Gergen, 1994). This paradigm views communication as a contingent, ongoing flow, jointly created between selves and others—referred to as the "self-other dimension of interaction" (Shotter 1993a, p. 10; 1995a, p. 164). The utterances that drive this interaction are regarded as co-constructed, as are the interpretations, stances, actions, activities, identities, emotions and other culturally meaningful realities they produce (Jacoby & Ochs, 1995). Co-construction refers to a "distributed responsibility among interlocutors" (Jacoby & Ochs, 1995, p. 177) for collaborative interactional processes, but does not assume affiliation or support (e.g., a disagreement is co-constructed).

A commonality among traditions of social construction, writes Shotter (1993b, 1995a), is that interaction is viewed as: (1) dialogic—no things exist in themselves but are created in dialogue through multiple (historical, present, hypothetical) voices/ perspectives; (2) indeterminate—flows in a direction that is unpredictable or unknowable prior to the moment of its occurrence; and (3) situated—located within particular situational and historical contexts, involving particular selves and others. Power relations are also taken into account within social constructionism, as it recognizes the ways in which all utterances are constrained, or limited ideologically, by the institutional discourses that mediate them (Foucault, 1979). This final point relates to agency, referring to the speaking or acting opportunities that are disproportionately available to and/or valued by certain interactants in social situations (cf. Wertsch, Tulviste, & Hagstrom, 1993).

A rhetorical-responsive version of social constructionism (Shotter, 1993a, 1993c) forms the theoretical framework of engaged research.[4] I was drawn to this version, and most notably its Bakhtinian roots, as it provided interpretive tools and ethical stances that matched my research interests. That is, it fruitfully guided qualitative-interpretative studies of the micro-level structure of naturalistic interaction, supporting the pursuit of meanings whose production researchers are intimately (biographically, emotionally) involved. More broadly, this theory resonated with my postmodern and feminist perspectives on research methods, and my desire to employ them to explore possible therapeutic and political realms of a familiar form of support group talk.

Within a rhetorical-responsive version of social constructionism, the appropriate units of analysis for studies of human interaction are "living utterances . . . voiced in concrete social contexts" (Shotter, 1993a, p. 7). These units include both interpersonal utterances (i.e., exchanges among support group members) and intrapersonal utterances (i.e., instances of self-talk within one support group post). Interpersonal types of living utterances may be addressed to two kinds of audiences. The first audience involves a generalized other—in Mead's (1934) terms, an imagined member of a community to which we (want to) belong. The second audience refers to an ideal other, or superaddressee—in a Bakhtinian (1984) sense, one whose "absolutely just responsive understanding is presumed, either in some metaphysical distance or in distant historical time" (cited in Morson & Emerson, 1990, p. 135).[5] A rhetorical-responsive version of social constructionism regards living utterances as "words-in-their-speaking," and distinguishes them from those "already spoken about" (Shotter, 1996b, p. 484). More concretely, living utterances are products of specific social, relational and historically situated interactions—namely, those born out of active involvement among particular persons in particular contexts.

Within a rhetorical-responsive branch of social constructionism, efforts to understand its basic units of analysis (living utterances) without such active involvement are thought to yield "decontextualized systems of conventionalized meanings and usages" (Shotter, 1993c, p. 468). "Passive" methods of Internet research (Eysenbach & Till, 2001, p. 1103) seem to represent such attempts, featuring, for example, the mining of support group discussions (or their archives) by investigators who are uninvolved in or unfamiliar with the group culture.[6] The prevalence of passive types of research may stem from the limitations of scientific discourse itself:

"In our concern, as first-person subjectivities with only a third-person objective world, this whole category of events, in which the responsibility for an outcome is shared between a 'you' and an 'I,' disappears. . . . As scientists we have lacked an intelligible vocabulary in terms of which to make sense of it" (Shotter, 1989, p. 16).

To remedy this omission, I support expanding research paradigms, privileging exclusively third-person perspectives (analysts) to include those of second-person (participant-experiencer), as well. From these dual positions, intricate understandings of living utterances—whose indeterminate outcomes are mutually shared by researchers and group participants—may result. Voloshinov (1973)[7] attests to the nature and authenticity of these types understandings: "Any true understanding is dialogic in nature; meaning is between speakers . . . realized in active responsive understanding" (p. 102). In short, according to a rhetorical-responsive perspective of social constructionism, living utterances become accessible to deeply mine and comprehend—structurally and emotionally—by researchers who are dually positioned as (third-person) analysts and (second-person) participant-experiencers.

The ethical core of the theoretical framework underlying engaged online research involves establishing dialogical relationships with study participants, while navigating between analyst and participant-experiencer positions. In doing so, researchers become jointly involved in interaction with and morally linked to participants in ways exclusively third-person analysts are not, states Shotter (1989). These ties are accomplished as researchers coalesce the interpretations formed from analyst and participant-experiencer positions. Following Katz and Shotter (1996), I refer to these interpretations as those emanating from "seen" and "sensed" realms of interaction, respectively. To elaborate, analyst positions reveal the "seen"—the systematic language patterns structuring interaction. These insights unfold as researchers employ methodological tools to examine online support group discussions. Participant-experiencer positions tap into the "sensed"—the affective and evaluative impressions formed through interaction. These senses are grasped as researchers attend to and map their emotional responses to their involvement in group discussions. In navigating these analyst and participant-experiencer positions, and in making that process public, researchers create ethical connections with group participants. That is, engaged researchers become uniquely responsible for their aesthetic activity (Morson & Emerson, 1990), namely, the situated, responsive interpretations of (self-other) interaction that they produce.

The writings of Bakhtin on the ethical dimensions of self-other interaction are integral to a rhetorical-responsive version of social constructionism. That is, his works extensively address the ethical links formed among interacting selves and others in historically-situated contexts. I next elaborate on two concepts advanced by Bakhtin, *dialogical intuition* and *creative understanding*, to further flesh out how a rhetorical-responsive version of social constructionism provides an ethical theoretical foundation for an engaged research approach. I highlight how these concepts may guide researchers in the taking up of participant-experiencer (second-person) and analyst (third-person) interpretive positions, the bases of forming dialogical relations and ethical ties with support group participants.

Bakhtinian Theory

First, Bakhtin describes dialogic intuition as "the ability to sense the inner dialogues of others in all their unfinalizability and then participate in that dialogue while respecting its openness" (cited in Morson & Emerson, 1990, p. 267). This intuitive and interactive capacity stems from *addressive surplus*, whereby two fields of vision enrich each other, and not *essential surplus*, whereby one vision independently defines the vision of others. With addressive surplus, each vision is shaped by an (often unspoken) apperceptive background in the moment-to-moment unfolding of interaction (e.g., in mutually sharing personal experience). This fleeting convergence, between situated speakers and utterances of prior contexts, is said to yield, as noted, "true understanding[s]" (Voloshinov, 1973, p. 102). Such a responsive process of understanding of self-other interaction, contends Bakhtin (1983), must inform all accounts of it:

"Any account of an utterance must, 'reproduce this event of mutual [simultaneous] reactions between speakers, must, as it were, restructure it with the person wishing to understand taking upon himself [sic] the role of the listener. But in order to carry out that role, he [sic] must distinctly understand the position of the other as well' " (cited in Holquist, 1990, p. 62).

Moreover, Bakhtin claims that this situated approach to interpreting human nature—essentially dialogical not just psychological—is "the only true ethical one" (cited in Morson & Emerson, 1990, p. 267).

Dialogical intuition fruitfully guides engaged qualitative researchers of public, online support groups in taking up the roles of analyst and participant-experiencer. For example, as an analyst, I came to understand the structure and function of support group interaction in reading, and contributing relevant personal experience to, discussions of participants' battles with their eating disorders. For example, amid my active involvement, I noticed and was drawn to use in my postings several salient metaphors, occurring within group discussions. These metaphors were routinely employed to present heated intra- and interpersonal quarrels with eating disorders conditions. A chief metaphor used to accomplish these portrayals was "eating disorder voice(s)." In-depth analyses of uses of this metaphor evidenced its central role within a larger narrative structure. This narrative enabled support group participants to achieve three important support group purposes, as stated in the group's Frequently Asked Questions document (FAQ). My ability to detect ("see") the structural and functional significances of this narrative largely stemmed from the apperceptive background that I shared with participants (e.g., as an eating disorder sufferer and ongoing member of the group).

Moreover, as a participant-experiencer, dialogical intuition supported my attending to and interpreting the feelings I experienced, while engaging in support group interaction. For example, when engaging in discussions of "eating disorder voices," I progressively tapped into the evaluative-emotional significances of this metaphor and narrative structure within which it was housed. That is, I sensed their role in giving discursive shape—as illness narratives (Frank, 1995)—to painful eating disorder problems, which may otherwise remain inchoate and thereby unresolved.[8] Thus, these metaphorical and narrative structures enabled group participants to vent anxiety, frustrations and anger at their eating disorder conditions and to appeal to group members for emotional support and practical help. These sensed meanings formed through attending to my own emotions when using these shared linguistic resources to discuss my own and others' eating disorder experiences.

A second concept featured in Bakhtinian theory, creative understanding, additionally guides engaged researchers in merging participant-experiencer and analyst interpretive positions, enabling responsive understandings and moral ties to be formed. Creative understanding primarily relates to the analyst role. For example, in creative understanding, researchers bring their "foreign" perspectives as social analysts to bear on dialogical processes to illuminate new meanings:

"In creative understanding, the interpreter creates a special sort of dialogue. 'A meaning only reveals its depths once it has encountered and come into contact with another, foreign meaning; they engage in a kind of dialogue, which surmounts the closedness and one-sidedness of these particular meanings, these cultures' (RQ, p. 7). The result of these dialogues is to enrich both the text and its interpreter. The exchange creates new and valuable meanings possessed by neither at the outset" (Morson & Emerson, 1990, p. 289).

Engaged researchers form creative understandings as they draw on disciplinary knowledge (theories and methodologies) to reveal the micro-level complexities of the social interactions they are investigating and in which they are involved. As a result, researchers may generate fresh perspectives on local phenomenon as both "insiders"— cultural members of the interactive contexts they are studying—and as "others," "located outside the object of his or her creative understanding" (Bakhtin, 1979, cited in Morson & Emerson, 1990, p. 55).

I see it as important to stress a vital, transformative potential of creative understanding processes. This promise is reflected, in my view, in the following passage by Bakhtin:

"For one cannot even really see one's own exterior and comprehend it as a whole, and no mirrors or photographs will help; our real exterior can be seen and understood only by other people, because they are located outside us in space and because they are others" (cited in Morson & Emerson, 1990, p. 7).

Bakhtin seems to point to the ways in which the creative understandings of engaged communication researchers may go beyond advancing scholarship to benefit participants in online support group studies. That is, the new perceptions of one's own "exterior" that creative understandings potentially produce may be especially helpful to support group participants, who are often caught in unfavorable states of self-awareness.

For example, "no mirrors or photographs" are likely to convince women and girls struggling with eating disorders of their talents or self-worth. With creative understanding, I came to focus on the problem-solving and supportive skills that group participants showed in employing a local narrative to accomplish group purposes—an impressive achievement that participants did not explicitly acknowledge themselves. Such foregrounding of group participants' competencies, in my view, may equip them to see from a "foreign" perspective their "own exterior," ostensibly affording opportunities for positive change (e.g., new forms of intra- or interpersonal interaction that enhance the recovery-seeking purpose of support group discussions). It is important to recognize that traditional types of studies of online talk may also reveal new local meanings and catalyze positive changes among group participants. However, their origin in "one-sided" (non-interactive) analyses of "the already spoken about" (Shotter, 1996b, p. 484) renders them "impoverished," from a Bakhtinian viewpoint (Morson & Emerson, 1990, p. 183). That is, divorced from situated dialogue, "one-sided" (or passive) analyses replace "interactive processes with consummated products, and thus sacrifices the eventness of events for a mere theoretical 'transcription'" (Morson & Emerson, 1990, p. 183). In other words, researchers engaged in creative understanding, amid dialogue with group participants, produce mutually enriching interpretations. Moreover, writes Bakhtin, these understandings remain open to alternative (or future) meanings and change-oriented possibilities (Morson & Emerson, 1990).

Creative understanding and dialogic intuition operate in harmonious tandem in engaged research of public online support groups. That is, these processes may be jointly actualized as researchers merge their interpretative lenses (as analysts) and apperceptive backgrounds (as participant-experiencers) to explore and illuminate "seen" and "sensed" dimensions of group interaction. Both activities essentially emerge out of researchers' engagement in the ongoing, indeterminate, contingent flow of interactions that they study, whereby dialogic relations are created between selves and others, and situated, responsive understandings are formed.

The ethical nature of the interpretive activities guided by dialogical intuition and creative understanding lies in the fact that specific persons are uniquely responsible for their results, as Bakhtin explains below:

"Ethical action is born of a sense that each act is unrepeatable and responsibility is nontransferable. 'What can be accomplished by me cannot be done by anyone else, ever'" (Bakhtin, 1986, cited in Morson & Emerson, 1990, p. 179).

Here Bakhtin stresses that the understandings derived from interpretive processes—or aesthetic activities—are products of particular actions, people, times, and places, [and] cannot be generalized away" (Morson & Emerson, 1990, p. 184). In short, ethical interpretive activity results from meanings emerging between interacting persons—as first- and second-persons—not only from "the point of view of a nonparticipating 'third person'" (Bakhtin, 1984, cited in Morson & Emerson, 1990, p. 249).

In summary, I argue that a rhetorical-responsive version of social constructionism, with its key Bakhtinian roots, provide a theoretical framework and ethical foundation for engaged communication studies of public, online support groups. Below, I elaborate how this theoretical framework may be mapped onto qualitative, interpretive methodologies.

METHODOLOGICAL FOUNDATIONS OF ENGAGED RESEARCH

Qualitative, interpretive methods well suit engaged research in public, online support group contexts, as they readily afford dialogic relationships between researchers and group participants. As noted, these relationships allow "seen" and "sensed" layers of data to be bridged and ethical ties to be formed. Qualitative-interpretive methods can be innovatively coalesced to conduct engaged research, as well. For example, I found it helpful to incorporate a range of such methods in my larger analysis of online eating disorder support group interaction. The specific ways in which I employed these methods are discussed at length elsewhere (Walstrom, 1999, 2000a, in press). Methods relevant to the present discussion include discourse analysis (Fairclough, 1989, 1992; Schiffrin, 1994; van Dijk, 1989, 1993)—specifically micro-level discourse analysis (Ochs & Taylor, 1992; Ochs, Smith, & Taylor, 1996; Taylor, 1995a, b)—interpretive interactionism (Denzin, 1989), narrative analysis (Labov & Waletzky, 1967; Langellier, 1989; Riessman, 1993), conversation analysis (Atkinson & Heritage, 1984; Goodwin 1981; Jefferson & Lee, 1981; Sacks, Schegloff, & Jefferson, 1974) and Grounded Theory (Strauss, 1987). In the spirit of Denzin and Lincoln's (1994) notion of "researcher-as-bricoleur" (p. 2), I chose and employed qualitative-interpretive methods in ways that were consistent with my theoretical orientation and that deepened my evolving understandings of support group interaction.

These qualitative-interpretive methodologies enabled an engaged research project to unfold out of what was a coincidental discovery of a research site. I briefly overview this process to further clarify the emergent nature and ethical orientation of an engaged research approach. To elaborate, I discovered the online eating disorder support group while perusing the new selections that had appeared in my newsreader program. I followed this group's interaction for one year, benefiting from the way it bolstered my own recovery. During this year, I began to save posts featuring several metaphors that group participants used to represent their eating disorders.[9] These salient metaphors attracted both my personal and analytical interests. Personally, I identified emotionally with these metaphors, as they strongly resonated with my eating disorder experiences. Analytically, these metaphors seemed to index important events, given their location in affectively- and evaluatively-loaded sequences. At the end of one year, I had collected 5,609 posts that contained the metaphors to which I had been drawn. At this point, I felt deeply inspired to formally launch a study of support group interaction that could benefit both research and eating disorder support group communities. During the second year, I systematically collected and analyzed group posts in the form of entire threads, enabling an analysis of interactional sequences.[10] While collecting data, I focused on the metaphors that I had noticed previously. I used a variety of qualitative-interpretive methods to closely examine the micro-level structure and function of 144 support group threads (comprised of 823 posts). During this year-long phase of research, I introduced myself, personally and professionally, to support group participants—a point to which I return below.

The primary methods that I employed in my analysis are summarized next. This summary provides an important backdrop for the forthcoming excerpts from my larger study, which serve to demonstrate how engaged research may unfold. Grounded Theory guided an analysis of the salient, systematically-used metaphors that I observed in group discussions. Resulting core categories led to an analysis of narrative activity within two-part exchanges (an initial post and the subsequent replies to that post). A central finding that emerged from this analysis entailed a collective linguistic resource to which I referred as a "public narrative" (Somers & Gibson, 1994, p. 62).[11] This narrative enabled many group participants to accomplish supportive, informational and recovery-facilitating group purposes. Specifically, my analysis demonstrated how one public narrative facilitated sharing emotionality and intimacy (creating a safe interactional context) as well as posing solutions to and solving eating disorder problems (Walstrom 1999, 2000b). Further scrutiny of this narrative with discourse analytic tools led to a study of group participants' self-other "positionings" (Davies & Harré, 1990). This discursive practice refers to the taking up of protagonist positions by group participants within narrative activity and the locating of other participants within such positions, as well. I focused on positionings involving action, thinking, feeling, evaluating and states of being. Close examination of these positionings showed a complex, collaborative process of identity co-construction, whereby eating disorder identities were negotiated, challenged and afforded opportunity spaces to be transformed (Walstrom, 1999).

With this overview of the methodological foundations of one engaged research project, I proceed to illustrate how this process evolved. Below follows two excerpts from my longitudinal study of one public, online eating disorder support group. In the first excerpt, I present the first central finding of the initial two analytical phases noted, namely, one public narrative routinely employed by support group participants to accomplish problem-solving and emotional support. The second excerpt features a discourse analysis of this narrative focusing on its micro-level complexities.

ENGAGED ANALYSES OF ONLINE SUPPORT GROUP TALK

Narrative Analysis: "Generic" Features of a Public Narrative

A narrative analysis of online eating disorder support group interaction evidenced four generic components of one public narrative, including *typical addressee, main characters, plot* and *(evaluative) point*. Below I present ways in which these components jointly facilitated problem-solving activity. I first briefly introduce Bakhtin's theory of speech genres to show how it helpfully guided this phase of my analysis (Walstrom, 2000a).

Bakhtin (1986) argues that all utterances are situated in one or more speech genres, including "everyday narration" (p. 60). These genres may be primary or secondary. Primary genres include "everyday stories, letters, diaries" (Bakhtin, 1986, p. 98) or more generally, dialogue "of the salon, of one's own circle, and other types as well, such as familiar, family-everyday, sociopolitical, philosophical, and so on" (Bakhtin, 1986, p. 65). Secondary genres include novels and dramas (and other literary genres), scientific discourse and exposition/commentary, namely, those that "arise in more complex and comparatively highly developed and organized cultural communication" (Bakhtin, 1986, p. 62). Bakhtin (1986) argues that primary speech genres are highly diverse and depend on the "situation, social positioning, and personal interrelationships of the particulars of communication" (p. 79). In such situations and relations, a typical addressee is understood: "each speech genre has its own typical conception of the addressee and this defines it as a genre" (Bakhtin, 1986, p. 95). In primary speech genres—in part composed of "intimate genres and styles" (Bakhtin, 1986, p. 97)—the addressee is seen as one who is safe to direct the depths of one's personal experience. "Intimate speech is imbued with deep confidence in the addressee, in his [sic] sympathy, in the sensitivity and goodwill of his responsive understanding. In this atmosphere of profound trust, the speaker reveals his internal depths" (Bakhtin, 1986, p. 97). The extent to which speakers reveal their internal depths is connected to their facility for invoking various speech genres: "the better our command of speech genres, the more freely we reveal our individuality in them (where this is possible and necessary), the more flexibly and precisely we reflect the unrepeatable situation of communication" (Bakhtin, 1986, p. 80).

Within speech genres, the unrepeatable (unique) situation of communication remains in ongoing tension with the givenness of those genres. Some of these givens—according to Shotter (1995a), expanding on Bakhtin and Wittgenstein—involve "invented concepts," that is, practical resources for both drawing our attention to and making "discussible" matters to which "otherwise we would not know how to attend" (p. 173). These concepts, or "perspicuous representations," are embedded in a larger category of "language games" (Wittgenstein, 1953, cited in Shotter, 1995a, p. 173) through which it "becomes possible [in their situated use] to sense how different (metaphorical) ways of talking create different realities" (Shotter, 1995a, p. 174; cf. Lakoff & Johnson, 1980).

Guided by these Bakhtinian concepts, a narrative analysis demonstrated that support group participants appear to invoke, negotiate and maintain a type of primary speech genre—a public narrative—characterized by four generic features. My ability to discern these features stemmed from the dialogical relations I formed with group participants as a dually-positioned researcher, attending to the "seen" and "sensed" aspects of interaction (e.g., repeated metaphorical themes and their emotional-evaluative significances, respectively). From this mobile analytical perspective, I traced the dynamic flow between the givenness and newness of shared personal experiences in support group interaction, namely the systematic ways in which participants invoked a public narrative through four generic features. This dynamic flow between givenness and newness appears to be key to the ability of myriad participants with unique eating disorder experiences to share and solve commonly-faced eating disorder problems through one support group public narrative. Below follows a summary of the generic features of this public narrative that a narrative analysis of support group talk evidenced—typical addressee, main characters, plot and point.

The typical addressee(s) of the support group public narrative are other group participants. This claim is evidenced by the ways in which group participants portray recipients of their posts who are not evidently addressees. For example, group participants expressed concern about the fact that their posts were being archived within Deja News (now owned by Google.com) and might be sold by this clearinghouse for profit. That other support group members are considered as typical addresses is indexed, in my view, by the use of personal pronouns, marked in italics below. Moreover, this post suggests that researchers are also considered as possible addressees.

I question what is Dejanews and why are they archiving our posts? I've saved some posts because I find it helpful to reread them. I can understand if someone is doing research, the information we share could be helpful. But if Dejanews is going to sell our posts or our e-mail addressees, I'd be pretty alarmed.

In short, group participants' reaction to the potential wider audiences of their postings demonstrates that they view their discussions as being primarily directed toward each other, as typical addressees.

The main characters of the public narrative include a protagonist (a group participant) and an antagonist (usually an eating disorder). Analysis revealed two strategies that group participants employed to portray antagonists (eating disorders) as a voice. The first is "personification" (Lakoff & Johnson, 1980, pp. 33-35), wherein the voice is explicitly displayed. The second is reported speech (Voloshinov, 1973), whereby eating disorders are cast as speaking entities, engaged in dialogues with protagonists (group participants). Exchanges with eating disorder voices may be implied, for example, where quotation marks serve to index them. The fact the group participants rarely questioned such representations (e.g., "Who is being quoted here?") suggests precisely the commonality underlying the public narrative, whereby the eating disorder as an antagonist is so widely known that it (or often "he") need not be explicitly identified. Personification and reported speech may appear together or separately in one post.

These main characters tend to be portrayed within a distinct plot, a third generic feature of the public narrative. This generic feature embodies a dynamic relation between givenness and newness. For example, Bakhtin states that the plot cannot completely structure a work or be known in advance. This view of plot structure as indeterminate is echoed by Shotter (1989): "no plot is the plot" (p. 236).[12] I follow Shotter and Bakhtin in viewing the plot of the public narrative as "a way of setting optionally favorable conditions for intense dialogues with unforeseen outcomes" (Morson & Emerson, 1990, p. 247). The unforeseen outcomes arising through the public narrative plot seem to provide enabling conditions for the main characters (group participants) to create new "extra-plot connections" (Bakhtin, 1984, cited in Morson & Emerson, 1990, p. 247). Such connections appear to emerge in and through the public narrative plot, as it affords group participants (in its generic features) opportunity spaces (in its protagonist positionings) for creatively posing and solving problems.

One way the givenness (generic nature) and newness of the public narrative seem apparent is in the way its baseline plot may be invoked and uniquely developed by myriad group participants. The baseline plot features the eating disorder, often portrayed as a voice, engaged in a relentless quest to win control over group participants' individual actions. Specifically, the voice seeks to incite[13] group participants to perform eating disorder-related activities—behavioral or verbal (the latter involving what one does or says to oneself). The voice also seeks compliance from group participants directly or indirectly. A direct attempt may involve a command ("Don't eat that!"). An indirect attempt may entail a negative self-evaluation ("Look at her, she's so much more skinny than you!").[14]

The complicating action of this baseline plot may develop in at least three directions, or plotlines, according to my analysis. The first two directions are similar, involving (1) group participant displays of compliance (or an intention to comply) with the eating disorder voice's aims (e.g., restricting food or eating disorder-related activities) or (2) group participant displays of a struggle to resist or protest the eating disorder voice's aims in conjunction with compliance. In the latter case, participants at times refer to their compliance with the eating disorder voice's aims as having "listened" or "lost a battle" to this voice. An example from my larger analysis shows one group participant's compliance with the eating disorder voice:[15]

Example 1

01   Right now I'm sitting here writing in an effort to stop myself from going and eating.
02   I feel like I'm actually fighting myself, it's an exhausting battle going on in my
03   head, "I want food"; "NO, NO, NO, YOU'RE TOO FAT TO EAT!!!!!"

.
.

10   Fighting, fighting, fighting, fighting,
11   stomping on the ED voice—he won't go away!!!

With repeated complicities (e.g., losses or listenings), it appears that some group participants' everyday experiences entirely revolve around the dictates of the eating disorder. One participant expresses such a view: "anorexia is more than what I do[;] it is what I am and without it I am nothing."

A third direction that complicating action may take within the public narrative baseline plot also involves battles between the main characters—the initial poster (protagonist) and the eating disorder as a explicit or implicit voice (antagonist)—however, this conflict develops differently. That is, the voice's influence on group participants' eating disorder-related activities loses force. For example, the complicating action involves group participants' displays of noncompliance with the eating disorder voice's aims. Women at times refer to these transgressions as "winning a battle" over the eating disorder voice or "not listening" to it. Noncompliance may also entail replacing the eating disorder voice with a different voice:

Example 2

33   I have no clue where the voice from inside of me came from. I
34   never hear a positive voice, but last night I did. I keep saying I don't
35   have the strength to fight, but I realized last night I DO!!!!!

Through these three plotlines of the public narrative, an (implicit or explicit) central point may emerge, a fourth generic feature of this narrative. This (evaluative) point—a displayed preferred objective of protagonists (group participants)—entails a separation of the eating disorder from the self.[16] One way this separation may be accomplished is through a combined noncompliance with the eating disorder voice's aims and the practice of recovery-oriented activities. Another way this separation may occur is through an affirmation of the worth, or inherent value, of a group participant and the rejection of the worth or value of the eating disorder voice (and/or the practices or behaviors it advocates).[17] This combined separation (indicated by single arrows) and affirmation (indicated by double arrows) sequence is illustrated in the following excerpt:

Example 3

| | 27 | > Fighting, fighting, fighting, fighting, stomping on the ED voice—he |
| | 28 | > won't go away!!! I want to go cry because I'm pathetic. Sorry. *sobs* |

—>	29	Keep fighting, love! Keep stomping! Take that bast*rd ED voice, put him
—>	30	in a blender and pureÈ... then take the sludge that he is and bury him so
—>	31	deep in the soil he will never bother you again.

| —>> | 32 | You are not pathetic ... you are in pain. I am wiping the tears from your |
| —>> | 33 | eyes Amy, and embracing you with the warmest Keats-Hug I can. |

My analysis showed that this point of the public narrative may appear in responses or initial posts. As Example 3 illustrates, a respondent took up the role of articulating the (evaluative) point on behalf of an initial poster to become that positive voice advocating recognition and separation from the eating disorder voice.

It is important to note that this central point might not emerge in group participants' invoking of the public narrative. Whether or not the point appears depends on the individual circumstances of the group participants' using it. This indeterminacy of the public narrative plot (and point) seems to underscore how this narrative may be creatively used by group participants to make sense of eating disorder experiences, in general, and to engage in problem-posing and -solving, in particular. Such creative use of this "given" structure affords group participants valuable, new opportunities to create "extra-plot connections" (Bakhtin, 1984, cited in Morson & Emerson, 1990, p. 247) and "different realities" (Shotter, 1995a, p. 174).

I next present a second excerpt from my larger analysis that I argue demonstrates how the public narrative is invoked through its four generic features: typical addressee, plot, main characters and point. This excerpt features a unique instance of the public narrative as a tool for solving eating disorder problems. That is, my analysis primarily evidenced uses of the public narrative by group participants to portray personal struggles with eating disorders. However, the present exchange reflects how the public narrative may be used to present a collective eating disorder problem, highlighting its versatile strength. It also suggests how the public narrative—when invoked wittingly or unwittingly—relies on an unspoken apperceptive background (Voloshinov, 1973) of eating disorder struggles common to many group participants. Tapping into this shared perspective as a participant-experiencer, and employing methodological tools as an analyst, guided an engaged micro-level discourse analysis of support group narrative activity. An excerpt from this analysis follows, featuring the problem-solving capacity of this activity through one public narrative.

It is important to first note that my analysis does not support the claim that all support group participants are familiar with or use the public narrative. Rather, the analysis—based on a select number of support group exchanges—seeks to shed new light on an everyday social process (solving eating-disorder problems). I argue that this process, as evidenced within one online support group, can be inferred to be similarly operating more broadly (e.g., in other online or face-to-face eating disorder support groups). This view is supported by the Sartrean (1981) notion of universal singular, an alternative to validity and generalizablity recognized by the interpretive-interactionist stance intrinsic to my engaged analysis. According to Sartre, the particular or individual case may be experienced as an "instance of more universal social experiences and social processes" (Denzin & Lincoln, 1994, p. 202).

Discourse Analysis: Public Narrative as Problem-Solving Device

In the following two-part exchange, a veteran participant, Jackie, responds to a question posted to the online, eating disorder support group by an ostensibly new group participant, Elaine. Elaine's question requests clarification of a term often used in support group discussions that is confusing to her ("eating disorder voices"). In the micro-level discourse analysis below, I detail how the public narrative is invoked through its four generic features, and serves as a problem-posing and problem-solving tool.

Example 4[18]

Elaine:

    04   >everyone keeps talking about the "eating disorder voices" and i don't
    05   >think i have them...in a sense, it's like right before i go into ed mode,
    06   >i hear/feel nothing at all. i don't know what that means..................?

Jackie:

    07   We don't mean "voices" in the sense that a schizophrenic might hear
    08   voices. We refer to the eating disorder as having a "voice" because
    09   our minds tend to give us—often—a steady stream of unhealthy,
    10   eating-disordered propaganda. ("You're so fat!" "Don't eat that!"
    11   "Look at her, she's so much more skinny than you!," etc.)

    12   The reason we call this the "voice" of the eating disorder is that
    13   otherwise, we tend to think of it as our *own* voice. It's not.
    14   It's a "voice"—that is, thoughts—that are part of a sick,
    15   disordered part of ourselves. It's the voice of our eating disorder
    16   —not our own voice.

    17   (Does that make sense?)

    18   It's important to recognize that the eating disorder is not YOU.
    19   Understanding that the e-d "voice" is not your OWN is a good way to
    20   isolate it as a *disorder*, rather than an integral part of your
    21   Self.

22   I hope this helps!

23   Jackie

In lines 04-05, Elaine contrasts group participants' eating disorder experiences ("everyone keeps talking about 'the eating disorder voices'") and her own ("and I don't think i have them ... "). This distinction appears to index a status of "not belonging" (Shotter, 1993b, p. 126) to the online discourse community, that is, a "newbie" status. Elaine indirectly requests information to reconcile this difference through a display of uncertainty ("I don't know what that means ...." in line 06). The response-evoking nature of Elaine's utterance is visually accomplished through extended ellipses and a question mark. In these senses, Elaine poses a problem to be solved. I argue that the public narrative is invoked as a tool for problem-posing in line 04 ("everyone keeps talking about the 'eating disorder voices' ..."). Here Elaine refers to the main character (antagonist) of the public narrative ("eating disorder voices"). This problem-posing activity ostensibly occasions a reply—namely, a solution—that draws on this narrative, as well.

Jackie's reply appears to invoke the public narrative to offer a solution to Elaine's problem. In line 07, she begins to answer Elaine's question by contrasting the eating disorder voices shared by support group participants ("We don't mean 'voices' in the sense ...") and the voices often associated with persons with schizophrenia, clarifying the term's context-specific meaning. Jackie's use of the first-person, plural pronoun "We," in my view, indexes a shared set of meanings (an apperceptive background) inherent in the public narrative plot, as well as points toward its typical addressees (group participants). Jackie further contrasts the eating disorder voice and schizophrenia-related voices in lines 07-08. She accomplishes this contrast by using the plural form of voice in line 07 ("We don't mean 'voices' ...")—mirroring Elaine's use—to refer to schizophrenia-related voices and a singular form of voice in line 08 ("as having a 'voice'") to refer to the eating disorder voice.

Jackie continues to provide requested information about the meaning of the eating disorder voice by offering a reason why support group participants use such a term ("because our minds tend to give us ... ." in lines 08 through 10). I argue that this utterance indexes the public narrative through the featuring of its main characters (eating disorder voice as antagonist and selves/group participants as protagonists). Specifically, the baseline plot of the public narrative appears to be invoked through a portrayal of the eating disorder voice's destructive aims. That is, the voice is depicted—through personification (Lakoff & Johnson, 1980) and reported speech (Voloshinov, 1973)— as continuously dispensing false information ("a steady stream of unhealthy, eating-disordered propaganda," in lines 09 through 10) in order to incite group participants' eating-disorder-related activities. This influence of the antagonist (voice) appears to be conveyed both directly, through a command ("Don't eat that!"), and indirectly, through negative self-evaluations ("You're so fat! Look at her, she's so much more skinny than you!") in lines 10 through 11. The persuasive force of the command and negative evaluations are indexed by the intensifiers "so" and "so much more," as well as by exclamation marks.

The public narrative baseline plot is further evidenced in line 11, where the abbreviation "Etc." appears after the quotes by the eating disorder voice. This abbreviation seems to cast the voice as a source of multiple (perhaps infinite) commands and negative self-evaluations.[19] This use of "Etc." also sheds light on how the public narrative invites and affords group participants opportunities to fill in gaps (Iser, 1978; Shotter 1995b) in the narrative plotline. That is, group participants who share an apperceptive background may infer additional eating disorder voice criticisms. Such inferences index and reconstitute the ability of the public narrative to serve as a vital and versatile problem-posing and -solving tool.

In line 12, the public narrative point is implied, as Jackie asserts another reason why support group participants use the term "voice" to refer to their eating disorders ("The reason we call this the 'voice' ..."). This reason serves to contrast—or separate—participants' "*own*" voices and the eating disorder voice. I see this contrast being intensified through Jackie's use of emoticons (asterisks). The significance of this emphasis in presenting this contrast seems to enable Jackie to raise a problem associated with the eating disorder voice—that the voice at times is mistakenly believed to be participants' own voices (" ... we tend to think of it as our *own* voice. It's not." in line 13). In lines 14 through 15, the contrast between—or separation of—the voice of the self and the voice of the eating disorder is reinforced through further description of the latter. For example, Jackie portrays the eating disorder voice in a negative light—namely, as a condition to be remedied ("a sick, disordered part of ourselves"). I argue that this contrast gains additional force as Jackie subordinates the status of the eating disorder voice in relation to support group participants' "selves." That is, the eating disorder voice is described as composed of "thoughts" (line 14), rather than as possessing full "personhood," remaining consistent with the voice's generic character ("our minds tend to give us ..." in line 9). The voice seems further subordinated in relation to group participants' "selves" through repeated minimization of its status: "part of a sick, disordered part of ourselves" (lines 15-16).

The public narrative continues to be invoked in Jackie's problem-solving activity in lines 14 through 16 ("It's a voice that ..." and "It's the voice of ..."). Here the status and nature of the eating disorder voice—again depicted as subordinate to and separate from the self—are presented as "facts" (Potter, 1996, p. 112).[20] In other words, the structure of these claims not only establishes the voice's nature (as separate from one's own voice) and status (as subordinate to the self) as true, but also applies, or generalizes, that hopeful truth to all group participants.

The point, or main evaluative clause, of the public narrative explicitly emerges in line 18 ("It's important to recognize that the eating disorder is not YOU"). In this utterance, Jackie asserts another factual claim that again contrasts, or separates, the eating disorder (voice seems implied) and the self. This contrast notably accomplishes evaluation ("important"), indexing the point of the public narrative. Although this utterance is similar in structure and function to lines 14 through 16—also beginning with statements of fact ("It's a 'voice' ..."; "It's the voice of ...") and accomplishing evaluation ("part of a sick disordered part of ourselves")—it differs in one important way. That is, from within the apperceptive background ostensibly shared by the users of the public narrative, this utterance may be seen as a potential outcome (or climax) of a process (complicating action) involving a battle with and ultimate overcoming of (separating from) the eating disorder voice. In other words, although the complicating action—conflict between the self and the voice—is not explicitly displayed in Jackie's post, I argue that it may be inferred through the generic plot central to the public narrative that she invokes (e.g., through the reported speech in lines 10 through 11).[21] That is, typical addressees of this post, support group participants ("We"), may fill in gaps in the plotline—namely, supply missing sequences of eating-disorder-related challenges preceding this separation. Although Elaine, the primary addressee of Jackie's post, seems not to be a typical addressee—given her uncertainty about the term "eating disorder voices"—and thus may not be able to fill in plotline gaps, the plot may become accessible to her with continued participation in the support group forum.

The point of the public narrative, to separate the self from the eating disorder voice, is rephrased and upgraded in lines 19 through 21. For example, Jackie repeats the point ("Understanding that the ed 'voice' is not your OWN ...") and then supports it with a second claim ("is a good way to isolate it as a *disorder*, rather than an integral part of your Self"). Like lines 14 through 16, this claim both establishes a fact and performs an evaluation ("good"). The evaluation has two valences: (1) the eating disorder voice appears negatively evaluated ("*disorder*"), and (2) the action, or goal, portrayed (the separating, or isolating, of the self from the eating disorder voice) appears positively evaluated ("is a good way"). The negative evaluation is intensified by emoticons, that is, asterisks ("*disorder*"). In other words, stressing the unfavorable condition of "disorder" seems to discourage an equating of the self with the eating disorder voice. Jackie again subordinates the status of the eating disorder voice through a description of the voice as a fraction of the self ("part" in line 20). This subordinate status seems accentuated by the capitalizing of the word "Self" in line 21, implicitly demoting the eating disorder in relation to the self. The last line of Jackie's post appears to transition out of the public narrative into personal narrative in order to indicate a preferred function of her reply—to solve a problem ("I hope this helps!"). This intention is enthusiastically and warmly conveyed by an affective stance marker (exclamation point), indexing emotional support and intimacy.

In sum, these excerpts aim to show how an engaged research approach may evolve as qualitative-interpretive methods are employed to yield data-driven and emotionally-informed interpretations of public, online support group interaction. That is, engaged research findings unfold from both analyst and participant-experiencer perspectives, which illuminate "seen" and "sensed" realms of interaction, respectively. This process stems from initially attending to personal and analytical interests in support group talk, and proceeds as salient "seen" and "sensed" themes (e.g., routine uses of highly-charged metaphors) are closely examined with methodological tools. This dual-perspective and aesthetic activity also connects researchers ethically to group participants. Specifically, through active involvement in and shared responsibility for interactional outcomes, engaged researchers (as "natives") become morally linked to group participants in ways traditional investigators ("outsiders") often are not. Thus, I contend that an intrinsic ethical foundation can be seen to undergird an engaged approach to public, online support group studies.

MEETING ETHICAL CHALLENGES IN ONLINE SUPPORT GROUP ENGAGED RESEARCH

Here I elaborate three features of engaged communication research that I argue bolster its ethical merit for public, online support group inquiry. These features aim to meet the ethical challenges of studying these research contexts, namely guarding against risks of participant harm. These three features involve concealing participant identities, establishing relations of care and trust, and the seeking of practical benefits. I contend that these practices provide a sound ethical ground to engaged research praxis within public, online support group contexts.

First, engaged researchers seek to conceal the identities of support group participants by removing salient identifying information from posts. For example, I stripped the names, subject headings, dates, e-mail addresses, sending organizations and other obvious identifying information (e.g., nicknames) from the posts appearing in accounts of my analyses. Full quoting is commonly done in discourse analyses to substantiate the claims being made about the form of social interaction (Herring, 2001). Quoting also is important in engaged research to invite alternative interpretations and critiques. Additionally, full quoting aims to honor the voices and perspectives of participants themselves, which can be especially empowering to disfranchised groups. Therefore, given these rationales for full quoting, engaged researchers strive to respect public, online support group participants' privacy by removing salient identifying information. Such omissions help to ensure that group participant identities remain anonymous.

It is nevertheless the case that anonymity cannot be guaranteed as postings may be traced via online search engines. However, I see the deleting of salient identifying information as a viable way to mask group participant identities, given the technological means available for concealing identities online and the "technical realities," as Herring (2001) notes, of the Internet (i.e., discussion archiving). To elaborate, support group participants may obtain anonymous e-mail accounts. These accounts work by "stripping identifying information from the header of an incoming e-mail and forwarding it to its intended recipient with a substituted header that disguises the original sender's name and electronic address" (Jacobsen, 1999, p. 130). Granted, users who desire anonymity may not be motivated to use anonymous accounts. While recognizing this limitation, I see educating group members about anonymous e-mail accounts—if not already provided—as a feasible way for engaged researchers to attend to privacy and possible harm concerns. As Herring (2001) writes, responsibility for such instruction is to be taken by "experienced internet citizens, including researchers and site owners" (p. 8).[22]

Second, engaged researchers of public online support groups form relations of caring and trust with group participants. Such relations can be forged by establishing cultural membership. Cultural membership in engaged research involves more than following routine "netiquette" guidelines. For example, netiquette guidelines typically include reading support group discussions (lurking), learning group norms and participating in discussions (Mann & Stewart, 2000, p. 36). While these practices build cultural familiarity, cultural membership in engaged research results from detailing one's personal background with the problematic issue central to group discussions. The shared emotionality that unfolds in this process helps build relations of caring and trust between researchers and group participants. Such relations are further forged by the open sharing of research aims.

A self-introduction to the online support group enables engaged researchers to initiate relations of caring and trust. As researchers disclose personal background and analytical foci in such correspondence, they also demonstrate social competence (e.g., of interactional norms) and emotional involvement in group interaction—both key to cultural membership. Researchers' replies to group participants' responses to their self-introductions enable dialogic relations of trust and caring to begin to form. These relations in turn fortify researchers' ability to "see" and "sense" the intricacies of support group interaction. That is, caring and trusting relations enriches the apperceptive background upon which researchers draw during analysis.

For example, I began an extensive, two-part self-introduction to the online eating disorder support group by describing my own struggle with anorexia nervosa. I also acknowledged the benefit I had received in following the group, and a desire to continue contributing to collective recovery efforts. I then discussed my initial research aim of shedding light on participants' ability to achieve support group purposes (as stated in the FAQ), in general, and to understand the specific role of communication in those processes, in particular. I additionally noted my wish to anonymously (as possible) quote discussion postings. I concluded with an enthusiastic request for feedback. Through this self-introduction, I displayed competence and interest in observing group norms for first-time postings (e.g., in offering a self-introduction featuring relevant personal experience). I also emotionally identified with group participants and conveyed a sincere desire to illuminate processes that they valued themselves. Such efforts to establish cultural membership and disclose research aims were foundational to creating relations of caring and trust with group participants.

All responses that I received to my self-introduction (those privately sent and posted publicly) welcomed me to the group and supported my study. I received such replies for as long as two weeks following my introduction. Additionally, no one objected to or criticized my study or my presence when they replied to the postings in which I later referenced my project. Because potentially hundreds of participants had learned of my dual roles (as member and researcher), I took the consensus of positive feedback and acceptance that I received as a reasonable index of group participants' endorsement of my participation and project. I subsequently contributed to numerous support group exchanges, both publicly and privately. I see the consistent replies that I received to my participation as indexing relations of caring and trust between myself and group participants.[23]

Third, engaged studies of public, online support groups seek benefits for group participants. Such an aim embodies a feminist, communitarian ethic, which broadly "entails a commitment to the common good and to universal human solidarity" (Denzin, 1997, p. 274). This ethic stems from researchers' shared emotionality with group participants and a genuine desire to conduct inquiry that promotes participants' well-being. That is, guided by a feminist, communitarian ethic, analysts strive to engage in "research that makes a difference in the lives of real people" (Denzin, 1997, p. 268). Participant benefits may include offering new, potentially transformative understandings of support group processes, such as those that enhance participants' abilities to achieve support group purposes. Another benefit may entail a critique of dominant institutional discourses that structure public representations of group participants' problematic experiences, which often constrain their ability to understand and cope with them effectively (Walstrom, 1996).

One benefit of the present analysis involved locating and recognizing the narrative skills through which group participants cooperatively solved destructive eating-disorder problems—a crucial process in eating disorder recovery efforts. I envision my larger study positively impacting both online support group members and the wider eating-disorder community by making research findings available in mainstream forms (cf.

Riessman, 1993; Tierney, 1995). Specifically both print and online translations of research findings may importantly contribute to the direly-needed resources for eating disorder prevention and recovery.[24] In seeking this aim, I follow several eating disorder researchers and clinicians who have enriched eating disorder resources through producing mainstream publications, supporting prevention and recovery efforts (Garrett, 1998; Claude-Pierre, 1997).[25]

Echoing Waern (2001), I underscore the importance of ensuring that research benefits outweigh possible risks to participant harm in engaged studies of public online support groups. The present study observed this crucial criterion in several ways. For example, in familiarizing myself with the FAQ document of the public, online eating disorder support group, I learned that procedures for obtaining anonymous e-mail accounts were well detailed as noted. Moreover, I observed within group interactions numerous, explicit discussions and routine uses of such email accounts during the time that I collected data. I viewed this information as evidence of low "perceived levels of privacy" of group discussions by participants (Eysenbach & Till, 2001, p. 1104). Stated alternatively, this information seemed to support the view, following Bruckman (2001), that no "reasonable expectation" existed regarding the privacy of group communication (p. 3). Additionally, attempts to minimize possible harm were done by ensuring that my study met institutional and discipline-specific standards for ethical research. As discussed by Suler (2000), this was accomplished by consulting senior colleagues about ethical issues of the study, having the study approved by a research ethics committee and demonstrating the scientific merit of the study. Careful efforts to address concerns for harm and sincere attempts to seek participant benefits reflects the third way engaged research meets the ethical challenges of public online support group analyses.

CHARTING FUTURE
ENGAGED RESEARCH DIRECTIONS

I have presented an engaged research approach to public online support groups in high-risk online contexts, which warrant heightened efforts to guard against risks to participant harm. This approach is rooted in researchers' navigating between analyst (third-person) and experiencer-participant (second-person) interpretive positions. These positions equip researchers to richly "see" and "sense" the meanings of local interaction, forming dialogical relations with support group participants. The ethical foundation of this approach lies in the moral and emotional ties that form through these relations. This foundation is guided by the theoretical framework at the heart of engaged research, based in a rhetorical-responsive version of social constructionism and, relatedly, Bakhtinian theory. A discussion of the evolving phases and qualitative-interpretive methods central to one online, support group analysis aimed to show how this theoretical framework may unfold to enable ethical, engaged inquiry. The ethical nature of such engaged studies can be fortified in three key ways: masking group participant identities, cultivating researcher-group participant relations of caring and trust, and seeking group participant benefits (both local and wider eating-disorder support group communities). These three essential features of engaged research join its dually-positioned interpretive core to address potential risks of participant harm in public, online support group studies. Thus,

I argue that engaged research provides a viable ethical alternative to traditional analyses of public, online support group interaction.

I see attractive academic and professional incentives for future engaged studies of public, online support groups. First, as noted, engaged research may advance understandings of communication processes online, as it delves into an interactional realm—"between first and second persons"—that is seldom researched, according to Shotter (1989). Specifically, important future discoveries may stem from the dual positions of engaged researchers, as "third-person" (analytical) lenses are brought to bear on "second-person" (participant-addressee) stances amid group interactions. That is, as Shotter (1996) contends, through active involvement in the development of the interaction researchers can "begin to grasp how ... the communication process works" (p. 63). These understandings, Shotter (1995b) writes, are derived from "perceiving otherwise unnoticed connections or relations between features of the everyday life activities we wish to study, not as third person outside observers of them, but from within them as (to some extent) second person involved participants" (p. 170). In addition to academic benefits, I see engaged research of public online support groups as enriching the practices of therapists and related health care professionals. That is, these groups may readily incorporate into their practices the advances made in public online support group research.[26] For example, refined understandings of support group problem-solving activity may enable clinical support group facilitators to improve the quality of therapeutic outcomes.[27]

In sum, I see rewarding benefits linked to increased engaged research of public, online support interaction. Those inspired to heed this call may further disciplinary knowledge and enrich the lives of those intimately linked to the processes they study. More broadly, engaged researchers may fuel the exciting, revolutionary changes occurring in healthcare worldwide by expanding understandings of avidly-sought, Internet medical resources.

REFERENCES

Atkinson, J. M. & Heritage, J. (Eds.) (1984). *Structures of Social Action: Studies in Conversation Analysis*. Cambridge: Cambridge University Press.

Bakhtin, M. M. (1984). *The Problem of Dostoevsky's Poetics* (C. Emerson, Ed., and Trans.). Austin, TX: University of Texas Press. (Original work published in 1973).

Bakhtin, M. M. (1986). The problem of speech genres. In C. Emerson & M. Holquist (Eds.), *Speech Genres & Other Late Essays* (V. W. McGee, Trans., pp. 60-102). Austin, TX: University of Texas Press. (Original work published 1979).

Barak, A. (1999). Psychological applications on the Internet: A discipline on the threshold of a new millennium. *Applied and Preventative Psychology, 3,* 231-246.

Barnes, S. (1998, November). *How ethical lessons learned on-line shape future research ethics*. Paper presented at the National Communication Association, New York, NY, USA.

Baym, N. (1995a). From practice to culture on Usenet. In S. L. Star (Ed.), *The Cultures of Computing* (pp. 29-52). Cambridge, MA: Blackwell.

Baym, N. (1995b). The emergence of community in computer-mediated communication. In S. Jones (Ed.), *Cybersociety: Computer-Mediated Communication and Community* (pp. 138-163). Thousand Oaks, CA: Sage.

Baym, N. (1996). Agreements and disagreements in a computer-mediated discussion. *Research on Language and Social Interaction, 29,* 315-345.

Bruckman, A. (2001). *Ethical guidelines for research online: A strict interpretation.* Retrieved from: http://www.cc.gatech.edu/~asb/ethics/.

Capps, L. & Ochs, E. (1995). *Constructing Panic: The Discourse of Agoraphobia.* Cambridge, MA: Harvard University Press.

Cavenaugh, A. (1999). Behavior in public?: Ethics in online ethnography. *Cyberpsychology, 6.* Retrieved from: www.socio.demon.co.uk/magazine/6/cavanaugh.html.

Chen, S-L. S., Hall, G. J., & Johns, M. D. (in press). Research paparazzi in cyberspace: The voices of the researched. In M. D. Johns, S-L. S. Chen, & G. J. Hall (Eds.), *Online Social Research: Methods, Issues, and Ethics.* New York: Peter Lang.

Claude-Pierre, P. (1997). *The Secret Language of Eating Disorders: The Revolutionary New Approach to Understanding and Curing Anorexia and Bulimia.* New York: Random House.

Colon, Y. (1996). The public forum: Chatt(er)ing through the fingertips: Doing group therapy online. *Women & Performance, 17*(9), 205-215.

Davies, B. & Harré, R. (1990). Positioning: The discursive production of selves. *Research on Language and Social Interaction, 20,* 43-63.

Denzin, N. (1989). *Interpretive Interactionism.* Newbury Park, CA: Sage.

Denzin, N. (1997). *Interpretive Ethnography.* Thousand Oaks, CA: Sage.

Denzin, N. (1999). Cybertalk and the method of instances. In S. Jones (Ed.), *Doing Internet Research: Critical Issues and Methods for Examining the Net* (pp. 107-125). Thousand Oaks, CA: Sage.

Denzin, N. & Lincoln, Y. (eds.) (1994). *Handbook of Qualitative Research.* Thousand Oaks, CA: Sage.

Edwards, D. & Potter, J. (1992). *Discursive Psychology.* London: Sage.

Ess, C. & Association of Internet Researchers (AoIR). (2002). *Ethical decision-making and Internet research: Recommendations from the AoIR ethics working committee.* Retrieved from: www.aoir.org/reports/draftFIVE.html.

Eysenbach, G. & Till, J. E. (2001). Ethical issues in qualitative research on Internet communities. *British Medical Journal, 323,* 1103-1105.

Fairclough, N. (1989). *Language and Power.* London: Longman.

Fairclough, N. (1992). *Discourse and Social Change.* Cambridge: Polity.

Ferguson, T. (1996). *Health Online.* Reading, Mass.: Addison-Wesley.

Ferguson, T. (1997). Health care in cyberspace: Patients lead a revolution. *The Futurist, 31*(6), 29-34.

Finn, J. (1996). Computer-based self-help groups: On-line recovery for addictions. *Computers in Human Services, 13,* 21-41.

Foucault, M. (1979). *Discipline and Punish: The Birth of a Prison.* New York: Random House.

Fox, S. A. (1998, November). *The uses and abuses of computer-mediated communication for people with disabilities.* Paper presented at the National Communication Association Convention, New York, NY, USA.

Frank, A. W. (1995). *The Wounded Storyteller: Body, Illness, and Ethics*. Chicago, IL: The University of Chicago Press.

Frankel, M. S. & Siang, S. (1999). *Ethical and legal aspects of human subjects research on the Internet*. Retrieved from: www.aaas.org/spp/dspp/sfrl/projects/intres/main.htm.

Garrett, C. (1998). *Beyond Anorexia: Narrative, Spirituality, and Recovery*. Cambridge, UK: Cambridge University Press.

Gergen, K. J. (1982). *Toward Transformation in Social Knowledge*. New York: Springer-Verlag.

Gergen, K. J. (1985). The social constructionist movement in modern psychology. *American Psychologist, 40*, 266-275.

Goodwin, C. (1981). *Conversational Organization: Interaction Between Speakers and Hearers*. New York: Academic Press.

Grohol, J. M. (1999). *The Insider's Guide to Mental Health Resources Online*. New York: Guilford Press.

Harré, R. (1983). *Personal Being: A Theory for Individual Psychology*. Oxford, UK: Basil Blackwell.

Herring, S. (October, 2001). *Ethical challenges to doing research on the Internet: The CMDA perspective*. Presented at the Second International Conference of the Association of Internet Researchers, Minneapolis-St. Paul, Minnesota, USA.

Holquist, M. (1990). *Dialogism: Bakhtin and his World*. London: Routledge.

Iser, W. (1989). The play of the text. In S. Budick & W. Iser (Eds.), *Languages of the Unsayable* (pp. 325-339). New York: Columbia University Press.

Jacobsen, D. (1999). Doing research in cyberspace. *Field Methods, 11*(2), 127-145.

Jacoby, S. & Ochs, E. (1995). Co-construction: An introduction. *Research on Language and Social Interaction, 28*, 171-183.

Jankowski, N. & van Selm, M. (2001). *Research ethics in a virtual world: Some guidelines and illustrations*. Retrieved from: http://www.brunel.ac.uk/depts/crict/vmpapers/nick.htm.

Jefferson, G. & Lee, J. (1981). The rejection of advice: Managing the problematic convergence of a "troubles-telling" and a "service encounter." *Journal of Pragmatics, 5*, 339-422.

Jones, S. (ed.) (1999). *Doing Internet Research: Critical Issues and Methods for Examining the Net*. Thousand Oaks, CA: Sage.

Kassirer, J. (1995). Transforming the delivery of health care. *Consumer Research Magazine, 78*, 27-30.

Katz, A. M. & Shotter, J. (1996). Hearing the patient's "voice": Toward a social poetics in diagnostic interviews. *Social Science & Medicine, 43*, 919-31.

Labov, W. & Waletzky, J. (1967). Narrative analysis: Oral versions of personal experience. In J. Helm (Ed.), *Essays on the Verbal and Visual Arts* (pp. 12-44). Seattle, WA: University of Washington Press.

Lakoff, G. & Johnson, M. (1980). *Metaphors We Live By*. Chicago, IL: The University of Chicago Press.

Langellier, K. (1989). Personal narratives: Perspectives on theory and research. *Text and Performance Quarterly, 9*, 243-276.

Mann. S. & Stewart, F. (2000). *Internet Communication and Qualitative Research: A Handbook for Researching Online*. London: Sage.

Mead, G. H. (1934). *Mind, Self, and Society: From the Standpoint of a Social Behaviorist*. Chicago, IL: University of Chicago Press.

Miller, J. K. & Gergen, K. J. (1998). Life on the line: The therapeutic potentials of computer-mediated conversation. *Journal of Marital and Family Therapy, 24*, 189-202.

Morson, G. S. & Emerson, C. (1990). *Mikhail Bakhtin: Creation of a Prosaics*. Stanford, CA: Stanford University Press.

Murphy, L. J. & Mitchell, D. L. (1998). When writing helps to heal: E-mail as therapy. *British Journal of Guidance & Counseling, 26*, 21-32.

Ochs, E. & Taylor, C. E. (1992a). Family narrative as political activity. *Discourse & Society, 3,* 301-340.

Ochs, E., Smith, R., & Taylor, C. E. (1996). Detective stories at dinnertime: Problem-solving through co-narration. In C. L. Briggs (Ed.), *Disorderly Discourse: Narrative, Conflict, and Inequality* (pp. 95-113). New York: Oxford University Press.

Pomerantz, A. (1978). Compliment responses: Notes on the cooperation of multiple constraints. In J. Schenkein (Ed.), *Studies in the Organization of Conversational Interaction* (pp. 79-112). New York: Academic Press.

Pomerantz, A. (1984). Agreeing and disagreeing with assessments: Some features of preferred/dispreferred turn shapes. In J. M. Atkinson & J. Heritage (Eds.), *Structures of Social Action: Studies in Conversation Analysis* (pp. 57-101). Cambridge, UK: Cambridge University Press.

Potter, J. (1996). *Representing Reality: Discourse, Rhetoric, and Social Construction*. London: Sage.

Riessman, C. K. (1993). *Narrative Analysis*. Newbury Park: Sage.

Sacks, H., Schegloff, E., & Jefferson, G. (1974). A simplest systematics for the organization of turn-taking for conversation. *Language, 50,* 696-735.

Schwandt, T. S. (1994). Constructivist, interpretivist approaches to human inquiry. In N. Denzin & Y. Lincoln (Eds.), *Handbook of Qualitative Research* (pp. 118-137). Thousand Oaks, CA: Sage.

Sharf, B. (1997). Communicating breast cancer on-line: Support and empowerment on the Internet. *Women & Health, 26*, 65-85.

Shotter, J. (1984). *Social Accountability and Selfhood*. Oxford, UK: Basil Blackwell.

Shotter, J. (1989). Social accountability and the social construction of you. In J. Shotter & K. J. Gergen (Eds.), *Texts of Identity* (pp. 133-151). London: Sage.

Shotter, J. (1993a). Becoming someone: Identity and belonging. In N. Coupland & J. Nussbaum (Eds.), *Discourse and Lifespan Identity* (pp. 5-27). Newbury Park: Sage.

Shotter, J. (1993b). *Conversational Realities: Constructing Life Through Language*. London: Sage.

Shotter, J. (1993c). Harré, Vygotsky, Bakhtin, Vico, Wittgenstein: Academic discourses and conversational realities. *Journal for the Theory of Social Behavior, 23,* 459-482.

Shotter, J. (1995a). Dialogical psychology. In J. A. Smith, R. Harré & L. VanLanganhove (Eds.), *Rethinking Psychology* (pp. 160-178). London: Sage.

Shotter, J. (1995b). In conversation: Joint action, shared intentionality, and ethics. *Theory and Psychology, 5,* 49-73.

Shotter, J. (1996). Talk of saying, showing, gesturing, and feeling in Wittgenstein and Vygotsky. *The Communication Review, 1,* 471-495.

Shotter, J. & Gergen, K. J. (1994). Social construction: Knowledge, self, others, and continuing the conversation. In S. Deetz (Ed.), *Communication Yearbook* (Vol. 17, pp. 3-33). Thousand Oaks, CA: Sage.

Siang, S. (1999, Fall). Researching ethically with human subjects in cyberspace. *Professional Ethics Report, 12*(4). Retrieved from: www.aaas.org/spp/dspp/sfrl/per/per19.htm.

Simblett, G. J. (1997). Leila and the tiger: Narrative approaches to psychiatry. In G. Monk, J. Winslade, K. Crocket, & D. Epston (Eds.), *Narrative Therapy in Practice: The Archaeology of Hope* (pp. 121-157). San Francisco, CA: Jossey-Bass.

Somers, M. R. & Gibson, G. D. (1994). Reclaiming the epistemological "other": Narrative and the social constitution of identity. In C. Calhoun (Ed.), *Social Theory and the Politics of Identity* (pp. 37-99). Oxford, UK: Blackwell.

Strauss, A. (1987). *Qualitative Analysis for Social Scientists*. Cambridge, UK: Cambridge University Press.

Suler, J. (2000). Ethics in cyberspace research. In *Psychology of Cyberspace*. Retrieved from: http://www.rider.edu/users/suler/psycyber/ethics.html.

Taylor, C. E. (1995a). *Child as apprentice-narrator: Socializing voice, face, identity and self-esteem amid the narrative politics of family dinner*. Unpublished doctoral dissertation, University of Southern California, USA.

Taylor, C. E. (1995b). You think it was a fight?: Co-constructing (the struggle for) meaning, face, and family in everyday narrative activity. *Research on Language and Social Interaction, 28,* 283-317.

Tierney, W. G. (1995). (Re)presentation and voice. *Qualitative Inquiry, 1,* 370-390.

van Dijk, T. A. (1989). Structures of discourse and structures of power. In J. A. Anderson (Ed.), *Communication Yearbook* (Vol. 12, pp. 89-59). London: Sage.

van Dijk, T. A. (1993). Principles of critical discourse analysis. *Discourse & Society, 4,* 249-283.

Voloshinov, V. N. (1973). *Marxism and the Philosophy of Language* (L. Matejka & I. R. Titunik, Trans.). Cambridge, MA: Harvard University Press. (Original work published 1929).

Waern, Y. (2001). *Ethics in Global Internet Research* (Rep. No. 2001.3). Linköping University, Department of Communication Studies.

Walstrom, M. K. (1996). "Mystory" of anorexia nervosa: New discourses for change and recovery. In N. Denzin (Ed.), *Cultural Studies: A Research Annual* (Vol. 1, pp. 67-100). Greenwich, CT: JAI Press.

Walstrom, M. K. (1997, November). *Identity co-construction in Internet-based support group narratives: Implications for recovery*. Paper presented at the National Communication Association Annual Convention, Chicago, Illinois, USA.

Walstrom, M. K. (1999). *"Starvation... is who I am": From eating disorder to recovering identities through narrative co-construction in an Internet support group*. Unpublished doctoral dissertation, University of Illinois, Urbana-Champaign, USA.

Walstrom, M. K. (2000a). "The eating disorder is not YOU": Applying Bakhtin's theories in analyzing narrative co-construction in an Internet support group. In N. Denzin (Ed.), *Studies in Symbolic Interactionism* (Vol. 23, pp. 241-260). Greenwich, CT: JAI Press.

Walstrom, M. K. (2000b). "You know, who's the thinnest?": Combating surveillance and creating safety in coping with eating disorders online. *CyberPsychology & Behavior, 3*(5), 761-784.

Walstrom, M. K. (2001, Fall). Eating disorder resources on the Web. *Feminist Collections: A Quarterly of Women's Studies Resources, 23*(1), 31-35.

Walstrom, M. K. (in press). "Seeing and sensing" online interaction: An interpretive interactionist approach to USENET support group research. In M. D. Johns, S-L. S. Chen, & G. J. Hall (Eds.), *Online Social Research: Methods, Issues, and Ethics.* New York: Peter Lang.

Wertsch, J. V., Tulviste, P., & Hagstrom, F. (1993). A sociocultural approach to agency. In E. A. Foreman, N. E. Minick, & C. A. Stone (Eds.), *Contexts for Learning: Sociocultural Dynamics in Children's Development* (pp. 336-356). New York: Oxford University Press.

White, M. & Epston, D. (1990). *Narrative Means to a Therapeutic Ends.* New York: W. W. Norton.

Winter, D. & Huff, C. (1996). Adapting the Internet: Comments from a women-only forum. *The American Sociologist, 27,* 30-54.

Winzelberg, A. (1997). The analysis of an electronic support group for individuals with eating disorders. *Computers in Human Behavior, 13,* 393-407.

Wittgenstein, L. (1953). *Philosophical investigations.* Oxford, UK: Blackwell.

ENDNOTES

1   Female-only, online support groups have been found to be particularly safe places on the Internet. See Walstrom (2000b) for an overview of research and analysis of various linguistic practices that characterize such fora.

2   The participant-experiencer stance reflects an interpretive interactionist view, which holds that inquiry essentially departs from the researcher's biography (Denzin, 1989). See Walstrom (in press) for a larger discussion of the interpretive interactionist dimension of an engaged research approach to public, online support groups.

3   These purposes, as stated in the support group FAQ document, include serving as a resource for those seeking information, support and recovery, a point further elaborated below.

4   See Schwandt (1994) for a discussion of other versions of social constructionism.

5   Shotter (1995b) writes that the superaddressee is "an ethically active, living entity beyond all those actually present" (p. 53).

6   Some studies of online, eating disorder support groups also feature passive approaches to research (cf. Finn, 1996; Winzelberg, 1997).

7   In recognizing the controversy over the authorship of Bakhtin and Voloshinov's work, I regard Bakhtin as representing the perspectives, if not the products, of the works attributed to Voloshinov.

8   Frank's (1995) writings on illness narratives have importantly influenced my analysis of online support group talk. I was especially struck by the transformative role of these narratives, according to Frank, as structures for presenting to, and having witnessed by, familiar others one's often otherwise unexpressed health traumas.

⁹   Group participants used a variety of metaphors to portray and dialogue with their eating disorders (e.g., "monster," "dictator," "committee," and "eating disorder voice").

¹⁰   A thread is one initial post and all replies to that post, identified by respondents' use of the same subject headers as initial posters.

¹¹   Somers and Gibson (1994) define public narratives as "those narratives attached to cultural and institutional formations larger than the single individual, however local or grand, micro or macro" (p. 62). These narratives—featuring plots, drama and selectively appropriated events—range from "the narratives of one's family to those of the workplace (organizational myths), church, government, and nation" (p. 62).

¹²   Following Shotter (1989), I argue that narrative cannot be structured—or emplotted—in advance, but rather is comprised of "actual facts" whose nature is not wholly determined. In a situated instance of narrative, these "actual facts"—also called "vague facts"—are given or lent a determinate nature and order (p. 235).

¹³   The use of "incite" here reflects a relentless panopticon-like (Foucault, 1979), self-monitoring activity in which I observed support group participants engaging through the public narrative.

¹⁴   Although the eating disorder and support group participants are portrayed as distinct protagonists, I recognize that the negative evaluations spoken by the eating disorder voice are nevertheless products of a "self" (group participants), and thus may be seen as self-evaluations. This view seems to expand on Pomerantz's (1978, 1984) study of self-deprecations, and suggests a promising prospect for future research.

¹⁵   Posts are presented in original form (including typos and spacing), pseudonyms replace all real names and heading information has been removed.

¹⁶   The separation process referred to by support group participants resembles the process that narrative therapists seek to initiate among their patients, including women with anorexia and bulimia (Simblett, 1997). This therapeutic technique is referred to as externalization (White & Epston, 1990).

¹⁷   The online, eating disorder support group FAQ document also featured, at the time of my analysis, an instance of this public narrative point—namely, the separating of the self from an eating disorder and the affirming of one's own worth. This instance seems to reflect the importance of this point, and its larger narrative structure, to the achieving of support group purposes:

*Believe this, because it is true: You are a dear and valuable
person. You are not your disease. You are a dear and valuable
person with a disease...*

¹⁸   To avoid redundancy, I omitted the quoting of Elaine's initial post (lines 1-3 within this example) in Jackie's reply. Such quoting represents "embedding" (Baym, 1995a, p. 40)—the incorporation of all or some segments of initial posters' messages within replies (each line of the embedded post beginning with the ">" sign). The use of embedding fashions a dialogue-like interaction out of a monologic electronic format, lending to Baym's (1996) observation of Internet interaction as a hybrid form of communication.

19   The abbreviation "Etc." also seems to powerfully index an unlimited capacity of the eating disorder voice to control, monitor and perpetuate eating disorder-related activities (e.g., through evaluating, ordering and shouting).

20   According to Potter (1996), accounts cast in the form of "X is a fact" (p. 112) require no further support or justification to establish their truth status.

21   Here a struggle between group participants' selves and the eating disorder voice may be inferred, as these utterances can be seen, in a Bakhtinian sense, as responses to prior utterances (e.g., ostensibly as denials to prior requests to eat).

22   The online, eating disorder support group FAQ document contains detailed instructions for obtaining anonymous email accounts.

23   Currently, the support group FAQ document includes a statement requesting that researchers refrain from conducting studies of discussions. This statement was not present during any phase of my participation or study. The presence of such a statement, and whether or not it is to be regarded as a barrier to research, reflects one of the current controversies surrounding public, online support group studies.

24   I see as critical the bolstering of online resources for eating disorders, because unlike many other forms of eating disorder assistance, they may be widely and privately accessed. See Walstrom (2001) for a review of an impressive array of online eating disorder resources currently available online of both professional and personal nature.

25   The Vancouver-based Anti-Anorexia/Anti-Bulimia League has created an impressive archive of recovery narratives. The potential for eating disorder prevention of these hopeful accounts is accomplished, according to eating disorder therapist Simblett, (1997), as women "discover elements [of eating disorders] both similar to and different from their own" (p. 158).

26   I see practitioners of narrative therapy (cf. White & Epston, 1990; Simblett, 1997) as key beneficiaries of future studies of public, online support group narrative activity, and regard this potential as a fruitful extension of the engaged analysis presented in part here (Walstrom, 1999).

27   I thank colleague and eating disorder therapist Barbara Murphy for acknowledging and underscoring this point.

Chapter XI

Peering into Online Bedroom Windows: Considering the Ethical Implications of Investigating Internet Relationships and Sexuality

Monica Whitty
University of Western Sydney, Australia

ABSTRACT

To date, there is a scarcity of literature available on the ethical concerns that accompany research into online relationships and sexuality. This chapter attempts to redress this balance. Questions are raised as to whether researchers should be permitted to lurk in chatrooms or take on different identities in order to obtain data. It is argued here that conceptions of cyberspace as one generic space is a narrow construction and that instead researchers need to consider the fuzzy boundaries between what constitutes a public and a private space online. How we perceive this space has important implications for future research.

INTRODUCTION

The focus on Internet relationships has escalated in recent times, with researchers investigating such areas as the development of online relationships (Whitty & Gavin, 2001, Whitty, 2003), the formation of friends online (Parks & Floyd, 1996) and misrepresentation online (Whitty, 2002a). The accessibility of online lascivious material has also been a popular area to study. For example, researchers have examined what types of individuals peruse the Web for erotic material, with an attempt to identify those addicted to accessing Internet erotic material (Cooper, Putnam, Planchon, & Boies, 1999). Moreover, others have been interested in Internet infidelity (Whitty, 2002b) and cybersex addiction (Young, Griffin-Shelley, Cooper, O'Mara, & Buchanan, 2000). Notwithstanding this continued growth of research in this field, researchers have neglected to stop and consider how one might best conduct research of this kind in an ethical manner. While many of the ethical issues raised in this chapter can be (and sometimes are) applied to online research in general, the focus here is on the concomitant ethical concerns of ongoing research into Internet relationships and sexuality. Given that the development and maintenance of online relationships, and the engaging in online sexual activities can be perceived as private and very personal, there are potentially ethical concerns that are unique to the study of such a topic area.

This chapter provides a brief background on the research conducted to date on Internet relationships and sexuality. It then proceeds to outline the benefits of studying this area and the advantages in recruiting participants online. Ethical concerns in respect to the types of methods social scientists employ to collect data online are discussed. For example, it is questioned whether lurking or deceptive strategies to collect data are ethical or even necessary, especially in respect to the study of online relationships and sexuality. The argument proposed here is that there are fuzzy boundaries between what constitutes a public and private space online and that when we debate concerns on virtual ethics we need to consider this ambiguity. Finally, this chapter considers practical concerns, such as informed consent, withdrawal of consent, confidentiality, psychological safeguards and cross-cultural differences.

REVIEW OF RESEARCH ON INTERNET RELATIONSHIPS AND SEXUALITY

Let me begin this chapter by providing an adumbration of research that has been conducted to date on Internet relationships and sexuality, while recognizing an exhaustive review of the literature is beyond the scope of this chapter. Early research into this area has mostly focused on the similarities and differences between online and offline relationships. Researchers have been divided over the importance of available social cues in the creation and maintenance of online relationships. Some have argued that online relationships are shallow and impersonal (e.g., Slouka, 1995). In contrast, others contend that Internet relationships are just as emotionally fulfilling as face-to-face relationships, and that any lack of social cues can be overcome. With time, they suggest, the reported differences between online and offline relating dissipates (Lea & Spears, 1995; Parks & Floyd, 1996; Walther, 1996). In addition, researchers have purported that the ideals that are important in traditional relationships, such as trust, honesty and commitment, are equally important online, but the cues that signify these ideals are different (Whitty & Gavin, 2001). Current research is also beginning to recognize that for some, online relating is just another form of communicating with friends and lovers and that we need to move away from considering these forms of communication as totally separate and distinct entities (e.g., Vayreda, Galvez, Nunez, & Callen, 2002; Whitty, 2003). Before highlighting key ethical issues that we need to consider when studying Internet relationships, this chapter provides some examples of the types of research questions and methodologies employed to examine Internet relationships and sexuality.

Internet friendships developed in chatrooms, newsgroups and MUDs or MOOs have been examined by a number of researchers. For example, Parks and Floyd (1996) were interested in how common personal relationships are in newsgroups. To this end, they randomly selected 24 newsgroups and within each of these newsgroups selected, again randomly, 22 individuals who had posted messages to the group over several days. These individuals were then e-mailed surveys, which asked if they had formed new acquaintances, friendships or other personal relationships as a consequence of participating in these newsgroups. Parks and Floyd (1996) found that personal relationships were commonly formed in newsgroups, with just over 60 percent of their sample forming some type of relationship with another person first contacted within the newsgroup. In a follow up to this study, Parks and Roberts (1998) examined relationships developed in MOOs. They were interested in the types of relationships formed within these online settings and the demographic characteristics of people who develop these types of relationships. Again they elected to investigate this question by developing a survey. To recruit participants they employed a two-stage sampling procedure. Initially seven different MOO groups were selected, and in the second stage 1,200 MOO characters who had connected to the MOOs within the previous 14 days were randomly selected; 200 MOO characters from the five largest MOOs and 100 MOO characters were selected from the two smaller MOOs. These researchers found that most (93.6 percent) of their participants had reported having formed some type of personal relationship online, with the most common type being a close friendship.

Researchers have also been interested in how the playful arena of the Internet impacts on the types of relationships formed in these places (e.g., Whitty, 2003). Turkle's (1996) research on swapping identities in MUDs is well known. Turkle researched MUDs by entering these places, observing the interactions that took place and interviewing some of the MUDs participants. She made the contentious claim that the role-playing aspect of MUDs actually creates opportunities for individuals to reveal a deeper truth about themselves. In my own research, using face-to-face interviews, I have found that while chatrooms do provide opportunities for people to lie about themselves, this does not necessarily lead to the formation of shallow relationships. Paradoxically, it can open a space for a deeper level of engagement with others (Whitty & Gavin, 2001). This is illustrated in the following quotes from an interview conducted with a 29-year-old man and a 17-year-old man, respectively:

You also lose the ability to be able to judge people's honesty effectively. It's a lot easier to do that in person, um, but there's a certain advantage to it. You lose your inhibitions, your insecurities. You can talk a lot more easily to people. It's a bit of an even cut of pros and cons (Whitty & Gavin, 2001, p. 629).

You can never be sure that anyone you talk to on the Net is telling the truth so there's very little trust. That can work both ways because you're free to be whatever you like, which means your not intimidated by what people think (Whitty & Gavin, 2001, p. 629).

While Turkle (1996) suggested that it is fairly common for people to lie on the Internet, more recent empirical data suggests that experimentation with one's physical appearance online does not occur as frequently as one might expect (e.g., Cooper, Delmonico, & Burg, 2000; Roberts & Parks, 2001; Whitty, 2002a). Moreover, I have found that men tend to lie online more than women, typically exaggerating aspects of themselves, such as education, occupation and income, which are aspects men often tend to exaggerate offline in order to attract women (Whitty, 2002a).

Social researchers have also examined the initiation and development of romantic relationships. These studies have ranged from observing interactions that occur online, to conducting interviews and administering questionnaires. The prime focus has been on whether individuals can develop genuine relationships online and then develop these relationships successfully offline. To give an example, Baker (2000) collected case studies to make comparisons between a couple who met online and are now married, with a couple who met online and are still apart. She asked the question "Why was one couple able to progress from online communication to meeting offline to marriage, yet the other couple with seemingly similar beginnings is not together now (though they now talk of joining up one day)?" (p. 238). To investigate this, she identified couples who met online with the intent of meeting offline, then requested these individuals complete an open-ended questionnaire, and followed this up with a phone interview. She concluded that two fundamental aspects affected the couples' ability to have an offline relationship: (1) physical appearance and shared values and (2) commitment, risk and resources. Taking these ideas further, McKenna, Green and Gleason (2002) were interested in whether individuals who are better able to disclose their "true" selves online than offline were more equipped to form close relationships online and then take these relationships offline successfully. To test this theory McKenna et al. (2002) randomly selected 20 Usenet newsgroups to include in their study. Over a three-week period, questionnaires were e-mailed to every fifth poster in each of the newsgroups (excluding Spam). Their first study found that indeed when people convey their "true" self online, they develop strong Internet relationships and bring these relationships into their "real" lives. Two years after this initial study, 354 of the 568 participants were e-mailed a follow-up survey (the remainder of the sample had e-mail addresses that were no longer valid). In line with these researchers' prediction, these relationships remained relatively stable and durable over the two-year period; however, one has to wonder how the 38 percent of the sample that were not followed up faired.

Other researchers have recognized the importance of examining the development of romantic relationships from a developmental perspective. For example, Clark's (1998) study considered teenagers' dating on the Internet. She examined these types of relationships within a much broader study, which examined the role of media technologies within domestic settings. To conduct this research she interviewed and observed

15 families and held two focus groups. From this initial study three teenagers were trained as peer leaders for discussion groups. They were selected on the basis that they represented "information-rich cases." The motive behind this methodology was to capture how teenagers "really" talk in the absence of adults. The three teenagers were requested to recruit six friends of the same gender, and these three teenagers were then expected to lead the group discussion and tape record the conversation. In addition, Clark lurked in teen chatrooms and used e-mail exchanges that she had obtained from one of the three teenagers. While it is perhaps difficult to generalize from three focus groups, Clark (1998) maintains that cyber-dating relationships were seen as emancipatory for many of the girls. The girls in her study were in a position to reject unwanted sexual advances, and, on the other hand, were able to adopt new physical personae to appear more attractive to boys. Clark (1998) also points to differences between teen chatrooms and adult chatrooms, stating, perhaps not surprisingly, that adults are typically more explicit about their sexual desires.

In addition to the examination of romantic relationships, researchers have focused their attention on sexuality on the Web. Cybersex addiction and the available treatment for these cybersex addicts and their partners has been an area of research and concern for psychologists (e.g., Freedman, 1999; Schneider, 2000; Shaw, 1997; Young, Pistner, O'Mara, & Buchanan, 1999; Young, 1998; Young et al., 2000). In my own research, I have examined what constitutes an online act of infidelity, which given that participants believed many online acts, such as cybersex, to be acts of betrayal, also has some important therapeutic implications (Whitty, 2002b). In addition to the examination of sex addicts and questions around online infidelity, some researchers have been interested in the types of people who peruse the Web for erotic material. Cooper et al. (1999) identified three categories of individuals who access Internet erotic material, including, recreational users, sexual compulsive users (these individuals are addicted to sex per se, and the Internet is but one mode where they can access sexual material) and at-risk users (these individuals would never have developed a sexual addiction, if it were not for the Internet). Cooper et al.'s (2000) research extended past anecdotal data of clinical cases to focus on individuals who access the Internet for sexual purposes. These researchers found that most of their participants, who surfed the Web for erotic material, did not experience significant problems in their lives.

ETHICAL ISSUES PERTINENT TO THE STUDY OF INTERNET RELATIONSHIPS AND SEXUALITY

While the aforementioned studies have each asked unique research questions, which have warranted varying research methodologies, one feature they all have in common is that they are researching a sensitive topic, which requires individuals to reveal personal and often very private aspects of themselves and their lives. This next section raises some ethical concerns by considering some of the research summarized above, and provides further examples from Internet relationship research to highlight and discuss these concerns in greater detail.

Are there any Benefits or Drawbacks to Conducting this Type of Research?

Before social scientists embark on any research they need to ask the question: What are the benefits of conducting such research and who will benefit from the findings of the study? This is quite a pertinent question in respect to the examination of Internet relationships and sexuality. One needs to ascertain whether the research is simply motivated by a voyeuristic curiosity about the types of interactions that take place online, or, if instead, the results will provide important insights from which others will benefit in the future. As illustrated in the research above, there is a plethora of important reasons and implications for conducting research on Internet relationships and sexuality. Issues concerning social support, trust, honesty, health, safety, infidelity, addictions and so forth all warrant attention by social researchers. If we subscribe to the view that Internet relationships and sexuality ought to be studied, then we next need to question how we should proceed to research this area.

Much of the research, to date, on Internet relationships and sexuality has been conducted online—either through interviews, surveys or by carrying out analysis on text that is readily available online. When we consider ethical concerns in respect to studying Internet relationships and sexuality, we need to consider whether collecting data via the Internet has any advantages over collecting data via more traditional offline methods. If we find that this is not the case, then perhaps we should abort attempts at gathering data online and turn back to more traditional methods, where ethical standards have already been established.

It is proposed here, however, that there are many advantages to conducting research online, as well as collecting text or data available online for analysis in one's research. Some of the practical benefits of conducting research online include: easy access to a population of individuals who do form relationships online and who do access sexual material, relatively limited required resources, as well as ease of implementation. I would like to expand further here on the first practical benefit.

Mann and Stewart (2000) and Nosek, Banaji and Greenwald (2002) have said that the Internet provides researchers with a population that is typically hard to reach (for example, people with disabilities, agoraphobia, mothers at home with infants, etc.). Mann and Stewart (2000) also suggest that computer-mediated communication (CMC) enables researchers to contact people in locations that have closed or limited access (e.g., prisons, hospitals, etc.). In addition to the strengths Mann and Stewart (2000) highlight, with respect to Internet relationships and sexuality, the Internet, it would seem, is an ideal place to recruit individuals. This is especially pertinent if assumptions held by some social researchers are true: that these individuals are potentially socially anxious, shy or simply do not have time in their lives to form relationships by more traditional methods.

In respect to Internet relationships and sexuality, it is proposed here that although in many instances an online survey or an interview is an appropriate way to acquire a sample, we still need to proceed with caution. For instance, we cannot expect that simply placing a survey online will automatically collect a large, diverse sample. Rather, as researchers, we need to consider what groups of people, from what types of backgrounds, are important to include in our studies, and then ensure that these individuals are made aware of our research projects. This method of recruitment was employed by some of the aforementioned studies, including, for example, McKenna et al. (2002). We should always bear in mind that our research questions should guide our sampling procedures. For instance, in researching attitudes towards Internet infidelity (Whitty, 2002b), it was imperative to collect a sample both online and offline, given that individuals who do not use the Internet may still have opinions on these relationships, especially if their partner is engaging in these activities. Had my sample been restricted to online participants, the results would have only been relevant and beneficial to a restrictive sample of the population.

COLLECTING ONLINE TEXT

As discussed earlier, a common reason for using the Internet for researching online relationships and sexuality is to analyze the text produced by people online. The text can be produced in a number of different forums, including, chatrooms, MUDs and newsgroups. One way researchers collect data is by lurking in these different spaces in cyberspace.

Lurking

A lurker is a participant in a chatroom or a subscriber to a discussion group, listserv or mailing list who passively observers. These individuals typically do not actively partake in the discussions in these forums. Some social scientists have opted to play the role of lurker for the purposes of collecting data. The development of online relationships (both friendships and romantic) and engaging in online sexual activities, such as cybersex, could easily be perceived by those engaging in such activities as a private discourse. Given the nature of these interactions, social researchers need to seriously consider if they have the right to lurk in online settings in order to learn more about these activities—despite the benefits of obtaining this knowledge. In some ways this could be perceived as "peering in online bedroom windows." I now turn to explore this issue further with some examples from past research.

Mehta and Plaza (1997) examined pornography in public newsgroups. They predicted that anonymous, noncommercial users would be more likely to post explicit material, compared to commercial distributors (who have a greater awareness of the legal ramifications of posting such material and are more easily traceable). A content analysis was performed on 150 randomly selected pornographic images from 17 alternative newsgroups, which they named. They found that their hypothesis was not supported, and that instead commercial users were more likely to post explicit pornography in public access newsgroups. They suggested that commercial users are perhaps motivated to take risks, such as publishing highly erotic material and sometimes illegal material (such as child pornography), because this is a means of attracting new customers to their private pay-per-use bulletin board services.

In a follow-up study, Mehta (2001) visited 32 Usenet newsgroups and randomly selected 9,800 pornographic images. These pictures were posted by commercial, anonymous and nonanonymous individuals and were images of the individuals themselves, their sexual partners and others. He rated the images according to whether they were commercial or noncommercial, rarity of a particular pornographic image, number of participants interacting sexually in an image, type of penetration, oral sex, masturbation, ejaculation, homosexual sex, bondage and discipline, and the use of children and adolescents. Mehta (2001) found some significant changes in the type of material being posted on these newsgroups since his previous study, including a greater proportion of images of children and adolescents.

While both these studies provide important information for psychologists, social scientists and criminologists, they also raise some important ethical and legal questions in respect to how we conduct our research online. Although it was not discussed, one might wonder if these researchers sought permission to use their institutions' servers to peruse Internet sites containing illegal material, and what the legal ramifications are if they did not. Another less obvious question, which I believe as social researchers we need to start asking is: Are these public Usenet newsgroups the same type of media as commercially sold erotic videos, pornographic magazines and comics (as these researchers allude to)? If not, then we can we apply the same ethical standards to this media as we would to offline content? Ferri (1999, cited in Mann & Stewart, 2000) has asserted that "private interactions do take place in public places" (p. 46). Sharf (1999) supports this view, stating that "despite widely announced admonitions concerning the potential for public exposure, there exists the paradox that writing to others via e-mail often feels like a private or, in the case of an online group, quasi-private act" (p. 246). Mann and Stewart (2000) make the point that men having sex in beats are quite private acts occurring within public spaces. Indeed it would be ethically challenging to justify observing such beats for the sake of our research. I am proposing here that there are fuzzy boundaries between what constitutes public and private spaces online. I would like to suggest that this is not a clear-cut issue, and that in addressing the issue, it would also be counter-productive for social scientists to answer this question in respect to the entire Internet. Instead, we need to acknowledge that there are different places online. For example, a chatroom might be deemed a more public space than e-mail. This is a crucial ethical concern that should not be swept under the carpet, and it would be arrogant for social researchers to debate this issue amongst themselves, without consulting the individuals who inhabit the Internet. Hence, while there is no answer offered here, it is strongly contended that the way forward in our research is to begin questioning the nature of this space. To this end, it is contended here that lurking in public newsgroups might be ethically questionable. We must, as researchers, debate how intrusive a method lurking potentially is. As Ferri (1999, cited in Mann & Stewart, 2000) contends "who is the intended audience of an electronic communication—and does it include you as a researcher?" (p. 46).

Miskevich (1996) has quite rightly raised the question of whether it is ethical for social scientists to play the role of lurker on the Internet, collecting any data that piques their curiosity. She also questions that if it is acceptable to collect data, what limits should be placed on the type of data collected and how this data is consequently analyzed. In the examples above, for instance, should the limits have been placed on analyzing the commercial material, and consent obtained from the rest of the participants?

As suggested above, in debating this topic we might want to distinguish between public and private spaces in cyberspace. If we are to make divisions between private and public spaces online, the demarcations are not so obvious. As previously raised by Ferri, private interactions can and do indeed occur in public places. It has been theorized that the Internet can give an individual a sense of privacy and anonymity (e.g., Rice & Love,

1987). The "social presence theory" contends that "social presence" is the feeling one has that other persons are involved in a communication exchange (Rice & Love, 1987). Since computer-mediated relating (CMR) involves fewer nonverbal cues (such as facial expression, posture, and dress) and auditory cues in comparison to face-to-face communication, it is said to be extremely low in social presence. Similarly, "the social context cues theory" (Sproull & Kiesler, 1986) proposes that online and face-to-face communication differ in the amount of social information available. Social cues, such as nonverbal behaviors, and the physical environment are not available online. The absence of such cues can lead to more uninhibited behavior, such as verbal aggression, blunt disclosure and nonconforming behavior. This type of behavior, known as "flaming," has been observed across a range of online settings, including business, governmental, educational and public networks (e.g., Lea, O'Shea, Fung, & Spears, 1992; Parks & Floyd, 1996).

The above-mentioned theories might aid us in our discussions on the ethical challenges involved in collecting text online for our research. Even if we conclude that these spaces are public spaces, the anonymity they afford can give the illusion that these are private spaces. Can we as researchers ethically take advantage of people's false sense of privacy and security? Is it ethically justifiable to lurk in these sites and download material without the knowledge or consent of the individuals who inhabit these sites? This is especially relevant to questions of relationship development and sexuality, which are generally understood to be private matters. It is suggested here that good ethical practice needs to consider the psychology of cyberspace and the false sense of security the Internet affords. It is quite naïve of researchers to simply equate online media with what on first thought might appear to be offline equivalents (such as magazines and videos). In the cases presented above, it is perhaps the commercial material that is more akin to the offline equivalents, such as commercially available pornographic magazines and videos.

Deception

While it might be unclear as to how ethical it is for lurkers to collect data on the Internet, there is less doubt as to whether it is acceptable to deceive others online in order to conduct social research, especially with respect to online relationships and sexuality. According to the Australian National Health and Medical Research Council (NHMRC), which set the ethical guidelines for Australian research:

"as a general principle, deception of, concealment of the purposes of a study from, or covert observation of, identifiable participants are not considered ethical because they are contrary to the principle of respect for persons in that free and fully informed consent cannot be given" (NHMRC, 1999).

They do, however, state that under certain unusual circumstances deception is unavoidable, when there is no alternative method to conduct one's research. However, in these circumstances, individuals must be given the opportunity to withdraw data obtained from them during the research to which they had not originally give consent. Moreover, the council stipulates that "such activities will not corrupt the relationship between researchers and research in general with the community at large" (NHMRC, 1999).

While many studies have adhered to such guidelines in respect to Internet research on relationships and sexuality, there are others who have not. Lamb's (1998) study is an example of a highly deceptive study, which did not entirely respect the rights of its participants (Whitty & Gavin, 2001). In this study he examined others in chatrooms by participating in the chat room. He mostly visited sites for adults seeking young men. In his interactions with his unsuspecting participants, Lamb adopted several identities, all of which were teenage bi-sexual males. He described himself as an honors student, who was athletic, sexually active, financially comfortable and curious. He also stated to each person he spoke to that he was either related to or acquainted with a psychologist with whom he discussed his chatroom experiences.

Lamb (1998) estimated that he chatted in total with approximately 1,000 screen personalities. In about half of the occasions, while chatting in a public chat room, Lamb's persona was invited into a private room, where the researcher and the unknowing participant engaged mostly in sexual conversations. From his experiences he divided the 1,000 screen names that he interacted with into three broad categories. These included: "The Browsers," genuinely curious people who were exploring the medium and expecting to contact real people, "The Cruisers," who were seeking instant sexual gratification through fantasized sexual relations and masturbation, and "The Pornographers," who wanted to gather and trade pornography.

The aims of Lamb's research were arguably important, that is, to explore whether deviancy is evident and possibly rampant in chatrooms. The implication being that these are places for pedophiles to abuse children. However, despite the utility of this information, it can be equally argued that the methodology that Lamb employed was unethical. Participants were deceived throughout the research, and while Lamb claims to have given hints to each participant (although he does not clarify what these hints were) that this might be recorded and later utilized in research, the intention behind the interactions were more covert than overt. In addition, Lamb does not state that he provided an opportunity for participants to withdraw data obtained from them during the research. While some have questioned whether deception and lurking are ethical ways to collect data, Lamb's research crossed this line when he decided to not simply observe but to also participate. Such research, despite all its good intentions, can create a virulent reputation for social researchers.

There are possibly alternative ways of obtaining the information that Lamb acquired. For instance, participants could be interviewed about the types of interactions that they have experienced in these chatrooms. These interviews could have taken place one on one in these private chatrooms, rather than presenting another opportunity for individuals to engage in highly erotic conversations. Alternatively, Lamb could have been up front about his identity and how he was going to use his data. He should have obtained consent from the individuals and the moderator (if there was one for this chatroom). In addition, he should have provided an opportunity for participants to withdraw consent.

At a recent psychology conference on relationships, I heard an interesting counter-view to obtaining informed consent or disclosing one's true identity as a researcher to participants in cyberspace. One psychologist remarked that everyone lies in cyberspace, it is the status quo, and it is quite simply expected. This academic concluded that it was permissible for researchers to not reveal all their cards, given that this is already a deceptive environment. In response, I would like to consider two main points. Firstly, as researchers is it our role to blend into the environments we research and to act the same way as our participants? Secondly, the so-named fact that everyone lies on the Internet is probably more myth than fact—especially when we begin to realize that individuals interact differently in some places on the Web (see Whitty, 2002a).

PRACTICAL CONSIDERATIONS

This next section considers suggestions for best practice in respect to studying Internet relationships and sexuality and can, in many ways, generalize to other forms of online research. It examines informed consent, withdrawal of consent, confidentiality, psychological safeguards and cross-cultural differences.

Informed Consent

Given the ethical dilemmas of being a lurking, deceptive researcher, in many cases the better alternative is to set up a reasonable system in place for our participants to give informed consent. Sixsmith and Murray (2001) have stressed that collecting data without informed consent can be potentially damaging to the research process, especially when these unknowing participants discover their words have been used without their consent or knowledge. In offline research individuals often sign a form to give their consent; however, this is not always achievable online. One way around this is demonstrated in Gaunt's (2002) study. Gaunt was interested in the types of friendships established in online chatrooms. He recruited participants by entering these rooms and asking whether individuals would be interested in conducting an online interview about their online friendships. If participants were interested in being interviewed and if they were over the age of 16 years, Gaunt directed the participant to a website, which contained information about his project. This website informed the participants about the purpose of the study, the procedure that would be employed and the ethics involved, as well as contact details of the researcher, his supervisor and the university's human ethics committee.

Participants were informed that if they continued by returning to the private chat room where the researcher was waiting, that this would be taken as being indicative of their informed consent to participate in the research. All this having taken place, the interview would commence (Gaunt, 2002).

In some cases, spaces on the Web are moderated. In these instances, it is probably also appropriate to contact the moderators of the site prior to contacting the participants. This is analogous to contacting an organization prior to targeting individuals within that organization. Wysocki (1998) was interested in examining "how and why individuals participate in sexually explicit computer bulletin boards; and to see if sex online is a way of replacing face-to-face relationships or a way of enhancing them" (p. 426). She researched this by considering the social construction of love and sexuality as constructed by users of a Bulletin Board Service (BBS) called the "Pleasure Pit." Rather than employ covert methods, Wysocki was up front with her identity as a researcher. She originally approached the systems operators and told them that she was a sociologist who was interested in using Pleasure Pit to collect data. The operators were enthusiastic about her research and she was invited to meet them and learn how the Bulletin Board Service operated. She found that the service had a system in place to ensure that no participants were minors. To recruit participants, a sign went up on the bulletin board stating:

There will be a female here at the Pleasure Pit office to do interviews with anybody who happens to be online ... she is doing research on BBS relationships and is interested in what happens to your inhibitions when your [sic] on the key board (we know what happens to them). Watch for more info on her activities. I may call your voice to set up a voice interview with her. If you volunteer you will be first called and you husband types (with spouses not into this) be sure to let me know that you do or don't want a call (Wysocki, 1998, p. 430).

Following from this, she placed her questionnaire, which contained forced choice and open-ended questions, in the Pleasure Pit. To ensure confidentiality, when Wysocki collected the respondents' answers, she separated the participant's name from the survey and assigned a number to each questionnaire. In addition, Wysocki interviewed some participants online. Participants that read her notices contacted her and she interviewed them in real time in chat mode.

While there are improvements that could have been made to Wysocki's procedure, it does provide a better alternative to downloading text without the participants' consent. The steps that Wyscocki carried out could, however, have been ameliorated. In her first notice, participants should have been given more details about the project so that they could make informed consent. The aims of the project and how the data were to be utilized needed to be included. Whether participants' responses were confidential or not should have been made clear in the initial notice. Moreover, Wysocki's contact details and the institution she was conducting the research at should have been provided from the very beginning of the project so that people could contact her about any questions they had about the project. The respondents should have been informed from the outset that their responses would remain anonymous and that their identities would not be revealed in any publication of the results. A project of this sort, as with many projects on sexuality and relationships, have the potential to cause distress for a participant—even when there is no malice intended from the researcher. Safeguards need to be put into place to ensure the participant has a professional to turn to if for some reason the interview or questionnaire causes some psychological distress. One further question raised by this research is: Should researchers expose the names of the chatrooms, bulletin boards and newsgroups from which participants are recruited?

While the above studies and suggestions potentially deal with consent in a fairly reasonable manner, we should also be aware that some European countries require written consent (Mann & Stewart, 2000). Mann and Stewart (2000) suggest that if written consent is required then the participant could download a form and sign it offline and then return it by fax or postal mail.

Withdrawal of Consent

We need to also consider the withdrawal of consent. In research about relationships and sexuality, in particular, there is the risk that the interview or survey has created too much stress for the participant to continue. As with offline research we need to consider up until what point a participant can withdraw consent. For example, it is obviously too late to withdraw consent once the results have been published—hence it is a little naïve to state the participants can withdraw consent at anytime. The end point of withdrawal of consent might be, for instance, after the submitting of the survey, or at the conclusion of the interview, the interviewer might find confirmation that the participant is happy to allow the researcher to include the transcript in the study. As social scientists, we should also be aware that the lack of social cues available online makes it more difficult for us to ascertain if the participant is uncomfortable. Thus we should tread carefully and make an effort to check at different points in the interview if the individual is still comfortable with proceeding.

There are other issues unique to Internet research with respect to withdrawal of consent. For example, the computer could crash midway through an interview or survey. Mechanisms need to be put into place to allow that participant to rejoin the research, if desired, and consent should not be assumed if it is not certain why the interview ceased. In addition, in circumstances such as the computer or server crashing, we might need to have a system to enable debriefing, especially if the research is asking questions of a personal nature. Nosek et al. (2002) suggest that debriefing can be made available by providing a contact e-mail address at the beginning of the study. They also suggest providing "a 'leave the study' button, made available on every study page, [which] would allow participants to leave the study early and still direct them to a debriefing page" (Nosek et al., p. 163). In addition, they state that participants be given a list of frequently asked questions (FAQs), since they argue that there is less opportunity to ask the sorts of questions participants typically ask in face-to-face interviews.

Confidentiality

There are various ways we might deal with the issue of confidentiality. As with offline research, we could elect to use pseudonyms to represent our participants or even request preferred pseudonyms from them. However, a unique aspect of the Internet is that people typically inhabit the Web using a screen name, rather than a real name. Can we use a screen name given that these are not real names? While they may not be people's offline identities, individuals could still be identified by their screen names if we publish them—even if it is only recognition by other online inhabitants. Again this is relevant especially to the study of online relationships, which is a more sensitive and private interaction. Gaunt (2002) proposed a sensible alternative in his research on Internet friendships. Not only did he replace the screen name with a pseudonym, but he also replaced these screen names with a similar theme. For example, if a participant used the screen name PSYCHOFELLA, he would replace it with CRAZYGUY in the publication of the results. He did this to demonstrate the themes of the screen names utilized in his study. While in all cases this may not exactly bear the same connotations, it most cases it will, and this is potentially a more ethical alternative than exposing people's online identities.

Psychological Safeguards

As mentioned earlier in this chapter, research into the areas of relationships and sexuality is likely to cause psychological distress for some. It is perhaps much more difficult to deal with psychological distress online and with individuals in other countries. It is difficult to provide names of psychologists in other countries available to counsel the participants. Nevertheless, it is imperative that we ensure that the participant does have counseling available to them, if the research has caused them distress—which sometimes might be delayed distress. This could mean that there are limits to the kinds of topics about which we interview participants online or that we restrict our sample to a particular country or region where we know of psychological services that can be available to our participants, if required.

Cross-Cultural Differences

While ethical standards are fairly similar across cultures, in particular across Western cultures, we need to consider that these might vary slightly when we are drawing from samples from across the world. In respect to studying Internet relationships and sexuality, we find that there are numerous cross-cultural differences. If we want to include a cross-cultural sample from the Internet, then as researchers we need to consider these potential differences prior to embarking on our research. If we do not want to consider these differences (which is the researchers' prerogative), then we should be clear to specify which countries we want to include in our studies. In addition to being sensitive towards cross-cultural ethical practice, we should also be aware of the variations in legislation worldwide in respect to content on the Internet.

CONCLUSION

While this chapter has provided examples of ways forward in our thinking about virtual ethics in respect to the study of online relationships and sexuality, it is by no means prescriptive or exhaustive. Rather, it is suggested here that debate over such issues should be encouraged, and we should avoid setting standards for how we conduct our Internet research without also considering the ethical implications of our work. To add to the complexity of this debate, we need to understand the nature of the Internet, and recognize that it is not one generic space. Furthermore, the boundaries are fuzzy between what is a private and public space online. The way forward is to not restrict the debate amongst social scientists, but to also consult the individuals we would like to and are privileged to study.

REFERENCES

Baker, A. (2000). Two by two in cyberspace: Getting together and connecting online. *CyberPsychology & Behavior, 3*(2), 237-242.

Clark, L. S. (1998). Dating on the Net: Teens and the rise of pure relationships. In S. G. Jones (Ed.), *New Media Cultures: Vol. 2 Cybersociety 2.0: Revisiting Computer-Mediated Communication and Community* (pp. 159-183). Thousand Oaks, CA: Sage Publications Inc.

Cooper, A., Delmonico, D. L., & Burg, R. (2000). Cybersex users, abusers, and compulsives: New findings and implications. *Sexual Addiction & Compulsivity, 7*(2), 5-29.

Cooper, A., Putnam, D. E., Planchon, L. A., & Boies, S. C. (1999). Online sexual compulsivity: Getting tangled in the net. *Sexual Addiction & Compulsivity, 6*(2), 79-104.

Freedman, L. S. (1999). Hot Chat: Virtual affairs can become very real emotionally. In R. Simon, L. Markowitz, C. Barrilleaux, & B. Topping (Eds.), *The Art of Psychotherapy: Case Studies from the Family Therapy Networker* (pp. 42-51). New York: John Wiley & Sons.

Gaunt, N. (2002, April). *Doing it live in cyberspace: Online interviewing for social psychological research?* Paper presented at SASP, Adelaide, Australia.

Lamb, M. (1998). Cybersex: Research notes on the characteristics of the visitors to online chat rooms. *Deviant Behavior, 19,* 121-135.

Lea, M. & Spears, R. (1995). Love at first byte? Building personal relationships over computer networks. In J. T. Wood & S. W. Duck (Eds), *Understudied Relationships: Off the Beaten Track* (pp. 197-233). Newbury Park, CA: Sage.

Lea, M., O'Shea, T., Fung, P., & Spears, R. (1992). 'Flaming' in computer-mediated communication: Observations, explanations, and implications. In M. Lea (Ed.), *Contexts of Computer-Mediated Communication* (pp. 89-112). London: Harvester Wheatshaft.

Mann, C. & Stewart, F. (2000). *Internet Communication and Qualitative Research: A Handbook for Researching Online.* London: Sage.

McKenna, K. Y. A., Green, A. S., & Gleason, M. E. J. (2002). Relationship formation on the Internet: What's the big attraction? *Journal of Social Issues, 58*(1), 9-31.

Mehta, M. D. (2001). Pornography in Usenet: A study of 9,800 randomly selected images. *CyberPsychology & Behavior, 4*(6), 695-703.

Mehta, M. D. & Plaza, D. E. (1997). Pornography in cyberspace: An exploration of what's in usenet. In S. Kiesler (Ed.), *Culture of the Internet* (pp. 53-67). Mahwah, NJ: Lawrence Erlbaum Associates.

Miskevich, S. L. (1996). Killing the goose that laid the golden eggs: Ethical issues in social science research on the Internet. *Science and Engineering Ethics, 2*(2), 241-242.

National Health and Medical Research Council (NHMRC) (1999). National statement on ethical conduct in research involving humans. Retrieved Sept. 25, 2002 from: http://www.health.gov.au/nhmrc/publications/humans/part17.htm.

Nosek, B. A., Banaji, M. R., & Greenwald, A. G. (2002). E-research: Ethics, security, design, and control in psychological research on the Internet. *Journal of Social Issues, 58*(1), 161-176.

Parks, M. R. & Floyd, K. (1996). Making friends in cyberspace. *Journal of Communication, 46,* 80-97.

Parks, M. R. & Roberts, L. D. (1998). 'Making MOOsic': The development of personal relationships online and a comparison to their off-line counterparts. *Journal of Social and Personal Relationships, 15*(4), 517-537.

Rice, R. E. & Love, G. (1987). Electronic emotion: Socioemotional content in a computer mediated communication network. *Communication Research, 14,* 85-108.

Roberts, L. D. & Parks, M. R. (2001). The social geography of gender-switching in virtual environments on the Internet. In E. Green & A. Adam (Eds.), *Virtual Gender: Technology, Consumption and Identity* (pp. 265-285). London: Routledge.

Schneider, J. P. (2000). Effects of cybersex addiction on the family: Results of a survey. *Sexual Addiction & Compulsivity, 7,* 31-58.

Sharf, B. F. (1999). Beyond netiquette: The ethics of doing naturalistic discourse research on the Internet. In S. Jones (Ed.), *Doing Internet Research: Critical Issues and Methods for Examining the Net* (pp. 243-256). Thousand Oaks, CA: Sage.

Shaw, J. (1997). Treatment rationale for Internet infidelity. *Journal of Sex Education and Therapy, 22*(1), 29-34.

Sixsmith, J. & Murray, C. D. (2001). Ethical issues in the documentary data analysis of internet posts and archives. *Qualitative Health Research, 11*(3), 423-432.

Slouka, M. (1995). *War of the Worlds: Cyberspace and the High-Tech Assault on Reality*. New York: Basic Books.

Sproull, L. & Kiesler, S. (1986). Reducing social context cues: Electronic mail in organizational communication. *Management Science, 32*, 1492-1512.

Turkle, S. (1996). *Life on the screen: Identity in the age of the Internet*. London: Weidenfeld & Nicolson.

Vayreda, A., Galvez, A., Nunez, F., & Callen, B. (2002). *Participating in an electronic forum: The difference gender makes*. Internet Research 3.0: Net/Work/Theory, Maastricht, The Netherlands (October 13-16, 2002).

Walther, J. B. (1996). Computer-mediated communication: Impersonal, interpersonal and hyperpersonal interaction. *Communication Research, 23*, 3-43.

Whitty, M. & Gavin, J. (2001). Age/sex/location: Uncovering the social cues in the development of online relationships. *CyberPsychology and Behavior, 4*(5), 623-630.

Whitty, M. T. (2002a) Liar, liar! An examination of how open, supportive and honest people are in chat rooms. *Computers in Human Behavior, 18*, 343-352.

Whitty, M. T. (2002b, July). Cybercheating: Attitudes toward online infidelity. Paper presented at *11th International Conference on Personal Relationships*, Dalhousie University, Halifax, Nova Scotia, Canada.

Whitty, M. T. (2003). Cyber-flirting: Playing at love. *Theory and Psychology 13*(3), 339-357.

Wysocki, D. K. (1998). Let your fingers to do the talking: Sex on an adult chat-line. *Sexualities, 1*(4), 425-452.

Young, K. S. (1998). *Caught in the Net: How to Recognize the Signs of Internet Addiction—And a Winning Strategy for Recovery*. New York: John Wiley & Sons.

Young, K. S., Griffin-Shelley, E., Cooper, A., O'Mara, J., & Buchanan, J. (2000). Online infidelity: A new dimension in couple relationships with implications for evaluation and treatment. *Sexual Addiction & Compulsivity, 7*, 59-74.

Young, K. S., Pistner, M., O'Mara, J., & Buchanan, J. (1999). Cyber disorders: The mental health concern for the new millennium. *CyberPsychology & Behavior, 2*(5), 475-479.

Chapter XII

Co-Construction and Field Creation: Website Development as both an Instrument and Relationship in Action Research

Maximilian Forte
University College of Cape Breton, Canada

ABSTRACT

Ethnographic research ethics involved in bridging offline and online modes of action research are the focal point of this chapter, written from an anthropological perspective. The specific form of action research in this case study is that of website development. The author argues that online action research, and Web development as a research tool and relationship in ethnographic research are still very much neglected areas of concern, with respect to both virtual ethnography and traditional forms of field work. In this chapter, the argument put forth is that while traditional offline research ethics are still applicable, especially in the offline dimension of research that precedes collaborative Web development, online modes of action research involve substantively different and more fluid conceptions of research ethics, rights and responsibilities for all parties concerned.

INTRODUCTION

Anthropologists are still in the process of determining whether or not ethnographies of Internet users raise new ethical questions or issues for researcher conduct. Publications in the Annual Review of Anthropology, intended as reflections of the "state of the art" with respect to particular fields of anthropological research and as a means of outlining future research directions, have paid scant attention to the question of ethics in Internet research (e.g., Wilson & Peterson, 2002). This is not a neglect that is confined to the work of Wilson and Peterson either, as they note: "the American Anthropological Association offers no ethical protocols or standards specific to online interactions in its Code of Ethics" (Wilson & Peterson, 2002, p. 461). What Wilson and Peterson (2002, pp. 461, 456) do argue is that the online world is embedded in the offline world from which it emerged, and is subject to its rules and norms, including codes of ethics developed in standard research settings. This basic corpus of ethical practices that applies just as much online as offline, according to the authors, are those outlined in the American Anthropological Association's (AAA) "Code of Ethics":

"A (2) Anthropological researchers must do everything in their power to ensure that their research does not harm the safety, dignity, or privacy of the people with whom they work, conduct research, or perform other professional activities. ... A (3) Anthropological researchers must determine in advance whether their hosts/providers of information wish to remain anonymous or receive recognition, and make every effort to comply with those wishes. Researchers must present to their research participants the possible impacts of the choices, and make clear that despite their best efforts, anonymity may be compromised or recognition fail to materialize. ... A (4) Anthropological researchers should obtain in advance the informed consent of persons being studied, providing information, owning or controlling access to material being studied, or otherwise identified as having interests which might be impacted by the research. ... the informed consent process is dynamic and continuous; the process should be initiated in the project design and continue through implementation by way of dialogue and negotiation with those studied. ... Informed consent, for the purposes of this code, does not necessarily imply or require a particular written or signed form. It is the quality of the consent, not the format, which is relevant" (AAA, 1998).

Essentially then, the primary ethical concerns reduce to norms that can be summarized as: no harm, anonymity (if desired) and consent.

What makes this issue suddenly more problematic and unclear is when other researchers (let me call them "the dissenters" for lack of a better term) take quite a different slant from the school of thought represented by Wilson and Peterson (let me call them "the conservatives"), and I count myself amongst the dissenters. The dissenters would not argue that basic research ethics, traditionally developed in offline research settings, are irrelevant, not worthy of respect or a burden to be shrugged off. "Dissent" is marked in this case by those posing perturbing issues: "undertaking research in cyberspace poses a greater risk to the privacy and confidentiality of human subjects than does conducting research in other contexts" (Young, 2001, p. A52). Jacobson (1999) concurs in noting, "questions about the identifiability of human subjects, the conceptualization of privacy, the need for and means of obtaining informed consent, and the applicability of copyright law to computer-mediated communication (CMC) pose special problems for doing research in cyberspace" (p. 127). Dissent in these instances is based on the recognition that there is something qualitatively different and substantively unique about Internet research, and that is in large part due to the technological parameters shaping communication practices. Researchers' responsibilities have become increasingly unclear, as Turkle (1995) noted, "virtual reality poses a new methodological challenge for the researcher: what to make of online interviews and indeed, whether and how to use them" (p. 324). Even so, online interviews are merely one case of an increasingly wide spread and diverse range of communication practices that constitute what we call "the Internet." In fact, the range of dissent can go as far as arguing that, "to the extent that the off-line identities of participants in cyberspace are not known or ascertainable to researchers, it would appear that [U.S.] federal guidelines regarding human subjects would not apply to such research," or that they may indeed apply if the subjects are identifiable (Jacobson, 1999, pp. 139-140).

While I agree that there are issues of basic research ethics that are special to, or altered by, the nature of CMC, I wish to strike a further note of "dissent" in this chapter. This is due to the fact that, firstly, I am addressing a different variety of ethnographic research, one that is applied and collaborative in nature, that is, action research. Secondly, my own work online (with its ethical peculiarities) grew from, and often fed back into, offline research where the prevailing ethical issues are those of traditional research (see Bruckman, 2002). Thirdly, on top of the special ethical issues of action research, online research and the online-offline nexus, I am dissatisfied with what seems to be a prevailing concern in discussions of Internet research ethics, with synchronous modes of communication (typically chat), or more dynamic forms of asynchronous communication (such as e-mail), being paid more attention than website development and research using Web pages.

In response, I would like to argue that online action research does not reduce to relatively neat principles of consent and anonymity. In fact, in my experience, anonymity is rarely an issue of importance to my collaborators. In doing research online, I am in agreement with Waern (2001, pp. 1, 8-9) that we should avoid unwittingly homogenizing the full range of media and practices that make up the Internet, with some forms entailing greater privacy, while others are very public. In the cases that I outline in this chapter, my own experience encompasses a bundle of activities: e-mail, message boards, online surveys, listservs, online publications, user tracking, online interviews and directories of hyperlinks. In order to begin sorting through some of the dominant ethical considerations that I face, I refer to Jacobson (1999, p. 128) and his concise summary of the issues, as I reformulate them in the chart in Figure 1.

My principal activity online consists of website development. Producing a Web page might not seem to be anything more dynamic or profound than typing a paper or designing a poster—after all, as some might say, these are simply the expressions of

Figure 1: Ethics and Communication Diversity Online

Mode	Characteristics	Examples	Ethical Issues
ASYNCHRONOUS	"static", "public", "stored"	Websites, newsgroup postings	Copyright
SYNCHRONOUS	"real time", "ephemeral"	Chat	Confidentiality

research, after the fact of the research itself, assuming that any research was involved at all. Indeed, from a mainstream anthropological perspective,[1] the notion that website development might be viewed as an instrument and as a process of ethnographic field research, let alone as a research relationship, is one that has received no attention in the extant research on ethnographic methods. However, this is also largely true of the extant research on "virtual ethnography" which, as a multidisciplinary enterprise, transcends the bounds of traditional anthropology. The idea that website development can be any of these things must seem, I admit, counterintuitive or, at the very least, obscure. My intention, therefore, is to describe and analyze how website development itself can serve as an instrument in both offline and online research, one that generates different yet overlapping research relationships, and that raises challenging questions that invite a revision of conventional understandings of ethics in ethnographic field research, while calling forth new perspectives on ethics in online action research, or what some might call "real world research" in the critical realist perspective (see Robson, 2002).

Important questions concerning research methods, the conduct of online research, trust and rapport building and, of course, ethics are addressed here through a case study of action research, where the Internet itself was used as a medium for conducting research and building relationships that bridged online and offline settings. These issues may become of greater relevance as more ethnographers, engaged in advocacy and applied research, embark on the kinds of projects discussed herein. Indeed, there is nothing far fetched about an ethnographer from a so-called "First World" society, having basic computer skills and being asked to build a website for his or her less privileged "native hosts," as a service in return for being allowed to study their group. When the relationship becomes elevated to a level higher than that of a simple exchange of goods, and when advocacy enters, then the most salient ethical questions that arise in this methodological framework are those of partnership, collaboration and transformation. Power relations are far more lateral than they are in traditional ethnographic settings; and the main mode of learning occurs from a sharing of expertise and knowledge, rather than the standard (native) give and (researcher) take relationship.

If forced to classify the type of action research in which I was engaged, I would probably adopt a variant of the concept "educational action research," i.e., applied learning in a social context with a focus on community problems (see O'Brien, 1998).[2] Given the plethora of terms, and their varying nuances, some might even call this an example of "technical action research" (see Masters, 1995), insofar as it involved a project instigated by a particular person (myself), who because of greater experience or qualifications (in Web design and information technology), is regarded by his collaborators as an "expert" (at least in this technical area). Mutual-collaborative action research, in a hermeneutic and ethnographic mode, is another, though somewhat ambiguous way, in which one could describe the type of research in which I was engaged.[3]

Whichever definition may be most appropriate, the "problem" at the focus of this action research was my (offline and online) collaborators' perceived need for greater recognition and public visibility. Visibility itself raises a central ethical issue in connection with anonymity. The "researched for" consisted of online public and likeminded Caribbean aboriginals. The "disadvantage" that this action research was meant to address consisted, in part, of the focus community's lack of access to information and communication technology (ICT), and the perception held by some that they, as a people, were extinct (see Forte, 2002).

The employment of website development as part of a program of collaborative research that moves from offline to online arenas (and back again), and that binds ethnographer and "informants" as partners, has transformative impacts on the research process and attendant questions of ethics. These transformations can be summarized as a series of moves from *participant observation* to *creative observation*, from field entry to *field creation*, and from research with informants to research with *correspondents* and partners. Ethnography has traditionally involved the sustained presence of an ethnographer in a physically-fixed field setting, intensively engaged with the everyday life of the inhabitants of the site. When the Internet enters into ethnography, and when ethnography itself acquires an online dimension, it becomes imperative that we reexamine the transformations of the researcher-researched relationship. In the process we need to rework established concepts of ethnography in order to pay due attention to cultural process in de-spatialized sites (see Gupta & Ferguson, 1992, 1997). I say that we require this in order to have a balanced appreciation of the interrelationship between online and offline modes of ethnographic work and the attendant ethical concerns that this raises.

This chapter is structured according to the three main "phases" of my research experience. The first consists of website development for an offline community (the Santa Rosa Carib Community of Arima, Trinidad), as a part of a collaborative research exercise in a traditional field setting. This resulted in the establishment of an online platform that extended the research experience in new directions. The second phase involved using the online platform to pursue offline goals, i.e., positive feedback and support for the Carib community. The third phase involved using the resultant online platform as a point of entry into online research and widened collaboration. In practice, there is a substantial overlap and circularity linking of these phases; and they are laid out here for analytical purposes without seeking to suggest that there is a linear chronology between these phases at all times.

In the first instance, I will briefly describe my relationship with the offline community at the centre of my field research in the "traditional" ethnographic sense, that is, an aboriginal organization called the Santa Rosa Carib Community, located in the Borough of Arima, on the Caribbean island republic of Trinidad & Tobago. I outline their stated aims and goals and the special requirements that these posed for researchers such as me; their aims and goals included their request for assistance in seeking greater national recognition, international support and supportive research. Given their emphasis on recognition and networking, their own processes of bureaucratization, documentary self-representation and brokerage, I had to devise the appropriate means of collaborative research allowing me greater insights into this organization, while assisting them. This is where the process of *co-construction* becomes relevant, especially in my devising forms of collaborative writing between informants and myself through the medium of website design. Websites were used to promote their own representations, present research about the community, and elicit support, at the very same time allowing me to learn more about them in the process. I had to first learn "their language"—i.e., their idiom of self-representation—and be able to appropriately manipulate their symbols and iconography before I could communicate their views to a wider public.

As a result, in the second phase of my research, I used the online platform—websites—to pursue offline goals. Here I will outline the specifics of the transformed participant observation that resulted, as well as an overview of the outcomes and effects of website development for my host community.

The third phase is quite distinct. This involves the creative effects emerging from the creation of online platforms that brought me squarely into action research online. In this section of the chapter I will detail and analyze my experiences leading up to and including the formation of the Caribbean Amerindian Centrelink (CAC). The CAC grew out of my awareness of other websites by and about Caribbean aboriginals, and my desire to unite them into a single directory for researchers and interested members of the online public. However, development did not stop there. Eventually the CAC grew into a proactive resource, featuring not just other sites, but also organizing online content, fostering communication between researchers, activists and cyber brokers, while engaging in research information outreach. As these processes helped to create a community of interest around the CAC, it then became possible to research researchers, to analyze and examine feedback by visitors and to develop regular online relationships. This is what I call field creation, and it involves creative observation, insofar as I am creating the site that attracts the prospective informants (unlike traditional fieldwork where one travels to a site that necessarily exists prior to the formulation of a research project), and I am observing users even while they observe me and the information that I construct. In other words, I am presenting research at the same time as I am researching those who engage the research. Suler (2000) immediately raises a pertinent ethical question here concerning transparency and accountability: "did the researcher himself create the group for the purpose of gathering data?" I must stress that my research about the CAC, as published in chapters such as this, was an after effect. The CAC was not created as a type of flypaper to attract users that would then be studied. Instead, I gradually began to reflect on the nature of the CAC and in time began to write about it, sometimes writing about it to the prime actors associated with it.

These processes, in fact, invert many of the traditional assumptions of offline anthropological ethnography. The researcher also becomes an informant in this situation, fielding questions from a wide public audience; the "site" is created by the researcher; and, "informants" are now more accurately "contacts" and "correspondents," and those whom we used to call informants are also acting now as researchers in their own right. Trust and rapport are also transformed by these changed research relationships, not necessarily developing into "friendship," but certainly entailing a form of collegiality in most cases.

Much of this chapter was not originally written as a philosophical examination of "truths" in the "established literature," a literature that is actually quite slim where online action research is involved; rather, it is written from an experiential, ethnographic and first person perspective. I am a participant in the processes that I describe and analyze, which can alter one's perspectives on some of the nuanced aspects of applied ethics. The utility of the case study approach in this instance is to develop, through practice, more illustrative examples and case studies to expand and focus our knowledge of ethical choices, an approach endorsed in the AAA's "Code of Ethics," which is itself intended simply as a guide. The National Association for the Practice of Anthropology (NAPA) adds, in its own code, "No code or set of guidelines can anticipate unique circumstances or direct practitioner actions in specific situations" (NAPA, 1998), thus further emphasizing the need for consideration of a range of concrete cases.

Before proceeding further, allow me to summarize my main positions on ethical research as developed in the sections that follow, and I present this for now as a simple and random list of points. (1) Ethics is a two-way street: an action researcher must also protect his/her credibility as a researcher and reflect the best of one's discipline, while also safeguarding his/her own intellectual property as produced online. (2) In bringing the offline into the online, one must get feedback, engage in consultation with one's informants/collaborators, seek their approval for placing materials online and, hopefully, work jointly on the actual production of materials to be published online. (3) In the online only realm of action research, relationships are a product of constant negotiation and reflexive monitoring; there is no recipe book apart from certain basics such as protecting one's collaborators from the harm of one's work, if there could be any, as well as protecting oneself from the possible harm of their activities. (4) In utilizing online resources for one's online work, especially in quoting websites, ethics that would govern private one-on-one and face-to-face relationships are largely inapplicable. Websites play the role of the voluntary, unsolicited, public informant and consent becomes redundant. Copyright, however, becomes critical. (5) E-mail that is private, or derived from private discussion lists, must remain confidential. Where newsgroups are concerned, however, these postings are all freely available on Google and authors of postings take their own reputation into their own hands, regardless of what a researcher does or does not do. I would maintain, however, that writing rarely demands that we go into "gory detail" and facilitate readers in tracking down our sources. (6) In traditional ethnographic research, participants are allowed to withdraw their participation and data at any time. On the Internet, where data may come in the form of a Web page volunteered for inclusion on one's site, this becomes almost impossible to guarantee, for even when a site is removed it remains archived in Google's cache or in webarchive.org's "Way Back Machine." (7) Researchers must limit and emphatically qualify their guarantees of confidentiality and privacy online, especially as surveillance, interception and hacking activities, beyond the control or knowledge of a researcher, are increasingly prominent and intrusive realities of life online.

ISSUES IN COLLABORATIVE ETHNOGRAPHY, ETHICS AND THE WEB

There is growing multidisciplinary concern with the conduct of "virtual ethnography" (i.e., Hine, 2000; Paccagnella, 1997), its specificity as a methodology and its import for issues of researcher conduct. Immediately, a bundle of knotted issues confronts us:

the conceptual relationship between the offline and the online; the conceptual nature of the "field" itself; fieldwork as science or advocacy—the now almost classical division between traditional information gathering approaches self-described as "scientific" versus those of the "barefoot anthropologist," combining activism and applied research (see Nader, 1972; Susman & Evered, 1978) and some of the ethical implications faced in doing ethnographic research on the Web. I will touch on all of these here, without having the opportunity for the exhaustive exegesis that each of these ultimately requires.

The Offline-Online Nexus

To start with, and in agreement with Miller and Slater (2000, p. 85), I do not adhere to a notion of strict discontinuity between the "real" and the "virtual." As I observed in my study, the Internet served to bring dispersed individuals back into a sense of rootedness with a particular place, that is, of finding and reaffirming a sense of themselves as Caribbean aboriginals. Online and offline practices were, at least initially, profoundly intertwined and online representation was first a deliberate projection and extension of offline cultural practice. This issue has implications, ultimately, for the way that we conceive of "virtual ethnography," and the manner in which "the field," at the focus of such ethnography, is methodologically and conceptually constructed. I agree with Ruhleder (2000) when she observes that, "some virtual venues support or enhance existing face-to-face settings and activities, while others provide alternatives to them" (p. 3). The move from offline to online in my case study tends to extend the face-to-face environments of the individuals concerned, while creating new opportunities for discussion, discovery and self-realization that fed back into the offline setting. While some also contend that, "online interactions are influenced by offline power relations and constructions of identity" (Wilson & Peterson, 2002, p. 457), I would not say that the offline determines the online unidirectionally.

The wider points to be grasped from a consideration of the offline-online nexus is that the "virtual" and the "real" overlap and interact, "to the extent that we are required to rethink the nature of a field site whilst also encouraging us to adapt traditional field methods to these settings" (Ruhleder, 2000, p. 4).

Thus far, much of the literature and possibly most discussions about virtual ethnography largely concern the study of online materials, often discontinuous with, or distinct from, offline contexts and the wider social milieu of such productions, or they may focus on the microsociological contexts of Internet usage (see Miller & Slater, 2000, p. 72; Paccagnella, 1997; Garton, Haythornthwaite, & Wellman, 1997). While the term "virtual" highlights the distinct nature of this type of ethnography, and thus its attendant research relationships and practices, I would hazard to argue that this area of study shares at least one assumption in common with traditional ethnography: both involve the detached study of a "site" that preexists the ethnographer and which the ethnographer comes to "visit" as an "outsider." Of course, when one remains straight jacketed in the role of outsider, this will beg questions as to one's conduct and responsibilities towards one's research "subjects."

The "Site" of Research

The second major analytical and methodological consideration that confronts us is the question of the research site, or "the field." This concern stems from the previous discussion concerning the offline-online nexus. While there may be no radical and absolute separation between the offline and online, the fact that the online exists does transform and expand the horizon of potentialities, now constituting the practical repertoires of thought and action among "real actors." As Ruhleder (2000) explains, the venues in which we carry out our fieldwork "increasingly intertwine real and virtual activities as participants move materials and interactions online," a fact that changes the nature of the field sites we observe, thereby requiring an "enhancement or even rethinking of traditional methodologies" (p. 3). Conventional notions of the field, especially in anthropology, which has been the premiere field-based discipline (see Amit, 2000; Gupta & Ferguson, 1992, 1997), involved basic assumptions of boundedness, the field was a strictly delimited physical place; distance, the field was "away," and often very far away as well; temporality, one entered the field, stayed for a time and then left; and otherness, a strict categorical and relational distinction between the outsider/ethnographer and the insider/native informant. The key mode of ethnographic engagement in the field was, and is, that of participant observation. Each of these elements of ethnographic field research specifically shapes and informs the ethical considerations confronting the ethnographer. This traditional methodology was inevitably intertwined with certain assumptions concerning ethical research and rapport, implicitly premised on dichotomous conceptual frameworks of outsider-insider, foreigner-native and taker-giver.

The researcher and his or her personal relationships are the primary means by which information is elicited (see Amit, 2000). The difficult issues raised are rapport and power relations, and the decidedly instrumentalist nature underlying the ways anthropologists build rapport with prospective informants:

"however sincere and nuanced the attachment they express, ethnographic fieldworkers are still also exploiting this intimacy as an investigative tool. Participant observation is therefore often uneasily perched on the precipice between the inherent instrumentalism of this as of any research enterprise and the more complex and rounded social associations afforded by this particular method" (Amit, 2000, p. 3).

As a result, even a cursory review of most of the statements on ethical research published by various anthropological associations will reveal an emphasis on the anthropologist's duty not to cause harm to his/her research "subjects," to protect the confidentiality of one's informants, and not to leave one's host community any worse off than one found it. The implicit understanding underpinning the overall perspective on the ethnographic enterprise is that of the ethnographer as an essentially intrusive, uninvited and potentially harmful figure who is out "to get," that is, to get information from "native informants," in order to advance the state of knowledge on a particular subject and, of course, to advance his or her career. One can of course become quite cynical in making negative assessments of researchers' instrumentalist approaches, unfortunately this sometimes mirrors opinions found in some host communities. In my case, as I suggested before, I discovered that leaders in the Carib community worked on the assumption that outside specialists would pursue their interests, without regard for them unless they proactively asserted a reciprocal exchange relationship.

Online research and action research online serve to transform if not erode the ways in which the field is constructed and the modes by which the ethnographer conducts research. We are then dealing with a quite different set of ethical considerations. It is in connection with these concerns that I speak of co-construction and field creation. However, some would argue that all field locations are constructed by ethnographers, which is an important conceptual transformation with import for current and future discussions of research methodology. As Amit (2000) explains:

"in a world of infinite interconnections and overlapping contexts, the ethnographic field cannot simply exist, awaiting discovery. It has to be laboriously constructed, prised apart from all the other possibilities for contextualization to which its constituent relationships and connections could also be referred. This process of construction is inescapably shaped by the conceptual, professional, financial and relational opportunities and resources accessible to the ethnographer" (p. 6).

Indeed, in situations where an ethnographer is seeking to observe interactions that can happen in his/her absence, interactions that are discontinuous and that may engage some or just a few, dealing with unique events that do not recur, "it may not be sufficient or possible for anthropologists to simply join in. They may have to purposively create occasions for contacts that might well be as mobile, diffuse and episodic as the processes they are studying" (Amit, 2000, p. 15). While we may then agree that, almost every field situation is constructed by the ethnographer, what happens when a research opportunity is co-constructed, and what relations and ethics do these entail?

Online Action Research

This is where this case study of co-construction and field creation becomes most relevant, as there is still little or no attention paid to the process of website development itself as a research method with its own specificities, whether in the literature on (traditional or virtual) ethnography, Internet research or even action research. Even though there is increased recognition of the use of information and communication technology as a potentially powerful adjunct to action research processes, some have rightly noted, "there is a dearth of published studies on the use of action research methods in such projects" (O'Brien, 1998).[4] It is not surprising, therefore, that a subdivision of that area of interest—website development—would receive even less attention than the area of online action research as a whole. From a logical positivist perspective, or at least from a perspective of one not engaged in action research, this area of interest is based on a seemingly counterintuitive premise: website development is an act of production, while research/data gathering is ostensibly an act of consumption. This distinction could also be framed as one between the classical Aristotelian notion of "praxis" (action) and "theoria" (knowledge for its own sake). The co-production of a website, between a researcher and his/her informants, not only permits the co-production of knowledge but also enables the researcher to gain greater insights into the world views of individuals and groups whose own cultural reproduction depends heavily on public recognition. This necessarily entails ethical responsibilities on the part of the researcher to recognize the social and political implications of information dissemination (cf. Watkins, n.d.).

While the AAA's "Code of Ethics" (AAA, 1998, C/2) makes the point that advocacy is a choice and not an ethical duty, advocacy in the form of action research certainly does encapsulate and help realize some of the basic ethical thrusts set out in the AAA "Code." For example, in section A/6 of the AAA "Code," researchers are called upon to "reciprocate with people studied," and, as I contend, reciprocity is the spinal cord of action research as discussed in this chapter. Watkins (n.d.), a member of the AAA ethics committee, urges researchers to involve their study populations throughout the entire process of their projects, from the formulation of research design, the collection and synthesis of data and even the publication of data, "in such a way that the cultural context of the population under study is represented within the project to as much an extent possible." This clearly echoes co-production as I discuss it here.

Co-production (or co-construction), therefore, is not simply an activity that has ethical consequences, as if we had to figure these out after the fact of the work conducted. It is not a method that is distinct from its ethical implications. Instead, it is an activity that is meant to embody certain ethical values—it is a value-driven mode of research. What kinds of values does co-production embody? One value is that of sharing knowledge and expertise in a common effort, presumably for a common good. In my case, especially with respect to my offline field work, it was also a means of delivering on an agreement. Co-production also involves some of the basic ethical assumptions relating to the protection of human subjects—those being beneficence, autonomy and justice (see Frankel & Siang, 1999, pp. 2-3). Co-production respects the principle of beneficence by seeking to maximize benefits to those whom we would ordinarily consider "research subjects," by enabling their voices to be heard. Autonomy is a key part of co-production to the extent that subjects *qua* collaborators are respected as autonomous subjects—likewise, the researcher-participant also maintains his/her autonomy and freedom to reserve endorsement of any particular message or act that may be troubling (see also AAA, 1998, sect/A/5). In line with the AAA "Code" (1998), an anthropological researcher must still "bear responsibility for the integrity and reputation of their discipline, of scholarship, and of science" sect. B/2). Justice is respected as a principle of co-production along the lines articulated by Frankel and Siang (1999), that is, "a fair distribution of the burdens and benefits associated with research, so that certain individuals or groups do not bear disproportionate risks while others reap the benefits" (p. 3). In broader terms, action research may be seen as adhering to a "common good" approach to science, challenging ethnographers and subjects/collaborators to view themselves as members of the same community, and with some higher goals in common, where knowledge, dialogue and change are some examples (see Waern, 2001, p. 2). The specificity of Internet-based or Internet-oriented action research, as suggested by Frankel and Siang (1999) is that the Internet "enables some individuals or populations, who might not be able to or willing to do so in the physical world, to participate in the research, hence giving some a voice that they would not otherwise have outside of online research" (p. 4; see also Allen, 1996, p. 186; Association for Internet Researchers (AoIR), 2002, p. 12). At the same time, those who were traditionally "the researched about" in offline settings, now have access to the works of researchers, can argue back (as they often do), and produce alternative materials in their own right. No longer is there a simple one-sided determination by the researcher over what research should be about, how it should be done and what its results should be—researchers, such as myself, are often called to account (cf. Wong, 1998, p. 179). As I have recognized, those who are researched want the power to represent themselves, and not have their representations hijacked by possibly insensitive or contrary academics. This fact is also recognized by Wilson and Peterson (2002) when they observe, "the Web has created a new arena for group and individual self-representation, changing the power dynamics of representation for traditionally marginalized groups such as Native Americans within the discourses of popular culture" (p. 462). I agree with Wilson and Peterson (2002, p. 459) when they contend that the new information technologies have helped to alter expert-novice relations—a point worth remembering when discussing the specificities of online research interactions.

Having said everything above, I would argue that "friendship" is actually not a necessary facet, or a *sine qua non,* especially of action research that occurs only online between individuals who have never met, and may never meet (cf. Wong, 1998, p. 181). Contrary to Wong (1998), I think we need to be careful in not reducing action research, friendship and reciprocity to interchangeable synonyms. Courtesy can be the basis for reciprocity, for example, even in the absence of palpable amiability. One can be engaged in action research for a particular cause or "on the same side" with people that one might find to be distasteful characters, while muting these personal dislikes for the sake of "the larger cause." In my own experience, there is a considerable amount of recurring personal friction between myself, fellow editors and local offline partners, hence the result being continuous negotiation. Where there is absolute agreement and single-mindedness, negotiation becomes redundant.

Having built-in ethical values does not exclude online action research from a consideration of issues such as confidentiality and copyright, as if these could be entirely dispelled by a warm glow of mutuality, courtesy and reciprocity. The Ethics Working Committee of the Association of Internet Researchers (AoIR) (AoIR, 2002, p. 8) makes the suggestion that when participants in a project act as authors whose texts/ artifacts are intended as public, then there are fewer obligations on the researcher to protect autonomy, privacy, confidentiality, etc. That does not mean that I as a researcher may, therefore, proceed to run rampantly against co-authors' interests; what it does suggest is that they also take charge of protecting their own rights and making their own decisions, with or without my guidance and assurances. The more public their chosen actions and representational outputs, the less I can protect their individual privacy and confidentiality—and, in practice, this appears to be readily understood.

The Nature of Consent in Online Action Research

In Wong's (1998) estimation, the aim of informed consent is to release the institution or funding agency from any liability and, at the same time, accede control and license of the research process to the researcher (p. 184). In Wong's (1998) view, diminished liability and increased license establishes a power relation between researcher and informant, one that attempts at "friendship" and "mutuality" can only try to mask, deceptively. The act of seeking and gaining consent thus institutes hierarchy (Wong, 1998, p. 188). Moreover, Wong (p. 189) questions whether consent even offers protection, say, from the subtle manipulations of the interview process that can expose and uncover the vulnerabilities of a research subject. From a legal standpoint, Jacobson (1999, p. 129) is troubled by the fact that seeking informed consent in online settings may involve a breach of anonymity, as the relevant guidelines require that an individual be identifiable in order to be counted as a human research subject and be protected, and thus the instrument of consent might itself be the one and only means of exposing the identity of an informant. Some might counter that, of course, all research online is with human subjects. I should interject here that not even that sentiment is a truth that we can entertain with safety any longer on this ever mutating, increasingly bewildering Internet, where sometimes one's chat partner turns out to be a robot.

If there appears to be a growing consensus on this subject, it seems to be that informed consent is context dependent. In the case of my online action research, participation is open to various autonomous agents, such as fellow academics and interested activists, and no consent forms have ever been exchanged. In this case, consent is implied.

OFFLINE-ONLINE: THE SOCIO-CULTURAL CONTEXTS OF CO-CONSTRUCTION

The group that I researched was the Santa Rosa Carib Community (SRCC), a group that claims descent from the aboriginal inhabitants of Trinidad that have come to be called Caribs. The SRCC, headed by President Ricardo Bharath, is a formal organization that was incorporated as a limited liability company in 1976. SRCC documents emphasize that the group's immediate needs are: (1) "recognition by society and government as a legitimate cultural sector"; (2) "research to clarify their cultural traditions and the issue of their lands"; and (3) "support from appropriate institutions in their perceived need areas" (Reyes, n.d.). Key SRCC brokers, such as Bharath, have progressively steered the group in the direction of greater formalization, bureaucratization, politicization and "cultural revival."

Gaining greater visibility has been a key issue for SRCC leaders in their quest to affirm their value in terms of having "contributed to the national cultural foundation," as they routinely state, and to gain recognition of this value. SRCC leaders and spokespersons work on two fronts: (1) gaining recognition as "true Amerindians" from other peoples and organizations abroad whose identity as "indigenous" is not questioned in Trinidad; and (2) in promoting themselves as the keepers of traditions that mark that "Amerindian cultural heritage" that has shaped the wider "national culture," where this is seen to exist. Visibility, not anonymity, is the overriding value at the heart of their engagement with researchers. When I mentioned constructing a Carib community website, which would end up exposing them to a wider international public, the reaction was enthusiasm and not fear. As one of the Carib community's own internal researchers put it, in grandiose terms perhaps: "Max is going to put us on the world map."

My research began with a pilot study with the group at the focus of my field research in 1995. I noted two strong themes in the statements that individuals made to me, especially by individuals who would become my key guides later on. One of these was their desire to receive greater recognition, locally and abroad. The second, and very much related to the first, was their constant emphasis on networking with a wide array of institutions and actors, locally and internationally, in seeking greater recognition, support and funding. The group itself, though small and consisting largely of members related by blood or marriage, was substantially bureaucratized, and had developed, and sought to further develop, a critical mass of documents, written representations of the group, project proposals, letters, historical statements and so forth, on the group itself and in connection with its wider networking. These observations seemed to suggest the following: that much of their time is spent in formalized activities of brokerage, and that much of their work consists of formal documentation, thus writing and graphic forms of self-representation. Lastly, my future guides and collaborators made it clear that they expected researchers to be of some assistance to them, to not "just come and take," and, in fact, some previous researchers had done a great deal to assist them in obtaining formal recognition by the state and annual subventions from different arms of the state. Transactionalism, pragmatism and brokerage surfaced as strongly suggestive keywords in describing their practice and their relationship with myself.[5]

As I was about to begin my two years of doctoral fieldwork in 1998, I struggled to outline areas of possible cooperation between informants and myself, as well as to envision the appropriate modes of participant observation, a mode of cooperation that would result in us becoming collaborators and co-constructors. As far as I could see, two of my strengths were my writing skills (especially in light of the fact that most members of the group did not receive a secondary education); and my access to funding that permitted me to acquire a computer suite, video and photographic equipment, added to my knowledge of how to use these things. Becoming an "insider," acting in some ways as an intern or even a consultant in terms of their brokerage processes, seemed to be a valuable means of gaining knowledge of this group. I was invited to assist in writing project proposals, letters and so forth, as a form of participant observation. In addition, I developed certain collaborative writing and representation exercises that would allow me even further access to the ways in which they perceive themselves, construct their identity and articulate their self-representations with a wider public. One of the platforms for collaborative writing was my proposal that we develop websites about the group, to further some of their aims for greater recognition, and to gain feedback from a wider audience, both locally and internationally.

As I mentioned before, anonymity never emerged as the dominant ethical issue. Indeed, even very personal internal disputes have been repeatedly aired in the national press over the years, due to their own public statements, so that the enforcement of privacy struck me as impressing them as "too little, too late." The point I wish to make is that their cultural and political practice is centered on respect, recognition and reputation. When offered anonymity during the more traditional early phases of my field research, they often waived this as an underhanded attempt at cheating them of their fame. In other cases, offering anonymity for their statements in interviews, or the choice of withdrawing their data at a later time, struck some as an expression of my lack of confidence in the "truth" of what they wished to say: "No, why should I wish to remain hidden? I stand by my words. I am a man of my word. I will retract nothing. I'm not ashamed about what I have to say." These were the words of one interviewee. In some respects, I could not even offer them some of the basics of anonymity. As the reader will have already seen in this chapter, I use their real names, due to the fact that there is only one Carib community in Trinidad, and only one president, and these entities are already very well publicized in the national press, or on other websites. My invention of personal names or a fictitious tribal name, or using an imaginary name for their location would have struck other social scientists that have studied in Trinidad as comical; members of the Carib community would have been offended at the erasure. What I did do was to follow, as a principle, the words scribbled by a supervisor into the margin of an early draft of a dissertation chapter: "no need for the gory detail." When quoting the name of an interviewee seemed to be of no meaningful value, I dropped it; when the details seemed to be too personal, I excluded them. These were the principles governing my "traditional" ethnographic writing for the dissertation. Where the production of collaborative websites was involved, we can see different emphases and concerns at work. Names of living individuals were not erased and photographs and sounds abounded. The value of being visible was at a premium. Yet, the fact remained that none of the parties wished to see their internal disputes aired in public. In fact, these disputes were almost entirely irrelevant to the generic purposes of these sites.

ONLINE-OFFLINE: THE EFFECTS OF HEIGHTENED VISIBILITY

The two websites, which involved collaboration between myself and my partners and required co-construction of their chosen type of representation, were the sites of the Santa Rosa Carib Community (Forte & Bharath, 1998-2002), and that of the Los Niños del Mundo Parang band (Forte & Adonis, 1999-2002), which is now defunct. These websites required research in advance, sitting down and discussing what should be shown and how, what should be said or not and what the scope and goals of the sites should be. As such, the websites represent collaborative writing exercises, emerging from meetings, conversations and interviews. While it is true that I took a leading role in the technical aspect of the work, without their interest and inputs, these projects would obviously not have come off the ground.

I created another website focused on the Carib community, but from a more distant and analytical perspective, and not as an attempt to enable the Carib community to represent itself, but more to showcase some of my own research and present some of my field data online (Forte, 1998-2002). Some of the leading members of the Carib community have seen this website, and generally responded with interest to the materials. In some cases they have wished to have selected items reproduced on paper for their own recently established Resource Centre. This website was still not designed in a way that would contradict the main elements of their self-representations. Yet, the dominant motivation leading me to produce it was to offer a more or less scholarly, independent resource, which I see as a duty to my discipline and to myself. This is not to say that I have been afraid to express my disagreement with my Carib collaborators. We have argued intensely many times, and have taken issue with each other's interpretations. On occasion, the friction was almost audible. If anything, the positive lessons learned from these exchanges is that collaborators are autonomous agents working together, not clones or puppets.

Santa Rosa Carib Community Website

This website serves to essentially tell people "we are here," and thus goes toward their effort to achieve recognition. This began as their official site, then became an "unofficial" site, and later became quasi-official. Why? After having left Arima, Trinidad, in 1999, and given the rapid changes that I knew were taking place in Trinidad and the different emphases they were placing in modifying their self-representations, plus the fact that visitors frequently complained that there was never anything new on the site, I decided that the site might have become more of a liability. From that standpoint, I added new materials, materials no longer directly sanctioned by the SRCC, and thus the site was retitled the "unofficial" website of the SRCC, so as to not expose them to even the slightest liability. If there is an ethical principle to be observed here, pertaining to Web development, it is the duty to be accurate and transparent.

Moreover, as I was the one to be asked questions about the SRCC by visitors, I had to ensure that no one thought that I was authorized to speak on behalf of the SRCC, and I took great pains to stress that. Acting as collaborator is fine; posing as a member is an act of misrepresentation. Correspondence between Arima, and Adelaide, Australia, was scarce and infrequent, given that my former partners did not have access to e-mail, and neither side was very devoted to letter writing. As it turns out, on my return to Arima, some of my former partners let it be known that they were not entirely satisfied with my manner of resolving the situation, naming their site "unofficial," as it now seemed that they lacked a real Web presence of their own. I was still not convinced that it was ethical for me to act as if I were a gatekeeper of the Carib community. However, having returned to Trinidad in 2001, I was able to resume more regular updates, with materials sanctioned by the SRCC. Yet, on the site itself, I still make it explicit that I am not a member of the SRCC and that I have no authority within the group, and thus any communications meant "for the eyes of the SRCC only" should be directed to them, not me. This helps to prevent potential embarrassment and loss of confidentiality, when people write very personal e-mail messages that then come through my computer. I do field questions of a general educational nature (i.e., "how do they make cassava bread?"; "what does the Queen do?" and so forth).

Los Niños del Mundo Website

This website was more ambitious than that of the SRCC. The intent was not just promotion and achieving recognition, but also involved educating the public about Parang music and Arima, fostering a network of contacts and seeking business opportunities. The irony here is that while the site had been maintained, the band itself dissolved roughly a year later. This situation is the opposite of the case with the SRCC site; in this case, ex-members of the group thought the site should, possibly, be removed. Not having the time or energy to significantly reshape the site, yet not wishing all that work to be lost, I contradicted myself and argued that the site should be maintained for historical purposes, while not stating this on the site itself in case the band ever got together again (i.e., no need to wash the day's dirty laundry in public). This has placed me in the awkward position of sometimes fielding enthusiastic messages for a group that no longer exists, an act of misrepresentation committed for the sake of history. However, I came to agree with the former band members, and this site has been dissolved, especially as it began to attract the serious interest of researchers wishing to study a nonexistent band. Maintaining the site, therefore, became increasingly an act of deception, especially as it became clear that the band would undergo no revival.

Offline Field Research Goals

Apart from being a tool of participant observation in the process of action research, my online activities furthered my offline field research goals in other ways. One of these involved observing the outcomes of having developed these websites with respect to the goals of the SRCC. For example, I witnessed other academic researchers learning about the SRCC online and traveling to Arima to study it further, often adopting some of the same key "informants"—and the fact of being studied by "foreign researchers" in itself helped to add to the SRCC's legitimacy. There was a perceptible increase in general interest expressed by Internet users, often Trinidadian expatriates, but also local journalists and students, and other individuals with Internet access—an observation that was also confirmed by my partners. Generally, there was an increased amount of activity generated around the SRCC and an increased number of in-person visitors who testified to having first learned of the SRCC via the Internet. Moreover, there has been an emergence of new websites on the SRCC, as well as other sites that have begun to highlight the SRCC, when they were not highlighted before. There has also been increased attention to the SRCC in the local print and television media, with journalists often using phrases, terms and sometimes even images that were adopted from the websites. The two sites have received over 20,000 visitors since their inception, several dozen e-mail messages and several commercial propositions oriented toward events and services produced or offered by the SRCC and its members. Moreover, they have also acted as a beacon for various expressions of local and national pride among the Arimian and wider Trinidadian diaspora overseas. Indeed, numerous Trinidad sites operated by such individuals routinely feature links to the SRCC. Finally, international gatherings of indigenous peoples held in Arima brought together groups that previously had only been aware of each other via the Internet.

There is a problematic side to this rapid development and heightened visibility. One of these concerns the inflation of expectations, or even inadvertently creating unrealistic impressions, amongst users who are swayed by symbols and images more than by the text that is provided. One possible example of this inflated expectation is that of a Canadian performance artist who visited Trinidad recently. She claimed Canadian First Nations ancestry, and remarked in a local newspaper interview that she was disappointed at not having come across any local First Nations people except for one who attended her performance. The journalist who wrote the article also bemoaned that "we had no representation of our own First Nations" (see Assing, 2002). Both the writer and the artist almost speak as if they expected "First Peoples" to be so numerous that they should be everywhere and at all times, and I am left to wonder to what degree the websites on the Caribs may have created this expectation.

ONLINE-ONLINE: ACTION RESEARCH IN AN INVISIBLE COLLEGE[6]

While creating websites for and about the SRCC, I investigated the existence and nature of other Caribbean Amerindian Websites, and other related online materials. Having already found a substantial mass of such materials online in mid-1998, I envisioned one central platform that researchers, activists and interested members of the general public could consult and utilize, rather than having to peddle through seemingly endless, sometimes obscure, search results that varied with the search engine used. Originally a mere gateway site without any original content, CAC was created. I soon started to use this venue for posting some of my preliminary articles, papers from conference presentations and so forth—indeed, sharing one's research, within reasonable limits, became one of the core values of this enterprise. These materials began to attract the attention of other interested researchers. Eventually, as a group, we reformulated and relaunched the CAC (1998-2002). The CAC has since evolved into an Internet-based information resource that specializes in research, publication and cataloging of Internet sites centered on the indigenous peoples of the wider Caribbean Basin, as well as helping to build wider networks of discussion amongst scholars and activists. In addition, it also led to the founding of KACIKE: The Journal of Caribbean Amerindian History and Anthropology (KACIKE 1999-2002), an electronic journal managed and edited by some of the leading international scholars in this field of study. The two sites are, to a certain extent, twins.

CAC

CAC, as its name implies, is a central link to a wide range of websites that either focus upon or shed light upon the native peoples of the Caribbean and circum-Caribbean. The CAC also endeavors to provide a venue for communication and mutual awareness among Caribbean aboriginal peoples. The CAC presents a variety of research, including histories, news and articles about native Caribbean peoples, educational resources, online surveys and discussions of problems and prospects for Caribbean Amerindians and their descendants. It aims to provide content and build a community-like platform at the same time. The CAC thus performs a dual function, meeting external demands for information (among students, scholars, teachers and the wider non-Amerindian public) and meeting internal demands for discussion and collaboration (amongst activists and scholars tied to the indigenous groups in question). It is at this juncture between the external and the internal that one's role as an action researcher/webmaster raises important issues of trust and ethical conduct.

The first point of ethical conduct that is relevant here is that as a researcher, and one privileged to have access to internal debates and discussions, it was incumbent on me to clarify my role to all visitors and participants. At all times, all users who were interested in checking the numerous materials on each site that described the site itself, its creators and aims would realize that I was acting as both researcher and producer. Indeed, I always make it a point to be as explicit as possible about my role, interests and activities, and I elaborated mission plans for the various sites, along with historical outlines of the sites' development. Much of my research online consisted of participation in listservs, one of which I created, e-mail interviews (some of which I published in the CAC newsletter), regular e-mail discussions and debates and content analysis of websites.

Modes for developing trust and building rapport, critical to the successful execution of all forms of ethnography, demanded that a series of exchange relationships be developed to facilitate action research within the internal dimension of the CAC that I identified above. One of the bases of trust and rapport depended on outlining common interests in Caribbean indigenous issues shared by both activists and scholars. The second involved enabling the production of related content on the websites of the different participants (essays on Taino history and culture, information on archaeological sites and language resources; sometimes sites will appropriate content from the

CAC—unethical yes—but also a reaffirmation of bonds and boundaries of interest and like-mindedness). Third, there had to be some degree of shared perspectives (exemplified by a shared idiom for discussing and presenting Caribbean indigenous issues, or, again, by the mutual appropriation and replication of content). Shared symbols in terms of images that are often recycled from one site to another (petroglyphic icons, figurines and animal figures seen as sacred symbols in Taino cosmology—i.e., the development of an online aesthetic), provided another means for the diverse actors' sites to become, in a subtle way, glued to each other. The fifth mode of building this internal network consisted of marking boundaries (formed by sites cross-referencing each other for users, the granting of awards and other typical examples being hyperlinks and Webrings). I must disagree with such assertions as, "hyperlinks are an impoverished and one-dimensional way to represent and express social ties" (Wittel, 2000). Hyperlinks can have multiple layers of meaning, can be of a wide variety, can be the sites of intense contestation, and can be as emblematic of social relationships as a handshake, an exchange of gifts, an embrace, an invitation to a birthday party or a "thumbs up" offered in praise. In my experience, owners of sites linked from the CAC are acutely concerned with where their links are placed, with informing us of updated links, demanding that we link to them, angrily protesting that we linked to certain sites and that we remove those links and so forth. In each case, CAC editors have to play a balancing act between their commitment to a cause writ large, and the specific interests of particular bodies that are active in this cause. A sixth mode involved recognition of mutual advantage (the legitimacy of each site is bolstered by the fact that other such sites exist as well, thus rendering any one site less of a one-click wonder, less of an aberration). The seventh mode consisted of regular information exchange (electronic newsletters, e-mail petitions, mailing lists, listservs, newsgroups, message boards, chat rooms and individual e-mail messages).

In terms of the external dimension of my work with the CAC, as defined above, I need to indicate that I was not only creating sites, but also organizing other sites into a directory. I was presenting my research, from the offline arena, while also conducting research online. I especially conducted research amongst the many different users of the CAC and KACIKE, so that my regular contacts and correspondents (rather than key informants), consisted of other academics, journalists, secondary school students, activists in non-governmental organizations, Caribbean Amerindian webmasters and other Caribbean Amerindian representatives, Trinidadian and many other Caribbean expatriates, other Webmasters in charge of either non-Caribbean and/or non-indigenous websites and a diverse array of general members of the Internet public who cannot be easily classed. Private messages have never been publicly cited. In fact, much of my interest focused on gross trends: traffic statistics, site usage patterns, repeated queries and requests for information, search terms used in navigating the CAC and so forth.

ETHICAL PROBLEMS:
SOLUTIONS IN CONTEXT

With an array of activities united under the CAC, and after four years of work online, I have accumulated a number of cases of conflict and controversial ethical problems that I have had to address, and that I will discuss here only in terms of their most essential aspects. In addition, I present these cases in random order. The main theme underlying the practice of CAC editors in addressing these problems as they arise is to attempt some resolution within the context of all conflicting parties, basically having a shared interest in highlighting Caribbean aboriginal survival and educating members of the public as to the various facets of this survival. It is only when conflicts reach a crisis point that participants will articulate positions with reference to wider bodies of thought on ethics, especially with reference to confidentiality and intellectual property rights, notions which have filtered into the wider public discourse through the work of academia, courts and the media.

The first ethical issue that the CAC has confronted is that of site credibility, in terms of transparency and accountability. First of all, in the spirit of collaboration and dialogue, other editors and I have made our actual research reports available online for inspection by those about whom we write. In correspondence with recommendations made by the Association of Internet Researchers (AoIR, 2002, p. 5), both the CAC and KACIKE have clearly posted editorial policies. Efforts are made at identifying the scholarly and collaborative nature of the sites through specific design elements, detailed contact information and links to sites that can help to verify the credentials of the researchers involved (see Hamilton, 1999, p. B7). Site credibility, especially in the case of the CAC, also derived from the fact that it emerged into a vacuum that was created, paradoxically, by the existence of other Caribbean Amerindian sites that, however, were sometimes in open conflict with one another. The CAC and its participants thus zealously guarded its position as a non-partisan, respectable, pluralistic and multi-audienced site.

A second major issue concerns the practice of the CAC and KACIKE in monitoring the ways visitors use the sites. The data gained is used to determine the countries where users are based, the pages which are most consulted and the referring links. There is no way for us to obtain personal information on the users, apart from resolving their IP addresses to host names, and the data is also only visible to me alone and to the sites that accumulate the data. The sites do not track users across the Web however, only within the CAC and KACIKE. We reserve this as our right, as the CAC and KACIKE are forms of intellectual property that merit protection. In a metaphorical sense, the CAC is our "territory," and the visitor is a guest, thus we have a right to protect our own interests by monitoring the movements of a guest in our "house." What is not clear to me is whether or not visitors view this tracking as a potentially harmful intrusion. According to a study of the Pew Internet and American Life Project, "Fifty-four percent of Internet users believe that websites' tracking of users is harmful because it invades their privacy. Just 27 percent say tracking is helpful because it allows the sites to provide information tailored to specific consumers" (Fox, 2000, p. 2). What remains unclear is whether or not the tracking to which the report refers is solely one site or across all sites that a surfer visits. While the latter tracking practice is indeed ethically dubious, I am not sure that a convincing case can be made for the former practice. The Pew report muddies the issue further by reporting the seemingly contradictory find that 68 percent of those polled were not concerned that "someone might know what websites you've visited" (Fox, 2000, p. 4).

Given that a very large part of the CAC's efforts consists of building and maintaining a unique and specialized directory of links to related sites, the ethics of the hyperlink has become a central issue. In two cases, sites with related content simply appropriated pages from the CAC directory without acknowledgment. I did not initially raise issues of copyright with the parties concerned, requesting only that some form of reciprocity be shown, either in an explicit acknowledgment and return link to the CAC, or by simply linking to the relevant page of interest on the CAC (see Snapper, 2001). The CAC's aim is to provide useful content for like-minded sites, and I did not wish to turn this into a copyright issue, but the issue of credit and honesty remained. After all, editors of the CAC had done the work of searching the Web, locating sites of value, categorizing them, writing descriptions and reviews and all of this on the basis of specialist knowledge of a field that enabled them to know in the first place what to look for and why. That labor deserves recognition for unlocking the value of widely spread and sometimes hard to find sites (see Spinello, 2001). Moreover, the parties that engaged in plagiarism were denying their visitors the opportunity of exploring additional sources of relevance that existed on the CAC that were not on their own sites. In the extreme, a site could undermine the CAC by simply copying it, and, in this extreme eventuality, I would take any reasonable measures available to redress the situation if the perpetrator(s) failed to respond. In most cases, when obtaining the services of a Web host, one is required to sign an agreement that stipulates that one will not engage in activities such as copyright violations, so this might be one place to start seeking redress as the host can potentially ban the guilty site.

However, the CAC also potentially exposes itself to ethical problems concerning our occasional practice of deep linking sites. Deep linking involves bypassing a front page of a given site, and pointing users only to a particular page within a site. Normally we also link to the front page as a means of providing a reference point to users. In most cases, argues Spinello (2001), "any arbitrary or unnecessary restrictions against deep linking should be eschewed for the common good of open communications, flexibility, and maximum porosity in the Internet environment" (p. 296). Where deep linking can be harmful, however, is in cases where sites are commercially oriented and contain the bulk of their promotional and advertising material on their front pages. What is noteworthy is that in the few cases that the CAC has received any messages concerning this practice, it has been from like-minded sites that apparently took the "more the merrier approach"; they were pleased to have several links to their sites, and took care in informing us when links to various pages had been altered or moved.

Power also enters as an issue in linking, especially in cases where one manifests power in making the decision to not link to a given site, to de-link or to crowd a link within a mass of links to sites with contrary views. The aim of the CAC, according to its site policy, is to provide a range of opinions, rather than to preach just one message to visitors. However, in a case where a site changed its content after having been listed in the CAC directory, where it specifically endorsed neo-Nazi messages and symbols while attacking Caribbean aboriginals for their purported cannibalism, the site was deemed too offensive and of too little value to be maintained in our lists. This was the opinion of some scandalized scholars who visited the site, as well as some indigenous activists. I therefore disagree, in this respect, with arguments that cultural integrity is difficult to protect in an Internet context (see Waern, 2001).

In the case of interviews conducted via e-mail, interviewees are immediately made aware of the objectives and intended publication venue for the interview (i.e., "The CAC Review: Newsletter of the Caribbean Amerindian Centrelink"), and they are able to examine past interviews and how they were conducted and presented online, then the exercise becomes one that is almost journalistic, that is, communication with a public audience in mind. In exceptional cases, I have not published an interview where, even though not at first obvious to the interviewee, great personal damage would have resulted. This is not even a difficult judgment call, as when an interviewee engages in attacks on government officials that are clearly slanderous and libelous on a personal level. I would also agree with Frankel and Siang (1999) that, "interviews conducted via e-mail allow for greater clarification of concepts and involvement and empowerment of the participants than face to face interviews" (p. 4; see also Murray & Sixsmith, 1998).

Editorial guidelines have proven to be a problematic issue for the CAC, from an ethical standpoint. Attempts at developing a constitution have failed (apparently through a shared disinterest in this degree of formalization), and developing common guidelines through customary practice has had mixed results. In one case, a prospective candidate for an editorial role forwarded him/herself on the basis of one editor unilaterally encouraging the person, in private and without the advance knowledge of the other editors, to come forward. Unfortunately, some of the editors had prior political conflicts with the candidate and basically took the stance of, "if that person comes in, I go out." In previous discussions, all the editors agreed that new editors should be incorporated as long as all of the existing editors voted in favor, and this discussion would preferably take place before indicating any sort of commitment to a prospective new editor. In this case, the candidate was inadvertently "set up" for a fall, a fact that resulted in some negative feelings that later seemed to be translated into a conscious effort by the individual to duplicate the role of the CAC and appropriate some of its contents. Needless to say, where online action research and partnership are concerned, this was a significant shortcoming on our part.

Privacy has emerged as another vital issue in the activities of the CAC. I agree with Fox (2000) in her endorsement of the view that sites need to delimit which parts are public and which are private before users can feel safe and informed in deciding what to disclose about themselves. The CAC has erected virtual boundaries around that which is public and that which is private. For example, participation in the Carbet-L listserv requires an application and an agreement to abide by the rules of the list, which require that all participants treat messages as confidential and as copyright-protected statements that may not be quoted or forwarded without permission of the authors. Messages to the list are archived, and available only for viewing by members of the list. The list has seen its problems as well, however. In one case, a flame war erupted between two members, drawing in members of the entire list, and was only brought to a rest when the weight of opinion of members of the list who were shocked at the level of discussion was brought to bear. In another case, one participant attempted to demand the "real identity" of a list member using a pseudonym, which also invited the intervention of an editor. Lastly, one list member copied the contact list that I, as a moderator, failed to edit out of another member's message to the list. That allegedly resulted in the Spamming of the individual's contacts by his/her rival on Carbet-L. Participants have a proprietary relationship to their lists of contacts, usually shown in the "CC" boxes of their e-mails, much like one values his or her little black book of phone numbers. The intervention of moderators has become more strict, having first been instituted as a result of that earlier flame war mentioned above. A policy for suspending and then banning anti-social members has also recently been instituted. Editorial discussions, conducted via e-mail are also kept strictly confined within the editorial group, without copies of our messages ever sent to non-editors. There is a shared understanding of the need to avoid what has happened to some of our anthropological colleagues with the exponential e-mail forwarding of a confidential message denouncing the work of a colleague (see Miller, 2001). I would recommend that others who wish to create lists first do so on the assumption that its members will behave in a civil manner, and only subsequently adopt heavy-handed regulatory measures as required to stabilize the list. Another private venue within the CAC concerns visitor feedback questionnaires, designed to solicit ideas on improving CAC content, and these are not published, circulated nor archived online. The responses are merely noted and tabulated.

With reference to e-mail, as a general rule, I do not wish to quote any specific e-mail message, whatever the source or venue, which helps to make writing less personal and anecdotal, while summarily dispelling any potential ethical crises. On the other hand, knowing how unsuitable this approach may be to diverse research projects, I do not advance this as a general rule that all should follow.[7] The wider principle of utmost import, in my view, is that even when a certain item is quoted, even if permission to quote is granted by the original author, one must ensure that it will not cause any personal harm to its original author. In some cases, especially where interaction occurs solely online, and where the only social context by which one can determine potential harm is the online context, "potential harm" can be difficult to estimate. Once again, this may not be satisfactory to all; my own resolution is simply to try to avoid the problem in the first instance by not creating the conditions that allow a problem to develop. Of course, one actually learns to sight potential problems by first making mistakes, an unfortunate consequence of "learning as you go." On the issue of quoting e-mail messages posted to a group, or messages posted in chat, I am in agreement with Liu (1999) who argues: "We can always stay on the cautious side by guarding the confidentiality of data unconditionally, by avoiding direct quotation of postings, and by not referring to any particular IRC [chat] participants in our writing."

ACTION RESEARCH ONLINE: CONSIDERATIONS FOR THE FUTURE

As more experiences and case studies of action research using online electronic communication media are recorded and published, one would expect further development of the preceding discussion concerning ethics, and ways of conducting research online via website development. My case study focused on research relationships with an offline community, brought online, leading to the development of a new online context of interaction, and with the result of new partnerships formed in what has become an online action research project. My relationship with the SRCC, in this context, is more of an offline action research project. My relationship as part of the CAC is an almost entirely online action research project.

My focus on website development as a research tool, process and relationship might not seem so relevant here were it not for the dynamic and transformative repositioning of the ethnographer that this context of interaction entails. To transform the ethnographic process is to transform its inherent research relationships. In online action research in the form of creative observation, the ethnographer, as gatekeeper of the sites that s/he creates, becomes an informant to others. The ethnographer creates the research field. The field post-dates the ethnographer. The ethnographer generates data and presents it online, and that itself generates data (visitor feedback, usage, etc.). Ethics becomes a two-way street as there is also a need to protect the ethnographer. The challenge, then, is for ethical conduct to itself become the negotiated product between partners, rather than a formalistic procedure in a hierarchy between scientific takers and native givers.

REFERENCES

Allen, C. (1996). What's wrong with the "Golden Rule"? Conundrums of conducting ethical research in cyberspace. *The Information Society 12*(2), 175-187.

American Anthropological Association (AAA). (1998). *Code of ethics of the American Anthropological Association*. Retrieved Oct. 10, 2002 from: http://www.aaanet.org/committees/ethics/ethcode.htm.

Amit, V. (2000). Introduction: Constructing the field. In V. Amit (Ed.), *Constructing the Field: Ethnographic Fieldwork in the Contemporary World* (pp. 1-18). London: Routledge.

Assing, T. K. (2002, March 28). Red libation at CCA7: Artist Rebecca Gilmore turns pain into art. *The Trinidad Guardian*, 5.

Association of Internet Researchers (AoIR). (2002). Ethical decision-making and Internet research: Recommendations from the AoIR ethics working committee. Retrieved Oct. 12, 2002 from: http://www.aoir.org/reports/ethics.pdf.

Bruckman, A. (2002). Ethical guidelines for research online. Version 4/4/02. Retrieved Dec. 10, 2002 from: http://www.cc.gatech.edu/~asb/ethics/.

CAC (1998-2002). *Caribbean Amerindian Centrelink*. Retrieved May 1, 2002 from: http://www.centrelink.org/index.html.

Forte, M. C. (1998-2002). *The First Nations of Trinidad and Tobago*. Retrieved May 1, 2002 from: http://www.centrelink.org/fntt/index.html.

Forte, M. C. (2001). *Re-engineering indigeneity: Cultural brokerage, the political economy of tradition, and the Santa Rosa Carib Community of Arima, Trinidad and Tobago*. PhD Diss. The University of Adelaide.

Forte, M. C. (2002, Spring). 'We are not extinct': The revival of Carib and Taino identities, the Internet, and the transformation of offline indigenes into online 'N-digenes.' *Sincronia: An Electronic Journal of Cultural Studies*. Retrieved from: http://sincronia.cucsh.udg.mx/CyberIndigen.htm.

Forte, M. C. & Adonis, C. (1999-2002). *Los Niños del Mundo Parang band*. Retrieved May 1, 2002 from: http://trinidadtobagoparang.freeyellow.com/.

Forte, M. C. & Bharath, R. (1998-2002). *The Santa Rosa Carib Community*. Retrieved May 1, 2002 from: http://www.kacike.org/srcc/index.html.

Fox, F. (ed.)(2000). Trust and privacy online: Why Americans want to rewrite the rules. *The Internet life report* Washington, DC: The Pew Internet & American Life Project. Retrieved Dec. 10, 2002 from: http://www.pewinternet.org/.

Frankel, M. S. & Siang, S. (1999, June). *Ethical and legal aspects of human subjects research on the Internet*. Report of a workshop for the American Association for the Advancement of Science, Washington, DC. Retrieved Dec. 10, 2002 from: http://www.aaas.org/spp/dspp/sfrl/projects/intres/main.htm.

Garton, L., Haythornthwaite, C., & Wellman, B. (1997, June). Studying online social networks. *Journal of Computer-Mediated Communication 3*(1). Retrieved from: http://jcmc.huji.ac.il/vol3/issue1/garton.html.

Gupta, A. & Ferguson, J. (1992). Beyond 'culture': Space, identity, and the politics of difference. *Cultural Anthropology, 7*(1), 6-23.

Gupta, A. & Ferguson, J. (eds.). (1997). *Anthropological Locations: Boundaries and Grounds of a Field Science*. Berkeley, CA: University of California Press.

Hamilton, J. C. (1999). The ethics of conducting social-science research on the Internet. *Chronicle of Higher Education, 46*(15), B6-7.

Hine, C. (2000). *Virtual Ethnography*. London: Sage.

KACIKE. (1999-2002). *Kacike: The Journal of Caribbean Amerindian History and Anthropology*. Retrieved May 1, 2002 from: http://www.kacike.org/.

Jacobson, D. (1999, November). Doing research in cyberspace. *Field Methods, 11*(2) 127-145.

Liu, G. Z. (1999, September). Virtual community presence in Internet relay chatting. *Journal of Computer Mediated Communication 5*(1). Retrieved July 8, 2002 from: http://www.ascusc.org/jcmc/vol5/issue1/liu.html.

Masters, J. (1995). The history of action research. In I. Hughes (Ed.), *Action Research Electronic Reader*. The University of Sydney, Australia. Retrieved May 10, 2002 from http://www.behs.cchs.usyd.edu.au/arow/Reader/rmasters.htm.

Miller, D. & Slater, D. (2000). *The Internet: An Ethnographic Approach*. Oxford, UK: Berg.

Miller, D.W. (2001). Academic scandal in the Internet age. *Chronicle of Higher Education, 47*(18), A14-A17.

Murray, C. D. & Sixsmith, J. (1998). E-mail: A qualitative research medium for interviewing? *International Journal of Social Research Methodology, 1*(2), 103-121.

Nader, L. (1972). Up the anthropologist: Perspectives gained from studying up. In D. H. Hymes (Ed.), *Reinventing Anthropology* (pp. 284-311). New York: Random House Pantheon Books.

National Association for the Practice of Anthropology (NAPA). (1998, November 8-9). National Association for the Practice of Anthropology: Ethical guidelines for practitioners. *Anthropology Newsletter*. Retrieved Dec. 10, 2002 from: http://www.aaanet.org/napa/code.htm.

O'Brien, R. (1998, April). An overview of the methodological approach of action research. Retrieved May 10, 2002 from: http://www.web.net/~robrien/papers/arfinal.html.

Paccagnella, L. (1997, June). Getting the seats of your pants dirty: Strategies for ethnographic research on virtual communities. *Journal of Computer-Mediated Communication 3*(1). Retrieved February 6, 1999 from: http://jcmc.huji.ac.il/vol3/issue1/paccagnella.html.

Reyes, E. (n.d.). The *Santa Rosa Carib Community of the Late 20th Century* (pp. 1-4).

Robson, C. (2002). *Real World Research: A Resource for Social Scientists and Practitioner-Researchers* (2nd ed.). Malden, MA: Blackwell.

Ruhleder, K. (2000, February). The virtual ethnographer: Fieldwork in distributed electronic environments. *Field Methods, 12*(1), 3-17.

Snapper, J. W. (2001). On the Web, plagiarism matters more than copyright piracy. In R. A. Spinello & H. T. Tavani (Eds.), *Readings in CyberEthics* (pp. 280-294). Boston, MA: Jones and Bartlett Publishers.

Spinello, R. (2001). An ethical evaluation of Web site linking. In R. A. Spinello & H. T. Tavani (Eds.), *Readings in CyberEthics* (pp. 295-308). Boston, MA: Jones and Bartlett Publishers.

Suler, J. (2000). *Ethics in cyberspace research: Consent, privacy and contribution.* Retrieved Oct. 12, 2002 from the Department of Psychology, Rider University website: http://www.rider.edu/users/suler/psycyber/ethics.html.

Susman, G. I. & Evered, R. D. (1978, December). An assessment of the scientific merits of action research. *Administrative Science Quarterly, 23,* 582-603.

Thomas, J. (1996). Introduction: A debate about the ethics of fair practices for collecting social science data in cyberspace. *The Information Society, 12*(2), 107-117.

Turkle S. (1995). *Life on the Screen: Identity in the Age of the Internet.* New York: Simon & Schuster.

Wadsworth, Y. (1998). What is participatory action research? *Action Research International,* Paper 2. Retrieved September 8, 2002 from: http://www.scu.edu.au/schools/gcm/ar/ari/p-ywadsworth98.html.

Waern, Y. (2001). *Ethics in global Internet research* (Rep. No. 3). Retrieved Oct. 12, 2002 from Linköping University, Department of Communication Studies website: http://www.cddc.vt.edu/aoir/ethics/public/YWaern-globalirethics.pdf.

Watkins, J. (n.d.). *Briefing paper on consideration of the potentially negative impact of the publication of factual data about a study population on such population.* Retrieved Oct. 10, 2002 from the American Anthropological Association, Committee on Ethics website: http://www.aaanet.org/committees/ethics/bp4.htm.

Wilson, S. M. & Peterson, L. C. (2002). The anthropology of online communities. *Annual Review of Anthropology, 31,* 449-467.

Wittel, A. (2000, January). Ethnography on the move: From field to Net to Internet. *Forum: Qualitative Social Research, 1*(1). Retrieved from: http://qualitative-research.net/fqs-texte/1-00/1-00wittel-e.htm.

Wong, L. M. (1998). The ethics of rapport: Institutional safeguards, resistance, and betrayal. *Qualitative Inquiry, 4*(2), 178-199.

Young, J. R. (2001). Committee of scholars proposes ethics guidelines for research in cyberspace. *Chronicle of Higher Education, 48*(10), A51.

ENDNOTES

[†]   This chapter stems from an earlier presentation that I was invited to make at a seminar on "Research Relationships and Online Relationships" at the Centre for Research into Innovation, Culture and Technology (CRICT) at Brunel University, Uxbridge, Middlesex, UK, on April 19, 2002 (see http://www.brunel.ac.uk/depts/crict/vmsem2.htm). I wish to thank Elizabeth Buchanan for her constructive comments and helpful reviews of earlier versions of this draft. Thanks also to Kevin Yelvington (Department of Anthropology, University of South Florida) for his generosity in suggesting and providing several additional sources.

[1]   I write this chapter as a trained anthropologist with a concern for field methods and research ethics in ethnography. A survey of all available field research methods in the various disciplines is largely beyond the scope of this chapter and even my knowledge. I thus largely restrict my comments to anthropological methods.

2   For that which makes research participatory action research, see the essay by Wadsworth (1998).

3   Masters (1995) outlines a set of features for this type of research, as follows. Its philosophical base is historical and hermeneutic; the nature of reality is seen as multiple and constructed; the "problem" is situationally defined, that is, not defined in advance by the researcher alone; the relationship between knower and known is dialogic; the approach is inductive; the type of knowledge produced is descriptive and ethnographic; values play a central role in the research process and the purpose of the research, from the standpoint of the researcher, is to "understand what occurs and the meaning people make of phenomena."

4   This is an electronic document and no page numbers are available.

5   Transactionalism in anthropology refers to a theory of social relations guided by concepts such as "negotiation," "exchange," "gain" and construction. Pragmatism is closely related, meaning a calculation of one's interests and the strategies needed to maximize one's position. Brokerage involves intermediaries working between "clients" or constituents, on the one hand, and an external audience on the other hand.

6   I encountered this term in Garton et al. (1997).

7   For a wider discussion on the ethics concerning research using public messages, as in chat rooms, see Paccagnella (1997) and Thomas (1996).

Chapter XIII

What If You Meet Face to Face? A Case Study in Virtual/Material Research Ethics

David Clark
University of Wisconsin-Milwaukee, USA

ABSTRACT

In this chapter, the author argues for a strict interpretation of research ethics when conducting online research, and in the process, discusses these four ethical categories: the presence of the researcher in the researched context, the blurring lines between "public" and "private," informed consent and confidentiality. In making his argument, he draws on examples from a case study in which he examined an organization that meets both online and face-to-face.

INTRODUCTION

Internet researchers have long struggled with the complexities of applying research ethics and methods based in material, face-to-face research to virtual research (Jones, 1994). In fact, scholars have widely asserted (if not widely agreed) that ethical models founded on face-to-face research are inadequate for the study of online communities, where among other difficulties the researcher must confront the following:

- **Researcher presence:** a renewed struggle with research effect because of the possibilities of "lurking" (cf. Association of Internet Researchers (AoIR), 2001; Frankel & Siang, 1999);
- **Public vs. private:** blurring lines between public and private (cf. Gurak & Silker, 1997; Frankel & Siang, 1999);
- **Informed consent:** complications in obtaining informed consent (cf. Reid, 1996; Bruckman, 2002) and
- **Confidentiality, risk and reciprocity:** old problems—risks and reciprocity—compounded by new difficulties in maintaining confidentiality in the digital realm (cf. Clarke, 2000; AoIR, 2001).

These are problems that cut across disciplines, and it is not difficult to find scholarship on Internet research from many diverse fields: psychology, sociology, library/information science, computer science and technical and professional writing. What all this work shares in common is a spectrum of ethical stances, varying from those with highly restrictive ethical views to those Charles Ess calls "deontological" ("[those] inclined to override subjects' protections in the name of research goals and its ostensible benefits," quoted in Suler, 2000). Another commonality is that scholars almost uniformly assert that Internet research requires new ethical structures (whether stricter or less strict) that acknowledge the new complexities inherent in virtual research. After all, many Institutional Review Boards (IRBs) are not up to date on the complexities of Internet research, and there is an anxiety in the Internet ethics literature that it is all too easy for researchers to take a position of "what can I get away with?" instead of dealing substantively with ethical issues. As a result, many organizations have stepped in to develop preliminary but thorough ethics codes, including the Association of Internet Researchers (AoIR) and the American Association for the Advancement of Science.

The Internet research ethics scholarship is still relatively young. It is still in the stage where a literature search turns up many, many articles making claims that are nearly identical rather than discipline specific. And there is little to no research on the complexities introduced by researching a context that is both virtual and material, such as my own work of a community that meets both online and in person. Research in a jointly virtual and material context raises unique questions. For example, the primary texts in my research are the community's listserv postings; how will participant perceptions of risk be impacted by physical meetings with me and others after I have written potentially critical things? Postings that seemed innocuous at the time could become a source of embarrassment. How can I best protect anonymity and confidentiality in an online community where participants actually know one another in person? How can I balance the private nature of group meetings (which no one would dream of studying without consent) with the apparently public nature of the listserv, which participants, along with many researchers, treat as free for public use? How should I manage informed consent?

As a first attempt at answering such questions as these, in this chapter I draw on my own virtual/material research project in attempting to explore what a joint virtual/material research ethics might look like. Why aren't virtual/material research ethics simply the same as face-to-face ethics? Are virtual/material ethics simply a matter of defaulting to the most restrictive ethical practices? Does a nuanced ethical stance require a unique construction for each context? In short, what happens when an Internet study involves meeting your participants face to face? In what follows, I survey the relevant literature in both virtual and material research ethics, pointing out the gaps that complicate my ethical decision making. As I do so, I explore the particulars of my work, supplying data and anecdotes from my research in supporting my overarching claim that virtual/material studies require their own unique ethical constructs.

CONTEXT

My research area is what my field (rhetoric and professional communication) calls the "rhetoric of technology," which can be broadly construed as the study of human discourse about the design, development, production and deployment of technology. Work in the rhetoric of technology borrows heavily from more traditional rhetorical studies but also from science and technology studies, anthropology and the history of technology, all fields that value discussions of discourse, while not focusing on it as explicitly as we do. Rhetoric of technology scholars have produced a significant body of work in a short span (the area was first named and distinguished only in 1998), much of it taking the form of ethnographic workplace studies. My own research work almost always relies on qualitative methodologies; I greatly value the messiness, complications and chaos that extensive field work, interviews, notes and occupational shadowing can introduce into research.

But while scholars in my field are rapidly learning to handle the complex and problematic research ethics of workplace studies, the ethical complexities of my next project have given me pause. This project addresses the controversial and contentious open-source software community and not only requires much consideration of virtual research ethics (about which I knew very little prior to this project) and material research ethics (with which I'm pretty familiar), but combines the two in novel and unprecedented ways that are giving me headaches.

To be more specific, my research design calls for the study of online and in-person discourse within a community of Linux[1] users, who I am studying to learn more about how self-described "technical" people conceive of and communicate about the relations between their work, their technologies and larger sociopolitical issues (cf. Feenberg, 1991; Downey, 1998; Winner, 1986; Johnson, 1998). A previous study examined software developers in an Internet startup company, noting that the company's developers—who code "censorware" designed to block Internet pornography—are immersed in work structures that oblige them to struggle not with the politics and ethics of their work but with drop-down menus and driver software (Clark, 2001). This focus is possible, I suggested, because these workers are culturally trained to see their machines not as political artifacts but as ideologically neutral "tools" that have political implications only in how they are used.

In my new study, however, I seek to complicate my own views of the relationships of politics and technology through observations of a very different community of technical people: those involved in the "open-source" movement, an enormous, politically charged community of computer professionals and hobbyists that seeks, through the distribution of free software and its source code (including open-source initiatives like the Linux operating system), to free themselves and the masses from the hegemonic corporations that control our desktops (e.g., Microsoft). These participants, I believe, think differently about the politics of technology than the censorware developers, but I am interested in how and in what ways: How do they articulate the politics of technology? Do they articulate technology as having a cause/effect relationship on an external social realm, or do they view technology as inherently political? And how do—or do—those articulations shape their work? In finding answers to these questions, I started with the Web, even though I'd never done online research before. I quickly latched on to the idea of studying the listserv of a Linux user's group. Open source, after all, is a textual community, and members of the user's group communicate primarily in text. A rhetorical study, then, seemed a logical choice for my analysis, and my research relied primarily on collecting, describing and analyzing texts.

However, the Linux user's group I elected to study is a virtual and material community; they have monthly in-person meetings where they meet to discuss issues, watch presentations and install and configure Linux. Getting a thick ethnographic description of the group, therefore, required both studying the listserv and attending meetings to observe and gain an understanding of their interactions. In addition, I believe that empirical anthropological research has taught us that qualitative data can most effectively and persuasively claim credibility when organized, interpreted and analyzed from not only the perspective of the researcher, but from the perspectives of participants and others (peer reviewers, code validators, etc.), in addition to those of the researcher herself. So I needed and wanted to combine virtual and material perspectives, requiring joint virtual/material ethical principles.

After much reading, reflection and interaction with my university's IRB, I arrived at ethical decisions that I believe reflect the most restrictive possibilities in terms of protecting the rights of participants, defaulting in many ways to the standards of material ethics. In short, I announced my presence as a researcher, I treated all publicly available documents—in my case, e-mail and Web page postings—as private documents. I obtained explicit, written permission for the use of these documents, and I'm in the process of constructing samples and new informed consent documents that will help my participants better understand the potential risks posed to them by my research. In what follows, I describe and argue for my ethical conclusions.

REVIEW AND DISCUSSION

I found that figuring out a virtual/material ethical stance was no easy task. The basic problems being explored in much of the literature on Internet research ethics are not unlike those explored in conventional research ethics. But four key issues emphasized as particular problems in Internet research also create unique problems in virtual/material research. At the significant risk of oversimplifying, I've grouped the primary concerns into four groups: researcher presence, public vs. private, informed consent and confidentiality, risks and reciprocity.

Researcher Presence

Material research ethics has long been concerned with the impact researchers have on the contexts they study. Where once ethnographers sought objective accounts of communities, they now acknowledge that their presence impacts a context and that all research reports come from a subjective, personal perspective. Qualitative researchers are by their nature participant-observers, and as Brueggemann (1996) suggests, participant-observers necessarily "traverse the hyphen," always in between, never wholly a participant/member of the community and certainly never an objective, detached observer (Dauterman, 1996). Guidelines on researcher presence are therefore fairly clear cut; formally, researchers must announce their presence and get permission for taking field notes, conducting interviews and using participant data. Many fields emphasize the importance of self reflection and acknowledging researcher positioning in writing up results.

However, virtual studies have further complicated the politics of researcher presence, because in some ways, virtual research has allowed the rebirth of the dream that researchers can be objective; by "lurking" a researcher can collect data without an obvious impact on a community's activities or perceptions. In virtual research, then, it really seems possible that researchers can remain completely detached from a context, observing without impacting the discourse. And this detachment is possible, right up to the point where they actually connect with or write about the context, thereby impacting community discourse in a substantive way. In one example, a researcher of an online sexual abuse survivor group downloaded, analyzed and published data from the group without permission, moving from an impact-free study to a "nightmare" for the privacy perceptions of the group in question (King, 1996). In another famous case, a researcher studied a community by pretending to be a female support group participant, only later revealing himself as a male researcher (much to the outrage of participants).

Obviously, these types of subterfuge are extreme examples and are ethically out of line; it's doubtful either research plan passed an IRB. But many scholars still do argue that one can and should maintain a distance from a virtual group. Bruckman (2002), in her widely cited "Ethical guidelines for research online," described by her and others as a "strict interpretation" of virtual ethics (cf. Suler, 2000; Jankowski & van Selm, 2001), indicates that researchers may freely use "publicly available" documents without seeking permission, and many others concur. What's more, she and others argue that the process of seeking approval can be "disruptive" to groups and therefore should be done selectively (Bruckman, 2002); indeed, in my own study, a list owner suggested that in seeking permission, I should be careful to keep my posts "on topic" to avoid disrupting normal list activities (Mike, personal communication, 2002).[2] I would point out, however, that the perception of "disruption" of normal activities can also occur when meeting face to face; at a user's group meeting, I explained my research to one member and he replied, "Oh, so you're a spy?" I think he was kidding.

So what should a researcher do when confronted with a jointly virtual and material community? According to the IRB guidelines at my institution (University of Wisconsin-Milwaukee, 2002), I don't need permission to quote or analyze "publicly available" documents, which are (in Bruckman's (2002) definition), documents that are "officially, publicly archived," requiring no password, on a topic that is not "highly sensitive," with no site or organizational policy prohibiting their use. The archives of the listserv I studied met this definition, so I could theoretically do as I liked with them. On the other hand, if I wished to collect data in person from the user's group, the IRB instructed that I need permission. I could, then, get permission to take field notes and interview participants in person, and use the listserv archives, written without any knowledge of my lurking or my research plans, in whatever way I chose, giving participants some input into my research (informed consent, interpretive reciprocity and free to withdraw) but no control over my use of their past words.

Ultimately, this solution is untenable if you wish to maintain balanced and ethical relationships with participants. The argument I ultimately find most compelling comes from Eysenbach and Till (2001), who argue that online participants "do not expect to be research subjects" (p. 2). For their article, they searched Web archives to find postings from researchers disclosing their work; searching for "research survey project health" turned up 85 messages, many of which were attached to negative responses from participants who felt like they were in "a fishbowl for a bunch of guinea pigs" (Eysenbach & Till, 2001, p. 2). Bruckman and others have argued that these reactions are a reason to avoid asking for permission, but given that research results are frequently public (whether presented, published, or posted online), I think we owe it to our participants to give them at minimum the freedom to withdraw from being studied. At the University of Wisconsin-Milwaukee, we are required by our IRB to allow the participants of any approved study to withdraw, and online participants deserve no less.

Public vs. Private

The theme of "public" vs. "private" runs throughout my above discussion of researcher presence. The notion that Internet texts, after having been "publicly, officially archived," are open to free use is both pervasive and compelling. Is it even reasonable to expect privacy on the Internet (Gurak & Silker, 1997), when users know (or should know) that their messages are being recorded, archived and preserved, and when scholars argue the Internet is "more public space than private given the conventions of behavior on Internet transmitted services" (Jones, 1994, p. 31)? It's common, if an unfortunate practice, for employers to search newsgroup postings for controversial or problematic postings (cf. Bowker & Star, 1999), and certainly government agencies and journalists have followed suit; should newsgroup posters expect different treatment from researchers? Are newsgroups and listservs public or private?

And what of a researcher studying a jointly virtual and material context? Again, as above, researchers studying material contexts are bound by their IRBs to obtain permission before researching even "public" face-to-face pronouncements within the confines of a community. In the Linux user's group, for example, I would never consider attending a meeting, taking careful notes on the discussions there and reporting those discussions without informing the group of my researcher status and obtaining permission to do so, even though the meetings are very much public gatherings of a self-selected membership. Is a listserv discussion really any different simply because (1) judges have ruled that there is an implicit consent to recording of chat and e-mail, unlike phone conversations (Kaplan, 2000); (2) the archived discussion happened in the past; and/or (3) the discussion was posted without participant knowledge of the researcher's presence?

Much of the public vs. private debate centers on the concept of "publishing." It's the idea that when works are "published," they are thereby freely available for public use and consumption. But this view is potentially problematic; what, after all, constitutes publishing? Some interpretations rely on a technological mindset (documents should be considered "public," if they are accessible to anyone with an Internet connection) (Frankel & Siang, 1999, p. 11), but if we're to follow Gaiser's (1997) call to consider ethics, rather than strictly relying on what's legal and what we can get past our IRBs, it's just as important to consider the sociocultural forces that influence participant conceptions about public vs. private. Is a self-posted Web page a public document? Probably. Is sending an e-mail to a listserv inherently public? Questionable, because although certainly the messages are in some ways intended for public consumption and although arguably the e-mailer knows the message is being saved in a public space, whether a listserv is "public" may be the wrong question. We must consider the limited context in which the messages are written, one in which the purpose is not the kind of public statement represented by a Web page, but the upkeep of an ongoing conversation in which the writer seeks to ridicule, help, tease or argue with another or others on a list.

I am not suggesting that we should not use listserv postings in our research. But I will suggest that researchers in the snare of sorting out virtual/material research ethics should again, in this case, default to the more restrictive set of ethical principles, if only for the continuance and richness of their data and research. In my own case, since I want to gather face-to-face information from my participants in addition to virtual, and since I am also specifically interested in the technological beliefs and ethics of my participants, it makes sense in terms of sustaining the goodwill of my participants for me to treat all data that I collect about and from the group as strictly private unless given permission to see it otherwise.

Informed Consent

Due to all of these decisions, early in my project I decided that my joint research ethics would default to asking for permission for everything. Getting consent in a way that ensures your participants are thoroughly informed and aware of their rights is difficult in any research project; participants may not thoroughly read the consent document, they may be seduced by researcher descriptions that minimize the possibilities of risk (Newkirk, 1996), they may lack the knowledge or interest to gain a full understanding or the researcher may be unable to fully explain a still-developing qualitative project (Moss, 1992; Doheny-Farina & Odell, 1985). Finally, participants who have developed a personal relationship with researchers are more likely to trust the researcher, minimizing the perceived risks of the research and making the researcher seem less ambiguous and more simply another group member.

All of these normal problems with obtaining informed consent are amplified by operating in a jointly virtual and material environment. As with the discussions above, I could arguably avoid the entire issue in the virtual realm, right up to the point where I started specifically requesting information from participants and/or conducting online interviews or gathering information through an online survey. As long as I stuck with just using the public listserv, no permission would be needed. But given that I'd already decided to ask for permission, what was the best strategy? Obviously, what I most wanted was permission to use the entire list, and some have argued that in many cases it is appropriate to ask for permission from the owner of the listserv, if one can be identified (Buchanan, 2002). In cases where group members cannot be easily identified or contacted, this may be an acceptable solution, but in others, the makeup and topic of the group, as well as the group's dynamics, structure and community orientation should be our guides in determining how far to go in obtaining consent.

In the case of the Linux user's group, by using the website I was able to track down a group e-mail address that was forwarded to the individual maintaining the site and the listserv. I asked for his permission and for advice, based on his own experience with the community, in contacting the others and getting their permission individually. This is important in this particular community because there are no obvious group officers or managers to appeal to; this user's group is a loose, individualistic collection of people who participate when they feel like participating, and so getting permission from only the person who maintains the listserv (who is not necessarily "in charge" and who himself rarely participates in the listserv) would be inadequate. In such a community, I can't assume that a system administrator has the experience, knowledge, power or authority to speak for the entire group, and I should not, if only because doing so might jeopardize my material relationship with my participants.

However, this ethical strategy raised new problems. Should I have written to list members individually? Or posted to the entire list? Which method was more likely to generate responses? Which was more likely to potentially create anger or a sense that they had been working in a fishbowl? At the advice of the list administrator, I posted one message to the entire list, carefully labeling it as [OT] (off topic) and writing and editing carefully to ensure that I didn't have to post any additional follow-up messages (see Appendix for the text of the message). The listserv members are readers and writers, and I knew they'd find the post at least interesting, if not relevant. I knew too that my past presence at meetings and on the listserv would grease the skids. Sure enough, I immediately received responses from most of the key members on the list; no controversies, no objections, no list postings, I simply received consent forms, and many additionally volunteered to be interviewed. Once I begin data analysis I would undoubtedly come across additional messages I hoped to use but didn't have permission to use, and that would necessitate follow ups. But in general it couldn't have gone better.

Still, I had to ask myself the following: Have I actually achieved informed consent? Did my participants actually read the full text, or scroll quickly past it and click "agree" as they have with so many software license agreements? Did my presence on the list and in person (although I didn't meet all of the respondents), make the participants trust me? One respondent took a copyright perspective in his response: "there's no copyright statement for the mail archives. Plus, if you are a list subscriber, I think you have the right to use what was given to you. Go for it" (Steve, 2002). Or do the participants simply not care that much? It would be easy not to view these issues as problems, but they connect in very real ways to the perceptions that participants have about the potential risk of their participation in my research.

Confidentiality, Risks and Reciprocity

First of all, I can't assure confidentiality. I will, of course, make every conventional effort (as stated in my "Informed Consent Document") to safeguard individual identities.

But no one can guarantee confidentiality, when anyone with an Internet connection could, while reading my work, type a quotation from an online source into a search engine and find out everything they would want to know about my research participants. My tech-savvy participants know this all too well. This new searchability of research is a nice hedge, in some ways, because in the case of online-only archival studies, the omnipresence of the data allows other researchers to more effectively investigate or question research conclusions. But to participants, it means that whenever a researcher writes about research conducted online, their worlds can be easily exposed and subject to further, unagreed-upon scrutiny. Even if they participate using only a pseudonym, their online world has the potential to be altered by my research, and in online communities like open source, where research indicates that participants trade primarily upon their reputations, the potential for embarrassment (or worse) should a participant or their peers not like what I write about them is very real.

And this risk is even more problematic in a jointly virtual and material context. In the case of this user's group, participants have the potential to have their online and face-to-face personas (which are sometimes very different) damaged, depending on their and their peer's reactions to the things I write. I have no plans, of course, to single out or purposely humiliate a participant. But ultimately only an individual can decide how they will react to a given situation; their embarrassment or humiliation is only partly within my control. And my work could potentially, if not intentionally, damage a participant's self perception and/or their position within the user's group.

For example, my research design, as explained in the "Informed Consent Document," calls for reciprocity in the form of my posting my writings to the listserv I'm researching. Every document I write about the group, including this one, will be sent to list members for their interest and their feedback, and I agree to make jointly agreeable changes to my representations of participants if requested. My focus, of course, is on the relationship of the participants to the technologies with which they work; what if my study unintentionally singles out an individual or a small group (perhaps a subgroup of which I'm unaware) as holding a particular controversial view? I suspect that many of my participants will be interested in what I write about them and their group—I know I would be—and will likely discuss and debate the issues I raise. Certainly, in terms of the richness and depth of my research, I hope they do. But how can I ensure that my participants have adequately understood the potential risks to their online and face-to-face personas of my work?

Of course my participants have the right to withdraw their consent at any point, but if the damage has already been done to their virtual or material persona, it's too late. The only adequate ethical solution in this context is to ask and ask again, in an effort to verify participant understanding of the risks by showing them examples, giving them possible embarrassing scenarios and, ultimately, sharing with them and including their responses to potentially controversial passages before publication in print or on the listserv. When I meet with my participants in person, therefore, I will ask them to again read and sign the informed consent document, which I will accompany with an explanation (perhaps from this article) that provides more detail into the kinds of risks they may expect. What if, as one participant related, they simply signed off because they do not care about my use of the archive, which is viewed as historical? What if they simply don't understand or can't imagine the representational possibilities for my representation and interpretation of their postings? As ethical virtual/material researchers, we owe it to our participants to make every effort to not harm the operation of the communities we study or the individuals within those communities.

CONCLUSION

This project is still in progress; I've yet to work through the archives that I have permission to study. I've yet to do any of the writing, a phase that, I suspect, will raise more virtual/material issues than I've anticipated in this essay. But I do think that my work thus far has pointed to a key principle that researchers should consider when conducting jointly virtual and material projects; in being most fair to our participants, a concern that should come before any considerations about our research results, we should in general default to the most restrictive ethical options, applying face-to-face standards to online research. It is possible to conduct these studies far more quickly and easily by simply running our designs past our local IRBs and leaving it at that, but IRBs, so many of which are behind the virtual times, should not be the final word on any research involving the treatment of virtual participants or data.

REFERENCES

Anderson, P. V. (1998). Ethical issues in composition research. *College Composition and Communication, 41,* 63-89.

Association for Internet Researchers (AOIR) Ethics Working Committee. (2001). *Preliminary report for ethics.* Retrieved July 12, 2002 from: http://aoir.org/reports/ethics.html.

Bowker, G. & Star, S. L. (1999). *Sorting Things Out: Classification and its Consequences.* Cambridge, MA: MIT Press.

Bruckman, A. (2002). *Ethical guidelines for research online.* Retrieved Oct. 30, 2002 from: http://www.cc.gatech.edu/~asb/ethics/.

Brueggemann, B. J. (1996). Still-life: Representations and silences in the participant-observer role. In P. Mortensen & G. Kirsch (Eds.), *Ethics and Representation in Qualitative Studies of Literacy* (pp. 17-39). Urbana, IL: National Council of Teachers of English.

Buchanan, E. (2002). Internet research ethics and institutional review boards: New challenges, new opportunities. *Advances in Library Administration and Organization, 19,* 85-99.

Clark, D. (2001). *A rhetoric of boundaries: Living and working along a technical/non-technical split.* Unpublished doctoral dissertation, Iowa State University, Ames, Iowa, USA.

Clarke, P. (2000). *The Internet as a medium for qualitative research.* Paper presented at the Web 2000 Conference, Rand Afrikaans University, Johannesburg, South Africa.

Dauterman, J. (1996). Social and institutional power relationships in studies of workplace writing. In P. Mortensen & G. Kirsch (Eds.), *Ethics and Representation in*

Qualitative Studies of Literacy (pp. 241-259). Urbana, IL: National Council of Teachers of English.

Doheny-Farina, S. & Odell, L. (1985). Ethnographic research on writing: Assumptions and methodology. In L. Odell & D. Goswami (Eds.), *Writing in Nonacademic Settings* (pp. 503-535). New York: Guilford Press.

Downey, G. (1998). *The Machine in Me: An Anthropologist Sits Among Computer Engineers*. New York: Routledge.

Eysenbach, G. & Till, J. E. (2001). Ethical issues in qualitative research on Internet communities. *British Medical Journal, 323,* 1103-1106.

Feenberg, A. (1991). *Critical Theory of Technology*. New York: Oxford.

Frankel, M. S. & Siang, S. (1999). *Ethical and Legal Aspects of Human Subjects Research on the Internet.* Washington, DC: American Association for the Advancement of Science.

Gaiser, T. J. (1997). Conducting online focus groups: A methodological discussion. *Social Science Computer Review, 15,* 2.

Gurak, L. J. & Silker, C. M. (1997). Technical communication research: From traditional to virtual. *Technical Communication Quarterly, 6,* 403-418.

Jankowski, N. W. & van Selm, M. (2001). *Research ethics in a virtual world: Some guidelines and illustrations.* Retrieved on Nov. 8, 2002 from: http://www.brunel.ac.uk/depts/crict/vmpapers/nick.htm.

Johnson, R. R. (1998). *User-Centered Technology: A Rhetorical Theory for Computers and Other Mundane Artifacts.* Albany, NY: State University of New York Press.

Jones, R. A. (1994). The ethics of research in cyberspace. *Internet Research, 4,* 30-35.

Kaplan, C. S. (2000, Jan. 14). Judge says recording of electronic chats is legal. *New York Times.* Retrieved July 14, 2002 from: http://www.nytimes.com/library/tech/00/01/cyber/cyberlaw/14law.html.

King, S. A. (1996). Researching Internet communities: Proposed ethical guidelines for the reporting of results. *The Information Society, 12,* 119-127.

Moss, B. (1992). Ethnography and composition: Studying language at home. In G. Kirsch & P. Sullivan (Eds.), *Methods and Methodology in Composition Research* (pp. 153-171). Carbondale, IL: Southern Illinois University Press.

Newkirk, T. (1996). Seduction and betrayal in qualitative research. In P. Mortensen & G. Kirsch (Eds.), *Ethics and Representation in Qualitative Studies of Literacy* (pp. 3-16). Urbana, IL: National Council of Teachers of English.

Reid, E. (1996). Informed consent in the study of on-line communities: A reflection on the effects of computer-mediated social research. *The Information Society, 12,* 129-174.

Suler, J. (2000). *Ethics in cyberspace research: consent, privacy and contribution.* Retrieved on Oct. 30, 2002 from: http://www.rider.edu/users/suler/psycyber/ethics.html.

University of Wisconsin-Milwaukee. (2002). *Institutional Review Board policy.* Retrieved July 14, 2002 from: http://www.uwm.edu/Dept/RSA/Public/IRB/Guide/index.html.

Winner, L. (1986). *The Whale and the Reactor: A Search for Limits in an Age of High Technology.* Chicago, IL: University of Chicago Press.

ENDNOTES

[1]   Linux is a popular "open-source" computer operating system. Open-source software is created and freely distributed by communities of developers; for more on open source as a cultural trend and/or a political movement, see http://opensource.mit.edu/ or http://www.opensource.org/.

[2]   All participant and organization names are pseudonyms.

APPENDIX

Informed Consent Document

To: XXX

From: Dave Clark [dclark@uwm.edu]

Subject: [OT] XXX Research

Hi! This is a tad off topic, but I've got another question for you all: How would you feel about my using the *** list archives in the pursuit of some research?

Here's the brief version. I'm an English professor (rhetoric and technical writing, to be more specific) at UWM, but I'm also a tech geek, and my current research is on software developers. My last project (my Ph.D. dissertation) was an examination of the technical politics of an Internet startup company that made censorware. My new research focuses on the politics (defined broadly) of open source developers and users. I'm interested because historically, many scholars in the humanities and social sciences—as well as mass-market critics—view technology workers as uninterested in the sociocultural implications of their work (for example, the censorware folks I studied spent their days struggling with drop-down menus and driver software, not struggling with the politics and ethics of their working for censorship).

I think open source communities and beliefs prove that the relationship of technology workers to politics is a lot more complicated than that. And that's what I want to write about, in both positive and critical ways: I want to complicate stereotypes about technology workers (poorly dressed, socially inept, strictly Libertarian) and also critique the way technology workers talk about politics, with an eye towards more democratic and egalitarian communication.

So what do I want? Permission to use the last year's worth of the *** archives in my study, so that I can study the way technology workers talk about politics. I want your OK because I think it's ethically important to ask permission when you're using someone's words for your research. And, I'd like some follow-up info (surveys/interviews/job shadowing [first-hand observation of technology work practices]) from folks who are willing to or interested in chatting some more (online or f2f).

So, specifically, I'd like permission from each of you to use your individual posts, and an idea of your willingness to be interviewed/job shadowed. I hope I can get most of you this way and save myself a lot of e-mailing :) Below I've attached the official permission form I wrote (in text below); key highlights are that (1) I will disguise all individual and organizational identities, (2) I will share my writing about *** with *** to solicit feedback, and (3) You can change your mind and withdraw your permission at any time.

If you're willing, please fill out the form following my .sig and return it to me at dclark@uwm.edu. And please e-mail me if you have any questions. Thanks much.

Dave

| dave clark

| assistant professor, department of english
| university of wisconsin-milwaukee
| http://www.uwm.edu/~dclark

form start

I have received an explanation of this study and agree to participate. I
understand that my participation in this study is strictly voluntary.

| Name | Date
| (type in name and date)
|
|----------------------------------

|I am willing to be (1) interviewed, (2) job shadowed
|(type in if they apply):
|
|----------------------------------

----
form end

Informed Consent Document (ICD)

I am Professor David Clark of the Department of English at the University of
Wisconsin-Milwaukee. I am conducting a study of how users and developers of open
source software talk and think about the politics of the technologies they use every day.
For example, I am interested in learning whether users of Linux see the operating system
and code itself as a political object or if, in contrast, they see only the discussion about
Linux as containing political content. I would appreciate your participation in this study,
as it will assist me in making contributions to scholarship in technology studies.

Research Procedures

In order to answer my questions about open source software, I will be collecting
and analyzing a variety of different kinds of data from publicly available documents, but
I also believe that there is no substitute for genuine participant response to research
ideas. Therefore, I will also collect data from between 15 and 20 open source users and
developers. To be more specific, I will do the following:

- Collect and code publicly available documents (books, magazines, Web pages,
  newsgroup and listserv postings, software code).
- Write extensive field notes on meetings, development activities, and interviews.
- Record and transcribe interviews.
- Record and transcribe responses to "think-aloud protocols," in which subjects
  read and verbally respond to documents.

- "Shadow" participants, which means taking extensive notes while watching participants work, attend meetings, etc.

Risks and Benefits

The risk associated with participating in this project is that you may not like what I write. I will use two means to protect your interests:

- Collecting your feedback. Before presenting or publishing from the data I have collected with your help, I will make a reasonable attempt (e.g., e-mailing you drafts with a request to respond within a reasonable time period) to obtain your feedback and incorporate it into my work, whether by changing or eliminating quotes or some other mutually acceptable compromise.
- Protecting your confidentiality and security. The data I collect using these procedures will be used to produce scholarly presentations and publications, in which I will discuss and describe individuals and their organizations. However, all participant and organizational identities will be kept strictly confidential; I will change all names and take whatever other measures are appropriate (disguising company products, for example) to ensure that people and organizations cannot be identified. In addition, all data will be kept secure, meaning that I store identity lists in a separate location from data files, store data on an un-networked, secure workstation. I will keep all data archived solely on CD-ROM in a fire safe box after completion of the study. All data will be kept indefinitely.

You may also benefit from participating in this project; you will get an opportunity to participate in discussions and scholarly publications that will shape the way academics and practitioners think about users and technologies.

Time and Location

The full scope of my data collection on this project will be approximately one year, starting in July 2002. However, your participation will not require overly extensive participation, falling into one of two categories:

- Interviewed. Interviewees will spend approximately half an hour to an hour on the project, including time spent being interviewed and responding to documents. Interviews will take place at times and places specified by participants.
- Shadowed. Participants who I shadow as they work with open source technologies can expect to spend significantly more time, perhaps several weeks, although the participation will require very little time and effort. I will primarily be observing and asking occasional questions. Shadowing will take place in participant workplaces (and of course will require my getting permission from your employer).

Freedom to Withdraw

Participation in this study is completely voluntary, and you may withdraw from the study at any time and for any reason without penalty; if you do so, I would hope to continue to use the data I have gained from your participation, but I will destroy it at your request. It is also possible I may exclude a participant from future participation due to conflicts of interest; if so, you will be notified and given the opportunity to determine the fate of any and all data I have gained from your participation.

Offer to Answer Inquiries

As stated above, I will share and request feedback on any and all presentations and publications that result from this research. In the meantime, if you have any questions, please contact me as follows:

Dave Clark, Ph.D.
Department of English
University of Wisconsin-Milwaukee
P.O. Box 413
Milwaukee, WI 53201
414.229.4870 (O)
dclark@uwm.edu

If you have any complaints about your treatment as a participant in this study, please call or write the following:

Jeanne M. Kreuser, JD
Human Protections Administrator
Institutional Review Board for the Protection of Human Subjects
Graduate School, University of Wisconsin-Milwaukee
P.O. Box 340
Milwaukee, WI 53201
414.229.3173

Although Ms. Kreuser will ask your name, all complaints are kept in confidence.

Chapter XIV

Fact or Fiction: Notes of a Man Interviewing Women Online

Michael D. Ayers
New School for Social Research, USA

ABSTRACT

This chapter examines conditions that participants of online qualitative research might give false answers to a researcher. As research was conducted with feminist activists who were online, a number of the responses were highly suspect as to how true they could actually be. Because the researcher was not face to face with these participants, he had to either take the responses as true or discard them. The researcher argues his lack of face-to-face presence made it difficult to generate a good rapport with these participants, and because of this, received answers based on the only social marker that was evident: his name, or that he was male. Interview data is presented to show apparent discrepancies in our electronic conversations. The chapter concludes by suggesting for future online qualitative research, the researcher should have a more reflexive research design and approach to the project.

INTRODUCTION

In late 2000, I found myself developing a research project that would compare two social movement groups: one that exists in cyberspace and one that exists in the physical world. I thought my research design was pretty straightforward: I would be interviewing feminist activists in these two different social spaces. My thought process led me to believe that my (yet-to-be determined) participants would be eager and willing to talk with me about their activism. After all, people love to talk about themselves, my optimism told me. As I was finalizing my design, nowhere did I question how my role as a researcher or a man would play out in this. With the online social movement group, I could utilize my years of writing tactful e-mails to interview these participants, even when the subject matter (politics) could, at times, be touchy. This lack of insight might have been a mistake. I was treated differently and the responses that I received could have been fabricated. In retrospect, I should have taken into account more about myself than I did.

Qualitative research methods, such as participant observation, the interview and content analysis, are all subject to different methodologies when looking at cyberspace because of the absence of a face-to-face presence the researcher typically has with participants. This chapter addresses the cyberspace interview. I explore the trials and tribulations that occur when conducting the interview in a strictly online environment, in this case, e-mail. My interviewees gave what I suspected were tailored responses, given that I presented myself online as a man, which I am, and asked them about feminist activism. I end the chapter with a discussion of a proposed solution to the perils I describe below: the reflexive study of cyberculture and cyberspace.

I conducted interviews in the spring of 2001, from (late) January to (early) April. My purpose was to examine whether or not an online feminist activist group had the ability to create a collective identity in the same fashion that a traditional social movement could, as the social movement literature describes[1]. I did a comparative study of one offline social movement group to a social movement group that existed in cyberspace. When researching the online group, I made initial contacts to 15 potential participants, with a total of five people agreeing to participate.

After receiving the e-signed institutional review board consent forms, I began interviewing these activists. E-mail was my last resort; I gave them the option to do the interview over the phone (on my tab), as well as the option to use instant messenger (IM), which I knew would provide the opportunity to have a "real time" conversation. Unsurprisingly, not one of the participants accepted my offer for the phone interviews, and as (bad) luck would have it, none of the participants used IM. So, I forged on with my only option: e-mail.

In the beginning, the participants replied with answers in a timely fashion. Rarely did I have to wait more than a few days to receive a reply. I always asked follow-up questions, as well as clarifying questions, when appropriate, to ensure I received the most accurate answers.

The back-and-forth e-mail continued for approximately three months. As the study progressed, the time I waited for responses increased as well. I had no explanation for why this was happening. But I did not want to risk any potential losses of participants, so I sat idle. The idleness led me to question my own responses to these women. Was I offensive in some shape or fashion? Was at any point, I being insensitive in my word choice or questioning? I found myself reading and rereading e-mails that I had already read several times, including the triple-check process that I did before left clicking the "send" button.

Alas, paranoia slightly being removed, the responses would trickle into my in-box. And although I can not prove any temporal correlations with what was said in the responses, many times my suspicions of my potential "misconstrues" were on target.

What happened in my case is unique compared to what has been previously published in regards to gender differences in online research. This is not to say that the interest in online qualitative techniques has not gone unnoticed. Many excellent ethnographers have shed much light onto a researcher's foray into uncharted virtual spaces, territories and communities (see Markham, 1997; Hine, 2000; Miller & Slater, 2000). Researcher transformation can be a very challenging and life altering experience, even in a virtual setting (Markham, 1997). Issues such as the lack of traveling to field sites, as well as the absence of face-to-face (FTF) interactions, make the virtual setting a tough one, at best (Hine, 2000). A traditional oral reliance that the ethnographer depended on in the past is no longer relevant in our case, the virtual case. Emphasis shifts from oral modes of speech to textual modes of speech, and with this, there are different ways of textual data interpretation with which the researcher must be concerned (Hine, 2000). The researcher must wrestle and contend with the shift from embodied participant observation to the disembodied; the body becomes less of a tool for research as it moves to passivity in a single space (the computer desk).

Ethnography as a qualitative technique allows for rich explorations of communities in hopes of unearthing unique cultural experiences specific to the group in question. I have highlighted a few of the concerns that virtual ethnographers have raised, as they are important when considering any qualitative research in cyberspace. The research that I discuss in this chapter, while ethnographic at times, was not a true ethnography in the sense I did not immerse myself in the community. I did not participate in the discussion group, nor did I lurk to a highly ethnographic degree to get a feel of what this virtual group was doing. I approached the respondents privately and conducted the research privately. I used a different qualitative technique, the semi-structured interview schedule to guide my research. As noted by Mann and Stewart (2000) in *Internet Communication and Qualitative Research: A Handbook for Researching Online,* perspectives vary in regards to establishing rapport, establishing trust and time-space issues during questioning. Simply, these different perspectives argue that computer-mediated communication (CMC) is a communication medium that can aid or hinder in generating rapport and building trust. Relationships formed online at times can become very personal and meaningful, and can be established rapidly. At the same time, the online researcher might not ever fully feel like a rapport has been established.

Mann and Stewart (2000) argue that through repeated e-mail communications, trust can be successfully built—at least prior research suggests this. The studies they cite examine topics that were personal at times, and they credit the trust building success to the notion of eager participants who were committed to research or wanted their voices to be heard (e.g. Dunne's (1999) study of gay fathers and Mann's (1998) cross-national study of families (cited in Mann and Stewart, 2000)). What happens if the research group is more overtly political? As I will demonstrate later, issues of rapport and trust issues become tricky when the stakes are higher.

What stems from these issues of rapport and trust is how valid the responses are, when using CMC and removing the FTF setting. It is typically assumed that the more comfortable a participant feels with the researcher, the more truthful and accurate the responses will be when engaging in the interview process. This is most likely applicable to both traditional FTF interviews, as well as CMC-conducted interviews. People tend to express more to people they feel comfortable with. CMC does throw in one caveat— the anonymity factor. Not a new topic by all means, the recognition of the increased ease of deceit and dishonesty as a result from human detachment should be considered whenever discussing CMC-based research. Julian Dibbell (1998) highlights this problem in his essay "A Rape in Cyberspace," where a LambdaMOO character virtually violates another virtual character; in the end we find out that the virtual rapist was not one person, but many acting together out of a New York University dormitory. The LamdaMOO inhibitors thought they were dealing with a person, not many people at once (11 to 30). As the most trustful relationships between researcher and participant can be developed online, in the forefront of our mind should always be "is this person who he/she says he/ she is?" And of course, we cannot ask that without risking offense, at least in a strict CMC-based research design.

Mann and Stewart (2000) also address gender issues that can arise in a CMC research environment. Their extensive review of online gender studies yield that CMC has the ability to create issues of power (as they describe it) between men and women online. Social cues that exist in written text through CMC tend to "give away" a person's gender, resulting in patriarchal interactions between male and females in cyberspace (Mann and Stewart, 2000, pp. 165-167). Examples of these cyberconstructed patriarchal hierarchies include men tending to dominate discussion groups, ignoring female queries or comments on a given topic and random sexual advances from men towards women in a non-sex related cybersettings. What is useful for this discussion is the power struggle that manifested during my research, between the male researcher and the female participant. Mann and Stewart (2000) offer the conclusion that "when e-mail is used as a mutually responsive medium it may evoke "rapport talk" not only between women, but also between men and women (and presumably other individuals who may be divided by social status differences) whose priority is to understand each other. As such, it offers an invaluable communicative tool to qualitative researchers" (pp. 174-175). I challenge this conclusion, as I will show that rapport building becomes increasingly difficult when the political stakes are higher in the group or people one is studying. Depending on what is being studied, there might not be a mutual priority to understand each other through e-mail.

THE SUSPICIONS RAISED

As the first few e-mails trickled in, I did not think too much about the researcher-participant interactions; I was more concerned with the focus of my study—collective identity formation. When I reached the data analysis stage, my suspicions of authentic data started to come into question. I thought that some of the answers that were provided to me seemed a little too clichéd, but I had no way of proving this. Also, I detected some level of annoyance with me from the participants' responses. Initially, this was surprising to me, because I had thought I was fairly successful in building rapport and creating a comfortable atmosphere for discussion.

The National Organization for Women (NOW) created a space through its website for anyone to participate in a Web-based discussion group. The group existed under the name "NOW Village." You did not have to pay or donate any money to NOW in order to use this particular portion of the website; you just had to create a screen name in order to post messages, thoughts, responses, etc., to whatever discussion was taking place. The topics that dominated these boards were highly political, ranging from abortion issues, to religious issues, to sexual issues, all in relation to women's rights. Often times, many people would post multiple messages and responses each day, giving this board a distinct group feel. As NOW is a political organization, it would be expected that the group members of NOW Village would also be political. It was no secret to my participants who I was in terms of gender and education. To them, I was male (my e-mail "from" line said Mike Ayers) and I was affiliated with a state university at the time (Virginia Tech). This, I believe, led to two types of responses I received: the possible fictitious response and the condescending response. I argue that this is due to no FTF interactions between the participants and I. This led to a weak rapport and established trust between the participants and I, which led to answers that could possibly have been given to my gender and not my research.

On Wednesday, February 21, 2001, at 1:13 a.m., my first response from Laura[2] made its way to my inbox. I was not up this late, so as I checked my e-mail after waking up later in the morning, I chose hers to read over everything else that had come in over night. I was excited to see how the responses came out. I did not expect this:

Mike Ayers (MA): Can you describe the relationship(s) that you have with other members of the (women's) movement, either local in your community, or online?
Laura (L): My community relationship(s) with any women might be described as sexual in nature at least to a certain extent.
MA: Can you describe the relationship(s) that you have with people that are online who participate in NOW's discussion forum (NOW Village)?
L: I have not picked up any lesbian lovers but I am developing relationships.

I thought this response was a little odd; the participants knew via the informed consent form that I was trying to "understand the people who participate in activist organizations and how they relate to one another in relation to furthering their organizations' goals in an online setting and offline setting." But these responses were a little more personal than political, but I did not question Laura's response or even clarify that I was not referring to any sexual relationships, knowing that the personal is political for some.

Wednesday, March 28, 2001:

MA: Are you involved with or a member of any specific organization that works for social change?
Carrie (C): Someone might say that I have made love to a good portion of the participants. Is there anything more exciting than yelling NOWWWWW!!!! during climax?
MA: If you are a member of a feminist organization, how long have you been a member of this organization?

C: My involvement in NOW has been for less than five years, but I have been involved in the battle of the rights of women for a long time. One of the things that women, even lesbians, can do is seducing members of the religious right and helping break up their families. Is there anything more exciting that seeing two crying children of a pastor after his wife has divorced him after he has had sex with a woman such as myself? Do I do that kind of thing? I could be accused of doing any time that I get the opportunity. That sort of thing can be soooo exciting. And some pastors are quite good in bed, though I would much rather have sex with a woman.

MA: Can you describe the relationship(s) you have with people that are online who participate in NOW's discussion forum (NOW Village)?

C: I have not had sex with most of them. Some of them might be males posing as women for all I know. I have all the sex that I want, than you without having to go on NOW boards for it. For that matter, a goodly amount of NOW members are not that much to look at.

MA: Describe any bonds or ties that you feel with other members of the NOW discussion boards.

C: Unless you mean things such as the joy of fisting publicly, why should I have bonds with anyone that I am not intimate with. Without intimacy, what good is a relationship?

   I started to think more and more after this response: Are these responses genuine? Is this really an accurate portrayal of someone's life? Or is this just a clichéd response to a non-involved researcher?

Friday, Feb. 23, 2001:

MA: If you are a member of a feminist organization, how long have you been a member of this organization?

Sharon (S): I am not officially a member of a feminist organization. Why should I be. Instead I infiltrate churches. And I am not going to deny right now that I have seduced both male and female pastors as well as getting people in a lot of trouble. I infiltrate, infiltrate, and infiltrate.

MA: By using online discussion boards, discuss who or what you are trying to change (if anything).

S: I am trying to change all incorrect ideas. Some people believe that people should be able to have more than two children. Should I not challenge that idea if it is wrong? Some people are against public fisting. Should I not strongly support and engage in public fisting as well as other public sex acts if I believe it is right?

   Whether or not these responses were true or false, I will never know the answer. If these answers were given to me in a FTF setting, I would have the chance to detect a wide range of factors that could give me a better idea of the truth in these responses. Factors such as facial expressions, tone of voice and body language—all of this would be noted by me and guide my interactions with these people in a FTF interview.

   The above responses seem to have a certain "shock" value behind them. Although possible, it is suspect that two different people are using "pastor seduction" as their mode of activism. Public fisting was also mentioned by two different respondents. And while this might be an acceptable form of activism for these people, most likely it is not actually happening. If people were committing these acts, the public would most likely be aware. These would be highly disruptive tactics that violate many norms as well as laws. Thus, I suggest that I received these responses based on the fact that I was a male researcher who had never met these people FTF.

My lack of physical presence led to another type of response that I received on more than one occasion—the condescending response. My "place" as a researcher should have led to assumptions of prior knowledge of what political activism these women are involved in. But I was treated in a different manner, as I will show below.

Thursday, March 1, 2001:

MA: Would you consider yourself involved in the current women's movement?
Maggie (M): Of course I am. Why ask a question like that? Why would anyone question my involvement. People like me need to be involved with fighting for women. I fight and fight and fight. I am emotionally involved, mentally involved, and volitionally involved. This is much more for me than writing some master's thesis to turn into the big shots. This is real life. And I am not so sure you know what real life is about.
MA: Describe any bonds or ties that you feel with other members of the NOW discussion boards. Describe any group dynamics that might be similar or different to any real life groups that you have participated in.
M: Did some Psychologist give you this question? Why not shove this question up your ass? Then why not feed it to your professor friend?

Friday, March 30, 2001:

MA: Please discuss any feelings you perceive when you are interacting with other participants who share your similar beliefs in the NOW discussion boards.
S: What other emotion should I have except love?
MA: Well, that's interesting ... and I don't know?!? So, would you say that you definitely feel a level of closeness to these people? Do you think that this closeness stems around your activism?
S: If you are trying to get me to talk about my sex life again, forget it. Are you trying to come on to me? If you are, let me let you know once and for all, MEN DO NOT TURN ME ON!!!!

———

MA: Describe any bonds or ties that you feel with other members of the NOW discussion boards.
S: If you want to know about my sex life, why should I engage in that kind of talk here? Sexual dynamics I guess would have some similarity. I like to be openly sexual both with a woman and on the board.
MA: Yeah, I wasn't really referring to that here. Another case of my vagueness. I was more referring to that feeling you get when you are a part of a group ... that sense of belonging, that you would be working for something you all have in common,

etc. Does that make sense? If not, let me know. That's what I was referring to in the above question …

S: Isn't this a case of a vague question by a sexist male who wants to get in my pants?

Needless to say, I did not follow up to this last series of interactions with Sharon. We can see assumptions made here in these statements based on my gender and education: that I am sexist, that I am interested in these women sexually and that I do not know what real life is about. They used the information they had knowledge of (gender and education) and tailored their responses towards this in a derogatory (at times) fashion.

I did not really know how to react to some of these responses I received. As we can see above, when I did try and follow up where it had appeared that I had been unclear, I was put down further.

WHAT COULD I
HAVE DONE DIFFERENTLY?

Lacking any FTF contact, and having e-mail as my only option, I was limited in the way I could interact with some of my participants. When the stakes are higher in the research population, as they are in political activist settings, building rapport can be more difficult. The responses above illustrate that there was a power issue at stake: the female activist versus the mail researcher (i.e., handing items in to the big shots). Because of the nature of how I conducted the research, what I have presented is left open for much interpretation, which I argue is central whenever discussing qualitative research conducted through cyberspace. This can be a rewarding actualization in the postmodern viewpoint of data collection and analysis, or on the other side, create controversial results and meanings. My data interpretation can be very different than the next person's; after all, it is all text based, and it depends on how each of us reads the responses. When researching cyberspace through cyberspace, we lose our ability to relate to people with our faces, our bodies and our tone of speech. This is where research in this setting becomes problematic and can lead to potential controversial conclusions about how people are actually using the Internet. In my case, I show that in a political arena, such as a group based around women's rights, we have to decide whether or not to take what is given to us as face-value truths. This applies to physical world qualitative approaches as well, but the removal of our bodies, our modes of speech and our presentation of self creates a more difficult task in creating a necessary rapport to ensure accuracy.

During my interviews, my gender position was clearly evident. I was assumed to be sexist and using this "research" for my own personal, sexual gain. Again, left up to reader interpretation, this can be viewed in different ways. First, the obvious, I was assumed to have ascribed personality characteristics of what "all" males think and do. A second interpretation, could be that these responses were just mere solutions to not wanting to answer the questions asked. Even during times of clarification, the questions were still avoided. There are most likely more interpretations to what was actually happening. I played the role of the passive; I did not question the participant's responses to a lengthy degree. I felt it was more important to keep what little peace (rapport) I had mustered up, rather than to risk having a participant retract everything they previously had divulged to me.

Cyberspace creates a place where the ethics of data interpretation are raised. When suspect data is presented to the researcher, such as in this case, one is faced with a slight conundrum. Should analysis continue with or without asking the participants about their honesty? If we take what is given to us as the truth, can we generalize our results? Do we recognize answers transmitted in cyberspace as more or less valid in terms of the participant's responses? Cyberspace has presented us with a unique, ethical dilemma. In my case, I did not become aware of the implications of possibly working with contrived data, until I was well into the analysis process. Worse off would have been to proceed with analysis without treating the research location as a unique, different social space than the real world.

There is no simple solution to what I have presented here. Cyberspace presents us with a very unique, yet tricky, sphere for analysis. When politics are added to the mix, the data can be even trickier. Just as in other forms of ethnographic research, cyber-research should incorporate modes of reflexivity, in Bourdieu and Wacquant's (1992) sense of the word. For Bourdieu and Wacquant (1992), a reflexive sociology (or social science, in general) allows an introspection that the researcher applies to his/herself. In an effort to control researcher bias and false interpretation, especially in cyberspace, we have to consider the relationship we have to our object of study has a distinct uncontrolled relation between researcher-research field. We must consider that when reporting data, a result of this uncontrolled relation is a projection of our researcher-research field relation on to the object of study (Bourdieu & Wacquant, 1992, p. 68). A reflexive cybersociology would in turn recognize the role of the researcher through introspection via writing and how he/she is actually projecting results. Cyberspace as a direct field of inquiry carries with it social markers that have a direct affect on the data being collected.

Heightened reflexivity in cyberspace research would allow for the acknowledgment of the validity in our actual results. From the initial starting point of data collection through the interpretation of results, consistent introspection should assist in controlling for questionable data. I failed to do this from my initial starting point and, only after receiving the responses that were seemingly off-kilter at times, did I finally start to question my approach. This resulted in an overly cautious interpretation of the data, which, in turn, greatly affected the degree to which these responses could have been generalized. As I have demonstrated here, cyberspace contains an element of uncertainty—it is a space with human presence without the physicality of a living body. This is not to say FTF interviews would not be questionable; the difference is that our senses are removed from the interview when we are left to read and interpret text. Reflexivity will allow data analysis to give a window into cyberlife, while at the same time acknowledging a sense of potential falseness. Cyberculture studies have been interdisciplinary since their inception; reflexivity in this field of inquiry will only heighten and strengthen the results and knowledge we have about the virtual space of the Internet.

The text above shows that certain gender distinctions meant I was possibly treated in a mocking fashion, based on nothing more than my name in the "from" line, which indicated my sex. At the same time, the information I received in turn could have been the truth as well. This is the reflexive course of action that should be applied to cyberspace research. As cyberculture studies incorporate multiple perspectives, so should our interpretations.

CONCLUSION

This chapter raises three main points. The first is that when involved in a cybersetting as a field of research, the lack of a FTF presence can cause problems in generating the necessary rapport with participants. In part, this is because the focus of the study has more of a political nature than previous studies where e-mail has been a source of interviews.

The second point that I argue is that the answers I received could have possibly been fabricated by the participants, based on my only social marker—my name, which was a marker of my gender. In addition to my lack of FTF presence, my gender could have also influenced how the participants responded.

Lastly, I argue that through my experiences in this research, the future of cyberculture research must be reflexive in nature. Reflexivity in cyberculture studies will not only allow for a critical introspective look in regards to the role of the researcher in data interpretation, it will also aid in compensating for the inherent problems with researching a space that is socially constructed, yet void of physicality.

Finally, I propose that the reflexive cybersociologist reports and creates meanings from textual data collection. How we create meaning from data is the backbone of social science research; how we present it to the public will be key to establishing and maintaining cyberculture research as a valid domain of study, both in academic and nonacademic spaces.

ACKNOWLEDGMENTS

I would like to thank Martha McCaughey and Jennifer Mahar for reading earlier versions of this chapter and providing insightful comments and feedback in an unprecedented short amount of time.

REFERENCES

Bourdieu, P. & Wacquant, L. (1992). *An Invitation to Reflexive Sociology*. Chicago, IL: University of Chicago Press.

Dibbell, J. (1998). *My Tiny Life: Crime and Passion in a Virtual World*. New York: Henry Holt.

Hine, C. (2000). *Virtual Ethnography*. Thousand Oaks, CA: Sage Publications.

Mann, C. & Stewart, F. (2000). *Internet Communication and Qualitative Research: A Handbook for Researching Online*. Thousand Oaks, CA: Sage Publications.

Markham, A. (1997). *Life Online: Researching Real Experience in Virtual Space*. Walnut Creek, CA: Altamira Press.

McCaughey, M. & Ayers, M. (2003). *Cyberactivism: Online Activism in Theory and Practice*. New York: Routledge Press.

Miller, D. & Slater, D. (2000). *The Internet: An Ethnographic Approach*. New York: New York University Press.

ENDNOTES

[1]   For complete results and discussion of this research, see "Searching for A Collective Identity in the Feminist Cyberactivist" in M. McCaughey & M. Ayers (Eds.), *Cyberactivism: Online Activism in Theory and Practice* (2003).

[2]   Names have been changed to protect participant's identities.

Section IV

Online Research
with Minors—
Special Considerations?

Chapter XV

Studying Adolescents Online: A Consideration of Ethical Issues

Susannah R. Stern
Boston College, USA

ABSTRACT

Despite the enormous potential of the Internet as a research tool and environment, implementing youth research in online environments raises significant ethical issues. This chapter addresses two quandaries that surfaced in the author's own research on adolescent home page authors. First, the necessity and feasibility of obtaining parental consent in online youth research is considered. Second, the chapter discusses the ethical responsibilities of Internet researchers who encounter distressing disclosure authored by youth online. The chapter aims to illustrate the contexts in which such ethical issues may arise and to provide suggestions for Internet researchers who focus on adolescent populations.

INTRODUCTION

Over the past several years, adolescents have increasingly embraced the Internet as a forum to express themselves, communicate with peers, meet new friends and find information. Indeed, recent surveys show that almost three-quarters of children between the ages of 12 and 17 go online (Pew Internet Project, 2001). In light of this rising number, researchers have begun to recognize the potential of the Internet as a tool to learn more about youth populations who have historically been difficult to investigate, as well as to shed light on how youth are using the Internet in their everyday lives. Because Internet researchers are able to overcome many geographic, time and physical barriers that traditionally restricted youth research, the potential content and scope of their inquiries is greatly expanded.

Despite the enormous potential of the Internet as a research tool and environment, it is important to recognize that conducting youth research in online environments raises significant ethical issues that differ somewhat from those raised in offline settings. Indeed, the very aspects of the Internet (e.g., its potential for anonymity and lack of authority) that make it an appealing place for kids to interact are also those aspects that introduce unique ethical quandaries for researchers. In this chapter, I will address two such quandaries that surfaced in my own research on adolescent home page authors (Stern, 1999, 2002a, 2002b). The first issue considered is the necessity and feasibility of obtaining parental consent in online youth research. The second discussion explores the ethical responsibilities of Internet researchers who encounter distressing disclosure authored by youth online. The purpose of this chapter is to illustrate the type of situations in which such dilemmas may arise and to provide some suggestions for Internet researchers as they attempt to ethically navigate their online inquiries about youth.

STUDYING HUMAN COMMUNICATION ON THE INTERNET

Despite the recent surge in Internet studies, the scholarly community remains at odds regarding the answer to a pivotal question guiding ethical decision making in online research: Does Internet research constitute human subjects research? Distinguishing whether certain research involves "human subjects" is important because human-subjects research is governed by specific laws and guidelines in American research institutions and universities. These laws and guidelines aim to protect research participants' rights. Traditionally, when deliberating this distinction, the United States Department of Health and Human services suggests researchers ask themselves (a) if there is some kind of interaction or intervention with a living person that would not be occurring, except for the research project at hand, or (b) if identifiable private data/information will be obtained for this research in a form associable with the individual (Office for Protection from Research Risks, 2000). Should either of these situations arise, a researcher's project would be categorized as human-subjects research.

While these demarcations seemed sufficient in years past, they are somewhat inadequate for Internet researchers, whose "virtual" data collection is more amorphously defined than typical offline research. Admittedly, for those who interact in some way with people in the online context explicitly because of their research endeavor (e.g., in interviews or surveys), the project clearly constitutes human subject research, just as it would in a real-life setting. But for those who study the communications of Internet users, yet who do not actually interact with any living person, the issue is less clear cut because of disagreement over the definition of "private." Indeed, Internet researchers not only debate whether cyberspace is a public or private space, but also whether online communications are public or private information (Frankel & Siang, 1999; Mann & Stewart, 2000; Waskul & Douglass, 1996). In brief, one side of the controversy encompasses those who believe Internet communications that are publicly accessible are "public" communications. On the other side are those who contend that simply because communications are publicly accessible does not mean that online authors consider their online discourse to be "public" information, or that they recognize the extent to which their communications can be accessed by others (Waskul & Douglass, 1996).

This debate is ongoing, with many recent scholars suggesting that the issue must be considered in more fluid terms (Binik, Mah, & Kiesler, 1999). That is to say, some types of information on the Internet should be considered more private than others, and this distinction should guide researchers' determinations of whether or not their research involves human subjects. For example, comments published to a bulletin board on an unmoderated World Wide Web (WWW) site may be deemed more public than information posted on a moderated, theme-specific listserv with a small and known membership. Consequently, the idea goes, the more that information is intentionally public (e.g., intended for a limitless audience, rather than a narrowly defined or conceived audience), the less that research should be considered as "human-subjects" research, which is accompanied by the need for extra safeguards and procedures, such as informed consent.

Determining whether one's research involves "human subjects" is important because such research is obligated to follow specific ethical guidelines. Indeed, most human-subjects research in the United States is directed by The Belmont Report, drafted by The National Commission for the Protection of Human Subjects of Biomedical and Behavioral Research in 1979. Three overriding principles are identified as central to conducting ethical human-subjects research: autonomy, beneficence and justice. I will discuss the first two of these principles in terms of their relevance to informed/parental consent and encountering distressing disclosure online, which are the main ethical issues pertinent to this book chapter.

AUTONOMY, INFORMED CONSENT AND CONDUCTING YOUTH RESEARCH ONLINE

The principle of autonomy refers to the idea that individuals should be treated as autonomous agents who should decide for themselves if they wish to participate in a research project. This principle typically finds its expression in the informed consent procedure, in which participants are made aware of their rights as participants and advised of the risks and benefits of their participation. Those persons with "diminished autonomy," including children, are entitled to special attention and protection (National Commission for the Protection of Human Subjects of Biomedical and Behavioral Research, 1979). Characteristically, this means that a parent(s) or legal guardian(s) of youth under the legal age of consent (usually age 18) must provide informed parental consent for the youth to participate in the research project (48 Fed. Reg. 9814, 1983). Youths who are able (e.g., who are developmentally competent) must also provide their assent to participate in a research project (Department of Health and Human Services, 1983, 45 CFR

§46.408(a)). Children are considered a special research population because they are expected to have greater difficulty than adults in understanding research due to a lack of real-world experience and more limited cognitive abilities (Thompson, 1992).

In terms of studying youth online, two important questions arise with regard to the principle of autonomy. First, when does one's youth research constitute human-subjects research, thus necessitating that parental consent be obtained by the researcher? Second, if parental consent is deemed necessary, how feasible is it, and what are potential barriers to obtaining parental consent?

Determining if informed consent is necessary is a complex issue for all Internet researchers, regardless of the population they study, as discussed earlier. It is even more complicated for those who study youth, in light of the special precautions researchers are encouraged to take on their behalf. Because youths typically have less fundamental knowledge about the world and less developed capacity to understand the risks and benefits of research participation, researchers are obligated to be particularly wary of youth's vulnerability. This means that some of the assumptions that we hold about adults' understanding of their actions may not be warranted for youths.

For example, we probably assume that anyone who publishes a personal home page to the WWW aims to reach a public audience and harbors few illusions about its accessibility by others. Indeed, Chandler and Roberts-Young (1998), with regard to home page authors' expectations of privacy, noted:

"[W]hile one may have a private conversation in a public park without expecting all and sundry to feel free to eavesdrop, you would not expect to restrict access to your diary to a few close friends if you chained it to a noticeboard in the park. It seems reasonable to assume that everyone who uses the Web does know that the material which they publish on their homepages is open to anyone and that the inclusion of material which they would prefer to regard as private is not obligatory."

However, children and adolescents who post home pages to the WWW may not fully grasp the concept of "public" in the same way we might expect adults to do so. For instance, while some scholars have suggested that adults think of their communication as "private" when it is transmitted in a theme-specific forum to a predesignated audience, my own research has indicated that teens think of their communication as "private," when the people they know in real life (e.g., parents, friends, teachers, etc.) do not see, hear or read it, regardless of who else does. This understanding of privacy is characterized by the words of one female adolescent whose home page I studied (Stern, 2002a), in her discussion of a recent self-cutting experience. She wrote, "I totally butchered my leg … I don't want sympathy from it … that's why I'm not telling anyone." The seeming irony of this comment is that she published this intimate information on a website accessible to a potentially worldwide audience. Nevertheless, her words suggest that she considered this information to be private, because she had not mentioned it to anyone in her offline life.

The notion that adolescents might regard their Internet communication differently than adults surfaced rather late in a series of studies I conducted that explored how adolescents were using WWW personal home pages as an alternative or complementary forum in which to engage in self-expression. Before I began those studies, I had concluded that the home pages I wished to address were public documents whose examination should not be considered human-subjects research, because their contents were intentionally published to a large, unfocused and unmoderated forum—the WWW. I reached this conclusion by following the guidelines offered by the Office for Protection from Research Risks (described earlier). Moreover, an initial exploration of teen's home pages demonstrated that the authors included multiple feedback mechanisms on their home pages (such as surveys, guest books and hot-lined e-mail addresses), which implied that they not only imagined, but also desired a public audience for their home pages.

Even though I perceived the home pages to be decidedly public documents, I began to wonder whether adolescents who published personal home pages were cognizant of the potentially limitless nature of their audience. Had it occurred to them, as they relayed some of their insecurities and intimate experiences, that the audience might, in fact, include a researcher who could identify them—even if only in terms of their publicly-assumed identities on the WWW—in a research publication? Were they able to grasp the vast expanse that was the Internet, and if so, would they have included the same amount of intimacy in their online communication?

In an effort to answer this question, I subsequently conducted face-to-face interviews with another group of adolescents to learn how "public" they understood their home pages to be. I found that those I interviewed were cognizant that whatever they posted could potentially be accessed by anyone with Internet service, even a researcher. The possibility that someone they did not know could find and even analyze their home page did not make them uncomfortable. Their comments thus provided validation for my initial conviction that teens' home pages constituted archival or textual research, rather than human-subjects' research.

Ultimately, we should be particularly mindful of our assumptions that youths define "public" and "private" in the same ways that adults do, since discrepancies may (or may not, as in my case) impact researchers' understanding of whether their research projects constitute human-subjects research. Since the requirement to obtain informed consent hinges on the distinction of whether the information under study is public or private, researchers who study youth would be well advised to explore the perceptions of the youth who have authored the communication they plan to study. One way to do this is to conduct pilot studies with such youth (or a sample of youth similar to those one aims to study), to learn more about their intentions and expectations with regard to their Internet communication. Such pilot work will help researchers determine if the communication they wish to study falls more on the side of public or private communication, as well as alert them to other issues that may impact the necessity and feasibility of acquiring parental consent.

Once it is decided that a research project does, in fact, require parental consent, the next issue concerns how researchers should go about obtaining it. This can be an arduous task for all youth researchers who must (1) share information about the project with both the youth participant and his/her parent or guardian, (2) make certain that the parent (and, when possible, the youth) understands the project and (3) garner parent's voluntary informed consent as well as the youth's voluntary assent (Frankel & Siang, 1999; Tymchuk, 1992). This procedure applies to both online and offline research, but it is much more complicated in online settings for a number of reasons, several of which came to light in one of my earliest projects on youth online.

To gain a better sense of the motivations for and gratifications of maintaining personal home pages, several years ago I devised a study that would allow me to conduct e-mail interviews with adolescent home page authors. My goal was to interview those authors whose home pages I had already analyzed, so that I could validate my impressions, as well as address specific components of their home pages I found particularly intriguing. I had located the teens' home pages on the WWW, and thus the only way for me to solicit their participation in my research project was through e-mail. This limitation did not trouble me, because I was eager to communicate with the teens in the same bodiless, virtual arena in which they had intended their original communication (on their home pages) to be experienced. Because all of the authors had indicated on their home pages that they were under the age of 18, it was clear that I needed to obtain parental consent, given that I wanted to interact with the teens via e-mail.

The procedure I designed to procure parental consent, I initially thought, was quite sound. First, I would e-mail a standard message to each of the teen authors, introducing myself and my interest in communicating with them. I would then ask them to visit a home page I had designed specifically for them to learn more about me and the project. On the site, I provided a biography page in an effort to make myself known as a real person who was genuine in her interests and could be trusted. I also provided a project page, which extensively described the research project, why I was conducting it and what the teen's participation in the project would entail. The project page linked to a parental consent form. Participants were directed to print out this form, ask their parents to sign it and mail it back to me through the regular post. The youth participants' assent would be indicated by the initiative in printing the consent form and giving it to their parents. In exchange for their participation, I offered a $15 gift certificate to an online retail store. The gift certificate would be delivered electronically to participants through e-mail.

All in all, this procedure seemed reasonable to me, my colleagues and to the university Institutional Review Board (IRB). Thus, with high hopes, I sent out my introductory e-mails to the teens and waited for a response. None was forthcoming. After two reminder e-mails and three months time, I received e-mail responses from only a handful of girls. Only one signed parental consent form was returned.

With the benefit of hindsight, these results are hardly surprising for a number of reasons, all of which demonstrate the complexity of securing parental consent, when conducting online youth research. First, I did not take into account the unique intersection between Internet use and adolescence that might deter teens from seeking parental permission to participate in my study. Adolescents are typically working to achieve greater autonomy, and they often disavow the need for authority in their lives (Steinberg, 1993). Thus, requiring teens to obtain parental permission can be insulting. This may especially be the case for teens who use the WWW precisely because of the power it affords them to be independent. Online, teens can go wherever they want, say whatever they want and rarely face limitations or consequences. And teen home pages—the very texts I was interested in understanding—comprise one of very few places for teens to have their own unmonitored, autonomous space. My request that teens obtain their parents' permission to talk about these personal spaces may have been perceived as a lack of respect for their authority in one of the few places they actually wield it. This was the case for at least one home page author, who signaled her interest in corresponding with me, but who was adamant that she did not need parental permission, despite my repeated explanations that it was necessary. She e-mailed: "[M]y parents could care less about who talks to me online, I mean its my computer, my web page, I pay for my own Internet and I talk to anyone I want in real life or online so they don't really care who I talk to" (sic). This perspective seemed to be common among adolescent home page authors, and inhibited some authors I contacted from seeking parental permission to participate in my online research project.

Moreover, adolescence is characteristically a time during which teens choose to keep parts of their lives private (Stanley & Sieber, 1992). Media use itself is often a private behavior (see Larson, 1995), and Internet use particularly so. Even for those teens whose Internet use itself is not completely private, many do not tell their families and friends about their personal home pages. Persuading teens to secure their parents' permission, when teens themselves do not wish for their parents to know about their home pages is, needless to say, a futile effort, and one which likely worked against the recruitment of participants in my project.

Second, the Internet has regretfully acquired a reputation for sheltering malevolent types, especially those who aim to harm children. This reputation likely hindered my ability to establish myself as a credible, nonthreatening researcher to potential participants, as well as to the parents of those teens who sought permission to participate in my study. Anticipating some skepticism, I provided extensive information about myself, my interests, background, university affiliation and contact information on the project website. However, many parents may not have seen this page, or perhaps, doubted its authenticity. Indeed, one adolescent girl who initially signaled her interest in participating, subsequently explained that her parents were uncomfortable with the prospect. Considering the publicity that online stalking and other predatory electronic behaviors have received, it is understandable that parents were reluctant to allow their teens to correspond with me, a stranger, over the Internet.

Finally, my solicitation of respondents was likely hampered by the heavy burden I placed on the girls and their parents to participate. Because it is difficult to validate parental consent online, I asked parents to sign and mail a physical document to me through the regular mail. This conservative technique was acceptable to my university IRB, but it required that a teen print out the consent form, (which may have been difficult if no printer was available), locate and address an envelope and purchase a stamp. This requires considerable effort on the part of the participant, effort that was probably not offset by the $15 incentive. To make things easier, I might have mailed a consent form and pre-stamped envelope (as is typical in offline research), but this was impossible, since I did not have any geographic addresses.

The irony of this seemingly rigorous procedure was that in order to comply, parents needed to sign the consent forms with their real identities (even though they could use their children's pseudonyms in reference to their child). Moreover, their geographic information would inevitably be included either in the return address or the envelope's postmark, which indicates the town/city from which letters are mailed. Given parents' existing skepticism about revealing real-life identities to a stranger on the Internet, the requirement that they identify themselves in a written document likely struck them as inconsistent and potentially hazardous. These issues likely reduced the motivation for any teen to ask for, or any parent to give, consent.

Ultimately, the early research design described here points to some of the major difficulties in securing parental consent in online youth research. First, part of the appeal of the Internet stems from users' ability to be anonymous, experiment with self presentation and navigate invisibly through the WWW. Adolescents who use the Web are particularly likely to enjoy this environment, since most other spaces they experience often seem unbearably restrictive. Moreover, establishing independence and experimenting with identity are developmentally appropriate tasks for adolescents, who may find the Internet a safe and fun place to engage in these activities. Consequently, researchers must determine how to show their respect for teens' privacy and autonomy, while at the same time adhering to guidelines requiring parental consent. This balancing act is unlikely to be easy, given the added difficulty Internet researchers have in establishing credibility in the online environment.

Next, the nature of the Internet as a mediator between researcher and subject introduces the more concrete problem of how parental consent can actually be obtained. Since online there are no signatures per se, and because real-life faces, phone numbers and addresses are typically absent, researchers will find it hard to follow established procedures for securing parental consent. IRBs will play a large part in determining how researchers can effectively obtain parental consent without significantly impacting the size and compilation of the sample of adolescents to be studied. For example, IRBs may consider accepting e-mailed consent from parents, rather than exclusively written consent. Digital signatures may also be deemed admissible, but the technology required for this procedure may be prohibitive, since many potential participants are unlikely to own the necessary equipment/software.

Perhaps the most dependable way to obtain informed parental consent is for researchers to solicit adolescent participants in an offline arena, rather than locating them online. For example, researchers might turn to computer clubs, youth community centers and after-school organizations to locate teens who are active Internet users. The ability to engage in an actual conversation with teens and their parents will likely make the informed consent procedure less arduous. Even when youth participants are located online, finding a way to move the research-participant relationship to an offline setting, at least initially (e.g., through a phone call) may be a fruitful option.

Some online researchers may find these strategies unproductive, because they inherently affect the type of participant who researchers are consequently able to study. Some of the most unique and fascinating people and phenomena to study may not be locally accessible. That is, in fact, the very reason the Internet holds so much promise—because it allows us to study those with whom we might not otherwise be able to communicate. Transferring all online correspondence to an offline setting for the purpose of securing informed consent will limit the usefulness of the Internet as a research tool. Although offline forums are privileged in the current informed consent procedure, many IRBs are starting to recognize that a reassessment of this procedure, in light of recent technological developments, is in order.

Ultimately, the principle of autonomy is useful as a guide for ethical research, but putting it into practice can be problematic for researchers who study online adolescents. The confusion over how to regard online information (as public or private) is just an initial obstacle faced by researchers as they seek guidelines for the ethical conduct of their research. When determinations are made that parental consent is necessary, the unique technology that is the Internet can make the most ethical course of action (e.g., soliciting written parental consent) infeasible. In the future, researchers will need to be more creative about how they gather information, and push IRBs to reconsider how to protect adolescent research participants while simultaneously encouraging research on this interesting online population.

BENEFICENCE AND ENCOUNTERING DISTRESSING INFORMATION IN ONLINE YOUTH RESEARCH

Another guiding ethical principle identified in *The Belmont Report* is beneficence, which essentially means that researchers should aim to do good to others. *The Belmont Report* explains, "Persons are treated in an ethical manner not only by respecting their decisions and protecting them from harm, but also by making efforts to secure their well-being." Internet researchers may find that the principle of beneficence leads them to question what responsibility they bear when they encounter distressing disclosure in the course of their online research. By "distressing," I refer specifically to disclosure that suggests an online communicant may harm him/herself or another/others. For example, in my own research on adolescents, I came across teens' discussion of suicidal feelings and narratives about self-cutting experiences. Although I did not encounter any in my own research, threats to kill, rape or hurt others should also be categorized as "distressing disclosure." Encounters with such disclosure will likely compel researchers to ask themselves if they should take any action, and if so, of what sort.

Although distressing disclosures are certainly not relegated to the Internet, two factors increase the likelihood that online researchers may encounter such distressing information (Stern, 2003). First, the Internet is a unique communication technology that allows users to communicate in private (e.g., in one's bedroom at home), and yet reach a potentially large, public audience. Moreover, Internet communication can be conducted anonymously. These factors actually seem to facilitate Internet users' self-disclosure (Childress & Asamen, 1998; Miller & Gergen, 1998; Reid, 1996; Thompson, 1999). Conceivably, the more users' self-disclose online, the greater the chances that researchers will encounter distressing self-disclosure in their online research. Moreover, the Internet allows researchers substantially more access to the expression and communications of individuals that previously may have gone unnoticed. Although distressing disclosures are admittedly expressed in offline settings quite frequently, they are much less likely to be intercepted by or expressed to a researcher. Given these unique circumstances, researchers who conduct their research in a virtual environment may find themselves especially likely to encounter distressing disclosure (Stern, 2003).

Given the inflated possibility online researchers may have for encountering distressing information online as well as the duty of beneficence, Internet researchers must contemplate the extent to which they have a responsibility to respond to such disclosure. Those who study adolescents, in particular, may find this issue especially perplexing, because adolescents (and children, more generally) are considered to be a more vulnerable population who deserve greater protection and care.

The importance of considering one's ethical responsibilities, when encountering distressing disclosure, was raised for me during the course of my research on adolescents' home pages. On their home pages, several of the adolescents I studied described intimate, and often tragic, personal stories. For example, almost every entry in Meg's Web journal relayed her desire to kill herself.[1] In one journal entry entitled "help me i wanna die," she wrote:

it seems as if the world has stopped turning today. i feel so cut off. ... i need to know why im here cause all i get is pain. pain that i hate, that i dont like i dont know what to do anymore. i have the knife to wrist right now but i dont know how to cut my wrist. i dont know how to die (sic)

Similarly distressing, Avery described her disillusionment with life, her visits to a psychiatrist, her battles with bulimia and a dangerously unhealthy obsession with her high school French teacher. Lorna's poetry indicated that she was lonely and depressed. An excerpt from one poem, "Ultimate Frustration," read:

Don't know why this happens to me
But I can't do anything about it.
I feel horrid, I want to die, I try to cry.
So many emotions
I just can't handle it anymore,
Someone take me away.

Overall, depression, suicidal feelings, loneliness, eating disorders and self-mutilation were frequently discussed on several of the teens' home pages I encountered. Such expression was likely prevalent because the WWW allows teens (and all home page authors) to speak both confidentially and publicly about what many consider inappropriate or uncomfortable topics in offline situations.

At the time, I saw little responsibility to respond to the distressing information I encountered on the teens' homepages. First, without training in psychology or counseling, I felt ill-prepared to react meaningfully to statements on depression or self-destructive behaviors. I was also very cautious about overstepping the bounds of the project I had received permission to complete from the university's IRB. Without written consent from the teens' parents, I was not entitled to communicate with the girls within the purview of my project. Thus, I deemed it inappropriate to communicate with or in any way "taint" the authenticity of the teens' home pages or their attitudes toward them. Third, I viewed myself as relatively powerless, since I did not know the authors' real names or geographic locations. I could not contact their parents, guardians or teachers. Moreover, I suspected that I would lack any credibility if I attempted to communicate since I, too, existed as merely a faceless stranger on the Internet. In short, I saw little recourse to address my concerns, and thus, felt no duty to respond.

On the other hand, it seems likely that I would have reacted quite differently to the distressing disclosure had I encountered it in a real-life conversation with actual adolescents. In other words, had I physically interacted with the teens (i.e., interviewed them face-to-face) and they had shared these same stories of tragedy (which they likely would not have), I may have considered intervening in some way. For example, I might have told Meg's parents or teachers about her preoccupation with suicide; or I might have referred Avery to an eating disorder support group.

The absence of direct communication between me and those who authored the disclosure I read online appeared to have created a sense of detachment that other Internet researchers have also noticed. That is, because of the lack of an actual body or perceptible voice in online research, researchers have commonly been tempted to view online disclosure strictly as "data." Waskul and Douglass (1996) articulated, "Although a certain degree of objectification will occur in any research scenario, the utter absence of flesh and blood can potentially result in extreme objectifications. Such objectifications will always impair a researcher's ethical judgement" (p. 137). King (1996) similarly noted, "Notes on a computer screen are simple to objectify. It is easy for researchers to fail to show respect for the very real people that make up the communities under study" (p. 127). Ultimately, it is the forum through which we learn about people that helps us individually to determine our response. In a face-to-face interaction, we may often take distressing disclosure seriously. Yet, likely because of our tradition in offline research and our uneasiness about taking that which we read on the Internet at face value, we are less likely to feel an obligation to respond to distressing disclosure online.

Despite this propensity, researchers would wisely remember that behind every online communication is a real, living, breathing person. The importance of this recognition was illuminated to me two weeks after I completed analyzing the home pages in the study described earlier. I learned then that Avery, a 17 year old whose home page was included in my sample, had committed suicide. My discovery was inadvertent; I had e-mailed Avery to ask her permission to use some of her home page images in my write up of the project. I received a reply from her friend, who, after explaining that she had taken responsibility for Avery's homepage, wrote, "Sadly [Avery] is no longer with us."

Such ambiguous words may have been confusing for someone who had never seen Avery's home page. However, I was fairly certain what they meant. I had spent hours on Avery's home page, learning about her struggles with bulimia and depression. I had read every sentence of the 35-page essay she wrote about her obsession with a teacher, who continually disappointed her by failing to pay her enough attention. I was familiar with her melancholy view of her life. In fact, in one journal entry, she had casually mentioned suicidal feelings:

One night in 10th grade, I was finished with work ... so I wandered all the way down to the road. ... Not many cars drive on that road, but I saw a huge truck coming towards me. As it got closer, I felt like stepping out in front of it. Instant death. But I'm a coward. Later I cried myself to sleep because I had missed my chance to die.

It is easy to look back at this home page and find "signs" of her depression. Yet researchers cannot know whether the communication they witness in online spaces is "real." Is it authentic? Is it exaggerated? Is it meant to alarm or as a joke or neither? For whom is it meant? And who actually authored it? Without knowing the answers to these questions, researchers are likely, as I did, to dismiss an obligation to respond. Yet much recent research has pointed to the Internet as a place where users can express themselves more fully and honestly. The possibility for anonymity is freeing, and the ability to draft text in the privacy of one's home can facilitate more openness and confession. One could argue that these factors provide researchers with even greater reason to respond to distressing disclosure, particularly when that disclosure is authored by adolescents, who are afforded special protection in research contexts.

These issues are, at least now, unresolved. However, even though most researchers are unlikely to encounter such a drastic scenario in the course of their online youth research, we would all be wise to begin our projects with a plan for how to handle any traumatic or questionable disclosure we encounter. For example, researchers may reply to online adolescents who disclose distressing information by referring them to online, regional or national support groups, or by suggesting they seek help from a friend, family member or counselor.

CONCLUSION

This chapter aimed to highlight two dilemmas researchers who study adolescents online may usefully contemplate. By providing detailed descriptions of my own research experiences, I hoped to demonstrate the importance and actuality of these dilemmas. Indeed, much of the discourse regarding online research ethics is abstract and hypothetical, pondering potential issues that may arise in the course of online research. Alternatively, this chapter aimed to illustrate specific dilemmas that grew out of actual research experiences, both to point out the seriousness with which they should be regarded and to highlight possible solutions.

Contending with the issue of parental consent and determining one's responsibility when encountering distressing information online are issues that grow out of identified principles of ethical research (autonomy and beneficence). These principles have successfully guided much of the research that has been conducted across disciplines for at least the past several decades. However, the practical application of these principles as traditionally directed by university IRBs and governmental funding agencies needs substantial reevaluation, given the growing number of studies of/on the Internet. Particularly when youth and their artifacts or communication are the subjects of study, re-examining such procedures as informed consent and devising guidelines for the ethical reaction to distressing online disclosure are particularly warranted. If such re-evaluation does not take place, we run the risk of discouraging researchers from conducting online youth research, for fear of violating expectations about ethical research procedures. Such a situation is highly undesirable, given the rich potential the Internet holds to better understand adolescents, and their uses of, relationships with and the effects of the Internet.

REFERENCES

Binik, Y., Mah, K., & Kiesler, S. (1999). Ethical issues in conducting sex research on the Internet. *The Journal of Sex Research, 36*(1), 82-90.

Chandler, D. & Roberts-Young, D. (1998). *The construction of identity in the personal homepages of adolescents.* Retrieved March 3, 2001 from: http://www.aber.ac.uk/media/documents/short/strasbourg.html.

Childress, C. & Asamen, J. (1998). The emerging relationship of psychology and the Internet: Proposed guidelines for conducting Internet intervention research. *Ethics & Behavior, 8*(1), 19-35.

Department of Health and Human Services. (1996). *Protection of human subjects, 45 D.F.R. Part 46, Subpart D – Additional DHHS protections for children involved as subjects in research.* (48 Fed. Reg. 9814, 1983)

Frankel, M. & Siang, S. (1999). *Ethical and legal aspects of human subjects research on the Internet: A report of a workshop.* Retrieved Feb. 1 2002 from: American Association for the Advancement of Science website: http://www.aaas.org/spp/dspp/sfrl/projects/intres/main.htm.

King, S. A. (1996). Researching Internet communities: Proposed ethical guidelines for the reporting of results. *The Information Society, 12*(2), 119-127.

Larson, R. (1995). Secrets in the bedroom: Adolescents' private use of media. *Journal of Youth and Adolescence, 24*(5), 535-550.

Mann, C. & Stewart, F. (2000). An ethical framework. In C. Mann & F. Stewart (Eds.), *Internet Communication and Qualitative Research* (pp. 39-63). Thousand Oaks, CA: Sage.

Miller, J. & Gergen, K. (1998) Life on the line: The therapeutic potentials of computer-mediated communication. *Journal of Marital and Family Therapy, 24*(2), 189-202.

National Commission for the Protection of Human Subjects of Biomedical and Behavioral Research. (1979). *The Belmont report: Ethical principles and guidelines for the protection of human subjects of online research.* Retrieved March 25, 2002 from: http://ohrp.osophs.dhhs.gov/humansubjects/guidance/belmont.htm.

Office for Protection from Research Risks. (2000). *Clarification of title 45 code of federal regulations part 46 (45 CFR 46).* Retrieved March 29, 2002 from Department of Health and Human Services website: http://ohrp.osophs.dhhs.gov/humansubjects/guidance/decisioncharts.htm.

Pew Internet Project. (2001). *Teenage life online: The rise of the instant-message generation and the Internet's impact on friendships and family relationships.* Retrieved August 19, 2002 from: http://www.pewinternet.org/reports/toc.asp?Report=36.

Reid, E. (1996). Informed consent in the study of on-line communities: A reflection on the effects of computer-mediated social research. *The Information Society 12*(2), 169-174.

Stanley, B. & Sieber, J. (1992). *Social Research on Children and Adolescents.* Newbury Park, CA: Sage

Steinberg, L. (1993). *Adolescence.* New York: McGraw Hill.

Stern, S. R. (1999). Adolescent girls' expression on WWW home pages: A qualitative analysis. *Convergence: The Journal of Research into New Media Technologies, 5*(4), 22-41.

Stern, S. R. (2002a). Virtually speaking: Girls' self-disclosure on the WWW. *Women's Studies in Communication, 25*(2), 223-253.

Stern, S. R. (2002b). Sexual selves on the World Wide Web: Adolescent girls' homepages as sites for sexual-expression. In J. Brown, J. Steele, & K. Walsh-Childers (Eds.), *Sexual Teens/Sexual Media: Investigating Media's Influence on Adolescent Sexuality* (pp. 265-286). NJ: Lawrence Erlbaum & Associates.

Stern, S.R. (2003). Encountering distressing information in online research: A consideration of legal and ethical responsibilities. *New Media & Society, 5*(2), 249-266.

Thompson, R. (1992). Developmental changes in research risk and benefit: A changing calculus of concerns. In. B. Stanley & J. Sieber (Eds.), *Social Research on Children and Adolescents* (pp. 128-142). Newbury Park, CA: Sage.

Thompson, S. (1999). The Internet and its potential influence on suicide. *Psychiatric Bulletin, 23,* 449-451.

Tymchuk, A. (1992). Assent processes. In B. Stanley & J. Sieber (Eds.), *Social Research on Children and Adolescents* (pp. 128-142). Newbury Park, CA: Sage.

Waskul, D. & Douglass, M. (1996). Considering the electronic participant: Some polemical observations on the ethics of on-line research. *The Information Society 12*(2), 129-139.

ENDNOTES

[1]   Names of home page authors in this chapter have been replaced with pseudonyms. All quotations from home page authors are unaltered.

Chapter XVI

Virtual Youth Research: An Exploration of Methodologies and Ethical Dilemmas from a British Perspective

Magdalena Bober

London School of Economics and Political Science, UK

ABSTRACT

By presenting findings from research into British online youth culture conducted by the author, the chapter critically evaluates how to study adolescents' use of the Internet and the ethical considerations facing the researcher. The methodologies applied include data collection with the help of Web server logs, online surveys, e-mail interviews, participant observation in online communities, as well as a "technobiography" of the author designing her own teenage website. Ethical problems discussed in the chapter deal with access to virtual sites of research, parental and informed consent, the role of the researcher, ownership of online data and issues of confidentiality.

INTRODUCTION

The rapid transformation of the Internet into a more commercial and consumer-oriented technology has opened up many gaps in our knowledge of how young people use online information and Web-based services. Recent research has begun to investigate these gaps (e.g., Tobin, 1998; Livingstone, 2001; Sandvig, 2001), though there are only a few publications applying online methodologies to study adolescents (e.g., Chandler & Roberts-Young, 1998; Tapscott, 1998). Researching this age group, in either the offline or online environment, calls for special care to be taken by the researcher. Yet still fewer publications deal with the ethical issues of collecting data about young people on the Internet (e.g., Abbott, 1998; Gaunlett, 2002b; Smyres, 1999).

In the last two decades, sociologists have tried to set up ethical guidelines for traditional child and youth research conducted in an offline environment (see Morrow & Richards, 1996). These revolve around access to the site of research, parental consent, power relationships between the researcher and the child, as well as issues of confidentiality and privacy. However, it is questionable whether these guidelines are applicable in a virtual context. Other researchers have already questioned the online usability of traditional ethical research codes that focus on adult subjects (see Frankel & Siang, 1999; Jones, 1994; Ward, 1999).

As Internet research progressively develops into a major field of academic inquiry and children as well as young people[1] are likely to become the subjects of online studies, as they constitute "the Internet users of the future," a discussion on the ethical issues regarding such research is required.

As a contribution to this evolving field, I will present one case study of online research in action, critically evaluating my experiences of investigating young people's use of the Internet. The research forms part of my work on the role of the Internet in contemporary British youth culture.

Such a discussion is less effective without an understanding of online methods and their implications for research involving young human subjects. Thus, I will illustrate the methodologies I applied to the online study of youth culture on a range of different virtual field sites, identifying problems and advantages in relation to traditional face-to-face methodologies.

Conducting research in a new field of study, such as the Internet, has its particular difficulties. Many areas still remain unexplored and there are no clear-cut guidelines for gathering data. A "hybrid approach" (see Sterne, 1999) has emerged, combining a range of methodologies and sites, of which the online aspects will be explored here. In particular, these include:

- interviewing producers of teen websites via e-mail,
- conducting an (informal) e-mail survey of young home page authors,
- designing a teen site, including a Web-based survey,
- conducting a participant observation in a teen online community, and
- collecting Web server data on young people's Internet use.

Before turning to virtual research, I studied young people's Internet use with traditional methods, conducting a paper survey of secondary school children in the northwest of England, observing Internet use in a school as well as a youth club, and furthermore, interviewing producers of teen websites face-to-face.

The research is an exploration of some new methodologies developed to study the role of the Internet in contemporary youth culture, which were developed during the research process. However, the applicability of these methodologies is not limited to the present topic and can equally be applied to the study of other issues in an online environment.

Using online methods raises particular ethical issues, and so far researchers conducting virtual studies have relied mostly on personal moral values, as ethical rules on how to obtain data from online respondents are only just emerging and far from consistent. For example, while certain research practices might be considered as ethical violations by some practitioners (e.g., "lurking" or not rendering respondents' identities anonymous), others would apply more "liberal" standards to online research. Furthermore, besides having to act as a responsible academic online, the researcher has to deal with the rules of netiquette as an Internet user during the research process.

I will attempt to point out potential ethical shortcomings in the protection of my subjects of study by means of a process of self-reflection and self-evaluation of my research and, by doing so, will contribute to the debate on establishing guidelines for ethical online research involving young people. Publications dealing with the ethics for offline research with children will be used as a starting point. It is important to stress that the chapter does not attempt to provide an "all encompassing" guide to conducting virtual research with young people. In line with Morrow and Richards (1996), it will be argued "that broad guidelines are [most] useful … as a way of helping researchers to consider potential ethical dilemmas … [allowing] room for personal ethical choices by the researcher" (p. 96).

Bringing together research from two perspectives, i.e., child and youth research on the one hand and Internet research on the other, the aims or this chapter are, in particular:

- to advance the understanding of the methodologies for youth research in an online environment;
- to explore the ethical dilemmas facing the online researcher when studying adolescents; and
- to contribute to the theoretical debate on establishing guidelines for virtual research, as some of the issues discussed are equally applicable to studies involving adult subjects.

The next part of the chapter introduces a selection of studies to exemplify the use of different methodologies in research involving young people and the Internet, and provides an overview of ethical considerations applied in offline studies with children.

The chapter then focuses on the virtual methodologies, which I applied to study youth culture online, and the problems that arose during the research. The advantages and disadvantages of online research compared to face-to-face research will be drawn out in relation to methods, such as interviews, surveys, participant observation and "technobiography" (see Kennedy, 2002), for investigating teen websites, personal home pages and online communities.

The chapter furthermore deals with the ethical dilemmas that arise when using these methodologies and how guidelines for real-life studies can be adapted in an online context. Issues raised include access to sites of research, informed and parental consent, power relationships between the researcher and the researched, ownership of online data and issues of confidentiality and privacy. Here, my experiences will be compared to other online studies on both children and adults.

THEORETICAL BACKGROUND
Methodologies for Studying Young People and the Internet

Existing studies of how young people use the Internet span a variety of topics and methods, applying to online as well as offline research and to the collection of both quantitative and qualitative data.[2]

Many British researchers rely on market surveys[3] or national statistics[4] for data on children's and young people's Internet access and use (e.g., Livingstone, 2001; Livingstone & Bovill, 2001; Williams, 1999), as these have been the first large-scale polls carried out in the UK on this topic. The first major academic survey on "Young People, New Media" in the UK has been published by Livingstone and Bovill (1999). Besides surveys, quantitative studies also include analyses of Web server data, such as the U.S. study on children's Internet use in public libraries (Sandvig, 2001).

Qualitative studies, for example, apply informal participant observation in order to investigate children's use of new technologies in schools (Williams, 1999) or in domestic contexts (Livingstone, 2001). Other methodologies include interviews, drawing techniques and time use diaries (Livingstone, 2001). Another example is the biographical account of a boy's life, analyzing the concept of young computer and Internet experts (Tobin, 1998).

Interviews and observations have also been conducted on the Internet. Studies utilizing virtual methods include online chat with young people to investigate their use of the Internet (Tapscott, 1998) or observations of teenage bulletin boards, e.g., on girls' body image (Smyres, 1999). Teen online communities have also been used to recruit respondents for research, e.g., on teenage sexuality, young women's print magazines (Gauntlett, 2002b) and young people's role models (Gauntlett, 2002a).

Furthermore, there are a number of studies, focusing on young people's personal home pages and their potential as a medium for identity construction (Chandler & Roberts-Young, 1998), for forming online communities (Abbott, 1998) and for emancipating girls' uses of new technology (Oksman, 2002). These authors study the textual representations on home pages and conduct e-mail surveys, as well as online or face-to-face interviews with young home page authors.

Ethical Considerations in Offline Child Research

Guidelines for research normally focus on adult subjects and are often inadequate for the protection of children. Children are perceived by society as being both vulnerable and incapable of making decisions, due to their physical and economic powerlessness, and are therefore understood to be in need of special protection (Morrow & Richards, 1996). The discussion about research ethics in offline studies involving children revolves around problems of access, parental consent, confidentiality and power relationships between the child and researcher.

Several UK authors stress the problem of access to the site of research with children (e.g., Hood, Kelley, & Mayall, 1996). The recruitment of young subjects for offline studies is usually institutionalized and takes place through schools (e.g., Alderson & Goodey, 1996), local authorities (e.g., Mauthner, 1997), health centers or youth clubs (e.g., Hood et al., 1996). These institutions function as gatekeepers for access, with the purpose of protecting the child (e.g., Morrow & Richards, 1996; Hood et al., 1996). However, several authors stress that at the same time as obscuring access, this pre-selective process does not take the young respondent's view into account, whether he/she wants to participate in the research (see Alderson & Goodey, 1996; Hood et al., 1996).

Before the researcher approaches the child, it is also recommended that written consent be sought from the parents. Morrow and Richards (1996) stress that "parental consent is often ... a key criterion for research to be seen as ethical" (p. 90). However, the presumption that children are vulnerable and incompetent and need to be protected from "exploitative researchers" excludes them from a democratic research process. Sociologists argue that it is less the child's age, which plays a role in his/her ability to consent to research, than the context in which the study takes place and the extent of consent (Morrow & Richards, 1996).

Therefore, researchers should ensure to inform their participants fully of the research purposes and, moreover, allow for their "informed dissent." Participants should not feel forced to take part in the research and should be given the opportunity to opt out, even though their guardians might have agreed to their participation (Morrow & Richards, 1996).

Furthermore, the researcher has the obligation to protect the identity of the respondent and deal with the collected data in a confidential way. However, if the information supplied makes the researcher aware that the child is at risk of harm, should promises of confidentiality be broken and the information be disclosed in order to protect the child, even if this means losing the trust of the respondent? Whereas the National Children's Bureau guidelines (as cited in Morrow & Richards, 1996) recommend doing so, Punch (2002) stresses "how important trust and confidentiality are for young people when deciding whether or not to reveal their problems" (p. 50). Alderson (1995) assumes an ethical middle ground and advises consulting the respondent first about which strategy to pursue should concerns about his/her safety arise.

Mauthner (1997) is concerned that during interviews, children are seldom given the same right to privacy as adults. Disruptions in schools or parents walking in during interviews at home might discourage the respondent from talking freely. The researcher might also influence the outcome of the interview, due to an unequal power relationship with the child subject, in so far as the child may give socially accepted replies during the interview (Hood et al., 1996; Mauthner, 1997). Factors influencing this power relationship are differences in gender, ethnicity and age between the researcher and the child. The first two factors can be matched; however, it is difficult to address the age difference. This age gap also puts researchers at risk of misinterpreting the data as they do not carry the same set of experiences as their young respondents.

Addressing the dilemma of research on children and adolescents, Morrow and Richards (1996) write, "in everyday social life, we (as adults, parents, or researchers) tend not to be respectful of children's views and opinions" (p. 91). To render the research process more democratic, they recommend that children are given more rights when participating in a study and are treated with respect, i.e., as the subjects, rather than the objects of research.

RESEARCHING YOUTH CULTURE ONLINE
Interviewing Website Producers

A starting point for the analysis of youth culture on the Internet is to investigate the cultural artifacts of this particular online culture, i.e., teen websites and personal home pages set up by young people.

Personal home pages have been recognized as a medium for identity construction and self-presentation by several authors (e.g., Chandler, 1998; Chandler & Roberts-Young, 1998) and can also provide an insight into the process of young people's identity construction.

Commercial teen websites usually consist of a noninteractive online magazine part (e-zine), similar to a print magazine, aimed at teenagers, including celebrity news, film and music reviews, human interest stories, advice on health and sexual issues, competitions, quizzes and horoscopes. This is often accompanied by an interactive part, featuring a chat room, bulletin boards, online games, downloadable mobile phone features and online shopping facilities (see Bober, 2001, 2002). Such websites are part of the discourse on contemporary youth culture. A starting point for their analysis can, for example, be found in research on teenage girls' print magazines (see McRobbie, 1991, 1997).

I analyzed the teen websites by conducting e-mail and face-to-face interviews with the (sometimes adult, sometimes adolescent) producers. In the case of the personal home pages, I chose to conduct an e-mail survey of the young authors, using open-ended questions to allow me to perform a qualitative analysis of the replies.[5]

When comparing the results of online methods with the face-to-face interviews I had conducted with some teen site producers earlier, several differences emerge. Whereas online interviews seemed to yield a higher response rate but shorter replies, face-to-face research produced more in-depth information, most likely due to the relative ease and speed of speaking compared to writing. Some face-to-face interviews took up to three hours, whereas the e-mail interviews only produced a couple of pages when printed out. As Gómez (2002) points out, e-mail interviews "require more time, even though they are clearer and less redundant (because of the use of writing instead of oral language)" (p. 15). Furthermore, the "richness that a face-to-face interaction would have" (Gómez, p. 15) is lost.

During face-to-face interaction, the researcher also has the opportunity to ask probing questions. In contrast, some of my online respondents did not reply to a follow-up e-mail. However, online data is still preferable, where on-site access is problematic. For example, obtaining access to the offices of teen websites to interview the employees posed a problem, firstly, because the staff were too busy, as they indicated, or because some websites were maintained from the homes of the owners, who, therefore, preferred e-mail questions.[6]

In the case of the personal home pages, I did not ask the respondents for face-to-face interviews as it is regarded as ethically problematic to seek face-to-face contact with young people over the Internet. However, before starting the e-mail survey, I was faced with the difficulty of finding young people's home pages to analyze (see also Chandler & Roberts-Young, 1998).

Conventional methods of finding information on the Internet, such as search engines and Web directories, were of no help as they only list personal home pages in general[7] but not specifically those of young people. In the end, I found teen bulletin boards to be a good source of home page addresses. There, the URLs of members' home pages are listed in the "member profiles" for other users to see. Via links, these home pages then led to other ones of friends.[8] An unavoidable downside of this strategy is that it introduces a sampling bias (Coomber, 1997), excluding those home pages that are less well publicized on the Web (see also Hine, 2000).

After overcoming these initial hurdles, the method produced a surprisingly large quantity of data. The home page authors seemed keen to take part in the research, and the response rate to the e-mail questionnaires turned out to be fairly high. Many personal home pages are being built with the hope of receiving feedback from viewers and frequently requests, such as "Please sign the guest book" or "E-mail me," can be found on them. Thus, the level of how much respondents feel personally affected by the topic of a study seems to influence the response rate (see also Witmer, Colman, & Lee Katzman, 1999). Home page researchers have the same advantage as researchers of fandom. "The very nature of fandom suggests willing informants: they feel strongly about the text(s) in question and have considerable interest in them ... [and] will either not mind or actually enjoy the interview process" (Gray, 2002, p. 10).

In essence, online methods have the disadvantage of producing less detailed interviews than those involving face-to-face interaction. However, this is compensated for by the ease of access to online data, hence providing a larger sample.

Designing My Own Teen Website—A Technobiography

Hine (2000) argues for a reflexive approach in Internet studies, i.e., that researchers should not only study how the Internet is consumed and produced by users and designers, but that they should also learn how to use the Internet themselves in order to understand the experiences of their research subject and to develop "an enriched reading of the practices which lead to the production and consumption of Internet artefacts" (p. 55).

So, in order to gain a deeper insight into Web production, I designed my own website (see Appendix). It was aimed at young people and included several interactive response forms, for example:

- a message board where users could discuss issues related to the Internet,
- a "quizlet," asking users whether they had bought something online before,
- an online questionnaire about use of leisure time, media and new technologies,
- a "fun-type" quiz, where users could find out about their "online personality type," and
- forms where they could vote for their favorite websites or submit their own home pages.

The online questionnaire was designed as a follow-up to the paper survey with students from schools and a youth club in the northwest of England about their use of and attitudes towards the Internet. Interactive forms for collecting data about users are a typical feature of most commercial websites. Nowadays "many researchers are turning their attention to the World Wide Web as a more suitable medium for administering questionnaires," as Mann and Stewart (2000, p. 70) note, due to its cost and time effectiveness, increased reach and the potential for generating high response rates.

But beyond providing additional survey data, designing my own website aimed at young people has added to my understanding of how the youth websites I was researching (i.e., teen sites and personal home pages) are set up and run, as I acquired the necessary skills while building my site (over a period of seven months). Hine (2000) argues that Internet researchers "can use their own data collection practices as data in their own right" (p. 54). This autobiographical process of a researcher reflecting on his/ her own experiences with new media technologies is referred to as "technobiography" by Kennedy (2002).

However, there are several problems with this new methodology, starting with the setting up of the site. My experience was similar to that of Yun and Trumbo (2000) who report that a "considerable time investment was required to establish and administer the website. But as many university researchers do, we invested our own labor in this effort" (p. 14).

"A further problem is how to target one's audience, i.e., getting visitors onto the site: There are a number of ways of attracting people who use the Internet to your research and some will be more successful than others. Simply having a Web page, for example ..., will not be sufficient. This is analogous to waiting for people to come to you, and while some will (maybe), many will not" (Coomber, 1997, para. 6.2).

A guide on how to "Create Web Pages in 24 Hours" recommends submitting the site to search engines, such as "Yahoo," and tell acquaintances about it via e-mail (Snell, 1999). Another possibility is to announce it in relevant online communities (Coomber, 1997).

However, publicizing one's website to a wide audience can pose problems if one does not have the necessary financial means. "Therefore, money provides a considerable advantage" (Gauntlett, 2000, p. 10). It is difficult to get listed in search engines and Web directories. Altavista's free submission service currently takes four to six weeks to review a site, which, even then, does not guarantee its listing.[9] For a seven-day-review, Yahoo currently charges a fee of GBP 199 (US $299).[10]

Announcing the website to respondents of the paper questionnaire survey by e-mail generated a low response rate in completed forms from the website. Having not installed a visitor counter on the website, I do not know how many visitors had accessed the site without completing any forms. There might be several reasons for this low response rate, in spite of the incentive of winning a shopping voucher from one's favorite store, such as the extra time and effort it takes to fill in a form, the reluctance to provide an extensive amount of information online due to a perceived security risk normally associated with e-commerce and the reluctance to take part in what might be perceived as market research. Moreover, the lack of success of the website was possibly due to the heavily text-based design, which was required by the nature of the research. My experience gives an insight into how difficult it is for website producers and home page authors to attract visitors to their site.

Witmer et al. (1999) stress that Internet surveys may yield lower levels of participation than traditional "paper-and-pencil" methods. This is supported by my observation that students who I asked to fill in a paper version of the extensive online questionnaire containing 24 questions did not mind completing it offline. Morrow and Richards (1996) note that "children who are required to participate in research in schools may not feel in a position to dissent, simply because most (if not all) tasks and activities in school are compulsory" (p. 101). For the online participants, on the other hand, the absence of the researcher made it easier to opt out of the survey.

I also announced the website on the message boards of a teen site I was researching – Angstteen.org.[11] This was, as I had discovered, a common practice among the users; however, it generated replies containing criticism and advice on the design of my site instead of more completed response forms, as the following posts by two different members illustrate:

Hmmm. Sorry to be blunt but what's it got that thousands of other sites haven't already done and done better? ... The layout of your site is fine. The colors of the forum are way too hard to read. It's empty, and you are competing with thousands of other sites out there, which already have hundreds and hundreds of pages of good content that makes interesting reading. So, the site is okay apart from the forum, but what's there to be worth visiting?[12]

Another thing often mentioned, it's easy to get visitors to visit your site, what's hard is making it worth their weight [sic] and wanting to come back. That's where good information, something different and unique comes into play... The most popular sites on the Internet are either very good information sites, software support or twisted/ black humor sites which people find amusing ... Be different, make your site easy to access and navigate around, people want information fast, time is money...

The above quotes demonstrate that Internet audiences have developed certain expectations of websites, concerning the look (e.g., layout, colors, readability and navigation) and the contents (e.g., good information, uniqueness and humor). Furthermore, users know that there is a wide range of websites competing for their attention.

On the bulletin boards on another teen site, Teen-Surfers.com, I was reprimanded for advertising my website, where it was possibly mistaken for competition:

*Are you just going to promote and then f*** off!?* (Site owner)

Why don't the topics that just open and advertise just get deleted! (Board moderator)

I had apparently disregarded the unwritten rules of netiquette of this online community, but later discovered that other messages announcing teen websites were treated similarly, as this selection of replies by the members of Teen-Surfers.com suggests:

Look at how crappy the design looks!

[Name of user], give it up, stop coming back here. No one cares about your sad site, and from the preview it does look really shite [sic] to be honest.

We don't care about your "stupid" site so just piss off.

I hate stupid advertisers and no teen website is better than Teen-Surfers.com.

I have been to the front page and I really couldn't be bothered to go any further. ... So bog off to your stupid site, at least Teen-Surfers.com has decent people!

Wow, that website is boring.

The above quotes demonstrate how difficult it is to establish a successful and convincing presence in the online youth market with its extremely critical audience.

Had I been more experienced, my website might have been more successful. However, due to the unregulated nature of the Web, professional websites have often been set up by amateurs. One such example is Teen-Surfers.com which started out as a small website founded by a teenager and has now become one of the leading UK teen sites (see Bober, 2002). Therefore, my experience is not far away from the reality of Web design aimed at young people, and the problems encountered did not only face me as a researcher but might also have been experienced by producers of teen websites themselves. This technobiographic experience has added to my understanding of teen sites and has demonstrated to me how difficult it is to create and maintain a successful website aimed at young people. That this is not an easy task is also proven by the recent closure of several youth websites in the UK, such as Swizzle, backed by Procter & Gamble and Wowgo, backed by Unilever (see Bober, 2001).

Participant Observation in Teen Online Communities

As part of my research, I also analyzed the bulletin board-type communities of six different teen websites.[13] Online communities have been the focus of several studies that have analyzed the behavior of members (e.g., McLaughlin, Osborne, & Smith, 1995), language use (Herring, 1996; Wilkins, 1991), community formation (e.g., Baym, 1995; Rheingold, 1994) and identity construction (e.g., Gómez, 2002; Turkle, 1995). Further-more, they have been used to research topics including, for example, teenage girls' body image (Smyres, 1999) and Goth culture (Hodkinson, as cited in Mann & Stewart, 2000).[14]

I found the bulletin boards to be a good source for data on issues related to young people's use of the Internet, as the following messages about broadband from a discussion on Teen-Surfers.com demonstrate:

Who has this? I love it ... yay I'm download mad lol now.[15]

Yep indeed, we just got it last week, it is sooo so so much faster.

I want it sooo much, it takes me two hours to download just one music video at the moment aarrgghh, stupid thing.

I have [the] broadband thingy but I have no idea what it's supposed to do differently. And for some reason our Internet isn't connected to the phone line, it goes into our TV thing with cable.

I really want broadband and I keep telling my mum the advantages but I think it costs a bit too much but I have Windows XP lol, not that it matters.

The above quotes exemplify how users make sense of a new technology when it is introduced into their domestic environment and during the course of its technological development. The young users are already familiar with the Internet, yet with the (expected) adaptation of broadband, the meanings and practices they associate with the Internet have changed (e.g., the possibility to download large files, such as music, faster connectivity vs. higher costs and skepticism towards or little understanding of the new technological development).[16]

On several sites, the owners or editors engaged in the discussions themselves. Their posts provide an interesting insight into the workings of the website, as illustrated by the following exchange between the (19-year-old) site owner of Teen-Surfers.com and a user:

Do you guys ever click on the banners at the top of the page? What sort of adverts make you look/which don't? Does it annoy you that there are a few sponsors? Do you shop online? Do you realize I earn money every time you click on a banner (18 pence)? (Site owner)

[Name of site owner], try and get Lush[17] or Amazon to sponsor you, I buy loads from them. (User)

[Name of user], I have e-mailed Lush re: a competition, and possible product reviews (which hopefully means freebies!). Amazon are a sponsor (well, I am an affiliate). I might stick a link up later! (Site owner)

These messages demonstrate a problem Internet entrepreneurs are faced with, i.e., how to make websites profitable. The Internet also allows for a closer relationship between producer and consumer, than in the traditional media, and user feedback can be incorporated much quicker.

I also decided to post questions related to my research on the boards, as I had seen this being done by other researchers (e.g., Gauntlett, 2002a, b). The following is an example of what I posted on Teen-Surfers.com:

Hi, I'm a student at Manchester Metropolitan University doing research on young people and shopping on the Internet and on the high street (what do teens buy, fav shops and sites, how do they pay, where do they get their money from).

It would be great if you could help me with this one:
What do you think about online shopping? Have you ever bought anything on the Internet or do you prefer "real" shops? Why (not)? Which site did you buy it from and

how did you pay? (Parent's credit card?) What did you buy? Or anything you saw and didn't buy because ... Or would you never buy online 'cause it's not secure?

Thanks very much four your help! E-mail me at [e-mail address] if you prefer.
Magda

More info about my research: [URL of departmental homepage]

The response rate and quality of the replies, however, was varied (see also Hine, 2000). Messages posted by members, who are part of the community, received more replies than the questions of a researcher or a student researching a particular topic, which is how I introduced myself on the boards. For example, I posted a request for the users to review other websites with youth-related content, which only received one answer. A similar topic posted by a member some time later, however, generated 12 replies. Thus, here the exclusive nature of the community becomes apparent, trying to guard itself against outsider intrusion.

Relying on the members to start a discussion on topics of interest to my research (as these posts generated more replies) limited the number of themes to be analyzed. However, it also produced new topics, previously not thought of, as the following questions posted by two different members show, which generated a large number of interesting replies on Teen-Surfers.com:

Who downloads music from post Napsterish programs such as KaZaA, Morpheus, BearShare, Audiogalaxy, etc.? Do you feel bad that you are downloading copyrighted material and it is someone else's property/illegal?

Where is everyone's comp [computer]? Mine is upstairs in my brother's bedroom, I would love it to be in my bedroom because he throws me out because the keyboard makes a noise and he can't get to sleep because of it, but the thing is my bedroom is too small grrr. Where are your comps? And do you hate them being there or don't you mind them as where they are now?

Leaving young Internet users to discuss issues of their choice among themselves and in an environment where they feel comfortable produces topics that the users consider important, without the researcher "artificially" imposing topics onto the group or the researcher's presence giving rise to socially desirable answers.

This methodology produces a large quantity of data, comparable to face-to-face interviews and, currently, I possess a stack of print outs that is more than three inches high from six different bulletin boards, collected over a period of nine months. It is convenient and relatively easy to record and save data when studying a virtual environment, as Ward (1999) reports. The researcher also has the ability to revisit the site after the original period of data collection, in order to incorporate new developments into the work, which is less common in real-life research (Ward, 1999). However, this creates a new problem, as Hine (2000) notes, i.e., when to stop data collection.

The disembodiment and (alleged) identity play of Internet users leads many researchers to question the validity of online data. The absence of facial expressions and bodily communication leaves fewer possibilities for the researcher to check the credibility of the respondents' answers than during face-to-face interviews (see Taylor, 1999; Paccagnella, 1997). To counter this problem, Turkle (1995) only uses online data from respondents she has met in real life. However, this is not very practical for most researchers.

When studying young people, the researcher is faced with an additional problem. Some authors stress that "[a]dults conducting research with children … inevitably invite particular kinds of 'approved responses' " (Sefton-Green & Buckingham, 1998, p. 75) and that young people "who respond to surveys may not give honest answers; for example, they may fear that they won't look good if they tell the truth" (Berger, 1998, p. 39).

Kendall (1999) claims that spending time in an online community and getting to know the particular norms of the group compensates for the absence of facial cues online and also increases the researcher's ability to evaluate the authenticity of responses.

Based on observation of young people's communication on bulletin boards for several months, I have come to the conclusion that the majority of postings represent the truth. Criteria of coherence of the argument presented in the message can be applied here, as well as an informal "system of checks" utilized by the message board members and moderators, who criticize messages that do not appear credible (see also Smyres, 1999). An example is this—somewhat upsetting—request for help posted on the bulleting boards of Teencybercafe.co.uk, another site I was researching:

Help, my dad is beating me up, punching me and throwing china bowls at my head. (hit)

While some users appeared concerned and urged the member to get help, others questioned the authenticity of this post:

I think she's joking … take my advice and buy him [your dad] an unsmashable present like a sponge ball.

Yeah, I agree with [the above reply]. Umm, how would anyone be able to type a message if someone (their dad!) was throwing china bowls at their head? I think she was "having a laugh"! If not then how … do you type a message on here while getting the sh*t kicked out of you?'

It appears that young Internet users are aware of the need to be critical about the genuineness of online conversation. They know of the possibility to create false impressions and identities on the Internet but seem very critical about people who do so. This is also demonstrated in the following quote by a young Internet user found in Tobin (1998):

"Unless I am playing a role playing game, I'm always myself on the Net. I never lie or make stuff up when I write to the [messaging] list. I'm sure there are people who do, but I despise them, just like I despise people who lie and boast in real life" (p. 123).

So, while a researcher can never totally prove the authenticity of online material, there should be no concern that material created by young people is less genuine than that of adults. With more experience and insight into the field a researcher will be able to judge the authenticity.

Investigating Sensitive Issues with Web Server Logs

Being confronted with emotionally difficult topics, such as the one described above, will undoubtedly not be a singular incident for researchers studying young people online. However, online communities might not be an ideal environment to investigate other sensitive issues, such as pornography found on the Internet and its effects on children and young people. As this is an issue of major concern in the public debate on children and the Internet, it needs to be addressed in academic research.

Yet on the teen bulletin boards I studied, I did not find any threads discussing the issue of online pornography during the observational period, although other issues of sexual nature, usually related to teenage sexuality, were frequently talked about there. I chose not to raise the topic myself by posting a question, thus, trying to avoid potentially upsetting or offending young respondents. On this issue, Livingstone (2002b) notes:

"Whether one can even research what children have seen, whether it upset them, and what it meant to them, is dubious. The researcher runs the ... risk of making more of an issue of such occurrences, or of putting ideas into children's heads. I asked my 12 year old if he'd seen pornography on the Internet, and found myself having to explain pornography in a way I hadn't had to with him before!" (p. 8)

However, in the paper survey I conducted with young people at schools and at a youth club, online pornography was mentioned amongst dislikes about the Internet by several respondents. In a survey by Allbon and Williams (2002), almost half of the participants stated having seen "unpleasant" material on the Internet, which shows that it is also an issue of concern among young people. Possible explanations that this topic was not raised on the bulletin boards might be embarrassment or fear of "virtual retribution" by other members for complaining about online pornography, as the boards usually tried to depict a typical adolescent attitude of coolness, cynicism and of being shocked by nothing.

In such a situation when it is difficult to raise a sensitive issue, it is possible for the researcher to utilize a more unobtrusive method of electronic data retrieval, i.e., to collect technical documentation about Internet use, in this case, from Web server logs (see McLaughlin, Goldberg, Ellison, & Lucas, 1999; Sandvig, 2001). I obtained printout reports from Internet monitoring software from a school in the northwest of England, where I was placed as a voluntary teaching assistant. It listed the "Top 30" banned categories students had tried to access. Among these, gaming and gambling sites were accessed most frequently, followed by adult material.[18] A separate report on banned adult sites revealed that the "Top 30" sites of this category had been accessed 341 times during one particular month of my stay at the school.

Those students who had tried to access banned sites repeatedly and even after having received a warning were denied Internet access. I did not speak to these particular students, but as informal conversations with the teaching and technical staff revealed, it was more a matter of testing the boundaries and the thrill of doing something forbidden that led the students to access pornographic pictures online. This method does not reveal the motives of these adolescents; however, it is an example of a more appropriate way to investigate a sensitive issue.[19] Dealing with such research questions undoubtedly raises ethical dilemmas. These will be discussed in the following section.

ETHICAL DILEMMAS OF
VIRTUAL YOUTH RESEARCH

Online vs. Offline Access

Before illuminating the ethical problems of access to children online, the difficulties of accessing real life research environments, in my case a school and a youth club, will be contrasted with the relative ease of access to virtual environments. As illustrated earlier, access to adolescents during offline research is often institutionalized and takes place through schools, youth clubs, children's care homes or their own homes, where the young participants are protected by teachers, youth workers, caregivers or their parents.

Before I could start my research at the school and the youth club, I had to undergo "security checks" to ensure the safety of the children and teenagers to be studied. This involved an interview about aims of the research and methodologies used for data collection, which had to meet the approval of the school and the youth workers, respectively. I was planning to hand out questionnaires and conduct an informal observation. The youth workers objected to the questionnaires, which asked for respondents' e-mail addresses, so they had to be assured of the confidential handling of the data. Another requirement was that the children were not allowed to be in my company without the presence of another youth worker in the room. At the school I was assigned to a teacher who would provide access to the students for me. I also had to provide two references and undergo a criminal record check for any past offences. These requirements were set by the local volunteers' bureau, which had helped to arrange both placements.

However, my experience of online research demonstrates that protection of children and adolescents is less effective in a virtual environment, and the researcher is left alone with his/her personal moral values. As the Internet is very popular with children and young people, it is fairly easy to gain access to this age group online. For example, e-mail addresses are available on some of the child- or teenage-focused bulletin boards that I used for my study. With no stringent checks present, which researchers normally have to face before being granted offline access to children and young people, online researchers are in danger of forgetting to take precautions to protect their subjects of study.

To recruit online respondents for my research, I posted a message on the bulletin boards of Angstteen.org, asking the members to visit my website, as described earlier. Recruiting participants on bulletin boards is a practice not uncommon among online researchers (e.g., Gauntlett, 2002a, b). However, the moderator of the bulletin boards, who had the role of a gatekeeper, objected to my message as demonstrated by the following reply:

If you are trying to get users to take part in your research, you need to ask the mods [message board moderators] first.

This reaction assumes that young people are more vulnerable online than in real life. The above site was run by a youth charity, and a similar attitude to protecting its young members was prevailing as in the youth club. Gauntlett (personal communication, March

8, 2002) recounts a similar experience when utilizing teenage bulletin boards for his research:

"I used a variety of sites and on a couple of them, I had your experience of being "told off" by a moderator for posting research questions to the board. Such rules generally do not become apparent until you break them. I simply stopped using those boards where moderators had objected to my presence."

In this discussion one cannot ignore the public fear of child molesters approaching young people on the Internet which might have influenced the moderators' reactions, as they see themselves in a position of having to protect children. Gauntlett (2002b) reflects upon the ethical issues of his research in the following way:

"Being a 30 year old man hanging out on teen websites for research purposes raises ethical concerns, of course—I was always careful to say who I was, what I was doing, and reminding teenagers not to disclose their address or other personal details to anyone on the net" (para. 7).

Mann and Stewart (2000) also recognize these concerns but take a more dogmatic position, advising researchers against direct contact with young participants, i.e., that contact should only be sought through gatekeepers, such as parents and schools. They stress that the "maturity, personality and possible vulnerability [of a disembodied child] may be unknown" (p. 53) which raises ethical difficulties.

Smyres (1999), on the other hand, contests that young people are more vulnerable when studied on the Internet. Exploring body image in a teenage girl online community, she claims that the users could discuss distressing issues, such as eating disorders, in an environment where they felt safe and comfortable as it was free of "apparent adult intervention" (para. 6).

Whether to seek direct access to young people on the Internet or only approach them through online gatekeepers should be made dependent on the subject matter of the research, the sensitivity of the topic under investigation and on the perceived maturity as well as potential vulnerability of the respondents.

Researchers should not shy away from studying children and young people online merely because they are perceived by society to be more vulnerable than adults. Special precautions still have to be taken, nonetheless one should not let moral considerations, aimed at protecting young participants, paralyze research projects.

Informed or Parental Consent?

Mann and Stewart (2000) stress that before starting to collect data, it is viable to obtain informed consent from participants. "Informed consent involves giving participants comprehensive and correct information about a research study, and ensuring that they understand fully what participation would entail, before securing their consent to take part" (Mann & Stewart, 2000, p. 48).

In face-to-face studies involving children and young people, it is recommended that consent is sought from the parents or legal guardians of the respondents, by having them sign a consent form. In online research this poses pragmatic problems, such as how to obtain an electronic signature, which possesses the same validity as a written one (see Mann & Stewart, 2000), especially if the identity of the person signing is unknown (see Frankel & Siang, 1999).

Furthermore, getting participants to fill in an online questionnaire is difficult enough. Adding the hurdle of obtaining a signature from their parents lowers the response rate dramatically. Therefore, I did not seek parental consent but chose to inform the participants sufficiently about the purposes of the research. In online studies, the researcher can accomplish this by directly writing to respondents by e-mail, by posting a message about the research on a bulletin board and/ or by providing a link to a website containing more information about the research, as I did, for example, when posting questions on the boards. However, the researcher cannot be sure if the participants have read the information and understood the implications of the research. During offline research, face-to-face dialogue can at least help to ascertain this, but in the case of a disembodied online respondent whose background, "age, competency, or comprehension" (Frankel & Siang, 1999, p. 10) and identity are unknown, it is questionable whether one can claim informed consent.

When studying young people, this issue can get even more problematic, as Gauntlett (personal communication, March 8, 2002) stresses. When agreeing to take part in research, they might be overruled by their excitement of being involved in a research project, rather than considering privacy issues. Referring to the participants of his study on "Media, Gender and Identity" (Gauntlett, 2002a), who he interviewed online, Gauntlett writes:

"I also made the point that 'I am writing a book about x' because they seemed to be excited that their words might end up in a book. Of course, there one has to be careful and to make it clear that their words may well "not" end up in the book and it is not going to make them rich and/ or famous!" (personal communication, March 8, 2002)

This assumption puts into question whether young respondents are capable of fully comprehending the implications of research and whether their giving consent is valid. In this case, it is then up to the researcher to adopt other strategies to protect respondents, i.e., rendering their identity anonymous or using pseudonyms, which will be discussed later.

However, the advantage of e-mail interviews or online research, in general, is that respondents experience less pressure to take part than during face-to-face research. Hodkinson (1999) stresses "the ease with which respondents can completely ignore questions" (as cited in Mann & Stewart, 2000, p. 152) and, thus, opt out of the research.

Online Power Relationships

Several researchers have argued that the virtual environment has the potential to balance out the unequal power relationship between the researcher and research subjects, which is present during face-to-face interaction (e.g. Frankel & Siang, 1999; Ward, 1999). Differences in age, ethnicity and social background are not exposed online due to the disembodiment of Internet users. For example, Ward (1999) reports on her research, "[a]s the participants were in a position to ask questions of me, the power relationships between the researcher and the researched changed radically. The researcher does not have so much control over the interview process" (para. 4.4).

On the other hand, due to the fluidity of online identities, new power relationships can emerge that researchers might use to their advantage. While conducting this research project, I was in the position of both a student and a researcher. Thus, when posting questions on the bulletin boards, I introduced myself as a student to the users, trying to minimize the age-gap and not wanting to appear too old as some of the boards demonstrated a hostile approach towards adult users in their (apparently) "adult-free zone." Being in my mid-20s, I might not have been too old to participate in the discussions myself, however the users did not know my age and introducing myself as a researcher might have made me appear even older in their eyes. However, when sending questions by e-mail, I tried to achieve exactly this effect and introduced myself as a researcher, thus, attempting to add more importance to the request for obtaining information about their home page, than an e-mail from a student might have done.

The new technology also makes it possible to balance out unequal power relationships, by studying virtual environments without the knowledge of the users. This strategy is also of advantage when observation of a real life environment poses problems. For example, the teenagers in the youth club, especially the older ones, felt uneasy being observed while using the computers and surfing the Net. Doing so would have interfered with their normal behavior. Yet on the bulletin boards the users were not aware of the presence of a researcher.

However, Mann and Stewart (2000) debate whether it is ethically justifiable to "lurk" on a message board as a hidden observer without the users knowing their messages are being monitored. Other researchers fear that introducing oneself as a researcher might influence the users' interactions; for example, Denzin (1999), who in his study openly declares that he did not ask for permission to quote from messages and did not introduce himself to the users; or Hodkinson (1999) who says that he was advised against announcing his presence as a researcher in a newsgroup because "as well as creating possible hostility it might well distort the "'natural' interactions [he was] seeking to observe and record" (as cited in Mann & Stewart, 2000, p. 53).

During my research, I adopted the strategy of "half-lurking," "half-participating" and made the respondents aware of my presence when posting questions on the boards. However, at other times, I did not tell them that I was observing the community as this might have influenced their behavior.

Online Data—Private or Public?

Online research raises the issue of who owns the data in newsgroups, bulletin boards chat rooms and personal home pages. Is it the system operator, the author or are the data public material (e.g., Kitchin, 1998)?

Mann and Stewart (2000) debate whether researchers should make message board postings anonymous by using pseudonyms or if it is justifiable to "simply … use the name that accompanied the original text on the grounds that, if people are happy for the Internet to see the association between their words and their name, why should they object to it in a book" (p. 46).

Each online community might have a different viewpoint on this issue. Wilkins (1991) reports that the members of the newsgroup she researched came to the conclusion that messages constituted public material and could therefore be used by others as long as the author was referenced appropriately. On the other hand, Gajjala (1999) writes that the users of her newsgroup agreed that computer-medicate communication is private and the researcher should obtain permission from the author before using any quotes.

In the case of personal home pages, one would be inclined to argue that by their very nature, and even more so than posts on bulletin boards, they constitute a conscious effort by the author to make the created content publicly available on the Internet. Therefore, it should be ethically justifiable to include content from home pages and their Web addresses in one's research without the permission of the author. However, Bassett and O'Riordan (2002) stress that the purpose and genre of each home page have to be considered, as well as the author's perception of his/her privacy; e.g., "is the site like a public forum modeled on a graffiti wall or a message board, or is it more like a newsletter intended only for members of a group?" (p. 16).

When children and young people create home pages, they might not be fully aware of the fact that online communication and publishing have the same status as print. This argument is supported by Chandler (1998), who notes that the boundaries between private and public are blurred on personal home pages and individuals might publish material that they would not disclose in face-to-face interaction (see also Frankel & Siang, 1999). Young people are considered especially vulnerable in these respects, being deceived by the privacy of sitting in front of a computer in their own bedroom and by the disembodiment of other users they encounter online.

However, on the bulletin boards that I studied, the users seemed aware of the public nature of the posts. This was demonstrated by a common practice of switching to private messaging (provided by the website), instant messaging (e.g., ICQ or AOL) or e-mail for private conversation. The site owners or board moderators had also adopted the practice of editing or deleting posts that might have infringed upon the privacy of one or several users. This is an ethical advantage to the users but a disadvantage to the researcher who misses out on part of the discourse.

Protecting Young People and Issues of Confidentiality

The question facing the researcher is therefore not whether to publish data collected online, but how to use the material in a responsible way, i.e., not to expose the author or publish material that might be harmful to or distressing for him/her.

Thus, throughout this chapter as well as in my research, data used from bulletin boards, e-mails and personal home pages (whether with or without the permission of the author) has been rendered non-identifiable, i.e., the writers' names have not been disclosed to protect the identity and pseudonyms have been used for website names. Equally, the schools and the youth club taking part in the research have not been identified by name or location.

The strategy of rendering data anonymous or using pseudonyms to preserve confidentiality has also been applied by other researchers (e.g., Abbott, 1998; Bassett & O'Riordan, 2002; Kendall, 1999). However, in hindsight Bassett and O'Riordan (2002) regret their decision to use pseudonyms during a study of a lesbian online community. "Overly protective research ethics risk diminishing the cultural capital of those engaging in cultural production through Internet technologies, and inadvertently contributing to their further marginalization" (Bassett & O'Riordan, 2002, p. 15). They had originally decided in favor of pseudonyms to protect the users who frequently shared private feelings on the website and of whom many were under the legal age of consent. Pseudonyms had also increased the readability of the article, in contrast to merely keeping names anonymous. Yet they feel that using pseudonyms for a group, which is underrepresented in the traditional media, such as the lesbian-gay-bisexual-transgender (LGBT) community, increases its marginalization and stereotypical view in society.

The need to protect young people also raises the question of how to treat sensitive issues. The author's research did not ask participants directly for potentially sensitive information, e.g., whether they were planning to arrange a meeting with someone from a chat room. However, as such issues might be discussed among the members of a message board, the researcher has to consider whether to get involved, warn the respondent of potential risks and possibly report the incident to the relevant parties (especially if an online community is not moderated by adults), or whether to retain a detached position in order to not influence the outcome of the study and preserve confidentiality.

Smyres (1999) describes her own emotional involvement while analyzing girls' body image in a teenage online community, describing her "primary desire ... to begin to type furiously and share [her] newfound self-assurance with these girls" (para. 7). However, she chose to remain unobtrusive and not to participate in the discussion.

Teen websites themselves also value confidentiality and their users' right to privacy. They recognize the importance of providing a space where users can discuss problems anonymously. On the bulletin boards of the girl's website Buzzingirls.co.uk, which I observed, the users sometimes discussed extremely distressing issues, such as self-harming or sexual abuse. In an e-mail the editor explained,

When teens feel alienated from their peer groups and their family it's often easier for them to open up to strangers on an anonymous board than confront their issues head on. Also one of the main worries of the teenager is that they are "the only ones" and they are "freaks." It helps to have scores of strangers tell you that you are not alone and they have been through the exact same thing. Plus it is an immediate, private and intimate way to discuss things you probably wouldn't talk about in public face to face.

This supports Smyres' (1999) argument, that online communities are safe spaces for young people to discuss private problems and also to be studied by researchers.

Furthermore, as I was told by the editor of Buzzingirls.co.uk, the moderator of the boards does not intervene in the discussions, i.e., does not give advice to the users or report potential safety issues to other parties: "[T]he chat moderator is [only] briefed to supply telephone numbers of relevant associations for them [the users] to contact for advice and help, e.g., Childline, etc."

Therefore, online researchers should also observe confidentiality and not infringe upon the users' right to privacy, especially if the adolescents might have believed to be in an "adult-free environment." However, if researchers are still concerned about the well being of the respondents, my observation of the boards reveals that other users post surprisingly mature and adequate replies. For example, the following reply advises a girl who was planning to meet up with an "online boyfriend" in real life:

You shouldn't have given him your phone number or address! ... Personally, I don't think you should meet him as he hasn't sent you a photo because for all you know he could be a 40-year-old perv or somewhat like that, but if you do decide to go and meet him then make sure to bring a mate. Next time you speak to him say, "I'm gonna bring a mate along" and see what he says about that. If he says "nope" straight away then you know it might not be safe to go, or go to a crowded place.

CONCLUSION

I have shown that the Internet is a valuable medium for the study of children and young people, possessing the same validity as face-to-face research. Without online methods, my data would have been very limited and would lack the richness it now possesses. After having "experimented" with different methods to investigate which one would prove most appropriate for the study of online culture (in this case, youth culture on the Internet), I argue that exactly this "hybrid approach" (Sterne, 1999), combining both quantitative and qualitative methods and investigating a range of different virtual field sites, has produced the most valuable range of data.

Although the disadvantages of online over face-to-face methods quickly become apparent, e.g., in the case of e-mail interviews, receiving less detailed data and fewer opportunities to ask probing questions, the advantages of access can compensate for it. Otherwise, I could not have interviewed a number of teen website producers and would not have been able to contact the young home page authors. By choosing a virtual site for observation (i.e., the teen bulletin boards), I was able to gather data that I would not have been able to access in real life, e.g., in the youth club, where the teenagers felt uncomfortable using the Internet in my immediate presence.

Previously "private" areas of youth culture are now discussed publicly in chat rooms or on bulletin boards and are easily accessible to the researcher. The Internet also makes it possible to apply unobtrusive methods to investigate sensitive issues, as was demonstrated in this study, i.e., to gain an insight into the use of online pornography with data obtained from Web server logs.

As more and more researchers become aware of the ease of access to children and young people through online environments and the advantages of virtual methods, it is likely that more child and youth research will be conducted over the Internet. Herein also lies the danger of this new research environment, since the relative novelty of the medium and a lack of guidelines for online studies could result in researchers acting with less consideration, and even behaving unethically, towards their study subjects.

Not all ethical considerations of the real-life research environment can be applied online. Institutional gatekeepers, usually present in offline research, cannot protect children as effectively on the Internet. Obtaining parental consent, which is seen as a precondition for ethical research with children offline, proves problematic online for pragmatic reasons. Thus, informing participants about the implications of the study should be regarded as vital by youth researchers. However, it has to be kept in mind that one cannot always be certain that children and young people understand these implications fully, and it is difficult to ensure this over the Internet. The identities of participants should, therefore, always be protected by rendering quotes anonymous or by using pseudonyms, especially when the research touches upon sensitive issues. This should also be observed in studies with adult subjects. However, exceptions can be made if the research involves politically or socially marginal groups whose voices need to be heard (see Bassett & O'Riordan, 2002).

Even when investigating adult online communities, the researcher might choose not to obtain consent from the users, keeping his/her presence covert in order not to influence user behavior. Lurking, as this practice is called, raises issues of unequal power relationships between researcher and researched, as the latter have no choice on whether to take part in the study or not. When participants are aware of being studied, however, they are in a stronger position online and can have a say in how the data is used by the researcher, i.e., whether it should be treated as public material and can be quoted directly, or whether it is seen as private dialogue and requires the researcher to seek permission from the author before being quoted.

It has been stressed that it is important to observe the confidentiality of information supplied by respondents, both online and offline. However, researchers might feel obliged to break these promises, if they perceive the young respondent's safety to be at risk. However, as I have shown, teen online communities are regarded by both researchers (e.g., Smyres, 1999) and practitioners as safe spaces where young people can talk about their problems anonymously, which they might be too embarrassed to do in a face-to-face discussion. Therefore, online researchers should also observe confidentiality and not interfere with the users' need for privacy.

Online environments have also been shown to be safe spaces to study children and young people, despite the public perception that young users are more vulnerable in an online environment. While special precautions still have to be taken, one should neither let moral considerations, aimed at protecting young participants, paralyze the research nor should ethically difficult questions be avoided. Moral concerns have to be weighed against pragmatic issues.

While Internet researchers have started establishing ethical guidelines for online studies involving adult subjects (e.g., Ess & Association of Internet Researchers, 2002; Frankel & Siang, 1999), it is difficult to accomplish this for research with children and young people at this stage. Instead of setting up a list of ethical principles, which might be too rigid for one piece of research and too lax for another, more sample studies using virtual methods and including young Internet users are needed. Researchers should be encouraged to conduct more research in this area, as most virtual studies deal with adult subjects. They should, furthermore, be urged to write about their consideration of the ethical issues and problems, as these undoubtedly play a part when setting up a study, but are rarely elaborated upon with sufficient detail in publications.

Moreover, in accordance with Frankel and Siang (1999), I argue for the creation of a forum or resource network so that researchers new to virtual methods will be made aware of existing studies and ethical considerations (in general and for young subjects or other groups in need of special protection, in particular) before starting their research in this relatively new field of academic enquiry (see Sharf, 1999). I also argue for the encouragement of a public debate about the benefits and potential dangers of online research so that potential participants, parents, legal guardians and "gatekeepers" (i.e., website owners, editors, moderators) are not discouraged from participating in online studies because of bad research practice.

ACKNOWLEDGMENTS

The author would like to thank John Cawood, Seamus Simpson and Matthew Reeves for their comments on an earlier version of this chapter.

REFERENCES

Abbott, C. (1998). Making connections: Young people and the Internet. In J. Sefton-Green (Ed.), *Digital Diversions: Youth Culture in the Age of Multimedia* (pp. 84-105). London: UCL Press.

Alderson, P. (1995). *Listening to Children: Children, Ethics and Social Research.* London: Barnardos.

Alderson, P. & Goodey, C. (1996). Research with disabled children: How useful is child-centred ethics? *Children & Society, 10,* 106-116.

Allbon, E. & Williams, P. (2002). Nasties in the Net: Children and censorship on the Web [electronic version]. *New Library World, 103,* 30-38.

Bassett, E. & O'Riordan, K. (2002, June). Mediated identities and the ethics of Internet research: Contesting the human subjects research model. Paper presented at *"Crossroads in Cultural Studies": Fourth International Conference of the Association for Cultural Studies, Tampere, Finland.* Also available in *Journal of Ethics and Information Technology,* 4(3), pp. 233-247.

Baym, N. (1995). The emergence of community in computer-mediated communication. In S. Jones (Ed.), *CyberSociety: Computer-Mediated Communication and Community* (pp. 138-163). London: Sage.

Berger, A. (1998). *Media Research Techniques.* London: Sage.

Bober, M. (2001, December). *Can the Internet replace the mall? How E-commerce affects the shopping experience for young people.* Paper presented at "Consumption and the Post-Industrial City": First conference in the series "The European City in Transition," Weimar, Germany.

Bober, M. (2002, June). *Boys and girls on the Net: The role of gender in the on-line practices and representations of young people.* Paper presented at "Crossroads in Cultural Studies": Fourth International Conference of the Association for Cultural Studies, Tampere, Finland.

Chandler, D. (1998). *Personal home pages and the construction of identities on the Web.* Retrieved April 4, 2001 from: http://www.aber.ac.uk/media/Documents/short/webident.html.

Chandler, D. & Roberts-Young, D. (1998). *The construction of identity in the personal homepages of adolescents.* Retrieved April 4, 2001 from: http://www.aber.ac.uk/media/Documents/short/strasbourg.html.

Coomber, R. (1997). Using the Internet for survey research. *Sociological Research Online, 2*(2). Retrieved Aug. 30, 2002 from: http://www.socresonline.org.uk/2/2/2.html.

Denzin, N. (1999). Cybertalk and the method of instances. In S. Jones (Ed.), *Doing Internet Research: Critical Issues and Methods for Examining the Net* (pp. 107-126). London: Sage.

Ess, C. & Association of Internet Researchers (AoIR) (2002). *Ethical decision-making and Internet research: Recommendations from the AoIR ethics working committee*. Retrieved Nov. 19, 2002 from: http://www.aoir.org/reports/ethics.pdf.

Frankel, M. & Siang, S. (1999). *Ethical and legal aspects of human subjects research on the Internet*. Retrieved Aug. 2, 2002 from the American Association for the Advancement of Science website: http://www.aaas.org/spp/dspp/sfrl/projects/intres/report.pdf.

Gajjala, R. (1999). Cyborg diaspora and virtual imagined community: Studying SAWNET. *Research Methodology Online, 6*. Retrieved April 18, 2002 from: http://www.cyperdiva.org/erniestuff/sanov.html.

Gauntlett, D. (2000). *Web Studies: Rewriting Media Studies for the Digital Age*. London: Arnold.

Gauntlett, D. (2002a). *Media, Gender and Identity: An Introduction*. London: Routledge.

Gauntlett, D. (2002b). *More about More! The sexual language of young women's magazines*. Retrieved Feb. 8, 2002 from: http://www.theoryhead.com/gender/more.htm.

Gómez, E. (2002, June). *"El Club" BBS: An ethnographic approach*. Paper presented at "Crossroads in Cultural Studies": Fourth International Conference of the Association for Cultural Studies, Tampere, Finland.

Gray, J. (2002, June). *Exploring new audiences: Anti-fans, non-fans and new fans*. Paper presented at "Crossroads in Cultural Studies": Fourth International Conference of the Association for Cultural Studies, Tampere, Finland.

Herring, S. (Ed.) (1996). *Computer-Mediated Communication: Linguistic, Social and Cross-Cultural Perspectives*. Amsterdam: John Benjamins Publishing.

Hine, C. (2000). *Virtual Ethnography*. London: Sage.

Hood, S., Kelley, P., & Mayall, B. (1996). Children as research subjects: A risky enterprise. *Children & Society, 10,* 117-128.

Jones, R. (1994). The ethics of research in cyberspace [Electronic version]. *Internet Research: Electronic Networking Applications and Policy, 4*(3), 30-35.

Kendall, L. (1999). Recontextualizing cyberspace: Methodological considerations for online research. In S. Jones (Ed.), *Doing Internet Research: Critical Issues and Methods for Examining the Net* (pp. 57-74). London: Sage.

Kennedy, H. (2002, June). *Technobiography: Researching experiences of ICTs*. Paper presented at "Crossroads in Cultural Studies": Fourth International Conference of the Association for Cultural Studies, Tampere, Finland.

Kitchin, R. (1998). *Cyberspace: The World in the Wires*. New York: John Wiley & Sons.

Livingstone, S. (2001). Children online: Emerging uses of the Internet at home. *Journal of the IBTE (Institute of British Telecommunications Engineers), 2*(1). Retrieved Jan. 25, 2003 from: http://www.lse.ac.uk/collections/media@lse/pdf/IBTE_article.pdf.

Livingstone, S. (2002a). *Children's use of the Internet: A review of the research literature*. Retrieved Aug. 2, 2002 from: http://www.ncb.org.uk/resources/lit_review.pdf.

Livingstone, S. (2002b, March). *Challenges and dilemmas as children go on-line: Linking observational research in families to the emerging policy agenda*. Paper presented at the 3rd Annual Dean's Lecture, Annenberg School for Communication,

University of Pennsylvania, Philadelphia, PA, USA. Retrieved Jan. 25, 2003 from: http://www.lse.ac.uk/collections/media@lse/pdf/AnnenbergLecture.pdf.

Livingstone, S. & Bovill, M. (1999). *Young People, New Media: Report of the Research Project, "Children, Young People and the Changing Media Environment."* London: London School of Economics and Political Science.

Livingstone, S. & Bovill, M. (2001). *Families and the Internet: An observational study of children and young people's Internet use.* (Final Rep. to British Telecommunications plc.). Retrieved Jan. 25, 2003 from: http://www.lse.ac.uk/collections/media@lse/pdf/btreport_familiesinternet.pdf.

Mann, C. & Stewart, F. (2000). *Internet Communication and Qualitative Research: A Handbook for Researching Online.* London: Sage.

Mauthner, M. (1997). Methodological aspects of collecting data from children: Lessons from three research projects. *Children & Society, 11,* 16-28.

McLaughlin, M., Osborne, K, &, Smith, C. (1995). Standards of conduct in Usenet. In S. Jones (Ed.), *CyberSociety: Computer-Mediated Communication and Community* (pp. 138-163). London: Sage.

McLaughlin, M., Goldberg, S., Ellison, N., & Lucas, J. (1999). Measuring Internet audiences: Patrons of an on-line art museum. In S. Jones (Ed.), *Doing Internet Research: Critical Issues and Methods for Examining the Net* (pp. 163-178). London: Sage.

McRobbie, A. (1991). *Feminism and Youth Culture: From Jackie to Just Seventeen.* London: MacMillan.

McRobbie, A. (1997). More! New sexualities in girls' and women's magazines. In A. McRobbie (Ed.), *Back to Reality? Social Experience and Cultural Studies* (pp. 190-209). Manchester: Manchester University Press.

Morrow, V. & Richards, M. (1996). The ethics of social research with children: An overview. *Children & Society, 10,* 90-105.

Oksman, V. (2002). "So I got it into my head that I should set up my own stable...": Creating virtual stables on the Internet as girls' own computer culture. In M. Consalvo & S. Paasonen (Eds.), *Women and Everyday Uses of the Internet* (pp. 191-210). New York: Peter Lang.

Paccagnella, L. (1997). Getting the seats of your pants dirty: Strategies for ethnographic research on virtual communities. *Journal of Computer Mediated Communication, 3*(1). Retrieved Aug. 2, 2002 from: http://www.ascusc.org/jcmc/vol3/issue1/paccagnella.html.

Punch, S. (2002). Interviewing strategies with young people: The "secret box," stimulus material and task-based activities [electronic version]. *Children and Society, 16,* 45-56.

Rheingold, H. (1994). *The Virtual Community: Finding Connection in a Computerized World.* London: Secker and Warburg.

Sandvig, C. (2001). Unexpected outcomes in digital divide policy: What children really do in the public library. In B. Compaine & S. Green Stein (Eds.), *Community Policy in Transition: The Internet & Beyond* (pp. 265-293). Cambridge, MA: MIT Press.

Saunders Thomas, D. (1997). Cyberspace pornography: Problems with enforcement [electronic version]. *Internet Research: Electronic Networking Applications and Policy, 7*(3), 201-207.

Sefton-Green, J. & Buckingham, D. (1998). Digital visions: Children's "creative" uses of new technologies. In J. Sefton-Green (Ed.), *Digital Diversions: Youth Culture in the Age of Multimedia* (pp. 62-83). London: UCL Press.

Sharf, B. (1999). Beyond Netiquette: The ethics of doing naturalistic discourse research on the Internet. In S. Jones (Ed.), *Doing Internet Research: Critical Issues and Methods for Examining the Net* (pp. 243-256). London: Sage.

Smyres, K. (1999). Virtual corporeality: Adolescent girls and their bodies in cyberspace. *Research Methodology Online, 6.* Retrieved April 18, 2002 from: http://www.socio.demon.co.uk/magazine/6/smyres.html.

Snell, N. (1999). *SAMS Teach Yourself to Create Web Pages in 24 Hours* (2nd ed.). Indianapolis, IN: Sams.

Sterne, J. (1999). Thinking the Internet: Cultural studies versus the millennium. In S. Jones (Ed.), *Doing Internet Research: Critical Issues and Methods for Examining the Net* (pp. 257-287). London: Sage.

Tapscott, D. (1998). *Growing Up Digital: The Rise of the Net Generation.* New York: McGraw-Hill.

Taylor, T. (1999). Life in virtual worlds: Plural existence, multimodalities, and other online research challenges. *American Behavioral Scientist, 43*(3), 436-449.

Tobin, J. (1998). An American Otaku (or, a boy's virtual life on the Net). In J. Sefton-Green (Ed.), *Digital Diversions: Youth Culture in the Age of Multimedia* (pp. 106-127). London: UCL Press.

Turkle, S. (1995). *Life on the Screen: Identity in the Age of the Internet.* New York: Simon & Schuster.

Ward, K. (1999). The cyber-ethnographic (re)construction of two feminist online communities. *Sociological Research Online, 4*(1). Retrieved Aug. 2, 2002 from: http://www.socresonline.org.uk/socresonline/4/1/ward.html.

Wilkins, H. (1991). Computer talk: Long-distance conversations by computer. *Written Communication, 8*(1), 56-78.

Williams, P. (1999). The net generation: The experiences, attitudes and behaviour of children using the Internet for their own purposes [electronic version]. *Aslib Proceedings, 51*(9), 315-322.

Witmer, D., Colman, R., & Lee Katzman, S. (1999). From paper-and-pencil to screen-and-keyboard: Toward a methodology for survey research on the Internet. In S. Jones (Ed.), *Doing Internet Research: Critical Issues and Methods for Examining the Net* (pp. 145-161). London: Sage.

Yun, G. & Trumbo, C. (2000). Comparative response to a survey executed by post, e-mail, & Web form. *Journal of Computer Mediated Communication, 6*(1). Retrieved Aug. 2, 2002 from: http://www.ascusc.org/jcmc/vol6/issue1/yun.html.

ENDNOTES

[1] In the present study young people are defined as being of secondary school age, i.e., 11 to 19 years old. Other studies quoted here, especially in the section on "Ethical considerations in offline child research," include younger children as well or refer to all persons under the age of 18 as "children." In such cases, the terminology of the author(s) in question will be adopted.

2   For a detailed overview, see Livingstone (2002a).

3   For example, see National Opinion Poll (NOP) at http://www.nop.co.uk

4   http://www.statistics.gov.uk

5   I also conducted a discourse analysis of the contents on websites and home pages. This will not be discussed here in favor of focussing on interactive methods, involving users and producers (for more information on discourse analysis of Web pages, see Hine, 2000).

6   Only three websites agreed to a face-to-face interview. Seven further sites answered questions by e-mail. A discussion of some of the findings can be found in Bober (2002).

7   For example, see Yahoo http://dir.yahoo.com/Society_and_Culture/People/ Personal_Home_ Pages, accessed Sept. 29, 2002.

8   A discussion of some of the findings is also available in Bober (2002).

9   http://addurl.altavista.com/addurl/new, accessed Jan. 25, 2003.

10   http://uk.docs.yahoo.com/ukie/express/splash.html, accessed August 29, 2002.

11   Pseudonyms are used for all four teen websites mentioned in this chapter (see also the sections on "Online data – private or public?" and "Protecting young people and issues of confidentiality"). At the time of writing, no websites with the names chosen as pseudonyms existed. It is not impossible, though, that websites with these particular names might be launched in the future. However, these sites do not bear any relation to the ones discussed in this chapter.

12   The spelling and punctuation in most of the bulletin board posts in this chapter was edited to increase readability.

13   Quotes from four of these are included in this chapter.

14   Online communities can, for example, be found on the Web (bulletin boards, message boards or chat rooms), as part of Usenet (newsgroups or discussion groups) and Virtual Reality (MUDs, i.e., Multi-User Domains or Dungeons) or can be e-mail based (mailing lists).

15   Used in online dialogue, the abbreviation "lol" stands for "laughs out loud" or "lots of laughs."

16   For a more detailed discussion on how meanings surrounding the Internet are constructed, see, e.g., Hine (2000).

17   Cosmetics' retailer

18   Apart from adult material, the banned categories included "glamour and intimate apparel," dating services, shopping, gambling and games, chat (and e-mail at certain times of the day), hacking, alcohol, drugs, weapons, violence, as well as hate speech.

19   For a more extensive discussion on children and online pornography from a British perspective, see Allbon & Williams (2002), or Saunders Thomas (1997) for a U.S. perspective.

APPENDIX

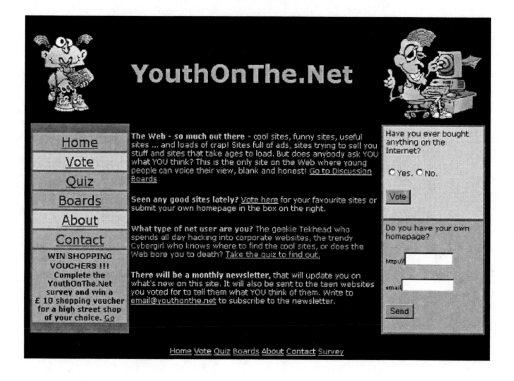

Section V

A Call to Researchers

Chapter XVII

International Digital Studies: A Research Approach for Examining International Online Interactions

Kirk St.Amant
James Madison University, USA

ABSTRACT

The constant diffusion of online communication technology increasingly allows individuals from different cultural backgrounds to communicate with each other directly and quickly. In its removal of more traditional communication obstacles, such as distance and time, these technologies may amplify cultural rhetorical differences. This situation might be particularly problematic as factors of both culture and media could confound the overall discourse situation. This chapter overviews a research approach—international digital studies—that offers a new method for exploring international online interactions (IOIs). The chapter also presents an argument for why it is crucial to begin studies of IOIs at this particular point in history.

INTRODUCTION

The Internet and the World Wide Web are making it easier to overcome the barrier of distance and to interact directly with persons located in different countries. Although this barrier is removed, individuals must remember that, when online, they could be interacting with persons from different cultures. This potential oversight could cause problems as cultures can have different expectations of how information should be presented. Such rhetorical assumptions, in turn, could result in confusion, miscommunication or accidental offense in international online interactions (IOIs).

Further complicating this situation is the fact that more businesses are using online communication technologies to develop international production processes. These new processes, however, rely on quick and effective cross-cultural communication via an online medium. Researchers interested in online communication trends, therefore, need to begin examining potential areas of conflict related to international cyberspace now, in order to anticipate potential online cross-cultural misunderstandings before they lead to unforeseen mistakes. Such research, however, can be cumbersome and complex as individuals try to determine what cultural factors could affect discourse via online media. Thus, research involving culture and online communication requires a new approach that can help isolate topics or variables that can then become the focus of further examination.

This chapter addresses this need by proposing a new research approach—the international digital studies approach—that focuses on examining how cultures interact via online media. The key to the international digital studies approach involves researching and understanding what factors individuals from different cultures associate with a credible presentation, an idea best embodied by the rhetorical concept of ethos. To help the reader understand the importance of this ethos-based approach, the chapter begins with an overview of how factors of both technology and culture can affect the credibility of the communication process. The chapter then explains how the international digital studies approach offers a research method that addresses credibility/ethos expectations in relation to both culture and online communication.[1]

CREDIBILITY, COMMUNICATION AND ETHOS CONDITIONS

Ethos, often defined as credibility, can be one of the most important aspects of a discourse situation. This credibility generally occurs at two levels: attention and acceptance. At the attention level, an audience must initially consider that presentation as credible—or worth listening to (it must gain the audience's attention), if that presentation is to be effective. At the acceptance level, presenters must prove that their ideas are credible—or worth considering, accepting or acting upon—once they have an audience's attention. If credibility is missing from either level of discourse, the presenter will be unable to achieve his or her overall objective for presenting information (e.g., to get the audience to consider, accept or do something they might not otherwise have done).

Because of these factors, ethos is perhaps the most important of the rhetorical concepts because it is only through ethos that other presentation factors become effective. If an audience does not find a presentation credible—or worth listening to/

reading—then they may stop listening or reading before other rhetorical devices, such as emotion (pathos) or logic (logos), are implemented. Additionally, the credibility of a presenter often affects how an audience perceives and interprets other rhetorical factors within a presentation. That is, ethos predisposes a given audience to view a presenter and a presentation in a positive or a negative way. This initial predisposition affects how positively or negatively audiences view other rhetorical aspects in a presentation (Johnson, 1984).[2] It is for this reason that the research approach presented in this chapter focuses on ethos and not on the other rhetorical factors as ethos greatly determines how effective those other rhetorical factors can be.

Credibility/ethos, however, is not a random process. Rather, audiences often look for certain factors—which I call ethos conditions—as indicating a credible presentation. The idea is that ethos conditions serve as a kind of checklist audiences use when establishing the credibility of a presentation. That is, audiences come to a particular presentation situation (forum) thinking, "This presenter must do or say x, y and z if I am to consider him or her credible or worth listening to." If all of these expectations and condition are met—and can be "checked off"—then the presenter and his or her opinion will be considered credible. If one or more of these conditions is not met, then the presenter will not have met the conditions required for that audience to consider him or her credible.

These ethos conditions, in turn, often relate back to the forum—the setting, context or genre—in which information is presented. The idea is that individuals come to a forum (setting or genre) for a specific purpose. For example, individuals come to the forum/genre of a progress report for the purpose of learning how the activities related to a particular process are progressing. If a presenter raises subjects or topics related to the purpose of that particular forum, then that presenter will gain that audience's attention (Aristotle, 1991; Miller & Selzer, 1985; Skinner, 1996; Walzer, 2000). For example, in the forum of a progress report, topics such as "due date" or "completion date" are items that readers of progress reports expect to encounter, for they directly relate to—and thus help with—the reader's/audience's purpose for reading a progress report. Thus, readers of progress reports will pay special attention to a discussion of a due date for such a discussion provides them with needed information.

These topics, moreover, are often particularly important when used in the forum of a progress report. When used in other forums/genres that have different purposes (e.g., an instruction manual), the mention of those topics will not merit particular attention as they do not related to the purpose at hand. Thus, ethos conditions tend to be forum/context/genre dependent in terms of their rhetorical usefulness. According to this perspective, if an audience's expected ethos conditions appear in a presentation, then that audience will view that presentation as credible—or worth listening to or considering. If these ethos conditions are not present, then chances are the audience will ignore the presentation or dismiss what is being presented.

CULTURAL EXPECTATIONS AND CREDIBILITY

Rhetorical expectations are by no means fixed. Rather, the ethos conditions one uses to evaluate the credibility of a presentation can vary from culture to culture

(Campbell, 1998; Tebeaux, 1999; Driskill, 1996). Such variation, moreover, can occur at a variety of levels within a discourse situation. Weiss (1998), for example, notes that the very nature of what constitutes a credible or a rhetorically valid argument can differ widely depending on the cultural background of the audience. That is, the ethos conditions that the members of one culture use to evaluate the credibility of a presentation might differ from those used by the members of another culture. In such cases, members of culture "A" have one set of ethos conditions—say 1, 2 and 3 must be met to create credibility. Members of culture "B," however, might determine credibility according to a different set of ethos conditions—say 2, 3 and 4. Imagine then that someone from culture A presents information to someone from culture B. The presenter (culture A) does 1, 2 and 3 and is convinced that his or her presentation is effective/credible. However, to the audience (culture B), ethos conditions 2 and 3 have been met, but not condition 4. As all of audience B's ethos conditions have not been met, presenter A's presentation is considered non-credible by audience B. In such a situation, person A would perhaps become confused by audience B's reaction to the presentation (i.e., audience B would be seen as dismissing a perfectly credible presentation). Audience B, in turn, might be confused or offended by presenter A's presentation (i.e., why did presenter A not take the presentation seriously and instead create an obviously non-credible presentation).

The difference in expectations between American and Japanese business memos can put this idea of ethos condition into a cultural context. Many Americans prefer memos to contain direct explanations in which all of the related facts are stated (Hall, 1981). In such a forum (the memo), the ethos conditions that must be met are directness and the presentation of facts related to the situation mentioned in the memo (Murdick, 1999). Conversely, many Japanese often appear to omit certain central facts. In their culture, directly stating such "self-obvious" information (e.g., the reason for which a business delegation is meeting) is considered rude (Murdick, 1999). In this case, a direct presentation of facts is not an ethos condition associated with this particular forum (the memo). As a result of these different cultural expectations, many Americans often consider the Japanese presentation style shifty and unfocused ("otherwise, they would get to the point more quickly"), while many Japanese often view the more direct American presentation style as rude ("why else would they treat us like children and state all of the self-obvious facts") (Murdick, 1999; Ulijn & St.Amant, 2000; Ferris & Hedgcock, 1998). In this example, each culture could see the other as lacking credibility, due to cultural differences on what one should or should not say in order to appear credible in a given situation.[3]

Such cultural differences related to ethos conditions and what factors constitute a credible presentation have been noted at a more micro level as well. As Driskill (1996) and as Murdick (1999) both note, persons from different cultures often use different organizational structures to establish the credibility of a presentation. In American professional communication, for example, paragraphs are generally arranged in a specific logical order, where one first introduces the basics or premise of an argument, and then the following paragraphs gradually and logically build upon this original premise to prove or establish one end or goal (Lunsford & Conners, 1997; Perelman et al., 1998). Individuals from Japanese or Latin cultures, however, often begin professional documents with a paragraph or section containing polite, solicitous comments that do not seem to relate to the logical development of the greater written presentation (Driskill,

1996). A formal Japanese business memo, for example, might begin with a statement such as "I am pleased to hear of the success of the Marui Trading Company in its various enterprises" (Murdick, 1999, p. 75). Without such an introduction, a Japanese reader might perceive these documents as lacking respect or unconcerned with building long-term relationships—two key cultural concepts in Japan (Murdick, 1999; Hofstede, 1997). Conversely, Japanese documents often do not include an introductory summary of the information presented in a given professional document (a common practice in American professional and scholarly journals). Rather, as Driskill (1996) puts it, the Japanese, "prefer a presentation of the data or evidence before the conclusion or recommendation, with no introductory summary" (p. 28). Driskill explains that many Japanese writers tend to omit such summaries, because they might encourage direct, logical debate—something the Japanese tend to avoid. Thus, a document that includes a summary at the beginning might create discomfort among or even offend Japanese readers who would consider such directness as ignorant or rude (Driskill, 1996).

These cultural expectations related to credibility can occur at a more micro level as well. As Ulijn and Strother (1995) note, different cultures can have different expectations of sentence length. Southern Europeans, for example, appear to associate longer sentences with credible presentations, while many Americans tend to view shorter and more direct sentences as indicating a more credible writing style. Such differences can cause cross-cultural communication problems involving the credibility of a presentation: "a Southern-European client, who might believe that the product is not a serious one because the sentences in the instructions telling how to use the product are too short" (Ulijn & Strother, 1995, p. 203). In other cases, Li and Koole (1998) and Li (1999) examined how cultural associations related to particular words can cause intercultural communication problems. In both cases, different cultural assumptions related to the word "support," caused credibility problems for Chinese and Dutch negotiators (Li & Koole, 1998; Li, 1999).

These cultural differences in credibility expectations, moreover, can also occur between individuals from the same linguistic background. Connor (1990) and Connor and Lauer (1988), for example, note certain rhetorical differences among the writing styles of native English speaking students from the U.S., the U.K. and New Zealand. American students, for instance, tended to use fewer appeals to data, tended to use passive voice less often and tended to use more formal syntactic constructions than their British or their New Zealander counterparts did (Connor, 1990; Connor & Lauer, 1988). Thus, it appears as if it is cultural rhetorical factors, and not language expectations, that have a greater effect on what audiences view as credible.

IOIs AND ONLINE MEDIA

While the rapid development of online communication has brought with it increased exposure to other cultures, relatively little has been written on how cultural expectations are affecting international online interactions, or what I call IOIs. At this point, it is important to draw a distinction between what I call IOIs as opposed to other online media. An IOI involves direct online contact between individuals from different cultures. This interaction can be immediate/synchronous—such as an online chat—or it can be time delayed/asynchronous—such as an e-mail. The key factor, however, is that individuals are interacting directly with one another in a two-way/back and forth/give and take communication relationship. Thus, IOI presentations are designed to be directly presented to a specific individual (e.g., an e-mail message) or a relatively limited group of individuals (e.g., an online chat group), rather than to a large, unknown and unspecified audience (e.g., a Web page).

While a good deal of literature has been written on international Web page design[4], that work focuses on designing one-way online displays for large cultural audiences, rather than focusing on conversations/discussions (two-way presentations of information), covering a limited group of interactors. In the limited research done on such IOI situations, however, there is evidence indicating that cultural rhetorical differences can cause miscommunication or confusion.[5] Thus, as worldwide online access increases, so does the potential for cross-cultural miscommunication related to credibility expectations. For this reason, it is imperative that individuals who study online communication patterns begin examining the effects cultural expectations can have on cyberspace communication now, as much of the world is just starting to get online. The reason for such exigency is that prospective problems areas related to IOIs can be identified and potential miscommunications can be avoided before such factors cause actual problems.

CULTURES, PROFESSIONAL TRAINING AND RHETORICAL EXPECTATIONS

At this point, it is important to note that one's cultural rhetorical expectations are not innate. Rather, as an individual grows up in a given culture, he or she learns—either through direct instruction or indirect observation—how to present and to evaluate information according to that culture's norms (Varner & Beamer, 1995). Thus, while culture shapes one's rhetorical expectations, these expectations are not absolute. Rather, one can learn to communicate with members of other cultures according to the rhetorical expectations of those cultures (Panetta, 2001; Campbell, 1998). Thus, problems related to culture and rhetoric could perhaps be avoided if individuals can find "common rhetorical ground." That is, can individuals from two different cultures, but who work for the same company, learn the same corporate cultural expectations for presenting information?

As Winsor (1996) points out, individuals are also acculturated or socialized into the communication norms of their related professions; "These professional writing contexts both created the demands that their [interns'] writing had to meet and provided support that helped them to do so in the form of experienced writers and established texts" (p. 21). In terms of ethos conditions, one's company/industry can tell that person what the forums/genres of that company/industry are and what ethos conditions to look for when assessing the credibility of the information presented in a given genre. As Miller and Selzer (1985) have noted, the engineers working for a particular industry seem to look for the same kinds of topics and headings when reading engineering reports. Thus, in telling employees what factors to look for when assessing the credibility of a document, one's corporate training could affect the ethos conditions he or she uses to assess the credibility of professional/job-related presentation. The question then becomes will individuals, who are from different cultures but who have similar jobs within the same corporate organization, have different rhetorical expectations?

To examine this relationship between culture and profession, Hofstede (1997) conducted a massive research project in which thousands of IBM employees in several different countries responded to a series of standardized questions. His findings reveal that, despite professional similarities, there is a distinct cultural character that accounts for why persons from particular cultures respond differently to similar situations (Hofstede, 1997). Thus, even in professional interactions, different cultural expectations of ethos conditions can affect cross-cultural discourse. For this reason, an ethos-based approach to IOIs would appear to be valid even when examining cross-cultural interactions among individuals working for the same company or the same industry. New production methods that focus on using online media to connect international co-workers could therefore be affected by different cultural communication expectations.

Other individuals may note that, in learning another language, one also learns the rhetorical expectations associated with the culture that speaks that language. Thus, if all of the individuals involved in an IOI use the same language for interacting, one might assume that cultural ethos differences should no longer be problematic. Ulijn's (1996) research in translation studies, however, suggests that individual appear to evaluate the effectiveness/credibility of materials according to the rhetorical norms of their native culture, apparently even when evaluating presentations done in another language. Some English as a Second Language (ESL) research, moreover, has noted similar trends revealing that, "we transfer our writing knowledge and skills [i.e., our rhetorical preferences] to a second language" (Perez, 1998, p. 59). Thus, the rhetorical expectations of one's native culture can still affect how one perceives information and interacts with others. An ethos-based approach to studying IOIs would therefore seem valid regardless of the professional or the linguistic similarities of the culturally different individuals participating in such an exchange.

DIMENSIONS AND
CROSS-CULTURAL COMMUNICATION

Comparing ethos conditions across cultures, unfortunately, can be a very complex process. The problem is that it can be difficult to isolate those particular factors (ethos conditions) that members of a culture associate with credible or acceptable presentations in all situations. For these reasons, effective cross-cultural communication research often involves a comparison of cultural communication behavior according to similar factors, conditions or variables that affect a wide range of communication behavior within a culture. These overarching factors with wide-ranging effects are often called dimensions. In the case of IOIs, then, it is important to determine:

- what dimensional factors could affect such exchanges and
- if the nature of online media alters the effects of such dimensions or contributes to the creation of new medium-specific dimensions.

The key to dimensions is that they can be used to rank how individuals from different cultures communicate in relation to the same concept in different situations. The idea is to prevent individualistic cultural comparisons of specific situations (e.g., culture A this, but culture B does this and culture C does this) by comparing all cultural groups in terms of how they respond to overarching concepts that affect communication practices in many or most situations. The concept of rank or status, for example, affects most kinds of communication situations from professional interactions (e.g., supervisor and employee) to familial interactions (e.g., parents and children). Thus, if one can determine how different cultural groups view status in terms of how important or unimportant it is as an overall concept, one can anticipate how the concept of status will affect the way in which various cultural groups behave in many different situations.

By evaluating how different cultures respond to these similar concepts, researchers can determine different degrees of responses to similar factors. For example, Edward T. Hall, one of the first persons to use dimensions in cross-cultural communication, examined how the context, or the setting in which information is presented, affects cultural communication expectations. Hall's focus was to determine how cultural perspectives on the setting in which information is presented affects what should and should not be directly stated in a given situation. Through observation, Hall determined that certain cultures (high-context) gained most of the meaning related to a presentation from the setting in which information was presented (Hall, 1981, 1983). Conversely, other cultures (low-context) could not rely on the setting to convey a great deal of meaning in a given situation.

Hall then compared and ranked various cultural groups according to how they differed on the dimension of context (Hall & Beoynd, 1981; Hall & Dance, 1983). At one end of this dimensional ranking system, the low-context Swiss Germans appeared to state most key information explicitly, instead of relying on the setting to convey implicit information about the nature of the exchange. At the other end of this scale, the high-context Japanese appeared to allow the setting in which one presented to convey the majority of the information related to the overall situation. In between these two end points were a series of other cultures that tended to lean slightly more one way or the other in terms of how much information should or should not be conveyed directly based on contextual assumptions. Individuals from Middle Eastern cultures, for example, appear to present relatively less information directly than Anglo North Americans do. (See Figure 1 for a relative cultural ranking based on Hall's dimension of context.)

Figure 1: A Limited Relative Ranking of Culture and Communication Styles Based on Hall's Dimension of Context*

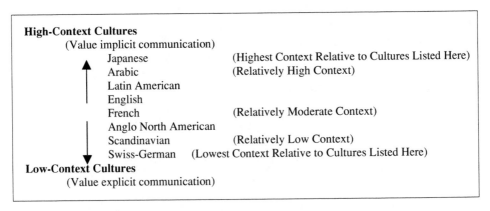

*Based on Hoft, 1995, p. 80

A dimensional approach thus allows researchers to anticipate how setting could affect the different ways in which members of different cultures presented information.[6] Such a relativistic approach can prove helpful in determining how various cultures might differ in their communication behaviors according to the same dimensional factors. For this reason, a dimensional approach can be a beneficial method for examining how cultures differ according to the same online communication situation or aspect. The question then becomes how might online media affect the communication expectations and practices of different cultural groups.

CREDIBILITY AND
ONLINE COMMUNICATION

While the aforementioned dimensions have proven beneficial in understanding cross-cultural interactions, they were developed in response to traditional, printed or spoken communication situations. Thus, the effects culture can have on two-way online interactions have remained relatively unexplored, especially in relation to dimensions. The assumption, perhaps, is that cultural communication patterns associated with traditional media can also apply to online interactions. Past research in online communication, however, has revealed that new kinds of rhetorical situations and new sets of ethos conditions appear to be emerging in online forums. Several of these new situations and conditions, in turn, result from limitations, or new kinds of conditions, related to communicating via cyber media.

As many studies in direct online discourse (where parties use media such as e-mail or chats to interact directly with one another) have noted, the notion of identity can change as a result of interaction through computer networks. As both Sproull and Kiesler (1986) and Hiltz and Turoff (1993) point out, in many cases, direct two-way communication via such networks generally reduces human interaction to typing words. As a result, individuals receiving online messages do not obtain any nonverbal cues about the sender's identity in terms of physical appearance—that is race, gender and status, both economic and social—so the sender seems faceless and anonymous (Sproull & Kiesler, 1986; Hiltz & Turoff, 1993; Herring, 1996; Kiesler et al., 1984).

Interestingly, in the online environment, notions of personality and identity, especially those related to authority and credibility—or ethos —often take on new forms. As Fernback (1999) notes, in online exchanges, the marks of status/credibility, which are marks that draw others to listen to you, are not, "brawn, money, or political clout," but rather are, "wit, and tenacity, and intelligence" (p. 213). Thus, one can use wit, tenacity and displays of intelligence in an online exchange for the purpose of appearing more authoritative or more credible than actual authority figures participating in the same exchange.[7] Displays of wit, tenacity or intelligence therefore become ethos conditions in online forums.

Fernback's (1999) notion that humor and wit contribute to a person's ethos in online discourse situations has been noted by researchers such as Baym (1997) in her study of a soap opera discussion list, Warnick (1998) in her discussion of online interactions and Zappen et al. (1997) in their studies of student interaction online. As all of these researchers note, individuals who use witty responses tend to be viewed more highly, or more credibly, than those participants who are more passive. Additionally, an individual's repeated use of quick and witty responses allows him or her to build up an online sense of presence, or ethos. As these individuals establish their online ethos, their opinions and viewpoints tend to be listened to more often and accepted more readily than are those participants who post less often or with less wit and verbal zeal.

In these cases, a particular set of ethos conditions—displays of wit, tenacity and intelligence—arise as a result of the particular nature of online communication media. Because these ethos conditions are so closely linked to creating credibility in cyberspace discourse, I choose to call these specific markers of online credibility digital ethos conditions. That is, one or more of these ethos conditions must be present in an online exchange for the audience participating in the exchange to consider presentations as credible. (As noted earlier, it is like a checklist—if the expected conditions are present, then the related presentation is identified as credible.) Such naming is important, for it can help researchers who study IOIs to focus on how online communication conditions affect cultural perceptions of what constitutes a credible online presentation. Moreover, such a distinction allows researchers to determine if certain cross-cultural online communication patterns result from the application of traditional cultural communication factors to a new situation, or if it is the new nature of the online environment that is giving rise to certain communication behaviors.

It now becomes the task of researchers to determine what factors—traditional rhetorical expectations or emerging digital ethos conditions—affect cross-cultural interactions in IOIs. Because these IOIs are affected by factors of both culture and technology, scholars in online communication will need to find a research method that can account for communication patterns related to both areas. The next section of this chapter proposes such a new research method that combines ideas from both online communication and intercultural communication. The purpose of such a method is to identify and to test how cultural ethos conditions relate to the new communication situations resulting from online media.

INTERNATIONAL DIGITAL STUDIES: A NEW RESEARCH AGENDA

To begin such an evaluation process, online communication researchers need to adopt a research agenda that examines how cultural rhetorical expectations affect IOIs. I call this approach international digital studies, as it focuses on how aspects of digital media affect international/cross-cultural communication practices. The goal of this evaluative research would be to determine how various cultural groups differ in their responses to a particular digital ethos condition. As such a comparative analysis examines how cultural responses to the same condition could affect communication behavior, each condition examined becomes an online communication variable, or a digital baseline, against which cultures will be compared. That is, these digital ethos conditions represent an overall concept that can affect a wide range of communication behaviors, depending on the value different cultural groups associate with that concept. Behavior in response to these dimensions can then be ranked (see previous example of Hall's context ranking), and this ranking can help researchers anticipate and understand how cultural factors could affect online communication situations. The new research objectives of the Internet researcher, therefore, become a two-fold process designed to explore the nature of these emerging digital dimensions in IOIs.

- The first objective of this new course of research is to identify and to isolate actual digital ethos conditions (presentation factors that actually seem to contribute to a presenter's credibility in online exchanges). Once isolated, these digital ethos conditions can become the variables/dimensions that researchers use to evaluate the ways in which different cultures communicate online.
- The second objective would be to determine if a potential variable/digital ethos condition is also an actual dimension—or a factor that varies in relation to cultural rhetorical expectations. That is, researchers need to find evidence indicating that cultures would differ on and would differ observably in how they responded to a particular digital ethos condition.

The pursuit of these two objectives would help researchers find key variables that could then be tested or examined to determine if a particular digital ethos condition actually has an effect on how different cultural groups interact in online exchanges. Should a particular variable affect how different cultures communicate in IOIs, then that variable would be considered a dimension that researchers could use to analyze, rank and anticipate the online communication behaviors of different cultural groups in relation to that dimension.

The key to this new line of Internet research thus becomes identifying potential variables that can serve as a foundation for a research project that examines whether certain digital ethos conditions are, in fact, digital dimensions—or aspects of online communication that vary according to cultural discourse expectations. To begin such a project, researchers must identify potentially conflicting ethos conditions in both Internet studies research and in intercultural communication research. For this reason, a two-part literature review would be the first major research step.

Performing a Dual-Field Literature Review

Achieving the objectives of the international digital studies process consists of a dual-field, or two-part, literature review designed to identify digital ethos conditions and evaluate their likelihood of serving as digital dimensions. The idea is to determine how factors of medium and of culture might create conflicting expectations of ethos conditions that could affect discourse in IOIs. Thus, researchers must begin by identifying these conditions through surveying the literature of both fields: Internet studies and intercultural communication. The first step in this literature review process would be to survey the literature generated by the field of Internet studies in order to identify digital ethos conditions in online discourse situations that involve direct, two-way interactions. These digital ethos conditions would be presentation styles/factors that individuals used to establish and assess the credibility or presentations in direct, two-way online exchanges. The focus of this review would be that reported behavior must result from conditions arising from online media and not simply be the transfer of ethos conditions from more traditional media to an online setting. Name dropping, for example, can be used to create credibility in both print and online media (where it indicates the user's intelligence). The use of emoticons (keystrokes used to produce a facial expression, such as :-) for a smiling face) to create credibility, however, is more restricted to online communication.

The reason for such a medium-based focus is to determine how conditions and situations created by the online environment are affecting cultural communication patterns. Again, the overall purpose of this new line of research is to identify and test new variables/dimensions resulting from a shift to online media, not confirm the use of previously existing ones found in other media. Thus, this first (Internet studies) literature review should focus on identifying ethos conditions resulting from the new discourse situation created by cyberspace.

Once this initial online ethos literature review has been completed and a potential digital ethos condition/variable has been identified, the researcher must next determine if that variable could cause confusion or conflict when two different cultural groups communicate via online media. The goal, then, becomes determining if this digital ethos condition is a point of contention. By point of contention, I mean situations where communication patterns documented in the literature of one field (Internet studies) seem to conflict with conventional communication expectations documented in the literature of another field (intercultural communication). That is, do findings in the intercultural communication research indicate that this digital ethos condition could cause problems—or contentions—because different cultural groups have different perspectives on that variable? For example, much of the Internet studies literature notes that online identity (who a presenter is) is plastic and easy to manipulate. Conversely, research in intercultural communication reveals that, for some cultures, a stable and discernable identity is essential to effective communication. Contentions, therefore, could result when individuals from cultures where a stable identity is important use online media to interact with individuals from cultures where a stable identity is not as important. In such cases, the members of one cultural group might wonder why the members of another cultural group are reacting in an "unexpected" way.

For this reason, the second part of the international digital studies process involves a second literature review—one of the intercultural communication research. In this second literature review, the researcher would look specifically for indications that digital ethos conditions identified in the initial (Internet studies) literature review relate to findings reported in the intercultural communication literature. If little or no mention—or no significant findings—on this variable are reported in the intercultural communication research, or if this variable appears to cause no real conflict in cross-cultural exchanges, then chances are that variable would be a weak point of contention. For example, if different cultural groups did not use or reacted differently to uses of wit in an IOI, then uses of wit would be a weak point of contention, for there is little evidence of different cultural expectations related to this digital ethos condition. If, however, the intercultural literature review reports that the ethos condition noted in the Internet studies literature can cause problems in cross-cultural interactions, then that factor is a strong point of contention that could affect cross-cultural interactions in cyberspace.

Researchers must then determine if a strong point of contention is a digital dimension. That is, simply because the two-part literature review indicates that a particular ethos condition could be a point of contention:

- Does that ethos condition actually affect cross-cultural discourse in IOIs?
- Do reactions to the uses of that ethos condition seem to vary depending on the cultural; groups interacting in the IOI? (e.g., Do some groups use it more than others? Are some groups more confused by its use than others?)

- Can we develop a relative ranking system that allows us to compare how specific cultural groups vary in relation to uses of and responses to this particular ethos condition?

Researchers then need to use these strong points of contention as the foundation for research projects or experiments designed to test if a strong point of contention is a digital dimension that has different effects on different cultural groups involved in IOIs. To put this international digital studies approach into context, the next section of this chapter presents an application of the international digital studies approach to the ethos condition/topic of identity. Through such a demonstration, the reader can better understand how to apply the international digital studies approach and will discover that identity is a strong point of contention worthy of further examination.

Identity: A Sample Strong Point of Contention

In the case of identity, a review of the Internet studies literature reveals that the concept of identity is a factor that affects discourse in online forums. Many researchers in online communication note that, in cyberspace exchanges, identity is not fixed or stable. Rather, it can easily change as a result of interaction through computer networks. As both Sproull and Kiesler (1986) and Hiltz and Turoff (1993) point out, communication via such networks often reduces human interaction to typed words. As a result, individuals receiving such communication receive few nonverbal cues about the sender's identity in terms of physical appearance—that is race, gender, and status, both economic and social. Thus, the sender's true identity is limited to what recipients can divine from the text of his or her messages.

This reduction of identity to texts, as VanGelder (1990) points out, allows individuals to use online media to create their identity on their own terms. Moreover, as VanGelder notes, the limits cyberspace places on identity cues has also led individuals to recreate who they are in online exchanges. In online occurrences of "gender-bending," for example, men pretend to be women, women pretend to be men, heterosexuals pretend to be homosexuals, etc. In other cases, as Turkle (1995) reports, the way in which online media limit identity cues to texts can even allow computer programs to masquerade as human beings. Turkle goes on to recount how one particular program—Julia—successfully duped several human participants in an online exchange into thinking the program was an actual human participant. What allows for such situations is that, by reducing identity to a single, non-verifiable attribute—texts—one has little way to confirm or deny the identity another claims to have. And unless some "slip" occurs in one's textual identity, there is no way to know otherwise.

Other research in online communication has examined how limiting identity to texts can allow other users to co-opt or to change someone else's text-based identity. Warnick (1998), for example, observes that the re-posting of electronic messages often blurs the notion of authorship—the identity of who wrote or who posted a particular text. Warnick also notes that when an individual encounters an online message/text, that individual may repost it to any number of persons sharing the same newsgroup. In reposting the message, however, individuals may cut or paste only portions of the original message (i.e., take items out of context) or modify the message by inserting new text or by deleting existing text. So, by cutting and pasting only parts of a message and by omitting the name of the person who originally posted it, an individual can separate what was said from the person who said it. Or, from an identity perspective, an individual can separate the traits that give an individual his or her online identity from the actual individual. The ability to separate posters from their original message gives cyberspace presenters a great deal of liberty, for they can:

- Attribute segments of forwarded postings to whomever they wish, and thus co-opt the online identity of someone else.
- Create new identities for themselves by co-opting the words or ideas of another.
- Alter what another said, creating a new identity for that author by putting words in that person's mouth and thus create a false identity.

In all three cases, by altering the textual factors individuals use to create and to maintain their online identity, co-opters of texts can change someone's online identity in one way or another.

From an ethos perspective, what is interesting about this online communication pattern is that even though it is very difficult to assess an individual's true identity in an online exchange, that lack of identity does not seem to detract from the credibility of an online message. On the contrary, as Gurak (1997) has noted, in some news groups, anonymous postings (texts that lacked any cue to the original presenter's identity) were often posted and circulated as if they were public service announcements. The question then becomes is there any evidence that the limited identity associated with online interactions could result in different reactions that vary along cultural lines? To answer this question, the researcher must review the intercultural communication literature in search of reports on cultural perspectives of identity.

A review of the intercultural communication literature does reveal that a fixed, or verifiable, identity (one that requires more than one item—texts—and more than one claim—the presenter's) is often essential to creating messages that will be viewed as "credible" by individuals from other cultures (Hall, 1981; Weiss, 1998; Richmond, 1995). This is not to say that there are cultures that don't value a verifiable identity. Rather, the members of different cultures seem to have varying levels of comfort in relation to interacting with persons who have "limited" identities. In some cases, different cultures use different factors, traits or cues to both determine the identity of a presenter, to determine the credibility of the presenter (based on that identity) and to determine their own identity in relation to others.

In some cultures, one's identity is not based on the claims or the proof that the individual himself or herself presents, but rather is based on the claims of others. For example, in parts of the Middle East and in parts of Eastern Europe, people interact within relatively large and complex social networks. These networks are often formed from long-term relations developed between individuals over time or from strong familial ties and based on trust and senses of family duty and family honor (Hofstede, 1997; Weiss, 1998; Richmond, 1995). In cultures that use these social network systems, the identity of the presenter often determines whether individuals decide to listen to or to ignore information presented by that individual (Hofstede, 1997; Weiss, 1998; Richmond, 1995). The distinction is essentially one of in-group vs. out-group. If one can be identified as a member of the in-group as confirmed by someone else in the social network, then certain behaviors are expected and a certain level of trust and disclosure is permitted. Additionally, a special authority—or credibility—is given to the information being presented. If one is identified as a member of the out-group (their identity cannot be confirmed by someone else in the social network), different behaviors are expected and different, more restricted levels of trust and disclosure are granted.

Also, in many of the cultures in which social networks are valued highly, outsiders—particularly members of a different culture—tend to be viewed with some degree of suspicion (Richmond, 1995). In this kind of communication system, being heard and being listened to often become a matter of having the proper introduction. In such systems, the right person—someone with a stable, known identity within the social network—needs to introduce an outsider to others in that network. If that "right person" says that outsider is someone who should be listened to, then the outsider is often identified as "credible," due to his or her identity being associated with a particular individual whose identity is known by and who is trusted by members of that system. With such an introduction the outsider's chances of successfully interacting with people in that network are much greater than they are if he or she attempted to approach these people un-introduced (Hofstede, 1997; Scharf & MacMathuna, 1998; Weiss, 1998; Richmond, 1995). Again, success in such a cultural communication system becomes a matter of identity—namely, does the recipient of a message know the identity of the sender/presenter and consider that identity a factor that indicates the credibility of the related message.

Social network perspectives on identity might also affect how individuals from such cultures use online communication technologies. For example, when an individual from a social network culture receives an e-mail message that lacks many of the nonverbal cues essential to establishing the identity of the sender, will that individual necessarily trust the identity the sender claims in the message (Richmond, 1995)? Moreover, if individuals from such cultures (cultures in which a person's word is often that person's bond) see how easily online messages can be altered and reposted, would those individuals be willing to use the online environment to introduce new people or new ideas, or to give earnest advice knowing that their words (and their reputations) might be altered and reposted by others? And how would resistance to disclosing information in cyberspace be perceived by individuals from other cultures who are more comfortable using online media?

According to such cultural expectations, the identity of the presenter affects his or her credibility, which in turn affects the degree of access that he or she has to certain kinds of information in social network cultures. Persons with a solid identity that is easy to confirm are considered credible and gain relatively open access in terms of the amounts and quality of data they may obtain. Individuals with a limited/text-based identity that is difficult to confirm, however, are often viewed as non-credible and are limited in terms of the amount and quality of information—particularly sensitive information (e.g., someone's actual thoughts or feelings)—to which they have access. In such cases, identity = trust/credibility while lack of identity = doubt. As a result, the limited identity resulting from an IOI situation could undermine the credibility of some participants and result in "unexpected" behaviors or reactions from members of social network cultures. (Such behavior might include ignoring important communiqués because the identity, and thus the credibility, of the sender is "suspect.") Such unexpected behavior, in turn, could lead to confusion or even offense. The notion of identity, therefore, appears to be a strong point of contention, for the limited nature of online identity seems to contradict the communication norms that members of certain cultures use to assess the credibility of certain communication behavior.

In other cases, cultural concepts of identity carry with them strict behavior cues and expectations. In the communication contexts of some cultures, knowing the identity of the individual with whom one is interacting can often be crucial to knowing how to act or to communicate. In his studies of intercultural interaction, Hall (1981, 1983) notes that the context, or setting, in which individuals from certain cultures communicate, can govern what is considered credible communication behavior. Moreover, Hall (1981, 1983) has noted that what is considered credible behavior within the same context, or setting, can vary along cultural lines. These setting-based variations of cultural communication behavior form the foundation of Hall's (1981, 1983) theory of high-context and low-context (see earlier discussion). According to Hall (1981, 1983), in low-context cultures, the setting in which information is presented has little effect on the shape a message will take. As a result, individuals from these cultures (e.g., the U.S., Germany and Scandinavia) tend to present information explicitly and directly. The idea is that according to their cultural communicative norms, speakers cannot rely on the context/setting of a situation to convey much standard, implicit information essential to understanding what is being communicated. In high-context cultures (e.g., Japan, Russia and Latin America), however, the context in which a message is communicated can sometimes convey as much, if not more, information about the topic being discussed than do the speaker's words. Additionally, in such high-context cultures, who is present (or the status of who is present) in a given communication situation can often have very different effects on behavioral expectations depending on the cultural background of the participants (Hall, 1981; Weiss, 1998; Richmond, 1995). Thus, in many high-context cultures, knowing how to behave or communicate credibly becomes a matter of knowing the identity—particularly the status identity—of the individuals presenting in a given setting.

What makes Hall's context model particularly interesting to online communication is that cues essential for determining identity related to status are often absent from online exchanges (Sproull & Kiesler, 1986; Hiltz & Turoff, 1993; Herring, 1996; Kiesler et al., 1984). Therefore, cyberspace forums often lack the particular kind of identity information that people from certain high-context cultures need to determine how to interact in a given communication situation. As a result, participants from such cultures may feel uncomfortable, frustrated or reserved in IOI situations. The reason for such behavior is that, without these identity-based context cues, it is difficult to establish who (from a status perspective) is present in the exchange.

Yet knowing the identity of who is participating in the exchange is often essential to identifying the context of that exchange, and the context dictates what is or is not acceptable communication behavior. Thus, individuals from high-context cultures might be unsure of how to act in the identity-limited discourse situation of an IOI. Therefore, these individuals might choose to remain silent or say as little as possible to avoid accidentally offending other participants in the exchange (Berry et al., 1992; Ng & Van Dyne, 2001). Such "passive" behavior, however, appears to detract from one's credibility in online exchanges involving the members of certain cultures (Warnick, 1998). In such a case, the credibility expectations of certain cultures appear to conflict with those observed in online media involving the members of other cultures (e.g., Anglo-Americans). Such conflicting expectations could, in turn, lead to miscommunication or confusion in an IOI. Again, the nature of identity appears to be a strong point of contention because the limited nature of online identity seems to contradict the communication norms that members of certain cultures use to assess the credibility of certain discourse behaviors.

The results of this two-part literature review, thus, indicate certain instances where differing cultural perceptions of identity and credibility could cause problems when individuals from different cultures exchange information in IOIs. As a result, the topic of identity appears to be a strong point of contention that merits further examination in order to determine if and how it might cause communication problems in IOIs. Thus, this dual-field literature review has identified a key variable that researchers can use as a focus for further study on how cultural factors might affect online communication behavior.

From this point, researchers can use different methods to examine how this strong point of contention—identity—might affect discourse patterns in IOIs. For example, some researchers may wish to conduct online case studies in which they observe how individuals from different cultural groups act and interact in online environments (e.g., online chats) where identity remains restricted to texts/typing. Other researchers may wish to conduct controlled experiments in which different cultural groups are asked to interact in situations where identity is known and stable and in situations where identity is limited and text based. The purpose of these various research approaches would be to determine if the point of contention—identity—is actually a factor that affects how different cultural groups interact in IOIs. Such research could also be used to establish a relative/comparative system for determining how various cultural groups differ according to this point of contention. Such a system would be like Hall's dimension of context, for it would allow researchers to identify and examine cultural patterns of online behavior as they relate to behaviors displayed by other cultural groups that are reacting to the same variable/concept. The overall objective, therefore, would be to determine if a strong point of contention could become a digital dimension that would allow for such a relativistic comparison of cultural behavior according to a similar concept—in this case, identity.

One key point to remember when conducting such research, presenting or applying such research is that all one can evaluate is overall group tendencies or group behaviors. Thus, research results based on a point of contention approach could not be an accurate indicator of the behaviors of individuals. Rather, it could only be used to examine the relative behaviors of different cultural groups in relation to a common variable or concept.

CONCLUSION

The rapid evolution of online communication technologies is constantly changing the way in which people think about space and time. Now, international communication often transpires in seconds or minutes, not days or weeks. This new degree of proximity, however, could lead to new levels of cross-cultural misunderstanding as many aspects of online interactions seem to contradict the communication expectations of certain cultural groups. This chapter has overviewed and exemplified how the international digital studies approach can serve as a foundation for examining the ways in which different cultural groups interact in IOIs. It now becomes the task of researchers to begin using new approaches to examine culture, technology and communication, in order to explore the true nature of this emerging area of online communication.

REFERENCES

Aristotle. (1991). *On Rhetoric* (G. A. Kennedy Trans.). New York: Oxford University Press.

Artemeva, N. (1998). The writing consultant as cultural interpreter: Bridging cultural perspectives on the genre of the periodic engineering report. *Technical Communication Quarterly, 7,* 285-299.

Baym, N. K. (1997). Interpreting soap operas and creating community: Inside an electronic fan culture. In S. Kiesler (Ed.), *Culture of the Internet* (pp. 103-120). Mahwah, NJ: Lawrence Erlbaum Associates.

Berry, J. W., et al. (1992). *Cross-Cultural Psychology: Research and Applications*. New York: Cambridge University Press.

Campbell, C.P. (1998). Rhetorical ethos: A bridge between high-context and low-context cultures? In S. Niemeier, C. P. Campbell, & R. Dirven (Eds.), *The Cultural Context in Business Communication* (pp. 31-47). Philadelphia, PA: John Benjamin.

Chu, Steve W. (1999). Using chopsticks and a fork together: Challenges and strategies of developing a Chinese/English bilingual Web site. *Technical Communication, 46,* 206-219.

Connor, U. (1990, February). Linguistic/rhetorical measures for international persuasive student writing. *Research in the Teaching of English, 24,* 67-89.

Connor, U. & Lauer, J. (1988). Cross-cultural variation in persuasive student writing. In A. C. Purves (Ed.), *Contrastive Rhetoric* (pp. 138-159). Newbury Park, CA: Sage.

Driskill, L. (1996). Collaborating across national and cultural borders. In D. C. Andrews (Ed.), *International Dimensions of Technical Communication* (pp. 23-44). Alexandria, VA: Society for Technical Communication.

Fernback, J. (1999). There is a there there: Notes toward a definition of cybercommunity. In S. Jones (Ed.), *Doing Internet Research* (pp. 203-220). Thousand Oaks, CA: Sage.

Ferris, D. & Hedgcock, J. S. (1998). *Teaching ESL Composition: Purpose, Process, and Practice*. Mahwah, NJ: Lawrence Erlbaum Associates.

Gillette, D. (1999, December). Web design for international audiences. *Intercom, 46*(10), 15-17.

Grundy, P. (1998). Parallel texts and diverging cultures in Hong Kong: Implications for intercultural communication. In S. Niemeier, C. P. Campbell, & R. Dirven (Eds.), *The Cultural Context in Business Communication* (pp. 167-183). Philadelphia, PA: John Benjamin.

Gurak, L. J. (1997). *Persuasion and Privacy in Cyberspace: The Online Protests Over Lotus Marketplace and the Clipper Chip*. New Haven, CT: Yale University Press.

Hall, E. T. (1981). *Beyond Culture*. New York: Anchor Books.

Hall, E. T. (1983). *The Dance of Life: The Other Dimension of Time*. New York: Anchor Books.

Herring, S. C. (1996). Introduction. In S. C. Herring (Ed.), *Computer-Mediated Communication: Linguistic, Social, and Cross Cultural Perspectives* (pp. 1-10). Philadelphia, PA: John Benjamin.

Hiltz, S. R. & Turoff, M. (1993). *The Network Nation: Human Communication via Computer Networks.* Cambridge, MA: MIT Press.

Hofstede, G. (1997). *Culture and Organizations: Software of the Mind.* New York: McGraw Hill.

Hoft, N. (1995). *International Technical Communication: How to Export Information about High Technology.* New York: John Wiley & Sons.

Johnson, N. (1984). Ethos and the aims of rhetoric. In R. J. Connors, L. S. Ede, & A. A. Lunsford (Eds.), *Essays on Classical Rhetoric and Modern Discourse* (pp. 98-114). Carbondale, IL: Southern Illinois University Press.

Kiesler, S., et al. (1984). Social psychological aspects of compute-mediated communication. *American Psychologist, 39,* 1123-1134.

Li, X. (1999). *Chinese-Dutch Business Negotiations: Insights from Discourse.* Atlanta, GA: Rodopi.

Li, X. & Koole, T. (1998). Cultural keywords in Chinese-Dutch business negotiations. In S. Niemeier, C. P. Campbell, & R. Dirven (Eds.), *The Cultural Context in Business Communication* (pp. 185-213). Philadelphia, PA: John Benjamin, 1998.

Lunsford, A. & Conners, R. (1997*). The Everyday Writer: A Brief Reference.* New York: St. Martin's.

Ma, R. (1996). Computer-mediated conversations as a new dimension of intercultural communication between East Asian and North American college students. In S. Herring (Ed.), *Computer-Mediated Communication: Linguistic, Social and Cross-Cultural Perspectives* (pp. 173-186). Amsterdam: John Benjamin.

Miller, C. R. & Selzer, J. (1985). Special topics of argument in engineering reports. In L. Odell & D. Goswami (Eds.), *Writing in Non-Academic Settings* (pp. 309-341). New York: Guilford.

Mitchell, D. A. (1998). Building a truly World Wide Web: A review of the essentials in international communication. *Technical Communication, 45,* 197-206.

Murdick, W. (1999). *The Portable Business Writer.* New York: Houghton Mifflin.

Ng, K. Y. & Van Dyne, L.. (2001). Culture and minority influence: Effects on persuasion and originality. In C. K. W. De Dreu & N. K. De Vries (Eds.), *Group Consensus and Minority Influence: Implications for Innovation* (pp. 284-306). Malden, MA: Blackwell Publishers.

Panetta, C. G. (2001). Understanding cultural differences in the rhetoric and composition classroom: Contrastive rhetoric as answers to ESL dilemmas. In C. G. Panetta (Ed.), *Contrastive Rhetoric Revisited and Redefined* (pp. 3-13). Mahwah, NJ: Lawrence Earlbaum Associates.

Perelman, L. C., et al., (1998). *The Mayfield Handbook of Technical and Scientific Writing.* Mountain View, CA: Mayfield.

Perez, B. (1998). Writing across writing systems. In B. Perez (Ed.), *Sociocultural Contexts of Language and Literacy* (pp. 49-65). Mahwah, NJ: Lawrence Erlbaum Associates.

Richmond, Y. (1995). *From Da to Yes: Understanding East Europeans.* Yarmouth, ME: Intercultural Press.

Scharf, W. F. & MacMathuna, S. (1998). Cultural values and Irish economic performance. In S. Niemeier, C. P. Campbell, & R. Dirven (Eds.), *The Cultural Context in Business Communication* (pp. 145-164). Philadelphia, PA: John Benjamin.

Skinner, Q. (1996). *Reason and Rhetoric in the Philosophy of Hobbes.* New York: Cambridge University Press.

Spears, R. & Lea, M. (1994). Panacea or panopticon? The hidden power in computer-mediated communication. *Communication Research, 21,* 427-459.

Sproull, L. & Kiesler, S. (1986). Reducing social context cues: Electronic mail in organizational communication. *Management Science, 32,* 1492-1512.

Tebeaux, E. (1999). Designing written business communication along the shifting cultural continuum: The new face of Mexico. *Journal of Business and Technical Communication, 13,* 49-85.

Trompenaars, F. & Hampden-Turner, C. (1998). *Riding the Waves of Culture: Understanding Diversity in Global Business.* New York: McGraw-Hill.

Turkle, S. (1995). *Life on Screen: Identity in the Age of the Internet.* New York: Touchstone.

Ulijn, J. M. (1996). Translating the culture of technical documents: Some experimental evidence. In D. C. Andrews (Ed.), *International Dimensions of Technical Communication* (pp. 69-86). Arlington, VA: Society for Technical Communication.

Ulijn, J. M. & Campbell, C. P. (1999). Technical innovations in communication: How to relate technology to business by a culturally reliable human interface. *Proceedings of the 1999 IEEE International Professional Communication Conference* (pp. 109-120). Piscataway, NJ: IEEE Professional Communication Society.

Ulijn, J. M. & St.Amant, K. (2000). Mutual intercultural perceptions: How does it affect technical communication? Some data from China, The Netherlands, Germany, France, and Italy. *Technical Communication, 47,* 220-237.

Ulijn, J. M. & Strother, J. B. (1995*). Communicating in Business and Technology: From Psycholinguistic Theory to International Practice.* Frankfurt, Germany: Peter Lang.

VanGelder, L. (1990). The strange case of the electronic lover. In G. Gumpert & S. L. Fish (Eds.), *Talking to Strangers: Mediated Therapeutic Communication.* (pp. 128-142). Norwood, NJ: Ablex.

Varner, I. & Beamer, L. (1995). *Intercultural Communication in the Global Workplace.* Boston, MA: Irwin.

Walzer, A. E. (2000). Aristotle on speaking "outside the subject": The special topics and rhetorical forums. In A. G. Gross & A. E. Walzer (Eds.), *Reading Aristotle's Rhetoric.* (pp. 38-54). Carbondale, IL: Southern Illinois University Press.

Warnick, B. (1998). Rhetorical criticism of public discourse on the Internet: Theoretical implications. *Rhetoric Society Quarterly, 28,* 73-84.

Weiss, S. E. (1998). Negotiating with foreign business persons: An introduction for Americans with propositions on six cultures. In S. Niemeier, C. P. Campbell, & R. Dirven (Eds.), *The Cultural Context in Business Communication* (pp. 51-118). Philadelphia, PA: John Benjamin.

Winsor, D. A. (1996). *Writing Like and Engineer: A Rhetorical Education.* Mahwah, NJ: Lawrence Erlbaum Associates.

Zappen, J. P., et al. (1997). *Rhetoric, community, and cyberspace.* Retrieved April 12, 2000 from: http://www.rpi.edu/~zappenj/Publications/Texts/rhetoric.html.

ENDNOTES

1   Please note that for the purposes of this chapter, the terms "cross-cultural" and "intercultural" communication are used interchangeably to mean situations where individuals from different cultures interact with or exchange information with one another.

2   It is this ability to predispose audiences that prompts the famous rhetorician Aristotle to note that ethos is perhaps the most powerful of the rhetorical proofs (Johnson, 1984).

3   Tebeaux (1999) notes similar kinds of cultural distinctions in Mexican-American business letters as does Grundy (1998) in his studies of business letters in Hong Kong.

4   See the works of Mitchell (1998), Chu (1999) and Gillette (1999) to name but a few.

5   See the work done by Ma (1996), Ulijn and Campbell (1999) and Artemeva (1998) for some examples of how cultural expectations seem to affect IOIs.

6   For an overview of different kinds of dimensions, see the works of Hofstede (1997) and Trompenaars and Hampden-Turner (1998).

7   See Spears and Lea (1994) and Sproull and Kiesler (1986) for a more in-depth discussion of status and communication patterns in online exchanges.

Chapter XVIII

User-Centered Internet Research: The Ethical Challenge

Maria Bakardjieva
University of Calgary, Canada

Andrew Feenberg
Simon Fraser University, Canada

Janis Goldie
University of Calgary, Canada

ABSTRACT

The current model of research ethics assumes an investigator, who holds expert status and superior knowledge, and a subject in a passive role. This model is meeting increasing resistance from subjects on the Internet. A collaborative model that recognizes the contribution of both researcher and subject is necessary for both practical and ethical reasons. We argue in this chapter that the history of the ethics and politics of research offers insight into our present situation and its dilemmas.

TWO MODELS OF ETHICS

The ethics of online research has received a great deal of attention from scholars in a variety of disciplines of late. The Internet is increasingly popular as a research site and it poses unique technological and methodological challenges. This has led to a renewal of the traditional themes of research ethics, such as the right of human subjects to give or withhold informed consent, protection of privacy and similar issues (see Ess, in press; Frankel & Siang, 1999; Thomas, 1996). Yet the ethical issues facing Internet researchers also involve some rather different problems that have not been addressed. We argue in this chapter that the history of the ethics and politics of research offers insight into our present situation and its dilemmas.

Research ethics originated from the concerns that surrounded the study of human subjects after the ghastly Nazi experiments in World War II. Following the war, public funding for research involving human subjects reached unprecedented levels, raising the issue of accountability to prominence ("Preface," 1969, p. v). Despite this early attention, it was not until the late 1960s that experimentation on human subjects drew widespread scholarly interest.

There are a number of similarities between the ethical issues that were discussed at that time and those faced by online researchers today. Both discussions identify the same actors as integral to ethical research procedures: the researcher, the participant, society at large, regulatory bodies (i.e., ethics committees, government, etc.) and publishing personnel all prove to be important to the process. Regulating the relationships among these diverse actors emerges as the ultimate mission of research ethics. However, opinions on how to fulfill this mission differ significantly depending on the analysis of the relationships among actors. Interestingly, sensitivity to the importance of this initial analysis seems to have been higher in the early debates. Contemporary accounts tend to assume a standard and unquestioned set of relations. To better understand this difference, it is helpful to review Freund's (1969) two models of research ethics.

In his introduction to a formative discussion of the ethics of experimentation with human subjects, published as a special issue of Daedalus (Freund, 1969), Freund distinguishes the "fiduciary" (p. ix), or law-model, from the "sociological model" (p. viii) as two distinct types of research ethics. In the law-model "a trustee, because of his superior competence and the trust and reliance placed in him, owes a duty of undivided loyalty and devotion to his client, the more so when [he] ... enjoys as a class certain exclusive privileges to carry on his calling" (Freund, 1969, p. ix). Medicine offers an excellent example of the trustee-client relationship. The doctor, because of his extensive schooling and mastery of the medical discipline, is more knowledgeable and competent than the patient. Thus the patient must trust the doctor to do the best he can. Invested with this immense trust, the doctor is responsible for fully protecting and serving his patient to his utmost capabilities. The asymmetrical power distribution in this relationship is compensated by the doctor's commitment to use this power for the betterment of the client (Freund, 1969, p. ix).

In contrast, the sociological model "underscores the communal aspect of the endeavor, the reciprocity of rights and duties, the positive values to be pursued, encouraged and facilitated, as well as the hazards, limitations and safeguards" (Freund, 1969, p. viii). Unlike the law model, which is based on a trustee-client relationship, the sociological model is patterned around the professional collegium, where everyone is granted equal status and works towards a common goal. In this model the doctor and the patient and, similarly, the researcher and the research subject, are construed as equally significant if not equally knowledgeable participants in a common project. Power and responsibility in this relationship, then, are fundamentally distributed.

It is noteworthy that current debates on Internet research ethics assume the law model. It is generally taken for granted that the researcher as trustee is ultimately responsible for the protection of the client. (Thomas, 1996; King, 1996). The researcher, because of her expert status, level of knowledge, competence, power and privileges, owes a special responsibility towards the participant. This responsibility is fulfilled by ensuring informed consent and protection of privacy (Waskul & Douglass, 1996). Furthermore, ethics review boards at most universities are primarily concerned with ensuring that the researcher in fact lives up to her trustee status. Thus they demand explanations as to the level of potential risk of harm to the participant, assurances and proof of informed consent and voluntary participation, as well as detailed descriptions of the recruitment processes and protection of anonymity.

While this process has been somewhat effective in protecting research subjects from questionable projects, it also places the subject in a passive position. The demand that the researcher should "inform" the participant about the goals and methods of the study guarantees that the participant is without agency in formulating research questions and project design. The obligation to allow the participant to withdraw from the study at any time locks him/her into a binary mode of participation—either in or out—with no power to negotiate and change the course of the research. The law model ensures that the unequal power structure between trustee and client remains intact—the trustee holds the superior knowledge and competence, while the client must blindly trust that his best interests are served. There is no distributed power relation with equal obligations and expectations. In essence, there is no room for an active participant. Instead, the participant is investigated by the researcher, who is presumed to have all the competences present in the research situation. This is, we contend, an unfortunate and unnecessary predicament for both researcher and participant, especially with regard to most Internet research. An alternative, collaborative model, proposed by Parsons (1969) and Mead (1969) in the aforementioned special issue of Daedalus, would be much more productive in this area. In what follows we will elaborate the early formulation of the collaborative model of research ethics and suggest directions for its further development and application to Internet research.

THE PROFESSIONAL COMPLEX

Parsons (1969) defines his concept of the "professional complex" as "a complex of occupational groups that perform certain rather specialized functions for others ('laymen') in the society on the basis of high-level and specialized competence, with the attendant fiduciary responsibility" (p. 331). The complex is broken down into three categories: research (the creation of new knowledge), practice (the utilization of knowledge in the service of practical human interests) and teaching (the transmission of knowledge to those classes of persons with an interest in its acquisition). Examples of such occupational groups include the clergy, who look after the spiritual welfare of the people via teaching; lawyers, who ensure justice by practicing law; and academics who attempt to uncover new knowledge through research.

Parsons (1969) sees the professional complex as embodying a collegial ethics where the different skills and knowledge of the members all contribute to the group's attempt to achieve a common goal, and power is widely distributed. The most interesting aspect of Parson's construct is that it is not constituted only of professionals but also lay persons (i.e., students, clients and research participants) as well. All of these diverse actors become involved in a common solidary collective, so that the research participant, and not just the researcher, belongs to the collegial group as a member of the professional complex, because of his or her knowledge, experience or personal attributes useful to the research enterprise. In this formulation, research becomes a team effort where mutual respect and support is offered to fellow members. Common values and goals are fundamental to the professional complex. By becoming a member of the group, each party implicitly acknowledges them.

According to Mead (1969) the collaborative model presented by Parsons as an ideal has long been an anthropological field practice (p. 361). The very nature of anthropological work, Mead (1969) claims, requires that the researcher build a stable relationship with the people among whom he or she seeks knowledge, and especially that s/he enlist the systematic collaboration of informants.

Thus, the "sociological" or collaborative, model attempts to incorporate the participant into the research process itself, recognizing the participant's place as an active member working towards the common goal. Insofar as this model implies not just the acceptance of certain duties and cooperation by research subjects, but also their input into the research process, it requires a willing, not simply informed, participant (see Jonas, 1969; Feenberg, 1995). The participant must identify with the overall goal of the study and, therefore, desire to be a part of the research process.

PARTICIPANTS' INTERESTS

Feenberg's (1995, 1999) work suggests a way to redefine the two models of ethics from the perspective of participants' rights, on one hand, and interests, on the other. The law model is centered on the notion of formal rights. Codes of medical ethics, Feenberg (1995) observes, are designed to guarantee the patient's right to refuse to lend his or her body for use by others, the right to information about risks, the right to withdraw at any time, the right to treatment for complications arising out of experimental participation, etc. (p. 102). This negative emphasis on rights has its roots in the revulsion against the abuse of patients and prisoners in Nazi wartime experimentation. Mead (1969), for her part, speaks about the powerful American cultural attitudes connecting the idea of experimentation to the word "guinea pig" (p. 367). The relationship between experimenter and his/her human subjects is thus perceived as a dangerous relationship in which human beings can be reduced to the status of experimental animals, stripped of their human rights and dignity. Against this background, true willingness to participate in experimentation is heroic and consent is suspect wherever it can be attributed to lower resistance, false hopes or captive circumstance (Jonas, 1969, p. 239).

And yet, as Feenberg (1995) has shown in his analysis of the case of AIDS patients, the emphasis on negative rights in current codes of research ethics has been challenged by human subjects who recognize important interests of their own in experimental participation. AIDS patients' movements have shown that the concept of participant interests can be the cornerstone of a new type of research ethics capable of realizing the positive inclusion of the participant as collaborator in the research enterprise envisioned by Parsons and Mead in the late 1960s.

In this light, the question of "what does the research subject get out of it," or, in other words, the question regarding the benefits of research for participants intrudes with new force. And this raises the further question: How are participants' needs and potential benefits to be known and incorporated into the research design? The law model assumes scientific expertise to be a reliable ground for design. In its terms, expert researchers already know the participants' and society's best interest. What this model demands beyond that is researchers' competence and benevolence in protecting individual participants' rights—freedom from harm, confidentiality, privacy, etc.

In the early versions of the collaborative model proposed by Parsons (1969) and Mead (1969), the question of participants' interests receives only cursory treatment. In Parsons' (1969) account the answer to the question "what does the research subject get out of it?" automatically follows from the recognition of the research subject as a part of the professional system. Given his or her status in the system, the research participant gets the same kinds of rewards as all other participants. However, the reward system is defined primarily by the interests of the investigators (Parsons, 1969, p. 339). Parsons (1969) identifies a range of motives for participation in research "bracketed" between the "highest" motive—the sense of contribution to knowledge—and the "lowest" motive of financial remuneration (p. 340). Intermediate motives include (in the case of medical research) the interest in the conquest of a preventable and curable disease and the sense of meaningfulness that an otherwise isolated and incapacitated sick person may gain out of his or her active contribution to a project (Parsons, 1969, p. 340).

Mead (1969) sees intrinsic value in the mere courtesy of treating subjects as collaborators which, she expects, will protect their human dignity. Such courtesy involves explaining to participants the purposes of the experiment and, generally, treating them as "intelligent, responsible, although not necessarily scientifically knowledgeable human beings" (Mead, 1969, p. 372). Compelling as this argument sounds, one notices the conflation between researchers' interest in "new knowledge" and participants' (informants') interests that are subsumed under those of the anthropologist. Research goals and techniques emerge out of the realm of expert knowledge and, in the best case scenario, collaboration-minded researchers manage to translate them into the language of potential participants, who, for their part, embrace these goals as their own. What kind of new knowledge does the anthropologist search for? Whom does this knowledge benefit and how? These questions do not arise in Mead's (1969) discussion of research ethics.

Feenberg's (1995) account of participants' interests offers insight into the question of "what does the research subject get out of it?" Feenberg points out that the needs research can potentially serve are not automatically credited as interests, but become so only through an authorized interpretation of some sort. Achieving recognition of these interests is in part a political process (Feenberg, 1995, p. 106). In his "sociotechnical" interpretation of medical ethics, Feenberg (1995) offers examples of how aspects of research (e.g., research goals and techniques) that appear "purely scientific" can be understood as a "technical mediation of a social interest" (p. 106). Feenberg (1995), therefore, claims that research is penetrated through and through by normative considerations without being "unscientific." This is explained by the availability of alternative research designs with equivalent scientific validity but different consequences for the participants.

Thus, a new dimension of research ethics emerges. Instead of simply offering a set of rules for the protection of individual rights arising at the interface between the professional and the lay participants in the research enterprise, ethics appears to be a "switching post between social demands and technical interventions" (Feenberg, 1995, p. 106). As such, ethics lies at the heart of the research enterprise and gives it legitimacy and direction. The extent to which participants' interests are recognized and addressed by the goals and techniques of research is a central ethical issue. A model of research ethics based on this interpretation would be collaborative in a more radical sense than the one developed by Parsons and Mead. Knowledge of participants' interests and the potential benefits they might derive from participation is not a question resolved by unaided scientific expertise. Such knowledge is held primarily by the research participants themselves.

It is, then, precisely this very dimension of collaboration in research that is the most interesting and potentially productive. When participants are perceived as passive, the opportunity to learn from their experience goes sadly unused. When they are invited to identify as collaborators with research objectives set by scientific experts, their intrinsic interests are often overlooked. On the contrary, by incorporating the research participant in the very process of formulation of research goals and designs, the issues that truly concern participants can be addressed.

THE STATE OF INTERNET KNOWLEDGE

How do these reflections inspired by earlier debates over medical ethics relate to Internet research today? There are some important similarities and dissimilarities between these two distinct research endeavors that have to be addressed before any parallels can be drawn. Medicine is a long-established field in which therapeutic practice and research have evolved hand-in-hand. The general utility of medical research—relieving human suffering and saving lives—is widely recognized, even if the specific objectives of concrete projects can occasionally be questioned. From this perspective, some potential participant interests in medical research are immediately recognizable. Parsons (1969) sums these up as "the interest in the conquest of preventable and curable disease and of premature death" (p. 340). Other interests, as Feenberg has shown, become known as a result of political process and struggle.

Internet research, on the other hand, has no such direct relation to practice. It has arisen as an afterthought in the course of the development of computer-network technology. Internet practice, understood as the design, engineering and construction of technical systems and their applications, has rarely relied on Internet research, i.e., social research involving human subjects. This disconnect between practice and research creates a significant difficulty in answering the question "what does the research subject get out of it." We argue that the difficulty can be overcome through a social constructivist approach to Internet development that acknowledges users' contribution to the shaping of the technology as a new communication medium. From such a position, numerous social groups are involved and have a stake, or interest, in how the Internet is built, employed and regulated. Identifying and articulating the diverse interests of all these groups, especially those that are typically deprived of voice and visibility, thus becomes a central task of research inseparable from Internet practice. We will examine this dynamic in more detail in the following section.

There is another specific feature of the field of Internet research that distinguishes it from medicine: the notorious "competence gap" (see Parsons, 1969, p. 336) between professional and lay members of the "complex," so glaring in medicine, is much less noticeable here. The "human subjects" of Internet research may themselves be designers, engineers, content-providers and seasoned users, who participate in creating the medium and often possess more knowledge of it than the researchers who study them. It is not atypical for researchers to "discover" Internet phenomena such as chat, online discussions, downloading of music, etc., long after those selected as subjects have learned and practiced the ins and outs of the new application. These subjects are then approached by the researcher and asked to share their practical knowledge so that it can be interpreted in the conceptual frameworks of an academic discipline. All too often the results are skewed by the ignorance of the researcher who is a newcomer to a well developed field of practice with a body of lore far more sophisticated, than anything an outsider can discover on the basis of a cursory study.

Nevertheless, whatever its flaws, Internet research is important and does serve to advance a scholarly discipline. What is less clear is the benefit for the participating subjects. It is unusual for the knowledge gained through research to return anything at all to the subjects who made it possible. It is this state of affairs, we believe, and not so much concern for individual privacy, that causes participants' outcry against "harvesting" (see Sharf, 1999) data from Internet forums.

In earlier publications we have argued that subjects react against alienation of their own online products, when these are appropriated by researchers (see Bakardjieva & Feenberg, 2000, 2001). This attitude seems to be spreading. A researcher looking for health-related discussions on the Internet recently noticed that most of the online forums dealing with the illness she wanted to study had "No research!" policies published on their websites (Solomon, 2003). We find this kind of aversion to Internet research highly disturbing and suspect that the current narrow notion of research ethics, with its indifference to fostering subjects' interests and goals, has something to do with it.

The lack of a pronounced competence gap between researchers and subjects as well as the vagueness of subjects' potential benefits configure the professional-lay relationship in the area of Internet research in a way quite distinct from that of medicine. This situation creates both opportunities and challenges for Internet research ethics. The preoccupation with individual rights and protection of subjects must be complemented with an adequate conception of participants' interests in the research process and its results. What is more, subjects' relatively high competence makes them potentially valuable collaborators in the research effort. To ensure their cooperation will require some major changes in research practice. It is necessary not only to inform subjects about the study, but to work with them at the stage of study design. In this lies the real opportunity for joining practice and research. Inquiry must be directed towards questions of actual concern to subjects, and this can only happen where the lay, but knowledgeable, subject is invited into the negotiations around research design presently open exclusively to "specialists."

USER-CENTERED INTERNET RESEARCH

As we have noted, medical researchers are aware that their efforts may someday save lives. But no such connection between theory and practice is evident in Internet research. The question, "why do the study in the first place?," is seldom raised. Researchers, in most cases, have remained surprisingly unreflexive with regard to their own practice. A strong case could be made that a big part of the research enterprise has been driven by the relative newness of the technology, by deterministic expectations of significant impacts on society or, let us face it, simply the ease and accessibility of the data. While, admittedly, there is less room to conceive of tangible, physical benefits for Internet users than for medical patients, the fact remains that Internet researchers have not conceptualized their own accountability to the populations they study.

This problem is not entirely unprecedented in the field of communication, where much of the research is done. It may therefore be useful to recall an earlier debate in that field over the distinction between "administrative" and "critical" research (Melody & Mansell, 1983; Smythe & Van Dinh, 1983). In the 1980s, communication scholars discovered that they raised different research problems, employed different methods and had different background ideologies as well (Smythe & Van Dinh, 1983, p. 117). Generally speaking, the administrative approach chooses its research problems with an interest in making an organization's actions more efficient. This approach usually aims at results that support, or at least do not seriously disturb, the status quo. Examples of administrative research include market research, behavioral research or survey research (Smythe & Van Dinh, 1983).

Critical research, on the other hand, addresses questions of power, inequality and exploitation in economic and political institutions and looks for ways to reshape institutions to meet the needs of the community. Critical research often advocates radical changes in the established social order.

It has been argued that the administrative research program, for example, in audience studies, serves those in power by delivering the audience as an object of control (see Ang, 1991). On the other hand, the critical approach unveils mechanisms of exploitation and alienation in media institutions and practices. It aims at consciousness raising and education of the exploited and encourages resistance. Yet, according to Melody and Mansell (1983, p. 110), scholars taking the critical approach, while excellent at exposing the problems, have generally failed to offer concrete solutions.

The utility of sharp dichotomies like this may be questionable, but nevertheless there is something instructive about the very effort to define the ideological, political and practical relevance of research, exemplified by the debate over these different approaches. Following this example, Internet researchers would be well advised to start explicating their motives, intentions and underlying ideologies: What are the interests and agendas behind any particular study? To whom do researchers report? Whose side are they on? These questions, we submit, define the relationship between the researcher and the participant from which all other, more narrowly perceived, ethical issues stem.

We find a useful model of reflexive and collaborative research in Smith's (1987) conception of sociology from the standpoint of and for women. According to Smith (1987), traditional sociology is locked into a professional, administrative and managerial apparatus to which women are outsiders. As women are excluded from traditional sociology, so Internet users are excluded from the knowledge-building process in the study of the Internet. They are most typically seen as objects to count and report on, with a view to increasing profit and system efficiency, or simple career advancement. Thus, a fundamental shift is necessary. A new model of Internet research for users must be devised. This is research that starts from the standpoint of subjects and their actual engagements with the technology in everyday life and aims to explicate for them the larger social matrix, in which they are implicated by virtue of their Internet usage. Subjects are naturally treated as collaborators in such a research paradigm, as they hold unique knowledge of their local situations and the life contexts into which the Internet is incorporated. The researcher, for his/her part, contributes the mastery of systematic techniques and conceptual vocabularies through which individual experiences are given significance transcending the local context. Thus the voices of the research participants can penetrate the specialized discourses that shape the Internet as a technology and social institution. Importantly, the problematic examined by this research does not stem from the specialized discourses of the academic disciplines, but is generated in the experience of subjects. Thus, Smith (1987) writes: "The purpose and direction of inquiry is in part (and particularly at the outset of this approach to sociology) an explication or codification ... of a problematic that is implicit in the everyday world" (p. 90).

The method of participatory action research (PAR) represents another useful source of ideas for the user-centered approach to Internet research we are advocating here. PAR prioritizes the democratization of social inquiry, by actively engaging subjects in the design and conduct of research (see Krimerman, 2001). It aims at achieving "cognitive justice" or inclusion in the knowledge-building process, exemplified by research involving groups that are typically marginalized and excluded from such practices. The second, equally important, goal of PAR is to help excluded groups to become conscious of their situation within the power structure and to emancipate them as reflexive actors capable of initiating change. Although PAR has been proven effective and has created a respectable tradition in fields, such as health care, social work and education, it has not yet been applied to Internet studies. Some promising first steps have been made in adapting PAR to ethnographic inquiry into information technologies, including the Internet. Slater, Tacchi and Lewis (2002), for instance, studied the Kothmale Community Radio Internet Project (KCRIP) in Sri Lanka, simultaneously developing what they called an "ethnographic action approach" involving local informants, in a variety of roles and in all stages of the project. The ethnographers saw their own task in the field not only as collecting data, but also as training local people into a "research culture" that would give them the analytical competency necessary for formulating and pursuing research questions.

PAR has usually been understood and implemented as research that benefits "the excluded, impoverished, marginalized, oppressed" (Krimerman, 2001, p. 63), for example, the mentally ill, battered wives, exploited children, homeless people, etc. It is not the approach that immediately comes to mind when studying Internet users, who are believed to be representatives of a privileged population with higher-than-average income and education. However, in all fields of human practice, specifically those related to science and technology, there exist characteristic monopolies of knowledge and expertise and, consequently, relatively marginalized populations. Internet users are one such relatively voiceless social category, to which PAR can open new opportunities for emancipation.

In the course of several research projects on the nature of online community, we became convinced that Internet research offers novel avenues for involving subjects as collaborators in this more radical way. The goal of our research was to discover how users appropriate the virtual space of the computer network as an environment for community life, and how technical features of groupware systems facilitate or obstruct this process. In order to achieve that, we needed to observe closely the interactions in diverse online groups and to ask community participants about their interpretations of what was going on in these forums. In the process of negotiating access to several virtual communities, we found that their members responded actively, and often critically, to our declared objectives. Taking advantage of the permanently open two-way communication channel, some participants engaged in a dialogue with us not only asking for clarifications, but also suggesting alternative directions for our inquiry. We believe this active interest in collaboration opens up new possibilities for elaborating a situated ethical approach, elegantly combining research objectives and methods with subjects' interests.

Participants in our projects were often not completely comfortable with the idea of lending themselves for observation. For example, one online group member responded to our invitation to take part in a project thus: "Interesting idea, much like watching the interactions in the monkey cages at the zoo (But excuse my sarcasm.)" But the same man went on to say:

I also think that the more important question you should ask is "How is discourse affected when traditional cultural contexts are deconstructed or not available? Does discourse proceed 'sans social context,' or is a new social context built to fill the void?" ... My own personal experience in online communities is that morality [our main focus of interest] is hardly an issue, but cultural norms and the lack of ability to convey interpersonal conversational clues, such as facial expression or tone of voice, create big obstacles.

Other participants also responded critically to the goals and procedures of our research and at some points demonstrated clear interest in influencing its course. Here for example is a new research objective suggested by one member of a health-related mailing list:

One thing I wondered about as a possible end-product of research like yours was making a case for funding for Internet access for many disabled people, shut-ins, etc. Pie-in-the-sky vision, of course, but if it could be shown that people used less medical care and fewer ER visits and saved gobs of money by having the support and info from the Net, who knows what might happen?

"Are you planning to include some of the negative effects of online communities in your study?" asked another woman, a member of a Web-based discussion group. She told us how she had become "overinvolved" with an online community for an extended period and had found herself spending huge amounts of time with it every day. Furthermore, her relationship with one of the community members reached the point where it could have endangered her marriage:

Now, I should clarify that I am a very independent, sensible individual, with no addictive tendencies, and a very strong marriage (believe it or not!) which is why I think it's important for you to look at these other aspects of online communities. It can affect *anyone* *this way.*

The everyday world of this woman, her family life, her responsibilities to her children who had been receiving less attention from her due to her obsession with the online group and her struggle to stay true to the kind of person she believed she was, all these things were connected to her experience as an Internet user and were charting a problematic divergent from our original intentions. Her experience suggested a need to add consideration of conflicts between online and face-to-face community.

In yet another case, a potential research participant, after looking carefully at our proposal to study the ethical aspects of online community life, wrote back to us to highlight those questions that had resonated with her own experiences with online group life:

I often wonder if, in fact, people are truthful or sincere. I say that as someone who periodically notes the inconsistency in what people write over time. The forums are, in a large respect, still virtually anonymous places ... a hide-a-way, if you will, for those seeking such a thing. Don't get me wrong, I've met some wonderful women on the forum but still remain somewhat skeptical of what I read.

Communications like these were extremely enlightening for us. Subjects were not content with being informed about the goals of the study. They initiated a negotiation in which our stated goals were critically examined, modified and reformulated in terms meaningful to those (still potential) research participants. The more or less conscious objective of this process was to align our (researchers') goals with participants' interests. Thus we were faced with the challenge to take our relationship with subjects to the level where the questions we investigate are influenced not just by scientific programs or other (commercial, political, etc.) agendas but also by participants' interests. Because this is a matter of accountability, respect, sincerity and honesty in relation to subjects, we believe it to be a matter of research ethics. It is, undoubtedly, also a political matter. The identification and recognition of participants' interests, as Feenberg (1995) has argued, is a political process in which research is deeply implicated. User-centered research has the potential to bring previously ignored or excluded interests into the process of social shaping of the Internet. It allows researchers to act as translators between abstract technical and social-scientific discourses and the lived experiences of the people who deal with the Internet on an everyday basis. This represents a higher-order motive for involvement in the research enterprise.

REFERENCES

Ang, I. (1991). *Desperately Seeking the Audience*. London: Routledge.

Bakardjieva M. & Feenberg, A. (2000). Respecting the virtual subject: How to navigate the private/public continuum. In M. Mowbray & C. Werry (Eds.), *Online Communities: Commerce, Community Action, and the Virtual University* (pp. 195-214). Upper Saddle River, NJ: Prentice Hall.

Bakardjieva, M. & Feenberg, A. (2001). Involving the virtual subject. *Ethics and Information Technology, 2,* 233-240.

Ess, C. (in press). Introduction. Special issue on Internet research ethics. *Ethics and Information Technology.*

Feenberg, A. (1995). *Alternative Modernity: The Technical Turn in Philosophy and Social Theory.* Los Angeles, CA: University of California Press.

Feenberg, A. (1999). *Questioning Technology.* London and New York: Routledge.

Frankel, M. S. & Siang, S. (1999). *Ethical and legal aspects of human subjects research on the Internet.* Retrieved Nov. 28, 2002 from the American Association for the Advancement of Science website: http://www.aaas.org/spp/sfrl/projects/intres/report.pdf.

Freund, P. A. (1969). Introduction to the issue 'ethical aspects of experimentation with human subjects.' *Daedalus: Journal of America Academy of Arts and Sciences, 98*(2), viii-xiii.

Jonas, H. (1969). Philosophical reflections on experimenting with human subjects. *Daedalus: Journal of America Academy of Arts and Sciences, 98*(2), 219-247.

King, S. (1996). Researching Internet communities: Proposed ethical guidelines for the reporting of results. *The Information Society, 12,* 119-127.

Krimerman, L. (2001). Participatory action research: Should social inquiry be conducted democratically? *Philosophy of the Social Sciences, 31*(1), 60-82.

Mead, M. (1969). Research with human beings: A model derived from anthropological field practice. *Daedalus: Journal of America Academy of Arts and Sciences, 98*(2), 361-385.

Melody, W. H. & Mansell, R. E. (1983, summer). The debate over critical vs. administrative research: Circularity or challenge. *Journal of Communication,* 33(3), 103-116.

Parsons, T. (1969). Research with human subjects and the 'professional complex.' *Daedalus: Journal of America Academy of Arts and Sciences, 98*(2), 325-359.

Preface. (1969). *Daedalus: Journal of America Academy of Arts and Sciences, 98*(2), v-vii.

Sharf, B. (1999). Beyond netiquette: The ethics of doing naturalistic discourse research on the internet. In S. Jones (Ed.), *Doing Internet Research: Critical Issues and Methods for Examining the Net* (pp. 243-256). London, New Delhi: Sage.

Slater, D., Tacchi, J., & Lewis, P. (2002). *Ethnographic monitoring and evaluation of community multimedia centres: A study of Kothmale Community Radio Internet Project, Sri Lanka.* (Rep.). U.K. Department for International Development, (DfID), in collaboration with UNESCO.

Smith, D. (1987). *The Everyday World as Problematic: A Feminist Sociology.* Toronto: University of Toronto Press.

Smythe, D. W. & Van Dinh, T. (1983, summer). On critical and administrative research: A new critical analysis. *Journal of Communication,* 33(3), 117-127.

Solomon, M. (2003). *Illness narratives: Sharing stories and support online.* Unpublished master's thesis, University of Calgary, Calgary, Alberta, Canada.

Thomas, J. (1996). Introduction: A debate about the ethics of fair practices for collecting social science data in cyberspace. *The Information Society, 12,* 107-117.

Waskul, D. & Douglass, M. (1996). Considering the electronic participant: Some polemical observations on the ethics of on-line research. *The Information Society, 12,* 129-139.

ENDNOTES

[1]   The three authors have contributed equally to the writing of this chapter in the spirit of the collaborative model discussed in the article. The authors wish to acknowledge the support for this research received from The National Science Foundation. Their names are listed alphabetically.

About the Authors

Elizabeth A. Buchanan is assistant professor and co-director of the Center for Information Policy Research at the School of Information Studies, University of Wisconsin-
Milwaukee, USA. She teaches and researches in the areas of research ethics and
methods, ethics and technology, information policy and distance education.

*   *   *   *

Michael D. Ayers is a Ph.D. candidate in the Department of Sociology of the Graduate
Faculty of Political and Social Sciences at New School University in New York City as
well as an adjunct professor in the Department of Sociology at Manhattan College in
Riverdale, NY. He is the co-editor of *Cyberactivism: Online Activism in Theory and
Practice* (Routledge 2003). His current research interests include the sociology of culture
in relation to media, music and art; social and cultural movements; and identity in
cyberspace. He received a Bachelor of Science (1998) and Masters of Science (2001) in
sociology from Virginia Tech and a Masters of Arts (2002) in sociology from the New
School. He is currently taking advantage of New York's music scene.

Maria Bakardjieva is assistant professor on the Faculty of Communication and Culture
at the University of Calgary, Canada. Her research focuses on users' creative involvement in the social shaping of the Internet. Her most recent articles have appeared in
Media, Culture and Society, *The Information Society* and *Ethics and Information
Technology*.

Magdalena Bober's research focuses on children's and young people's use of the Internet. She is currently based at the London School of Economics and Political Science in the UK, working as a research officer on a project about the opportunities and dangers of children going online. Her chapter is based on research carried out at Manchester Metropolitan University in the UK where she was researching British youth culture online with a focus on personal home pages designed by young people, teen websites and online communities. She formerly studied communications, psychology and politics at Mainz University in Germany and mass communication research at the University of Leicester, UK.

David Clark is an assistant professor in the Professional Writing program in the University of Wisconsin-Milwaukee's (USA) Department of English. His research work seeks to study, understand and improve organizational communication in for-profit and nonprofit enterprises, in particular through focus on qualitative research, knowledge and content management, the rhetoric of technology and management theory. He teaches document design, information architecture, knowledge management and the rhetoric of technology.

Charles Ess is distinguished research professor, Interdisciplinary Studies, Drury University, Springfield, MO, USA. He studied at the University of Zürich and completed his doctoral dissertation on Kant at Pennsylvania State University. He researches, lectures and publishes on Internet research ethics and, with Fay Sudweeks, organizes conferences and edits publications on cultural attitudes towards technology and computer-mediated communication (e.g., *Culture, Technology, Communication: Towards an Intercultural Global Village*). He has also published in comparative and applied ethics, history of philosophy, feminist biblical studies and philosophy of computing and information.

Andrew Feenberg holds the Canadian research chair in Philosophy of Technology in the School of Communication of Simon Fraser University. His most recent books are *When Poetry Ruled the Streets: The May Events of 1968* and *Transforming Technology*.

Douglas P. Flashinski completed his bachelor's degree at the University of Wisconsin-Eau Claire in December 2003 with a major in psychology and a minor in juvenile rehabilitation. He has received intramural grants to do research on the methods and ethics of Internet research, neuropsychological mechanisms of food motivation, subsidizing health club costs for the prescription of exercise and perceptions of mental illness and the insanity defense. He and Blaine Peden have collaborated with Tom Moore (Department of Computer Science) to develop an online lab for use by faculty and students at the University of Wisconsin-Eau Claire, USA. In the future, he will attend a doctoral program in forensic psychology.

Maximilian Forte, editor of the *Caribbean Amerindian Centrelink* and founder of *KACIKE: The Journal of Caribbean Amerindian History and Anthropology*, completed his doctorate in anthropology at Adelaide University in Australia in 2002. His research interests include the uses of website development as a method of participant observation in both virtual and traditional ethnography. His related publications focused on the revival of Caribbean indigenous identities via the Internet, the building of online communities and human interactions with Web-based artificial intelligence entities. His broader interests in the anthropology of culture, science and technology include the wider field of "Internet anthropology" and the anthropology of robotics.

Janis Goldie is currently completing her master's degree in communications at the University of Calgary, Canada. Her thesis explores how online group participants understand and experience privacy risks on the Internet. Goldie conducts user-centered research by addressing users' concerns in regards to current policy and technological issues in Canada.

M. Hoskins is an associate professor in the School of Child and Youth Care in the Faculty of Human and Social Development at the University of Victoria, Canada. Her research interests include adolescent girls and identity challenges, and the application and development of constructivist theory in educational and therapeutic settings. She is particularly interested in qualitative inquiry as a means for understanding human experience.

Steven Jones is professor and head of the Department of Communication at the University of Illinois at Chicago, USA, and research associate in the university's electronic visualization lab. He is also adjunct professor in the Institute for Communications Research at the University of Illinois at Urbana-Champaign. He serves as senior research fellow for the Pew Internet & American Life Project and is co-founder and president of the Association of Internet Researchers.

Sandeep Krishnamurthy is associate professor of E-Commerce and Marketing at the University of Washington, Bothell, USA. He received his doctorate from the University of Arizona in marketing and economics. He has developed several innovative courses related to e-commerce to both MBA and undergraduate students. He has written extensively about e-commerce. He recently published the 450-page MBA textbook, *E-Commerce Management: Text and Cases*. His scholarly work on e-commerce has appeared in journals such as *Journal of Consumer Affairs*, *Journal of Computer-Mediated Communication*, *Quarterly Journal of E-Commerce*, *Marketing Management*, *First Monday*, *Journal of Marketing Research* and *Journal of Service Marketing*.

Danielle Lawson is an American currently finishing a doctorate in the Faculty of Education at Queensland University of Technology in Brisbane, Australia. She was awarded an Australian Postgraduate Award in 2001, and looks forward to continuing research and teaching upon the completion of her degree. Her research interests include: gender performance and IRC, Internet research ethics, gender and sexuality issues online, synchronous computer-mediated communication, sociolinguistics and Internet sociology.

Peter Lunt is a senior lecturer in the Department of Psychology, University College London. He was educated at the universities of London and Oxford, receiving his doctoral degree in 1988. Since then he has taught at the universities of Kent and London, currently teaching social psychology at University College London. His research interests cover a wide range of topics, including the social psychology of consumption and saving, e-commerce, media and communication and social theory. He served as director of a number of research programs, including an EC-funded ESPRIT project examining psychological techniques in website development and an ESRC project "The virtual consumer: Broadening the scope of teleshopping" as part of the Virtual Society Program. He is associate editor for the *Journal of Economic Psychology*.

M. Maczewski is an interdisciplinary doctoral student at the School of Child and Youth Care and the Department of Computer Science at the University of Victoria, Canada. Her research interests include the sociology of childhood, young people's use of information and communication technologies, identity formation and qualitative research methodologies. Her professional background is in nursing and child and youth care.

Nadia Olivero is assistant professor at the Department of Psychology, University of Milan - Bicocca, Italy, and a doctoral candidate at the Department of Psychology at UCL, London, UK. She received her bachelor's degree, cum laude, and distinction, in psychology at University of Turin, Italy, in 1998. Since 1996 she has been experimenting with online research methods for both academia and the market research sector. She received an NCR grant to serve as research fellow at UCL for the project "Privacy negotiation and self-disclosure in e-commerce exchanges." She was awarded the student prize for best conference paper at the European Conference on Psychology and the Internet, British Psychological Society in November 2001. Her scholarly interests include the social psychology of computer-mediated communication, consumer behavior, self-disclosure and privacy in e-commerce, and Internet research methodology.

Blaine F. Peden completed a bachelor's degree at Fresno State College and a doctoral degree at Indiana University with a specialization in animal learning and behavior. Since 1977 he has taught and conducted research with undergraduates in the Department of Psychology at the University of Wisconsin-Eau Claire, USA. His research interests include topics in animal learning and behavior, such as autoshaping, learned performance in open and closed economies and foraging. Other research interests include classroom instruction, group matching, research ethics and the psychology of cyberspace.

Robert E. Ployhart is an assistant professor in the Industrial/Organizational Psychology program at George Mason University, USA. His research interests lie primarily in personnel selection (validity, test-taker perceptions, etc.), job performance (stability, typical/maximum, cultural influences, etc.), statistics and measurement (Web-based testing, factor analysis, etc.). His publications have appeared in the *Journal of Applied Psychology, Personnel Psychology, Organizational Behavior and Human Decision Processes, Journal of Management, Human Performance, Journal of Personality and Social Psychology* and *International Journal of Selection and Assessment*. He currently serves on the editorial boards of the *Journal of Applied Psychology, Personnel Psychology* and *Journal of Management*.

Clare Pollock is a senior lecturer in psychology at Curtin University of Technology, Perth, Western Australia. Her research areas relate to how people interact with technology and how human and technological systems interact.

W. Benjamin Porr graduated from Hofstra University in Hempstead, NY, with a bachelor's degree in psychology. He is currently a second-year doctoral student in the Industrial/Organizational Psychology program at George Mason University in Fairfax, VA, USA. His main research interests include the effects of computers on organizational research and testing. His research includes measurement issues of selection tests, effects of the Internet on attraction and recruitment of employees and motivation issues within the organization. He is also currently the website administrator for the GMU I/O program (http://www.gmu.edu/org/iopsa) and the Personnel Testing Council of Metro-Washington, DC (http://www.ptcmw.org).

Lynne Roberts is a research fellow with the Crime Research Centre at the University of Western Australia. Her doctoral research with the School of Psychology at Curtin University of Technology, Perth, Western Australia, examined social interactions in virtual environments. She has conducted both qualitative and quantitative research online in virtual environments. Roberts has published two journal articles and three book chapters, as well as presented papers at local, national and international conferences on social interaction in virtual environments and conducting research online.

Leigh Smith is head of the School of Psychology at Curtin University of Technology, Perth, Western Australia. His research interests include research methodology, disaster research, work and psychological well-being, cognitive architecture and deficits, addictions, unemployment and industrial democracy.

Kirk St.Amant is an assistant professor with the Institute of Technical and Scientific Communication at James Madison University, USA. He has a background in anthropology, international government and technical communication. His research interests include intercultural communication with a focus on how online communication technologies affect intercultural interactions. He has taught courses in intercultural communication for Mercer University and has taught courses in e-commerce, international business, and business communication in the Ukraine as a part of the USAID-sponsored Consortium for the Enhancement of Ukrainian Management Education (CEUME).

Susannah R. Stern is an assistant professor of Mass Communication at Boston College, USA. She received her doctorate from the University of North Carolina at Chapel Hill. Her research focuses on electronic and new media, adolescence and gender. Stern's work has appeared in such publications as *Women's Studies in Communication, Convergence: The Journal of Research into New Media Technologies*, *New Media & Society* and *Sexual Teens, Sexual Media*.

M.-A. Storey is an assistant professor of Computer Science at the University of Victoria, Canada. She leads the Computer Human Interaction and Software Engineering Lab (CHISEL) at the university. Her main research interests involve understanding how people solve complex tasks and designing technologies to facilitate the navigation and comprehension of large information spaces. She is a fellow of the British Columbia Advanced Systems Institute (ASI) and a visiting researcher at the IBM Centre for Advanced Studies. She has participated as a committee member, co-chair or chairperson of many conferences related to visualization and empirical software engineering.

Malin Sveningsson is a researcher and lecturer at the Department of Media and Communication at Karlstad University, Sweden. She received her doctorate from the Department of Communication Studies at Linköping University, Sweden. Her publications include *Creating a Sense of Community. Experiences from a Swedish Web Chat* (2001), and she is a co-author of *Digital Borderlands: Cultural Studies of Identity and Interactivity on the Internet* (2002). As a participant in a collective project that deals with Internet research methods, she is also publishing a Swedish textbook in that area. Her research interests include computer-mediated communication, social interaction, popular culture and subcultures.

Mary K. Walstrom, who received her doctorate from the University of Illinois, Urbana-Champaign in 1999, specializes in discourse analytic studies of public, online support group interaction. Her publications focus on the therapeutic potential, gender dynamics and ethical investigation of such interaction. She teaches a variety of university and college courses in the departments of Women's Studies and Communication Studies in northern California, USA. She also facilitates support groups for females recovering from anorexia and bulimia as a staff member of an outpatient eating disorder clinic. Additionally, as a health education consultant, she conducts public workshops and seminars that prevent body-image and eating-disorder problems.

Monica Whitty graduated with doctorate in psychology from Macquarie University in 2000. She is a lecturer at the University of Western Sydney and is a member of the Social Justice, Social Change Research Center at the university. She lectures in social and developmental psychology and research methods. Her research is often cited in the media, both in Australia and internationally. Her research interests include: Internet relationships and sexuality, the development of online relationships, Internet flirting, Internet infidelity, cyber-stalking, Internet and e-mail surveillance in the workplace, misrepresentation of the self online, cyber-ethics and young people hopes and dreams for the future.

Index

NEW Titles
from Information Science Publishing

30-Day free trial!

InfoSci-Online
Database
www.infosci-online.com

Provide instant access to the latest offerings of Idea Group Inc. publications in the fields of INFORMATION SCIENCE, TECHNOLOGY and MANAGEMENT

During the past decade, with the advent of telecommunications and the availability of distance learning opportunities, more college and university libraries can now provide access to comprehensive collections of research literature through access to online databases.

The InfoSci-Online database is the most comprehensive collection of *full-text* literature regarding research, trends, technologies, and challenges in the fields of information science, technology and management. This online database consists of over 3000 book chapters, 200+ journal articles, 200+ case studies and over 1,000+ conference proceedings papers from

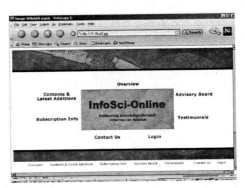

IGI's three imprints (Idea Group Publishing, Information Science Publishing and IRM Press) that can be accessed by users of this database through identifying areas of research interest and keywords.

Contents & Latest Additions:
Unlike the delay that readers face when waiting for the release of print publications, users will find this online database updated as soon as the material becomes available for distribution, providing instant access to the latest literature and research findings published by Idea Group Inc. in the field of information science and technology, in which emerging technologies and innovations are constantly taking place, and where time is of the essence.

The content within this database will be updated by IGI with 1300 new book chapters, 250+ journal articles and case studies and 250+ conference proceedings papers per year, all related to aspects of information, science, technology and management, published by Idea Group Inc. The updates will occur as soon as the material becomes available, even before the publications are sent to print.

InfoSci-Online pricing flexibility allows this database to be an excellent addition to your library, regardless of the size of your institution.

Contact: Ms. Carrie Skovrinskie, InfoSci-Online Project Coordinator, 717-533-8845 (Ext. 14), cskovrinskie@idea-group.com for a 30-day trial subscription to InfoSci-Online.

A product of:

INFORMATION SCIENCE PUBLISHING*
Enhancing Knowledge Through Information Science
http://www.info-sci-pub.com

an imprint of Idea Group Inc.